*In Memory of the families
and the men and officers
who fought in the American War of Independence*

and

*for Ann, Belinda, Bill, and Paula
With Thanks.*

THE THIRD VIRGINIA REGIMENT OF FOOT
1776-1778

With Flags Flying and Drums Beating

VOLUME ONE: A HISTORY

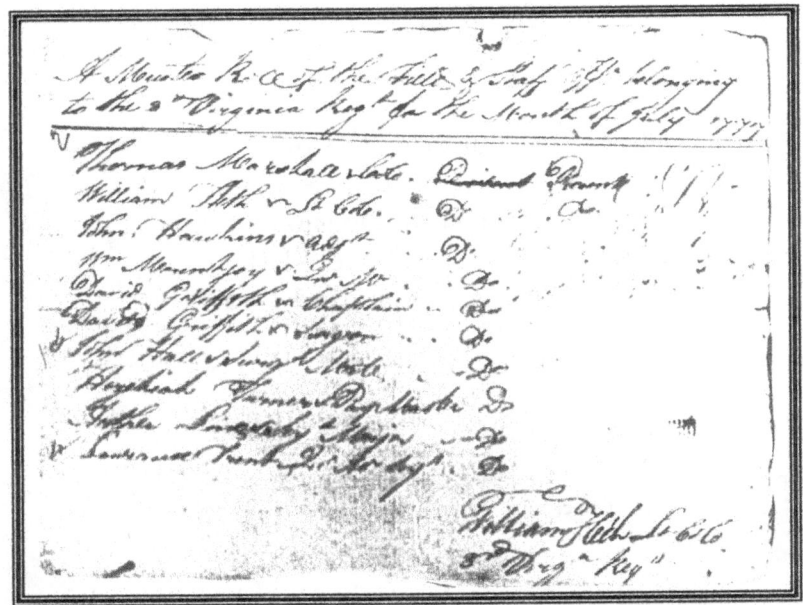

By Joan W. Peters, C.G.

HERITAGE BOOKS
2008

HERITAGE BOOKS
AN IMPRINT OF HERITAGE BOOKS, INC.

Books, CDs, and more—Worldwide

For our listing of thousands of titles see our website at
www.HeritageBooks.com

Published 2008 by
HERITAGE BOOKS, INC.
Publishing Division
100 Railroad Ave. #104
Westminster, Maryland 21157

Copyright © 2008 Joan W. Peters

Cover illustration by Debbie Parker Wayne

All rights reserved. No part of this book may be reproduced or transmitted in any form or by any means, electronic or mechanical, including photocopying, recording or by any information storage and retrieval system without written permission from the author, except for the inclusion of brief quotations in a review.

International Standard Book Numbers
Paperbound: 978-0-7884-4754-9
Clothbound: 978-0-7884-7296-1

Acknowledgments

Thanks is such an inadequate statement to express my appreciation to those individuals and institutions without whose assistance this history could never have been written.

In June 2006, I attended Samford University's Institute of Genealogy and Historical Research, or IGHR as it is more familiarly known, in Homewood, Alabama, having signed up for Advanced Library Research: Law Libraries & Government Documents. The information presented in this class opened up a whole primary record base with which I was unfamiliar.

It included online resources and first-hand accounts, letters, and journals available in the library's general and special collections. Much of this material has found its way into this book. A very special thanks go to Ann, Ben, and Kay who gave us a perfect hands-on experience in the law and government documents record base.

Carla Waddell, the reference and government documents librarian at Samford was also extremely helpful, pointing out other types of resource material in the general and special collection that would be helpful to my research.

Ann Fleming pulled double-duty when she shifted roles from a Samford instructor to a post Institute proof reader. She consented to read the manuscript, spending hours patiently making suggestions for changes to bring my endnotes into the present century and presenting impressive ideas which had the effect of making substantial alterations to the book's final appearance.

Belinda Wisnoski has been a colleague and associate since early 2004. One of Belinda's earliest projects was the compilation of a time line for the regiment for 1776. When completed, this chronology helped lay the framework for the regiments earliest movements in those heady, first days of the war.

Belinda has worked along side me as we spent countless hours at area libraries researching the men and officers of this regiment. We have gone through reams of microfilm rolls containing the compiled service records of the 3rd Virginia and the 3rd and 4th Virginia regiments, muster and pay rolls, and brigade returns, collating information on each of the officers and men who served between 1776 and 1778.

In two different research trips, Belinda was able to locate a source for the George Weedon letters, at the Library of Virginia; and the Gustavus Brown Wallace letters at the University of Virginia. She has acted as a sounding board where we could bounce ideas off one another, continually looking for ways to improve the final product.

My husband Bill also deserves my thanks. I began this project six years ago. During the five years of research and one year of writing, he has offered encouragement, steady and unwavering support, along with helpful suggestions regarding the contents of this history.

Paula Curran has been my fellow traveler to the National Archives. She was a willing and eager volunteer, ready to drive at a day's notice. Without her assistance in abstracting the pensions of 3rd Virginia veterans, this project quickly would have become unwieldy and impractical from the standpoint of time. Her dedication to the pension project enabled us to complete it in a timely fashion.

While most of the institutions in Virginia and Washington, D.C. were accommodating and helpful, there were two historical societies who were not nearly so cooperative.

George Weedon's revolutionary war letters were housed at the Chicago Historical Society according to the late John Gott and Dr. David Hackett Fisher. It took nearly four months for the Chicago Historical Society to respond to a request for copy costs for photocopies of these letters. They quoted an exorbitant cost structure on a per page basis for mailed copies, with no assurance it could be done in a timely fashion. It then proved impossible to find a researcher who was even willing to travel to Chicago to copy the records and mail them to me.

The second society was the New Jersey State Historical Society which owns a box of correspondence for William Alexander, Lord Stirling. I wrote this society asking for a cost structure to copy these letters in November 2006. They never even bothered to respond. I cannot help but wonder whether the late John Gott or Professor Fisher, the University Professor at Brandeis, had the same problem with historical societies which housed letters they needed for their books. Somehow, I think not. (Ahh … but I digress).

Fortunately, the experience was far different when dealing with libraries, universities, historical societies and local Circuit Courts in Virginia. The library of Virginia, the University of Virginia, Gregory Stoner at the Virginia Historical Society, Beverly Veness, Tish Como, and Don Wilson at the Bull Run Library's R.E.L.I.C room, and Phyllis Scott at the Fauquier County Circuit Court were all particularly accommodating in sending along copies of requested records in a timely fashion. So were Bill Peters of the Southern Fauquier Historical Society and Cheryl Sheppard of Millennium Preservation.

Another extremely helpful resource was the online records at the Library of Congress, University of Virginia and the Colonial Williamsburg Foundation. These sites provided primary source material, including letters of delegates, Continental Congress Journal entries, Washington's Writings, and *Virginia Gazette* articles.

Last, but far from least, is the assistance I have received from the National Archives. My request for microfilm of compiled service records for the 3rd Virginia and the 3rd and 4th Virginia regiments on M 881 MR 951–970 came in a very timely fashion. So did the revolutionary war rolls for the 3rd Virginia on M 246, MR 97, 98, and Brigade Returns on MR 136 and 137. Furthermore, the staff at the National Archives in Washington, D.C. was unfailingly helpful in my frequent trips into the city to retrieve pensions for 3rd Virginia veterans.

Thanks, too, go to Debbie Parker Wayne who created the cover. The scanned illustration of a Field and Staff Muster Roll found on the title page was taken from NARA's *Revolutionary War Rolls*, M 246 MR 97, Rolls of the 3rd Virginia Regiment.

Another note of acknowledgment must go to Emerson Peters, who was of exceptional assistance in the final proofing of the biographies in volume two.

One more individual must be added to this list to whom I owe so much. This is Craig Scott, who has been consistently patient with me throughout the writing process. His suggestions regarding the narrative for the men and officers along with suggestions regarding the appearance of the biographies have helped these accounts to remain manageable in their scope.

As these acknowledgements have demonstrated, while an author may write the narrative, it takes a collective, collaborative approach from people and institutions to bring that endeavor to fruition.

Preface

I have written this history of the 3rd Virginia Regiment of Foot, Continental Line with two purposes in mind. First, I wanted to honor the families of the men and officers of those who fought for this country's liberty and freedom. The 3rd Virginia was one such regiment, whose courage, resolve and perseverance could represent any of the troops who fought in the various theatres of this war.

Many of these soldiers and officers came home as heroes. Slowly, that perception changed. No doubt families of 3rd Virginia veterans grew tired of hearing about the "day I fought at Harlem Heights" or "I saw Captain Chilton die at Brandywine" or hear of comrades who died of small pox, or the hardships at Valley Forge without clothes, shoes, and blankets or even to experience the thrill of victories at Trenton and Princeton. These veterans and their regiments' exploits gradually sank into oblivion.

Only soldiers who were disabled in the war could apply for pension benefits. Families, whose husbands had been killed in the war, who applied, were ignored by both the state and the federal government. Sometimes the county court intervened and assisted parents, widows and orphans in financial need because of the service of their husband or son(s).

At other times, old officers intervened. Henry Knox, the Secretary of War, under President Washington, personally intervened for the deceased Major Andrew Leitch's family and obtained a half pay pension for seven years for his services. For the most part, however, these men were forgotten ... as was their service. Many of the veteran soldiers, and some officers, were left to slide into poverty.

It was not until 1818, nearly thirty-six years after the end of the war, that veterans could apply for a pension, and then, only for those in so-called "reduced circumstances." By 1818, these men would have been in their mid to late fifties, if born between 1759–1765. Others would have been in their sixties if born before 1765. By any standards of the time, these men were considered old. Between 1818–1821, these impoverished veterans found themselves placed on, then taken off, pension lists not because they owned too little property but because they owned too much!

By the time pension legislation had been enacted for service in 1832, many veterans had either died or were upwards of sixty-seven years old, if born between 1759–1765. Their memories of these events were more than a half century old and proof of their service or discharges from their units long since misplaced or lost. It is my hope this history will serve to endorse these men's achievements.

The second reason for a history of a revolutionary war unit is more complex. The revolutionary war has become one of America's forgotten wars. There is no memorial to these men in our nation's capital, already filled with war memorials; nor are there ones in front of courthouses in America's towns and cities. Even finding the graves to honor these men in death is difficult.

In all of the days set aside to honor those who died to preserve our nation, there is no day to honor the men who made it happen. There is no national holiday to honor their achievements. Only the 4th of July celebrates the revolutionary era and this day pays tribute to the *politician's* efforts in drafting and signing the Declaration of Independence. We seem to have forgotten that if it were not for all those men who fought for our freedom, there would be no nation and thus no reason to celebrate.

We owe these officers and soldiers a debt and a reaffirmation that their service has *not* been forgotten. Writing the history of the 3rd Virginia Regiment of Foot, Continental Line is my way of doing that.

Abbreviations

Sources:

Am.Archives	Peter Force's *American Archives*
Anc.com	Ancestry.com
BDUSC	*Biographical Dictionary of U.S. Congress*
CSR	Compiled service records
FCBC	Fauquier County Bicentennial Committee
FCDB	Fauquier County Deed Book
FCMB	Fauquier County Marriage Bond
FCWB	Fauquier County Will Book
Index, USIP	*Index, United States Invalid Pensions, 1801–1815*
JCC	*Journals of Continental Congress*
LC	Library of Congress
Letters	*Letter of Delegates*
LVA	Library of Virginia
MR/ Military Records	*Military Records from Fauquier County Virginia Minute Books, 1759–84, 1784–1840, 1840–1904.*
NARA	National Archives & Records Administration
N&F	*Neglected & Forgotten, Military Records from Fauquier County Virginia Clerks Loose Papers, 1759–1824*
PL 1792–1795	*Pension List, 1792–1795*
PWCOB/MB	*Prince William County, Virginia Order Book/ Minute Book*
Va Rev Bounty Warrants	*Virginia Revolutionary Bounty Warrants*
Va Rev Rejected Claims	*Virginia Revolutionary Rejected Bounty Claims*
RWP & BLWt Apps	Revolutionary War Pension & Bounty Land Warrant Applications
RWR	Revolutionary War Records
VGS	Virginia Genealogical Society
VHS	Virginia Historical Society
Virginia RW State Pensions	*Virginia Revolutionary War State Pensions*
UMW	University of Mary Washington
UVa	University of Virginia
WW	*Writings of Washington*

Other abbreviations found in narrative:

Adjut^t; Adj Gen	Adjutant; Adjutant General
Battn	Battalion
Brig^d	Brigade
Brig^{dr}	Brigadier
B.G. /Brig. Gen/	Brigadier General
M.G.	Major General
bef	Before
Capt	Captain
Com'd	Commissioned
Comd	command
Corp	Corporal
depreciat^n	Depreciation
Dischgd	Discharged
Enl	Enlisted
F&SMR	Field & Staff Muster Roll
Genl(s)	General(s)
Gdn	Guardian
GN	Given Name
Gov^{mt}/Gov^t	Government

Inf/Inft^y	Infantry
Jan to Dec	January to December
Jan^y	January
Jr.	Junior
Lt; Lt Col	Lieutenant; Lieutenant Colonel
KY	Kentucky
mo	month
MR	3rd Virginia company Muster Roll
No	Number(s)
NC	North Carolina
n.g.	Not given
P^a	Pennsylvania
Penna	Pennyslvania
Phila.	Philadelphia
PM	Paymaster
PR	3rd Virginia company Pay Roll
Prvt	Private
QM	Quartermaster
QM Sgt	Quartermaster Sergeant
Receiv'd	received
Regmt, Rgt	Regiment
Ret^d	Returned
Rew^d	Reward
SC	South Carolina
Serv'd	served
Sgt	Sergeant
Sold^r	Soldier
Sr.	Senior
VA	Virginia
VF	Valley Forge
wag^r	wagoner
w/o	wife of
wid/o	widow of
yr(s)	Year(s) (Note-- years 1776-1778 may be abbreviated: 76, 77, 78.) dates may also be abbreviated: January 15, 1777 = 1/15/ 77 etc.
^words between carrots^	interlined text from a quoted passage

TABLE OF CONTENTS

Acknowledgments

Preface

Abbreviations

Introduction — i

Chapter 1. Evolution of the 3rd Virginia — 1

Chapter 2. Organization & Structure of the 3rd Virginia — 27

Chapter 3. Tracking the 3rd Virginia — 53

Chapter 4. Skirmishes & Battles 1: September 1777 to April 1777 — 77

Chapter 5. Skirmishes & Battles 2: April 1777 to October 1777 — 121

Chapter 6. Skirmishes & Battles 3: October 1777 to June 1778 — 159

Chapter 7. The 3rd Virginia & Colonel Morgan's Light Infantry — 197

Index — 209

Bibliography — 231

Plates, Figures, & Tables

Plates

Plate 1. Muster Roll, Captain John F. Mercer, April 1777	v
Plate 2. Payroll, Captain David Arell, January 1778	vi
Plate 3. Muster Roll, Captain John Chilton, September 1777	vii
Plate 4. Muster Roll, formerly Captain Chilton, October 1777	viii
Plate 5. Pay Roll, Captain John Ashby, April 1777	ix
Plate 6. Muster Roll, Captain Valentine Peyton, April 1778	x
Plate 7. Muster Roll, Captain John Blackwell, February 1778	x
Plate 8. Muster Roll, Captain Robert Powell, May 1778	xi
Plate 9. Pay Roll, Captain Phill Lee, May 1777	xii
Plate 10. Pay Roll, Captain Gustavus B. Wallace, September 1777	xiii
Plate 11. Muster Roll, Captain William Washington, July 1777	xiv
Plate 12. Muster Roll, Captain Charles West, June 1777	xv
Plate 13. Pay Roll, Captain Reuben Briscoe, December 1777	xvi
Plate 14. Field Return of Brigades, Coryell's Ferry, June 178	51
Plate 15. Field & Staff Muster Roll, Officers, 3rd Virginia, July 1777	52

Figures

Figure 1. On the March to Trenton	99
Figure 2. The Action at Cliveden	146
Figure 3. Marching to Valley Forge, December 1777	166
Figure 4. Winter Quarters, Valley Forge, December 1777 to May 1778	167
Figure 5. Conditions of Troops at Valley Forge	168
Figure 6. Monmouth	187
Figure 7. Washington Relieving General Lee of command	187
Figure 8. Von Steuben Drilling troops at Valley Forge	189
Figure 9. Soldiers, Continental Line	191

Tables

Table 1. Woodford's Brigade Returns 12 January 1778 to 18 April 1778.	44
Table 2. Deaths in Captain John Chilton's Company, January to April 1777	110
Table 3. Deaths in Captain John Peyton's Company, January to April 1777	110–111
Table 4. Deaths in Captain Wallace's Company, December 1777 to April 1778	111
Table 5. Deaths in Captain Ashby's Company, December 1777 to April 1778	111
Table 6. Casualties in 3rd Virginia at Brandywine, 11 September 1777	135–137
Table 7. Sickness in 3rd Virginia, November 1777 to April 1778	169–170
Table 8. Deaths & Desertions in 3rd Virginia, December 1777 to April 1778	172
Table 9. Woodford's Brigade Returns May 1778	179–180
Table 10. 3rd Virginia veterans at Monmouth	189
Table 11. 3rd Virginia Men in Colonel Morgan's Light Infantry	205–206

Introduction

Historical Overview

The 3rd Virginia Regiment, Continental Line included officers and men from a variety of disparate military organizations. Many had previous military experience, either as part of a Virginia military unit that fought with the British, between 1754–1763, in the French and Indian War or as part of Minute Battalions and independent companies formed to respond to Lord Dunmore's attacks on Norfolk, Hampton and Great Bridge between October 1775 and January 1776.

When Virginia's royal governor, John Murray, fourth Earl of Dunmore escaped to the safety of his fleet, leaving the colony's government in disarray, a de facto colonial government fell to the third Virginia Convention which met in July 1775 to discuss Virginia's military situation.

Nearly six months had passed since Lord Dunmore had removed the colony's gunpowder from Williamsburg, and three months since he fled the colony for the safety of his war ships.

In July 1775, the convention authorized two regiments of regular troops and sixteen Minute battalions "for the better protection and defence of the country against invasions and insurrections." [1]

Then came Lord Dunmore's attacks on Norfolk and Hampton in September and October 1775 and the colony's armed response.

It was not until December 1775 that the Continental Congress confirmed the Virginia Convention's authorization of two regiments of regular troops by a resolution calling for the raising of six Battalions in Virginia.

On Thursday, December 28, 1775 Congress authorized the creation of these battalions, which were "necessary to be immediately raised in Virginia"; they were to be paid as the continental forces at the Camp in Cambridge, unless the convention could raise them on better terms. [2]

The 3rd Virginia was one of these six continental battalions and went on to engage the British at the Battle of Long Island in August 1776, at Harlem Heights, in September 1776; they participated in a skirmish outside of New Rochelle with the intent of capturing Major Robert Rogers in November 1776 and at least one company, under the command of Captain John Thornton, took part in the Battle of White Plains. After going into winter quarters at Valley Forge, the 3rd participated in the excursion into Trenton in December and Princeton in January 1777.

The Regiment took the brunt of attacks at Brandywine and Germantown in September and October 1777. After another stay in winter quarters, they moved out with the main army to play a part in the battle at Monmouth Courthouse in June 1778. In September 1778, the Virginia continental line was reorganized and the 3rd Virginia was consolidated with other Virginia regiments.[3]

Organization and Content

I have organized the first volume of this history of the 3rd Virginia into these seven chapters:

Chapter 1 conveys in greater detail the evolution of the 3rd Virginia from Minute Battalions and independent companies organized to counter Lord Dunmore's attacks in the winter months of 1775 and early 1776. The armed response to Dunmore's attack on Norfolk, Hampton and Great Bridge are detailed here. I have used contemporary accounts of these battles, taken from letters of the participants and Congressional delegates as well as eighteenth century newspaper accounts.

I have also made use of Washington's writings and the Journals of the Continental Congress in dealing with the details of these attacks and their aftermath. Future 3rd Virginia officers and men with prior military experience detailed in this chapter are found in **bold face** type.

Chapter 2 describes the structure and organization of the 3rd Virginia, from its inception as a regiment through its absorption into several brigades, first, briefly under George Weedon, then transferred to William Alexander, Lord Stirling's brigade and finally as part of General Woodford's Brigade.

Chapter 3 is entitled "Tracking the 3rd Virginia". I have put together the route the regiment took from Virginia in the summer of 1776 through the battle at Monmouth Courthouse in June 1778.

I have drawn on weekly and monthly returns, muster rolls and payrolls, diaries and letters to track the 3rd Virginia. There is information to be had in Orderly Books. It is also useful to know where the

Commander in Chief was since the 3rd Virginia was with the main army. When this information is lacking, I have used other historians' beliefs relating the whereabouts of the 3rd Virginia during this time period.

Chapter 4 relates the skirmishes and the battles in which the 3rd Virginia participated during the campaigns from September 1776 to April 1777. The regiment was part of Weedon's and Stirling's brigade during this period. Here again, I have drawn on contemporary newspaper accounts, and letters from 3rd Virginia officers, some of which describe the battles in graphic detail.

Chapter 5 continues the description of skirmishes and battles in which the regiment was involved when the 3rd Virginia became part of Brigadier General William Woodford's brigade in May 1777. The chapter concludes with Germantown and its aftermath in October 1777.

Chapter 6 continues in the same vein, beginning in October 1777, after Germantown and describes the problems facing the regiment in the fall and winter of 1777–1778. Morgan's men, along with the men from the 3rd Virginia selected for that fighting unit, returned in November 1777 and were involved in the skirmish at White Marsh. Many of the men in the regiment were discharged between December 1777 and March 1778.

New recruits eventually came on throughout 1777 and the first months of 1778 to replace the veterans, many of whom returned home during the early months of 1778. Many of these were inexperienced and received their baptism by fire at Germantown. Von Steuben's training during the long winter encampment at Valley Forge helped transform the men into a cohesive fighting unit. During the spring of 1778, detachments from the 3rd Virginia went with Lafayette to scout the British and, in May 1778, became involved in the skirmish at Barren Hills. Monmouth was the last battle for the 3rd Virginia before the reorganization of the regiment in September 1778 at White Plains.

Chapter 7 describes the part Colonel Daniel Morgan's rifle company played at Saratoga in October 1777. Colonel Morgan received permission from General Washington to go through the American camp in June 1777 to raise companies of rifle men to serve in his command. The 3rd Virginia sent twenty-three men as a detachment for this command.

An every name index and bibliography completes the first volume of this history.

The second volume consists of a short introduction and three chapters relating to bounty land and pension laws information, biographies of officers of the 3rd Virginia from 1776–1778 and biographies of the men of the 3rd Virginia regiment for the same dates. **Chapter 1** gives a synopsis of pension and bounty land laws which are necessary in understanding the role local, state and federal governments played in assisting the 3rd Virginia veteran's return to civilian live. **Chapter 2** is an alphabetical listing of the officers of the 3rd Virginia Regiment. I have summarized their military experience and included a synopsis of any pension records extracted from the National Archives or other derivative sources.

This chapter may also contain contents of letters and diaries from officers to family and friends. End notes appear at the end of the biographical listing of the officers.

Chapter 3 includes an alphabetical listing of all the men in the 3rd Virginia. They include the men who enlisted in 1777 and 1778, which were found on NARA's compiled service records for the 3rd & 4th Virginia regiments. These listings contain the same information as that found in the officer's chapter: the mens' military service records, whereabouts in 1810, pension or other local records which detail information about them. Endnotes appear at the end of each alphabetical letter.

The plates that appear in the narrative have been scanned from revolutionary war rolls on microfilm from the National Archives.[4] The soldier "at the ready" watermarked on the first page of the Table of Contents came from a book of Dover electronic clip art.[5] The Continental Line soldiers pictured on page 191 came from the same source.[6] Figures 1 through 9, spread throughout the narrative have been taken from John Grafton's *The American Revolution, A Picture Sourcebook.*.[7]

Finally, an index and bibliography can be found after the biographies of the officers and men in the regiment.

The Use of Primary and Derivative Sources

Whenever possible, I have used contemporary accounts and microfilmed military sources and pension papers found at the National Archives, the Library of Congress, state libraries, historical societies and regional libraries and online newspaper collections to describe the momentous events in which the 3rd Virginia Regiment was involved between September 1775 and September 1778.

When necessary I have made use of historians' rehashing of these campaigns, although I preferred the actual accounts of the participants who lived through them.

There are, of course, many historians who have written their interpretation of these revolutionary war battles. For readers who are more comfortable with a derivative source I recommend these books, among the many that have been written, for their historical understanding and analysis of these campaigns:

- David Hackett Fischer, *Washington's Crossing* (New York: Oxford University Press, 2004).
- John Gott & Triplett Russell, *Fauquier County in the Revolution* (Warrenton, Virginia: Warrenton Printing & Publishing Company, 1976).
- Richard Ketchum, *The Winter Soldiers: The Battles for Trenton & Princeton* (New York: Henry Holt & Company, 1973) and *Saratoga* (New York: Henry Holt & Company, 1997).
- Thomas J. McGuire, *The Surprise of Germantown: October 4th, 1777* (Gettysburg: Thomas Publications, 1994).
- Brendan Morrissey, *Monmouth Courthouse, 1778* (Great Britain: Osprey Books, 2004).
- Stephen Taafe, *The Philadelphia Campaign, 1777–1778* (Lawrence, KS: University Press, 2003).

The Biographies of the Officers and Men

The military biographies in volume 2 were taken from NARA's M 881 MR 951–956, *The Compiled Service Records, 3rd Virginia 1776–1778* and M 881 MR 957–970, *The Compiled Service Records, 3rd & 4th Virginia* in Record Group 93 at the National Archives; Francis Heitman's *Historical Register of Officers of the Continental Army* (Baltimore: Genealogical Publishing Company, 2003), W. T. R. Saffell's *Records of the Revolutionary War* (1894 Reprint, Baltimore: Charles T. Saffell, 1894), and John Gott & Triplett Russell's *Fauquier County in the Revolution* (Warrenton: Warrenton Publishing Company, 1976).

I used Virgil White's four volume *Genealogical Abstracts of Revolutionary War Pension Files* (Waynesboro, Tennessee: The National Historical Publishing Company, 1990) and Patrick Wardell's five volume *Virginia/West Virginia Genealogical Data from Revolutionary War Pension and Bounty Land Warrant Records* (Bowie: Heritage Books, 1996) as my finding aids for possible pension records for 3rd Virginia veterans. Once I had that information, I used the pension papers at the National Archives on M 804, *Revolutionary War Pension and Bounty Land Warrant Applications Files, 1800–1900* to verify pensions for 3rd Virginia service.

Occasionally, there were other easily accessible records which assisted in shedding more insight into the veteran in question. This was particularly true for Fauquier County men as I had already abstracted the military records from the County Court Minute Books and the County's Clerks Loose Papers. That information is included here as are any final pension vouchers from A. T. Pierce's two volume *Selected Final Pension Payment Vouchers 1818–1864*.(Athens, Georgia: Iberian Publishing Company, 1996).

Caveats

While I have kept the eighteenth century spelling true to its time period, I have used modern punctuation and paragraphing when quoting from historical sources. I have found it easier to understand the writer if words are not capitalized in the middle of the sentence and accounts are broken into paragraphs from the page long paragraphs in the original.

End notes are found at the end of each chapter. A list of abbreviations for my sources is found in the front of this history.

There are at least ten different ways to cite sources found in published works, according to the *Modern Language Association*, (MLA), The American Psychological Association (APA), Turabian's *A Manual for Writers*, the *Chicago Manual of Style* (CMS), the National Archives, the *Virginia Genealogical Society's Journal*, the *New England Historical and Genealogical Society's Journal*, the Virginia Historical Society, the Library of Virginia, the University of Virginia and Elizabeth Shown Mill's *Evidence*.

While each form is similar, they all differ in some way from one another. Since the objective is to be consistent and to make it easy for the reader to find the source, source citation has become a quagmire for an author. This is especially true for those of us who write for the general public rather than the academic community.

A common, simple and consistent standard appears, as of this writing, to be nonexistent. Some say to begin with a government agency. Other say to begin with the document in question. Most of these authorities, when using online records, want authors to use the entire online citation for the record in question rather than the more familiar abbreviated version.

Since it is obviously not possible to please all of these experts, I have adopted the following policy for my end notes. I have used the Library of Congress's online *Citation Guide* whenever possible. So the first time the source is cited, I have begun with the government agency, whether the Library of Congress, the National Archives or the county court. The title of the document or record of the soldier is next, which I have italicized. If the record is from a microfilm collection at the Archives, the Micro publication and roll come next, followed by the title of the document. For example: National Archives and Records Administration, *Edward Abbey's Service Record*, M 881 MR 951, *Compiled Service Records, 3rd Virginia*.

In special cases, such as letters from 3rd Virginia officers in special collections at the University of Virginia or the Library of Virginia, I have followed their own guide to how they want their sources cited. In all other instances I have cited the source as described above.

It is my understanding that access dates for online publications need not be cited if they are more than two years old. Since the research for this book took five years to complete and nearly two years to write, I have not included these dates in my citations. I have also abbreviated websites after their first citation, for personal convenience and space considerations. For example: Journals of Continental Congress, A Century of Lawmaking for a New Nation: U.S. Congressional Documents and Debates 1774–1875, 3: image 403, was taken from www.loc.gov/ ammem/amlaw/lwjclink.html. Any recurring instance of that online form will be an abbreviated one. There is only one exception to this rule—if the web site does not contain the initials www; then I have used the hypertext protocol. Colonial Williamsburg Foundation website for the Virginia Gazette is http://research.history.org and that is how I have cited it.

I have used several online sources, among them, the Library of Congress, the University of Virginia, and the Colonial Williamsburg Foundation for primary records. The University of Virginia has Fitzpatrick's complete *Writings of Washington* online. They are cited two ways in my endnotes. If I looked for a specific name, a search of the Writings ensued. This search furnished volume and page numbers for the name being searched. As a result, the web citation reads etext.lib.virginia.edu.

For the most part, however, it was more effective to search by the volume number of Washington's Writings. Then an index of each piece of correspondence or general orders, arranged by date, in that particular volume became available. There were no page numbers associated with these records. Because of that, the citation for records retrieved in each volume of Washington's Writings reads slightly differently—etext.virginia.edu.

Finally, I have used James Lester and James Lester Jr's *Writing Research Papers: A Complete Guide* (New York: Pearson & Longman, 2005) which contains the footnote and endnote system according to the *Chicago Manual of Style* (CMS) for citing the more traditional derivative sources.

Conclusion

At the present time, there is but one other history of a Virginia continental line regiment. It is my hope that this history of the 3rd Virginia will supplement our knowledge of these now-forgotten battles and skirmishes and provide insight into the motives, courage, perseverance, intrepidity, and resolve of those who served in the War for Independence.

End Notes
Introduction

1. Mary Steven Jones, ed. *An Eighteenth Century Perspective: Culpeper County, Virginia* (Culpeper, Virginia: Culpeper Historical Society, 1976), 23.
2. *Journals of Continental Congress, 1774–1789*, December 28, 1775, 2: 463, Library of Congress, (www.memory.loc.gov/ammem/lwjc). Hereafter *JCC* (www.memory.loc.gov).
3. See details in Chapters four through six for information relating to the regiment's battles and skirmishes.
4. See the National Archives and Records Administration, *Revolutionary War Rolls*, M 246 MR 96–97, *3rd Virginia Regiment* and MR 137 *Returns of the Army*.
5. ---, *American Historical Illustrations and Emblems: CD Rom and Book.* (New York: Dover Publications, 1998), 4, image 035.
6. Ibid., 9, image 071.
7. John Grafton, *The American Revolution, A Picture Sourcebook.* (New York: Dover Publications, 1975), 64, 66, 76, 77, 79, 83, and 85.

Plate 1

M 245 MR 98 Muster Roll,
Captain John Francis Mercer, April 1777

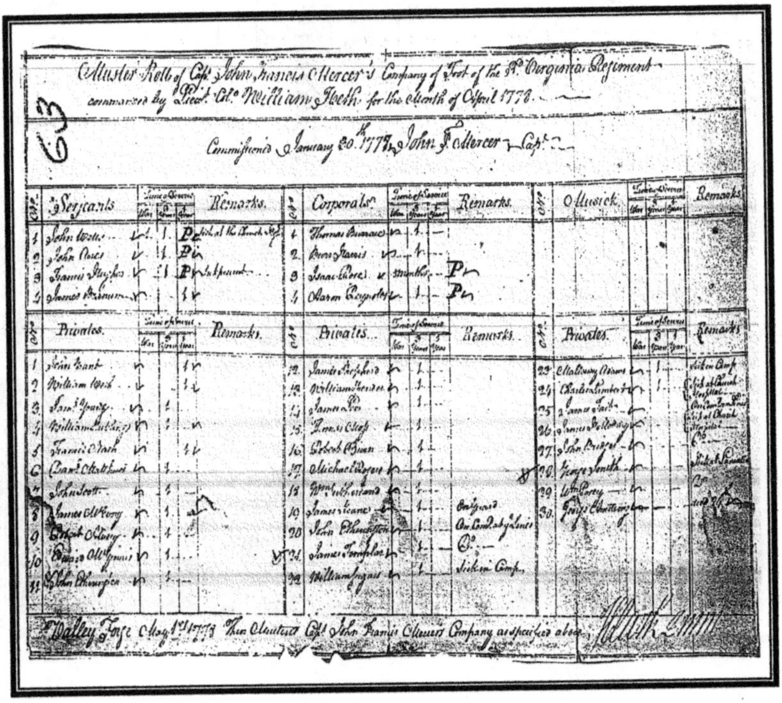

PLATE 2

M 246 MR 97 Pay Roll,
Captain David Arell, January 1778

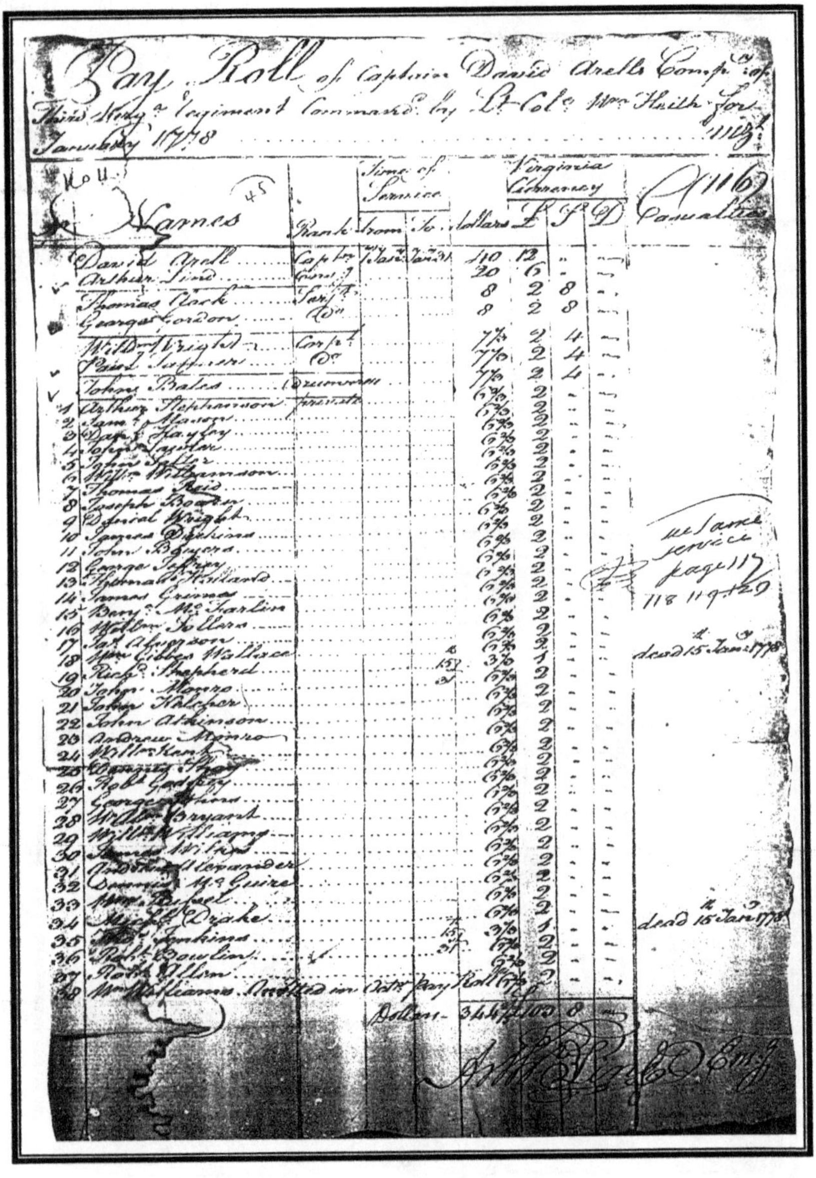

Pay Roll of Captain David Arells Compy of Third Virgª Regiment Commanded by Lt Col. Wm Heith for January 1778 ... 1116

	Names	Rank	Time of Service From	To	Dollars	Virginia Currency £	S	D	Casualties
	David Arell	Captn	1 Jany	Jany 31	40	12	"	—	
	Arthur Lind	[illegible]			20	6	-	—	
	Thomas Clark	Sarjt			8	2	8	—	
	George Gordon	Do			8	2	8	—	
	Willm Wright	Corpl			7 1/3	2	4	—	
	Paul [illegible]	Do			7 1/3	2	4	—	
	John Bates	Drummer			7 1/3	2	4	—	
1	Arthur Stephanson	private			6 2/3	2	-	—	
2	Saml Mason				6 2/3	2	-	—	
3	Danl Hayfey				6 2/3	2	-	—	
4	[illegible] Taylor				6 2/3	2	-	—	
5	John [illegible]				6 2/3	2	-	—	
6	Willm Williamson				6 2/3	2	-	—	
7	Thomas Reid				6 2/3	2	-	—	
8	Joseph Booker				6 2/3	2	-	—	
9	Daniel Wright				6 2/3	2	-	—	
10	James Dickins				6 2/3	2	-	—	
11	John Boyers				6 2/3	2	-	—	
12	George Jeffrey				6 2/3	2	-	—	
13	Thomas Hillard				6 2/3	2	-	—	see same service page 117 118 119.129
14	James Grimes				6 2/3	2	-	—	
15	Barry McFarlin				6 2/3	2	-	—	
16	Willm Fellers				6 2/3	2	-	—	
17	Jas Afurgson				6 2/3	2	-	—	
18	Wm Gibbes Wallace			15	3 1/3	1	-	—	dead 15 Jany 1778
19	Richd Shepherd				6 2/3	2	-	—	
20	John Monro				6 2/3	2	-	—	
21	John Hatcher				6 2/3	2	-	—	
22	John Atkinson				6 2/3	2	-	—	
23	Andrew Monro				6 2/3	2	-	—	
24	Willm Hanky				6 2/3	2	-	—	
25	[illegible]				6 2/3	2	-	—	
26	Robt Godfrey				6 2/3	2	-	—	
27	George [illegible]				6 2/3	2	-	—	
28	Willm Bryant				6 2/3	2	-	—	
29	Willm Williams				6 2/3	2	-	—	
30	James Wilson				6 2/3	2	-	—	
31	Andrew Alexander				6 2/3	2	-	—	
32	[illegible] McGuire				6 2/3	2	-	—	
33	Wm [illegible]				6 2/3	2	-	—	
34	Micjl Drake			15	3 1/3	1	-	—	dead 15 Jany 1778
35	[illegible] Jenkins				6 2/3	2	-	—	
36	Robt Dowlin				6 2/3	2	-	—	
37	Robt Allen				6 2/3	2	-	—	
38	Wm Williams. Omitted in Octr Pay Roll				6 2/3	2			
				Dollars	344 2/3	103	8		

[illegible] Cmy

Plate 3

M 246 MR 97 Muster Roll,
Captain John Chilton, September 1777

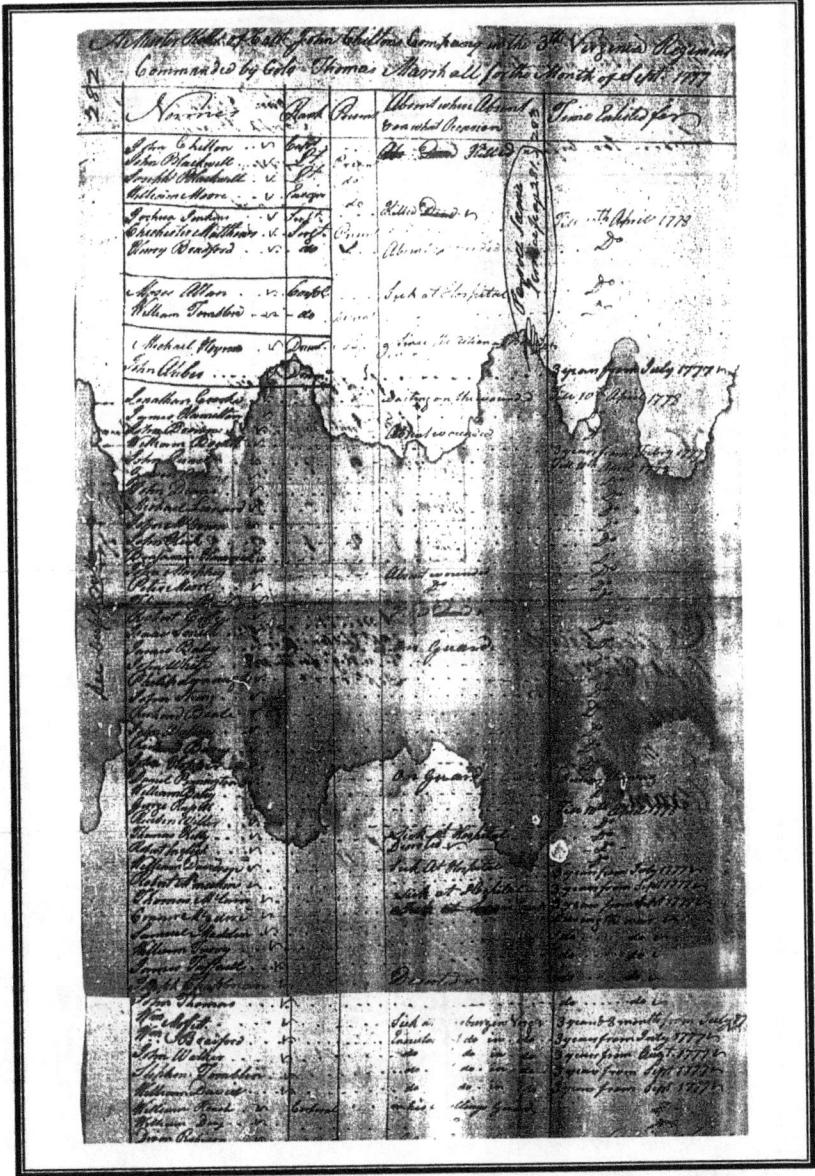

PLATE 4

M 246 MR 97 Muster Roll,
formerly Captain John Chilton, October 1777

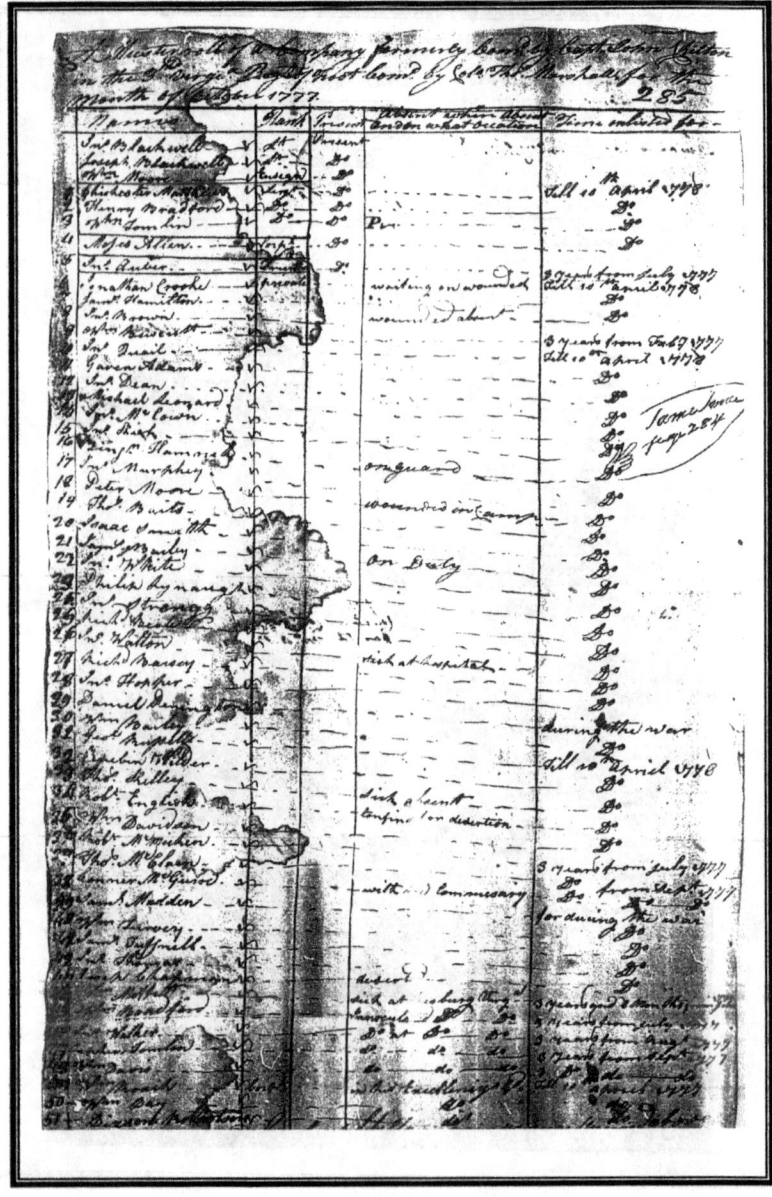

PLATE 5

**M 246 MR 97 Pay Roll,
Captain John Ashby, July 1777**

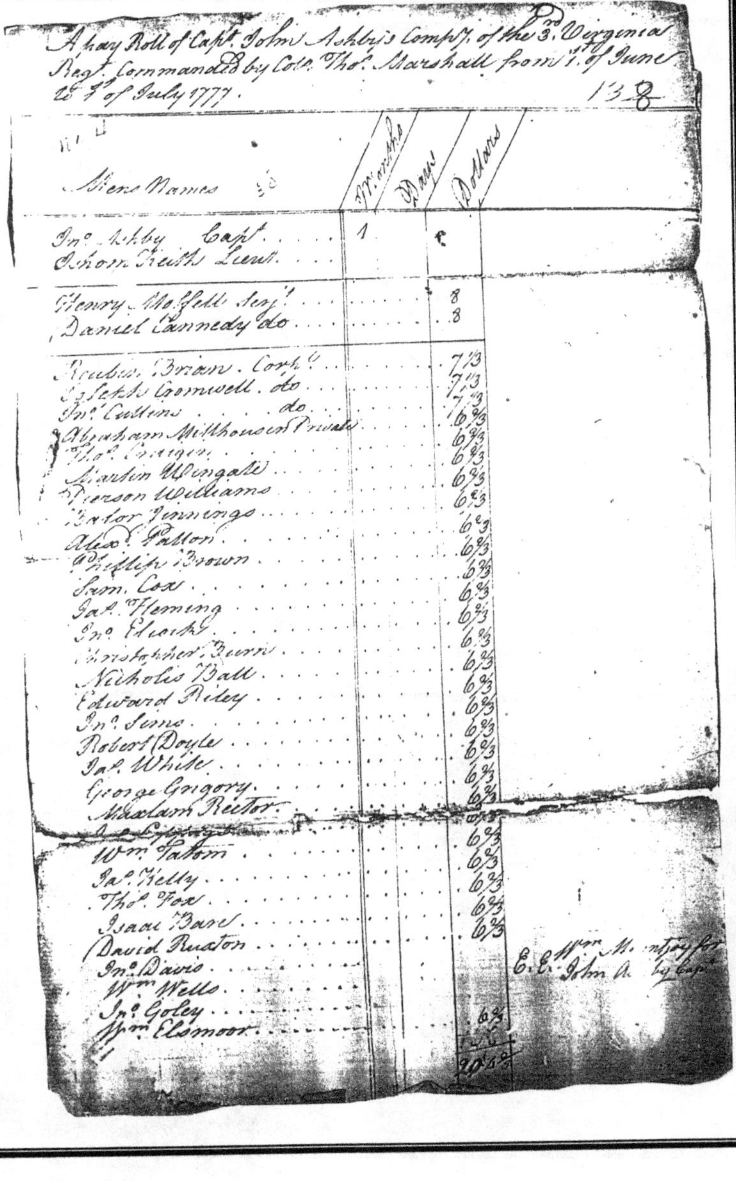

A Pay Roll of Capt. John Ashby's Compy. of the 3d. Virginia Regt. Commanded by Coll. Thos. Marshall from 1st. of June to 1st of July 1777.   138

Mens Names	Months	Days	Dollars
Jno. Ashby Capt.	1		8
Solomon Treuts Lieut.			
Henry Mozfeld Serjt.			8
Daniel Cannedy do			8
Reuben Brian Corpl.			7 1/3
Joseph Cromwell do			7 1/3
Jno. Collins do			7 1/3
Abraham Millhouse Private			6 2/3
Thos. Craven			6 2/3
Martin Wingate			6 2/3
Pierson Williams			6 2/3
Tavtor Jennings			6 2/3
Alexr. Patton			6 2/3
Phillip Brown			6 2/3
Sam. Cox			6 2/3
Jas. Fleming			6 2/3
Jno. Elcock			6 2/3
Cristopher Burns			6 2/3
Nicholis Ball			6 2/3
Edward Riley			6 2/3
Jno. Sims			6 2/3
Robert Doyle			6 2/3
Jas. White			6 2/3
George Gregory			6 2/3
Absalom Rector			
Wm. Tatum			6 2/3
Jas. Kelly			6 2/3
Thos. Fox			6 2/3
Isaac Bare			6 2/3
David Ruxton			
Jno. Davis			
Wm. Wells			
Jno. Goley			
Wm. Elsmoor			6 2/3
			200 2/3

PLATE 6

M 246 MR 97 Muster Roll,
Captain Valentine Peyton, April 1778

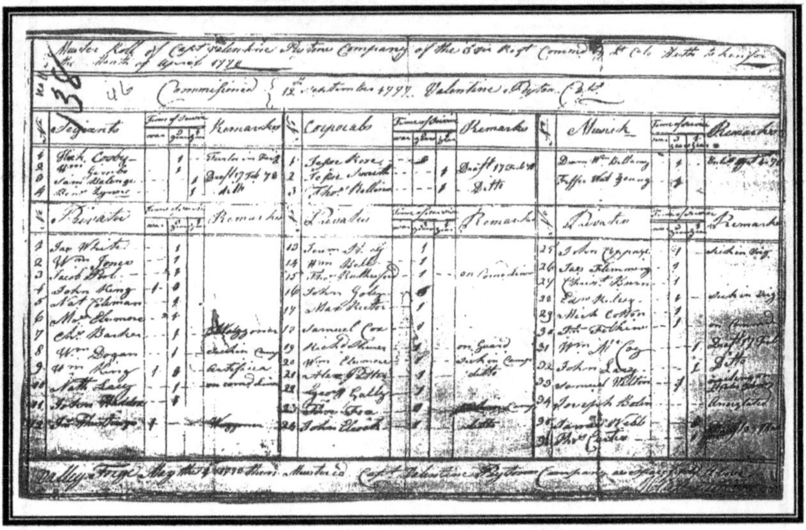

PLATE 7

M 246 MR 97 Muster Roll,
Captain John Blackwell, February 1778

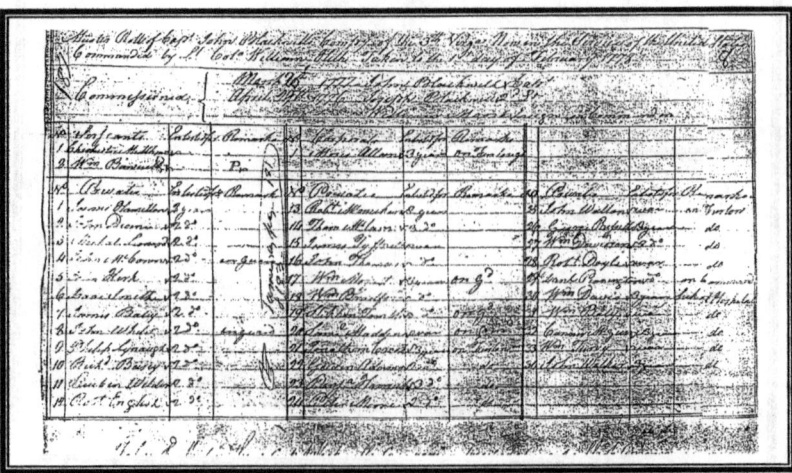

Plate 8

M 246 MR 97 Muster Roll,
Captain Robert Powell, May 1778

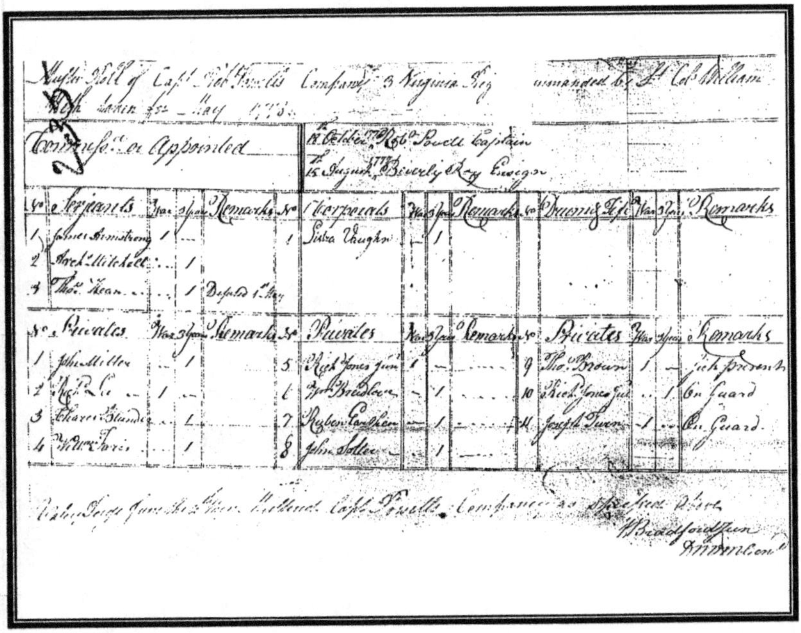

PLATE 9

**M 246 MR 97 Pay Roll,
Captain Philip Richard Francis Lee, May 1777**

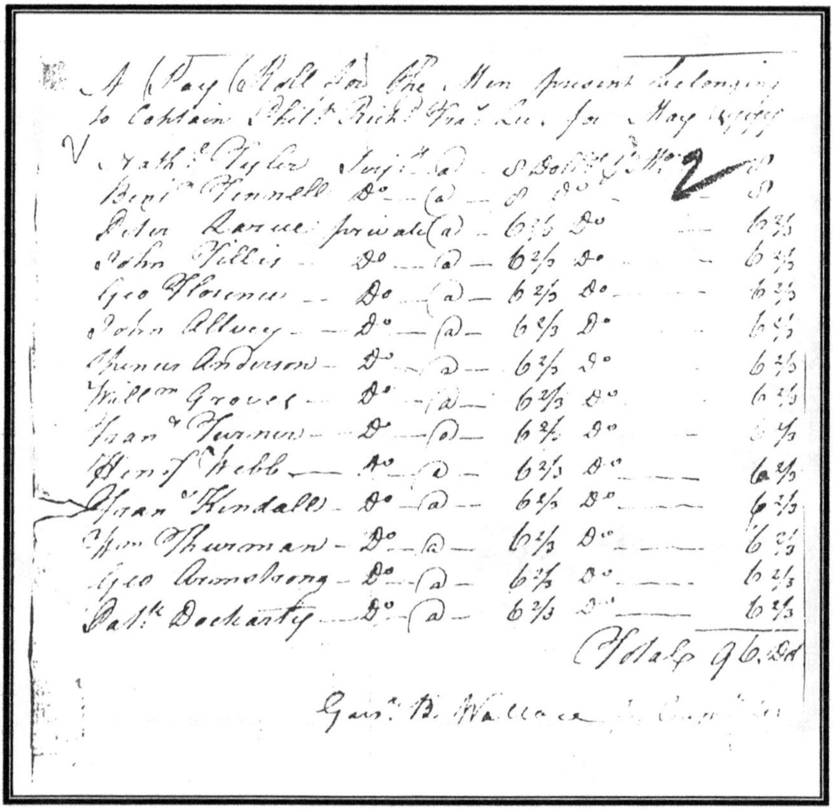

A Pay Roll for the Men present belonging to Captain Phil.t Rich.d Fra.s Lee, for May 1777

Nath.l Tyler	Serj.t	@	8 Dolls. p. M.o	8
Benj.n Pennell	D.o	@	8 D.o	8
Peter Larue	private	@	6 2/3 D.o	6 2/3
John Willis	D.o	@	6 2/3 D.o	6 2/3
Geo Florence	D.o	@	6 2/3 D.o	6 2/3
John Allvey	D.o	@	6 2/3 D.o	6 2/3
Thomas Anderson	D.o	@	6 2/3 D.o	6 2/3
Will.m Groves	D.o	@	6 2/3 D.o	6 2/3
Isaac Turner	D.o	@	6 2/3 D.o	6 2/3
Henry Webb	D.o	@	6 2/3 D.o	6 2/3
Isaac Kendall	D.o	@	6 2/3 D.o	6 2/3
Thom Thurman	D.o	@	6 2/3 D.o	6 2/3
Geo Armstrong	D.o	@	6 2/3 D.o	6 2/3
Pat.k Dockarty	D.o	@	6 2/3 D.o	6 2/3

Totals 96 Dol

Gav.n B. Wallace [illegible]

Plate 10

M 246 MR 98 Pay Roll,
Captain Gustavus Brown Wallace, September 1777

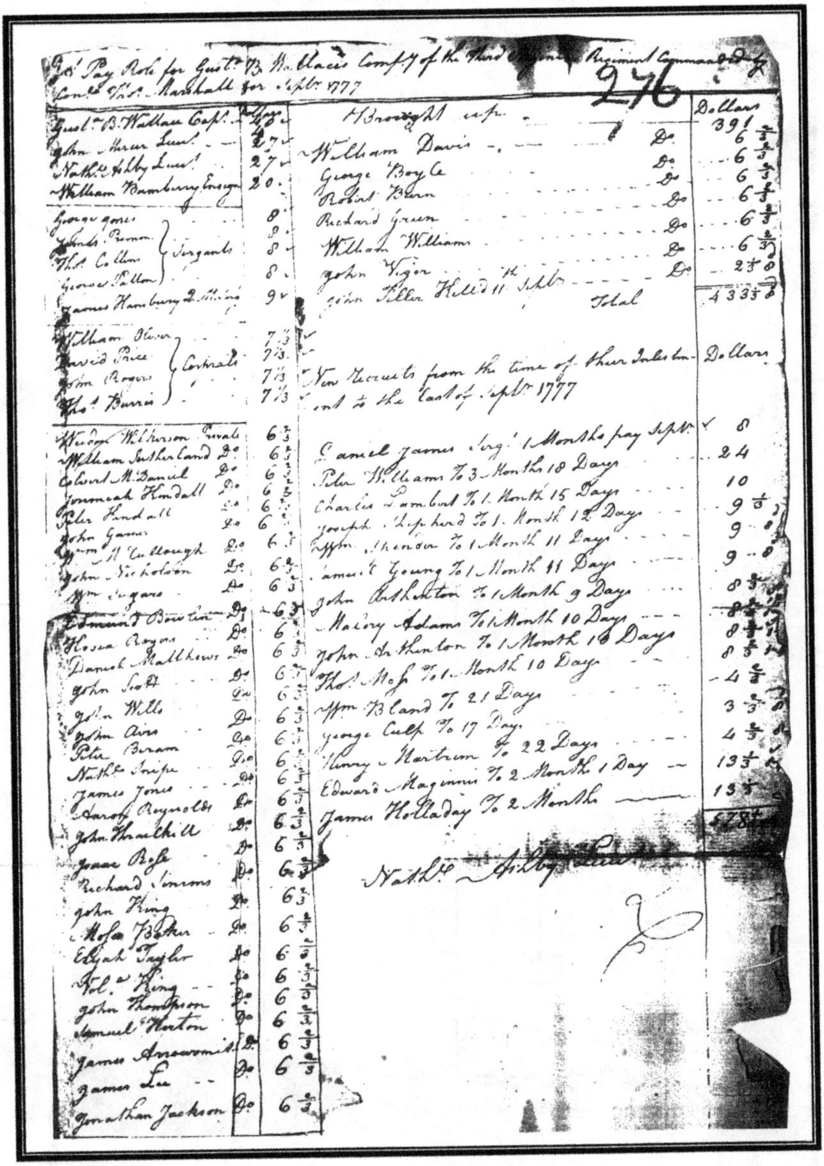

Pay Roll for Gust. B. Wallace's Comp.y of the third Virginia Regiment Commanded by Coll. Thos. Marshall for Septr. 1777

276

Gust. B. Wallace Capt.		Brought up		Dollars 391
John Mercer Lieut.	27	William Davis	Do.	6 2/3
Nathl. Ashby Lieut.	27	George Boyle	Do.	6 2/3
William Bambury Ensign	20	Robert Bern	Do.	6 2/3
George Jones	8	Richard Green	Do.	6 2/3
Jonas Brenon — Serjeants	8	William Williams	Do.	6 2/3
Thos. Collin	8	John Vigor	Do.	2 5/8
George Patton	8	John Tiller Killed 11 Septr.		
James Hambury Drumming	9		Total	433 5/8
William Oliver	7 1/3			
David Price — Corporals	7 1/3	New Recruits from the time of their Inlistment to the last of Septr. 1777		Dollars
John Rogers	7 1/3			
Thos. Barris	7 1/3			
George Wilkerson Private	6 2/3	Samuel James Serg. 1 Months pay Septr.		8
William Sutherland Do.	6 2/3	Peter Williams To 3 Months 18 Days		24
Edward McDaniel Do.	6 2/3	Charles Lambert To 1 Month 15 Days		10
Jeremiah Kindall Do.	6 2/3	Joseph Shepherd To 1 Month 12 Days		9 1/3
Peter Kindall Do.	6 2/3	John Shender To 1 Month 11 Days		9
John James		Samuel Young To 1 Month 11 Days		9
Wm. McCullough Do.	6 2/3	John Atherton To 1 Month 9 Days		9
John Nicholson Do.	6 2/3	Malory Adams To 1 Month 10 Days		8 2/3
Wm. Sugars Do.	6 2/3	John Atherton To 1 Month 10 Days		8 8/9
Edmund Bowtin Do.	6 2/3	Thos. Moss To 1 Month 10 Days		8 8/9
Hosea Rogers Do.	6 2/3	Wm. Bland To 21 Days		8 8/9
Daniel Matthews Do.	6 2/3	George Culp To 17 Days		4 2/3
John Scott Do.	6 2/3	Henry Martrim To 22 Days		3 2/3
John Wills Do.	6 2/3	Edward Maginnis To 2 Months 1 Day		4 2/3
John Aires Do.	6 2/3	James Holladay To 2 Months		13 1/3
Peter Buram Do.	6 2/3			13 1/3
Nathl. Snipe Do.	6 2/3			578
James Jones Do.	6 2/3	Nathl. Ashby Lieut.		
Aaron Reynolds Do.	6 2/3			
John Thrailkill Do.	6 2/3			
Isaac Rose Do.	6 2/3			
Richard Simms Do.	6 2/3			
John King Do.	6 2/3			
Moses Baker Do.	6 2/3			
Elijah Taylor Do.	6 2/3			
Vol. King Do.	6 2/3			
John Thompson Do.	6 2/3			
Samuel Horton Do.	6 2/3			
James Answorth Do.	6 2/3			
James Lee Do.	6 2/3			
Jonathan Jackson Do.	6 2/3			

Plate 11

M 246 MR 98 Muster Roll,
Captain William Washington, July 1777.

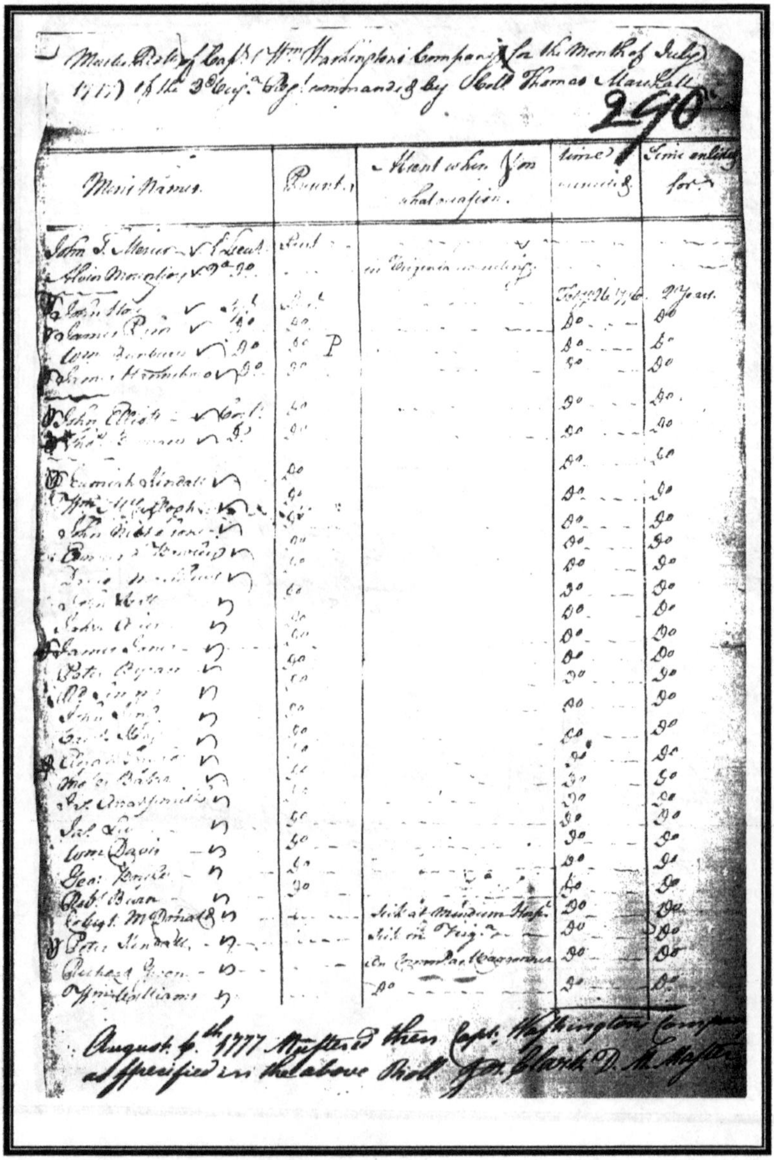

Muster Roll of Capt. Wm. Washington's Company for the Month of July 1777 of the 3d Virg.a Regt. commanded by Coll Thomas Marshall

290

Men's Names	Present	Absent when & on what reason	time enlisting	Time enlisted for

August 4th 1777 Mustered then Capt. Washington's Company as specified in the above Roll Jn. Clark D. M. Master

PLATE 12

M 246 MR 98 Muster Roll,
Captain Charles West, June 1777

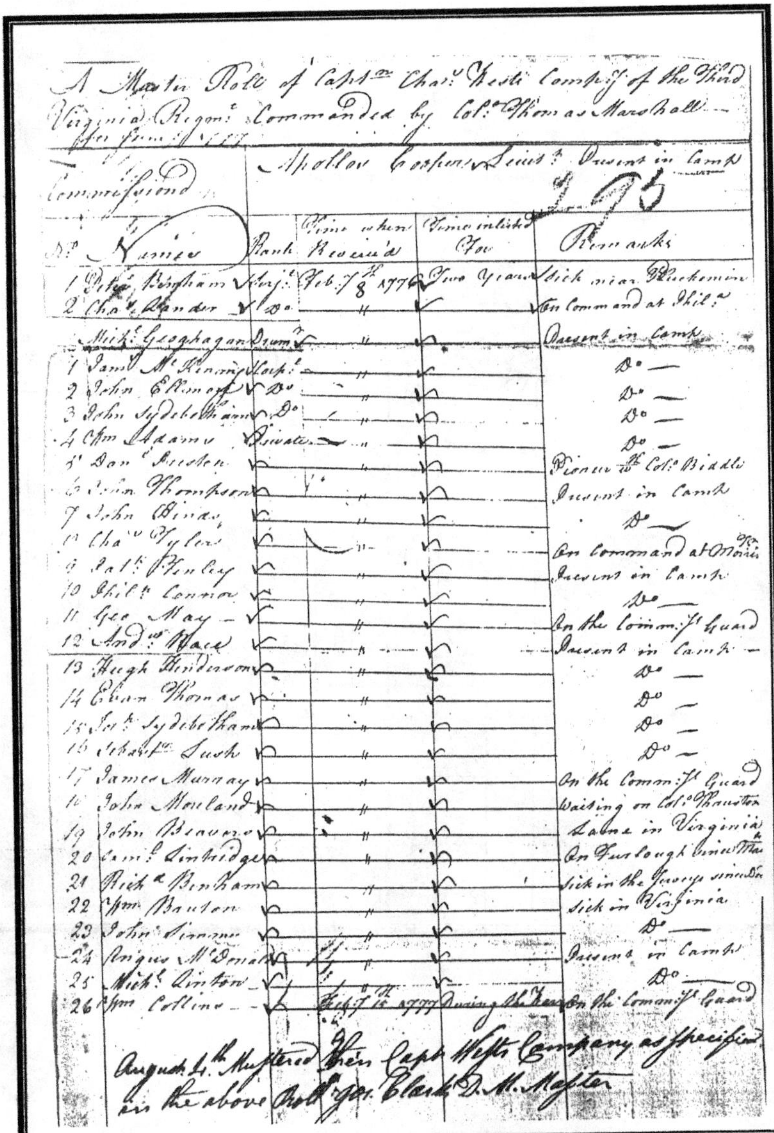

A Muster Roll of Capt.n Cha.s West's Comp.y of the Third Virginia Reg.t Commanded by Col.o Thomas Marshall for June 1777

No	Names	Rank	Time when Received	Time inlisted For	Remarks
	Commission'd	Apollos Cooper Lieut. Present in Camp			
1	Peter Bingham	Serj.t	Feb.y 8th 1776	Two Years	Sick near Puckemin
2	Cha.s Bander	Do	"	"	On Command at Phil.a
	Mich.l Geoghagan Drum.r				Present in Camp
1	Jam.s McKenning	Corp.l	"	"	Do —
2	John O Rimoy	Do	"	"	Do —
3	John Sydebetham	Do	"	"	Do —
4	Chr.n Adams	Private	"	"	Do —
5	Dan.l Preston		"	"	Prisoner to Col.o Biddle
6	John Thompson		"	"	Present in Camp
7	John Binds		"	"	Do —
8	Cha.s Tyler		"	"	On Command at Morris &c
9	Pat.k Henley		"	"	Present in Camp
10	Phil.p Connor		"	"	Do
11	Geo May		"	"	On the Comm.y.s Guard
12	And.w Wace		"	"	Present in Camp
13	Hugh Henderson		"	"	Do —
14	Eben Thomas		"	"	Do —
15	Jos.h Sydebetham		"	"	Do —
16	Sebast.n Lush		"	"	Do —
17	James Murray		"	"	On the Comm.y.s Guard
18	John Moreland		"	"	Waiting on Col.o Thruston
19	John Beaver		"	"	Lame in Virginia
20	Sam.l Sinbridge		"	"	On Furlough &c
21	Rich.d Bingham		"	"	Sick in the Jerseys since &c
22	W.m Banton		"	"	Sick in Virginia
23	John Simms		"	"	Do —
24	Angus McDonald		"	"	Present in Camp
25	Mich.l Linton		"	"	Do —
26	W.m Collins		Feb.y 8th 1777 during the war	On the Comm.y.s Guard

August 4th Mustered then Capt. West's Company as specified in the above Roll ⅌ Geo. Clark D. M. Master

PLATE 13

M 246 MR 98 Pay Roll,
Captain Reuben Briscoe, December, 1777

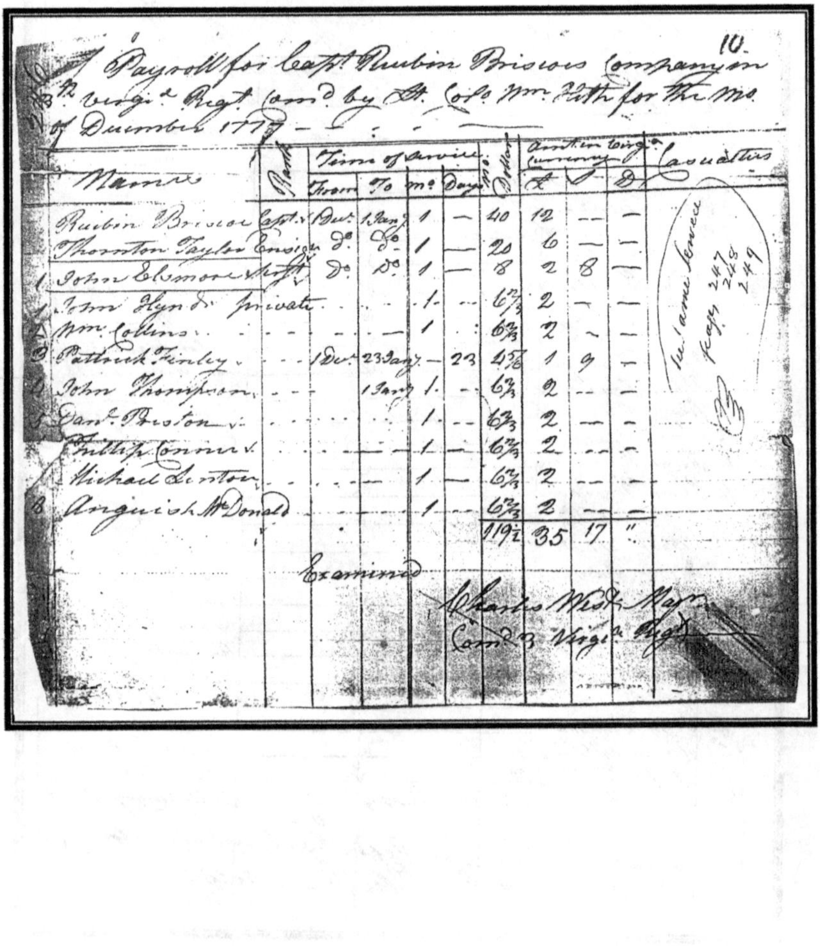

10.

A Payroll for Captn Rubin Briscoes Company in 3d Virga Regt Comd by Lt Colo Wm Heth for the Mo of December 1777

	Names	Rank	Term of service From	To	Mo	Days	Dollars	Amount in Virga currency £	S	D	Casualties
	Rubin Briscoe	Captn	Decr	1 Jany	1	—	40	12	—	—	See same service Copy 247 248 249
	Thornton Taylor	Ensign	Do	Do	1	—	20	6	—	—	
1	John Elsmore	Serjt	Do	Do	1	—	8	2	8	—	
1	John Flyn	private			1		$6\frac{2}{3}$	2	—	—	
2	Wm Collins				1		$6\frac{2}{3}$	2	—	—	
3	Pattrick Finley		1 Decr	23 Jany	—	23	$4\frac{5}{6}$	1	9	—	
4	John Thompson			1 Jany	1		$6\frac{2}{3}$	2	—	—	
5	Danl Preston				1		$6\frac{2}{3}$	2	—	—	
	Phillip Conner				1		$6\frac{2}{3}$	2	—	—	
	Michael Linton				1		$6\frac{2}{3}$	2	—	—	
8	Anguish McDonald				1		$6\frac{2}{3}$	2	—	—	
							$119\frac{1}{2}$	35	17	"	

Examined

Charles West Majr
Comd 3 Virga Regt

CHAPTER 1

EVOLUTION OF THE 3RD VIRGINIA REGIMENT, CONTINENTAL LINE 1776–1778

HISTORICAL BACKGROUND
1775 REVAMPING THE VIRGINIA MILITARY ESTABLISHMENT

A number of the officers and men of the 3rd Virginia Regiment on Continental Establishment actually had prior military experience before December 1775 when the Virginia Convention authorized the formation of the regiment. Many of these men were part of the colony's military response to Lord Dunmore's removal of gunpowder from the Williamsburg magazine in the spring of 1775.[1] While authorized in December, the 3rd Virginia was not, in reality, organized until the last of February 1776 at Alexandria and Dumfries.[2]

The events leading to the Battle at Great Bridge in January 1776 and the burning of Norfolk played an important part in Virginians' motivation to enlist in the 3rd Virginia. The Regiment was recruited primarily from the northern Virginia counties of Prince William, Fauquier, Loudoun, Culpeper, King George, Spotsylvania, along with Westmoreland and Louisa counties, which were outside the Northern Virginia and Piedmont locale.[3] In order to appreciate the outstanding quality of leadership found in the 3rd Virginia it is necessary to recount the actions taking place in 1775 which led to the enlistment of experienced veterans into the 3rd Virginia in February 1776.

In March 1775, the second Virginia Convention met at St. John's Church on the James River. At this convention, Patrick Henry proposed the establishment of an independent militia, to serve in defense of the colonies. Thomas Marshall, a future officer in the 3rd Virginia, was a delegate. So was George Washington.[4]

The Convention passed a resolution to set up independent militia units and recommend that each county raise at least one infantry company, to be trained and ready for any emergency. An infantry company was to be composed of sixty-eight men with a captain, two lieutenants, an ensign, four sergeants, four corporals and drums and colors. Each soldier was to be provided with a rifle, a bayonet, cartridge box and tomahawk, as well as a pound of gunpowder and four pounds of ball, fitted to the bore of his gun. The men were to be clothed in a hunting shirt and to become acquainted with military exercise appropriate for an infantry company.

The convention also recommended the formation of cavalry units, to consist of thirty men, excluding officers; each trooper was to be provided with a good horse, bridle, saddle, and pistols and holsters, a carbine or other short firelock, a saddle pocket for his rifle, a cutting sword or tomahawk. He was to be provided with a pound of gunpowder and four pounds of ball. The cavalry was to use "utmost diligence in training and accustoming his horse to stand the discharge of Fire-arms and in making himself acquainted with military exercise for cavalry."[5]

In April 1775, Governor John Murray, Lord Dunmore attempted to remove the arms and gunpowder from the magazine at Williamsburg and transport it to the schooner *Magdalen* anchored at Burwell's Ferry. The keeper of the magazine gave up the keys and then warned town authorities that the Governor had ordered the locks removed from the muskets and was going to carry off the powder.[6]

British troops had entered Williamsburg quietly on 21 April 1775 with the express purpose of transferring the colony's gunpowder from the capitol to a British ship, anchored four miles away in the James River. Lord Dunmore had ordered the seizure, hoping to put an end to any armed resistance to British policies in Virginia. He began looking for troops to restore royal authority although calls for loyalists to take up arms did not bring about the return for which he hoped.[7]

This brought about an immediate a chorus of disapproval which moved Dunmore to even greater antagonism. He was determined that, "by God, he would let them see that he could fight against them!"[8]

Once the removal of the arms had become known, independent militia throughout Virginia, authorized by the 2nd Virginia Convention, prepared to march on the capitol. Lord Dunmore, concerned about the extent of the public outcry, attempted to defuse the affair by agreeing to pay for the gunpowder.

This action did not measurably end the public concern and the situation remained volatile throughout May.[9]

By the end of May, however, cooler heads prevailed. The Governor realized he was in no position to fight without British help while the Virginian patriot leadership recognized that the minute service was in no condition to engage any kind of British armed response.[10]

In June, Dunmore decided to leave Williamsburg, with his family, for the safety of the British Navy. With the British focusing on Massachusetts, the royal governor realized that little aid would be forthcoming from that quarter. Nor was Dunmore successful in arousing loyalist opposition to undertake an uprising on his behalf, especially after he promised slaves freedom if they enlisted in his cause.[11]

In July 1775, the Virginia Assembly appointed a Committee of Safety, who was charged with putting together the defense of the colony. The Assembly authorized two regiments of regular troops and fifteen battalions of minute men to defend the colony against invasion and insurrection.[12]

The convention recommended the formation of fifteen companies of sixty-eight men each. Eight of these companies would form the 1st Virginia Regiment. The regiments were subject to service outside Virginia's borders. The commander of the 1st Virginia would also command all of the Virginia troops. The remaining companies were to form the 2nd Virginia Regiment. The four western districts were asked to recruit only riflemen so that each regiment would have two companies for use as light infantry.

The Convention considered four men to be the commander of the 1st Virginia: Patrick Henry, Thomas Nelson, Wm. Woodford of Caroline County and Hugh Mercer of Fredericksburg. Patrick Henry, the convention's choice so annoyed Hugh Mercer, who was easily the most experienced military leader, that he withdrew his name from consideration as commandant of the 2nd Virginia. The convention then turned to Wm. Woodford as the commander of that regiment.[13]

Now that the Governor had fled to the British lines, the de facto government of Virginia fell to the third Virginia Convention. Delegates met in *August 1775* and formed a new military establishment for the colony. The Convention gave orders to replace the independent militia companies organized in March by the second Virginia Convention with a three-tier military system.

At the top were two 500 man Battalions—the 1st and 2nd Virginia Battalions. These battalions were made up of full-time soldiers raised through out the colony to serve a one year term. The battalions were a throw-back to Virginia's military during the French and Indian War, some twenty years earlier.[14]

The second tier was a newly-created minute service. The Convention divided Virginia into sixteen recruiting districts, with each district responsible for raising a battalion of 500 minute men.[15] These minute men were so-called because they were men who were ready and able to serve at a minute's notice. Men were to be recruited into the minute service who were between the ages of sixteen and sixty. They were better trained and prepared than militia men, which made up the last tier of this new military establishment. Free white males between sixteen and fifty could also belong to the county militias.[16]

The largest Minute Battalion was organized in the Culpeper District, made up of men from Culpeper, Orange and Fauquier. The flag of the Culpeper Minute Battalion consisted of a rattlesnake, in the center of the flag, coiled to strike with the motto "Don't tread on me!" below it. "Liberty or Death" adorned the sides of the flag while the top of the standard bore the name of the unit: The Culpeper Minute men.[17]

Colonel Patrick Henry, remembered for his stirring "Give me Liberty or Give Me Death!" speech at the second Virginia Convention in March 1775, had been appointed commander in chief of the colony's military forces. He ordered the separate minute companies in the Culpeper district to form a battalion under Colonel Lawrence Taliaferro of Orange, Lt. Colonel Edward Stevens of Culpeper and Major Thomas Marshall, of Fauquier. The companies and battalion were to rendezvous near present-day Culpeper Court house.

In the fall of 1775, 350 men of the Culpeper Minute Battalion marched to Williamsburg to join the main body of the Virginia troops. The original companies in the battalion grew to fourteen. Thomas Marshall, young John Marshall, John Chilton, John Blackwell, and others were in this contingent and gained valuable military experience before they joined the 3rd Virginia Regiment.[18]

Culpeper County may have raised as many as five companies of sixty-eight men; Orange County, two companies; and Fauquier, no less than seven companies. Some of these companies may have been under strength.[19] Anyone who could recruit sixty-eight men would automatically become a captain of a company in this battalion.[20] As it turned out, enlistment in both minute and militia companies was strong and soldiers throughout the counties in the colony moved toward Williamsburg. By autumn, residents of Williamsburg had grown accustomed to seeing armed men around the town.[21]

While this flurry of activity dominated Virginia's soldiery, events had also taken place in Philadelphia where the second Continental Congress had been meeting since May. Delegates, back in the spring, had agreed to put the colonies in a state of military readiness. By June 1775, Congress voted to raise six companies of expert riflemen—two from Pennsylvania, two from Maryland and two regiments from Virginia. Congress believed that these regiments could march north to support the Massachusetts troops then attempting to relieve Boston. At the same time, they named Colonel George Washington as a commander-in-chief of the now Continental forces. He took command in Cambridge in July. Bunker Hill had already taken place. The two Virginia rifle companies were raised in Berkeley and Frederick counties, under the command of Hugh Stephenson and Daniel Morgan.

Daniel Morgan, thirty-nine years old in 1775, had already seen service in the French and Indian War as a teamster and later service in the militia, and as a commissioned officer in Pontiac's war near Detroit. Morgan raised his company in ten days and marched northward to New England.[22] Daniel Morgan also had a connection with the 3rd Virginia. In June 1777, he received permission to recruit riflemen from the 3rd Virginia who went on to play a decisive part in the American victory at Saratoga.[23]

VIRGINIA'S NEWLY CREATED MILITARY VERSUS LORD DUNMORE

THE IMPORTANCE OF LEADERSHIP IN THE INDEPENDENT COMPANIES, VIRGINIA BATTALIONS AND THE MINUTE BATTALIONS IN THE FUTURE 3RD VIRGINIA OFFICER CORPS.

One: The formation of Independent Companies.

In the aftermath of Lord Dunmore's seizure of gunpowder in April 1775 from the Williamsburg magazine, young gentlemen through out the colony organized independent companies and planned to march to Williamsburg to recover the powder.

Some of these companies had been formed as early as 1774 as "gentlemen independents", supposedly to prepare for an attack by the Shawnee. By the time they were ready to march, events had overtaken preparations and Andrew Lewis's Augusta militia had defeated the Shawnee at Point Pleasant. "After discovering the fun of being peacetime soldiers, however, the youths were loath to disband, so a few of the volunteers in Prince William and Norfolk counties remained mobilized."[24]

Prince William's Independent Company was one of those companies formed in November 1774 among young members of the gentry in the county.[25] Known as the Independent Company of Cadets, William Grayson was their chairman; Their motto was *Aut liber, aut nullus*. ("Either freedom or nothing") The minutes of the company for 11 November 1774 note resolutions for Thomas Blackburn, Richard Graham, and **Philip Richard Francis Lee** to request George Washington to take command of their company as their field officer and "direct the fashion of their uniform."[26]

George Washington noted in his diary for 13 November 1774, the appearance of Colonel Blackburn, Mr. Lee and Richard Graham as a Committee from the Prince William Independent Company.[27] Washington accepted their request. By the late spring of 1775, he had also accepted the commands of the independent companies of Fairfax, Fauquier, Richmond and Spotsylvania counties.[28]

Philip Richard Francis Lee went on to become a captain in the 3rd Virginia. His death was recorded in the Compiled Service Records of the 3rd Virginia as having occurred on 29 January 1778,[29] from wounds suffered at Brandywine.[30]

Other independent companies also provided officers for the future 3rd Virginia Regiment of Foot, Continental Line and other Continental and State lines. The Independent Company of the Town of Fredericksburg was formed in April 1775. They vowed to recover the powder abstracted from the Williamsburg magazine by Lord Dunmore. The Fredericksburg Company was equipped as a light cavalry company. They were led by **Captain Hugh Mercer, 1st Lieutenant George Weedon**, 2nd Lieutenant Alexander Spotswood, and Ensign John Willis.[31]

Captain Hugh Mercer was to become the first colonel of the 3rd Virginia; 1st Lieutenant George Weedon was to become the second colonel of the regiment when Mercer was promoted to Brigadier in

June 1776.³² Wounded at the Battle of Princeton, in January 1777, Hugh Mercer was captured and bayoneted to death by the British.³³

Lieutenant Alexander Spotswood, while not part of the officer corps of the 3rd Virginia, later became a Major in the 2nd Virginia, commissioned on February 13, 1776, promoted to lieutenant colonel of the regiment in May 1776 and finally colonel of the 2nd Virginia in February 1777. He resigned his commission in October 1777. Colonel Spotswood died in December 1818.³⁴

John Willis also joined the 2nd Virginia Regiment, commissioned as a 2nd Lieutenant in September 1775. He was promoted to captain in June 1776 and captured at Brandywine, in September 1777. He was not exchanged until November 1780. In May 1779, Willis was promoted to major of the 5th Virginia Regiment although he did not see service in this regiment.³⁵

The independent company of Caroline was also organized in either February or March 1775. Their first Captain was William Woodford.³⁶ Woodford became the colonel of the 2nd Virginia Regiment.³⁷ He had the overall command of the military during the campaigns against Norfolk and Great Bridge.³⁸ In November 1777, he became the commander of the 3rd Virginia Brigade which was composed of the 3rd Virginia, 7th Virginia, 11th Virginia, and 15th Virginia.³⁹

The independent company of Fairfax was originally formed in September 1774 by a committee of "Gentlemen and Freeholders" of Fairfax County. This group of young men had become alarmed by Indian incursions and troubled by threats to their civil rights and liberty. A young 2nd Lieutenant, **John Fitzgerald**⁴⁰ in this company, was later to become Captain John Fitzgerald of the 3rd Virginia⁴¹ and then Major Fitzgerald, an aide de camp to General Washington.⁴²

The independent companies of Fairfax, Fredericksburg, and Prince William, on the way to Williamsburg in April 1775 to confront Lord Dunmore, were persuaded by Colonel Washington to return to their counties. They did so reluctantly.⁴³

Two: The value of leadership in the two Virginia Battalions, vis-à-vis the future 3rd Virginia officer corps.

The Virginia Convention, meeting in July 1775, in its arrangement of military forces for the defense of the colony, set up two 500 men battalions, known as the 1st and 2nd Virginia Battalion on Provincial Establishment.⁴ Both battalions would later become the 1st and 2nd Virginia Regiments, on service for the United States or on the Continental Establishment.⁴⁴

The 1st Virginia Continental infantry regiment was raised as a provincial or state defense unit according to the 3rd Virginia Convention. This battalion's original colonel was Patrick Henry. Since he proved to be a better politician and orator than military man, the command passed to **William Woodford**. Woodford became the field officer in charge of operations in Norfolk and Great Bridge in the late fall and early winter of 1775.⁴⁵

Initially, the 2nd Virginia's formation and organization followed the pattern of the 1st Virginia. This battalion saw considerable service in Norfolk. William Woodford, of Caroline County, became the "de facto commander in chief of Virginia forces from October through December 1775."⁴⁶

While these two battalions did not provide officers for the 3rd Virginia, William Woodford did have a connection to the 3rd Virginia. His brigade was made up of the 3rd, 7th, 11th, and 15th Virginia in November 1777.⁴⁷

Three: Influence of leadership in the Minute Battalions on the future 3rd Virginia Regiment.

While the two Virginia battalions were mobilizing, the Minute Battalions were also busy. The Convention had organized the colony into sixteen Minute districts. The Caroline, Culpeper and Prince William Minute Battalions all contributed officers to the 3rd Virginia.

The Caroline District Battalion was formed from officers and men recruited from Caroline, Spotsylvania, King George and Stafford. Hugh Mercer became the Colonel of this battalion.⁴⁸ Their adjutant was **John Francis Mercer**.⁴⁹

At a September 12, 1775 meeting at Spotsylvania Court house, **William Washington** was selected as one of the Captains in the Stafford County minute company.⁵⁰ At the same meeting, **Reuben Briscoe** became an ensign for a company of King George minutemen.⁵¹

The Culpeper Minute Battalion was the largest minute battalion, recruited from Culpeper, Orange and Fauquier Counties. By September 1775, more than 300 men had been raised and divided into companies. Culpeper County alone raised five companies. Among the field staff of the Culpeper Minute Battalion was **Major Thomas Marshall**, another future filed officer of the 3rd Virginia.[52] Two more companies were raised in Orange. Seven companies were recruited in Fauquier.[53] **Captains John Chilton**[54] and **John Blackwell**[55] both of Fauquier, became Captains in the 3rd Virginia, although John Blackwell initially was commissioned as a 1st lieutenant in the regiment.[56]

The Prince William District Battalion was made up of officers and men from Prince William, Fairfax and Loudoun.[57] Their surgeon, **David Griffith** was to hold two field staff positions in the 3rd Virginia: that of Surgeon and Chaplain.[58] Captains **Charles West**,[59] **Andrew Leitch**,[60] and **John Fitzgerald**[61] were all to become officers in the 3rd Virginia.

From this exposition of the officer corps of the various military units described above who were deployed to Williamsburg, Norfolk and the Great Bridge before February 1775, it can be seen that the future 3rd Virginia Regiment on Continental Establishment claimed field staff and officers who were already battle-hardened; the younger group of men had been tested at Norfolk and Great Bridge. The older group, like Hugh Mercer, George Weedon, and William Woodford, had seen previous action in the French and Indian War.[62]

Four: September to October 1775 – The mobilization and march of the Culpeper Minute Battalions to Williamsburg.

The Fauquier contingent of the Culpeper Minute Battalion was drilling during August and apparently did not rendezvous with the Orange and Culpeper minute companies until early September.[63] The rendezvous took place at Colonel Philip Clayton's home near Culpeper Court house.

Once the battalion met, they adopted a yellow flag with a rattlesnake coiled and ready to strike. Beneath the rattler were the words "Don't tread on me". The words "Culpeper Minute Men" appeared above the rattlesnake while "Liberty or Death" was found on either side of the icon.[64]

Young Philip Slaughter, a private in Captain John Jameson's Culpeper Company of the Battalion, kept a diary of the events in which he was involved. He noted that the battalion

> ... appeared according to orders in hunting shirts made of strong, brown linen, dyed the color of leaves of the trees, and on the breast of each hunting shirt was worked in large white letters the words 'LIBERTY OR DEATH'... All those [men] who could procure for love or money bucks' tails, wore them on their hats. Each man had a leather belt around his shoulders, with a tomahawk and a scalping knife ...[65]

The *Virginia Gazette* reported in its October 20, 1775 edition of the expected arrival of the "Culpeper battalion of minute-men, all fine fellows, and well armed (near one half of them with rifles)... now within a few hours march of this city ..."[66]

Philip Slaughter thought the residents of Williamsburg "seemed as much afraid of us as if we had been Indians". They were apparently taken aback by the Battalions "savage-looking equipment—tomahawks and scalping knives."[67]

Among the captains of Fauquier companies of the Battalion arriving in Williamsburg in October were William Pickett, James Scott, John Chilton, William Blackwell, and William Payne.

Captain John Chilton decided to transform the appearance of his Fauquier company into something more traditional and less frightening to the town's inhabitants. So he outfitted his men with Osnaburg cloth for hunting shirts;[68] this was a coarse linen cloth stocked by most dry-goods stores.[69] He bought a pound of thread along with dozens of small and large horn buttons.[70] He also purchased blue half thicks, coarse wool dyed indigo blue, to be used as leggings to protect his soldier's ankles and legs.[71]

Five: October 1775 – Events leading to the Battle of Hampton

Meanwhile, Lord Dunmore, on the British ship *Otter*, was unhappy about the arrival of all these troops into his capital.[72] As the fall of 1775 faded into winter, more and more companies of regulars and minute battalions entered the city.

While the Culpeper minute battalion did not arrive in the capital until late October, the *Virginia Gazette* reported three companies of regulars and a company of minutemen entering the city and being reviewed by the Williamsburg Committee of Safety.[73] On 21 October 1775 two more companies of regulars arrived from Henrico and Mecklenburg. Added to these troops was the report of "A body of about 600 men in the minute service (mostly riflemen) from one of the upper districts, [who] are within a short distance of this city, and hourly expected."[74]

Williamsburg had begun to take on the appearance of an armed camp. Tents dotted the gardens behind the capitol and William & Mary College. Streets, because they were unpaved, were impassable due to mud and ruts. Taverns were crowded.

By the end of October, reports reached Dunmore that "shirtmen digging in the Palace garden had found a store of gunpowder."[75] His temper did not improve when he heard of the amount of troops arriving, seemingly daily, in the capital.

He was also annoyed at the events surrounding the American seizure of one of the British sloops at Hampton in late September and their refusal to return the goods confiscated from it. Among the impounded goods were six muskets, five cutlasses, two powder horns, two cartouche boxes, thirty-six swivel shot, six swivels, an anchor and grapnel with two cables and hawser, some lead and a seine. (A seine was a fishing net that hung vertically in the water, with floats at the upper edge and sinkers at the lower one.)[76]

Even more unhappy was the sloop's commander, Matthew Squires, who wanted "the king's sloop, with all the stores belonging to her ... immediately returned." The "people of Hampton, who committed this outrage," he blustered, "must be answerable for the consequence ..."[77]

The next day, Squires sent a letter to the printer of the *Norfolk Gazette*, written aboard the *Otter*:

> You have, in many papers, lately taken the freedom to mention MY NAME and thereto added many falsities. I now declare, if I am ever again mentioned therein with any reflections, I will most assuredly seize your person and take you on board the Otter...[78]

The Americans quickly countered this verbal attack saying that, far from being on His Majesty's service, the sloop was actually on a "pillaging or pleasuring party." On the contrary, the vessel and its stores were **not** seized by the inhabitants of Hampton. The vessel, stores and seine were given as a reward to a man called Finn, near whose house the sloop was driven, as a reward for entertaining him with "respect and decency."

The Committee of Safety offered the following terms: 1) the restitution of all slaves to their owners, including one named Joseph Harris. Harris was employed, with Squire's knowledge, in pillaging the town, under the cover of darkness, of sheep and other livestock. 2) the return of all other goods detained by the British under his command; 3) Free passage of persons and property in and out of Hampton without fear of insult, molestation, interruption.

Once these conditions were complied with, the Committee would "endeavour to procure every article left on our shore and shall be ready to deliver them to your pilot and gunner..." This letter was signed by the Committee of Elizabeth City County and town of Hampton.[79]

They committee of safety from Hampton had also sent out a plea for assistance for troops to defend the city. The response was immediate with 100 volunteers sent out from Williamsburg to confront Captain Squire, should he "attempt anything hostile" against its inhabitants.[80]

On 16 September 1775, at a meeting of the Committee of Safety for Elizabeth City County and the town of Hampton, a resolution was passed unanimously to thank Major James Innes[81] and the several volunteer companies who marched to their assistance and defense on the alarm occasioned by Mathew Squire's response to the seizure of a sloop and its intendant detention of stores found therein.[82]

In a move perhaps to distract the citizens of Hampton from a proposed attack, Lord Dunmore, disembarked at Kemp's landing, some ten miles from Norfolk with 140 men. Their intent was to retrieve military supplies and gunpowder they believed was stored there.

The British landed at Newtown, just as darkness was falling, marched to Kemp's Landing and proceeded to break and enter a blacksmith's shop, destroying some fifty muskets left for repair. The British then pillaged a number of other houses and managed to capture two officers in the minute service and four privates. The redcoats were unable to find any gunpowder, however, "which luckily had been carried off some time before."[83]

In retribution, as his own response to these events, Lord Dunmore decided to attack Hampton, which was small port town across the James River from Norfolk. This port had some strategic importance as well: it was the patriot's access to the Chesapeake and "commanded a sweeping panorama of the Roads." If a British attack on Norfolk were to be successful, then Hampton would have to be in British hands.[84]

On 26 October 1775 Lord Dunmore began firing incendiary shot into the town.[85] A company under Captain Nicholas of the second regiment along with Captain Lynn of the minutemen[86] and some county militia, without any cover, on the open shore, withstood a discharge of cannon from a large schooner commanded by Captain Squire. The rebel forces "stood coolly till the vessels were near enough for them to do execution, when they began a brisk and well-directed fire, which forced the little squadron to retire."[87]

During the night, under cover of darkness, British tenders forced their way through vessels sunk in the mouth of the river, and fired upon the town. They were also repulsed with the loss of nine men killed on the schooner and many wounded. Two were killed on the tender which was boarded by the Americans and taken.

Colonel Woodford had entered the town as the firing began, bringing with him a reinforcement of fifty "fine riflemen under the command of captain Bluford, an experienced and brave riflemen ..."[88]

Captain Abraham Buford and his Culpeper Minute men, along with "a substantial number of Captain William Blackwell's company of Fauquier rifles and some local militia, about 100 men in all,[89] had had a hard twelve hour night's ride in a driving rain to reach the town the next morning. They took positions along the shore and began returning fire on the ship's gunners. "Since the guns on board the British ships were unprotected by netting, the Virginians' marksmanship eventually discouraged Dunmore's marines, and they abandoned the shelling of the town."[90]

"The colonel [wrote] that all the men behaved with great resolution and were too eager. The troops in town are in high spirits, and wish for an attack in this quarter; they are all excellent marksmen and fine, bold fellows ..."[91]

Another more detailed account appeared in the 2 November 1775 *Virginia Gazette* of the battle and the part played by the minute service and regulars.

> ... Last Wednesday nigh a party of men from the [British] tenders went on shore and robbed several houses on Mill Creek, nigh Hampton. We heard of this the next morning and observed the tenders at anchor, no great distance from the place where several vessels had been sunk in the channel of Hampton river, to prevent their surprising us. The channel was not completely stopped, and we imagined, from their situation, they intended to prevent our compleating the work, or perhaps might intend to land, to be at their old trade.
>
> However, to observe their motions particularly, captain Lyne, in the minute service, rode round nigh where the tenders lay, and left orders for his lieutenant (Mr. Smith) with 30 men, to come over to him, by crossing one of the branches of Hampton river.
>
> In a short time after captain Lyne had fixed himself on the point, lieutenant Smith was over with the men, and then two vollies of musquetry were discharged from the tenders, and answered by captain Lyne from his post by a rifle, which was answered by a four pounder from one of the tenders; then began a pretty warm fire from all the tenders. Captain Nicholas, observing this, soon joined with about 25 of his men. The fire of our musquetry caused the tender nighest to us to sheer off some distance.
>
> The fire consisted of 4 pounders, grape shot, &c. for about one hour. Not a man of our's was hurt. Whether our men did any damage is uncertain. They could not get nigher than 300 yards. Some say the saw men fall in one of the tenders. After waiting under cover nigh the shore, and finding they would not land, the men were ordered to retreat to the woods, to try whether that would not induce them to land; but all in vain as long as we stayed.

The men were then marched into Hampton, and about 5 o'clock in the afternoon, some of them landed, and burnt Mr. Edward Cooper's house. In the night they cut a passage through the vessels that were sunk, and the next morning, about 8 o'clock (which was about half an hour after colonel Woodford and captain Bluford [Buford] arrived with a rifle company) 5 tenders, to wit, a large schooner, 2 sloops, and 2 pilot boat, passed the passage they had cleared, and drew up a-breast of the town; they then gave 3 chears, and began a heavy fire.

Colonel Woodford immediately posted captain Nicholas with his company on one side of the main street and captain Bluford [Buford] with his riflemen on the other, who were joined by the town company of militia; captain Lyne with his company, was ordered to march to the cross roads just out of town to sustain any attack that might come from James or back river. The colonel had been informed that men were landed from both these rivers. The musquet and rifle balls soon began to fly so thick that few men were seen upon the decks. The engagement continued very warm for some time.

At length, they began to cut and flip their cables, and all cleared themselves, except one, which was boarded and taken by some of our men. They took in her, the gunner and 7 men, 3 of whom were wounded, 2 mortally (both since dead), 1 white woman, and 2 negro men; lieutenant Wright, who commanded the prize, after receiving a ball, jumped overboard, and it is thought he was not able to reach the tenders. Several more jumped overboard; but it is not known what is become of them, or what damage is done on board of the other tenders.

In those 2 different actions, Mr. Printer, officers and soldiers of the regular, minute and militia, acted with a spirit becoming free men and Americans, and must evince that Americans will die, or be free! [92]

Following the cannonading of Hampton, Captain Buford and his company of Culpeper Minute men, along with the rest of the detachment, rejoined their battalion in Williamsburg.

Six: December 1775 – Prelude to the Battle at Great Bridge

In the meantime, Lord Dunmore was attempting to shore up his support. John Connolly, his agent in Pittsburg, procured blank military commissions from General Gage in Boston and set about recruiting loyalists from the Pennsylvania and New York to join Dunmore's forces in Virginia. By mid November, his forces included British regulars, Royal Marines, runaway slaves, indentured servants, and some of the leading merchants of Norfolk.[93]

Lord Dunmore published this proclamation because, in his opinion, a body of armed men, unlawfully assembled, fired on His Majesty's Tenders. An army was formed which was now marching to attack British troops and destroy the "well being of the Colony."

Dunmore wanted to defeat these "treasonable purposes," bring the traitors to Justice, restore the peace and good order; so he promulgated the following when he 1) declared martial law and 2) required any man capable of bearing arms to join the British or be regarded as traitors, liable to every penalty of the Law—forfeiture of life and lands among them.

He rounded out the proclamation with a bold declaration that "all indentured Servants, Negroes, or others (appertaining to Rebels,) free that are able and willing to bear Arms" if they joined the British as soon as possible. Dunmore also ordered and required that all British subjects retain their Quitrents and other taxes in their own custody until peace can be restored.[94]

With Dunmore's recruitment of loyalists, declaration of martial law, his military operations and the proclamations freeing Virginia's slaves if they joined British forces, war looked to be inevitable. The proclamation itself intensified a growing distrust between master and bondsman. It fueled fear of a slave uprising. The declaration of martial law had the practical intent of reminding the rebel forces they were now regarded as traitors. This upped the stakes considerably for all those who opposed Lord Dunmore and had the effect of polarizing the colony into loyal and rebel camps.

Lord Dunmore may have hoped that this efforts and the proclamation would motivate moderates to act as mediators. If so, this proved to be a serious miscalculation. For the well-born, the emancipation of slaves was a direct attack on property. For others, it brought about fear of a social disruption to the well-to-do planters and gentlemen of the colony. Its end result was to remind the moderates that they shared the same beliefs as their more radical counterparts. Furthermore, there was a realization in both groups that their beliefs should and would be defended against any British attempt to suspend them.

This proclamation produced concern among the Virginian delegates to Congress. Richard Henry Lee wrote Catharine Macauley from Philadelphia on 29 November 1775:

> Lord Dunmore's unparalleled conduct in Virginia, has, a few Scotch excepted, united every Man in that large Colony. If administration had searched thro the world for a person the best fitted to ruin their cause, and procure union and success for these Colonies, they could not have found a more complete Agent than Lord Dunmore...
> The last Post produces a proclamation from Ld. Dunmore declaring Liberty to the Slaves and proclaiming the Law martial to be the only law in that Colony------ And all this he says is done ' in virtue of the power and authority to me given by his Majesty.' Is it possible that his Majesty could authorize him thus to remedy evils which his Lordship himself had created? [95]

In early December, Francis Lightfoot Lee, another of the delegates to the Continental Congress from Virginia, wrote to Robert W. Carter that

> ... it will require very vigorous efforts, to put a stop to the proceedings of Lord Dunmore. We are extremely alarm'd by an express from the Comtee of Northampton County to Congress informing that he has issued a Proclamation, declaring military Law in Virg^a & offering freedom to all servants & slaves, who shall repair to the King's standard which he as erected; that the inhabitants of Norfolk & Princess Ann Counties have taken an Oath to oppose, to the last drop of their blood, any of their country men who shall come in arms into their Counties... [96]

On 10 November 1775 more "fine rifle-men" arrived at camp in Williamsburg, under the command of Captain Fontaine.[97] Another 100 minute men also arrived from Chesterfield and companies continued to arrive in Williamsburg on a daily basis.[98]

By mid November, no doubt as a result of a surfeit of regulars and minutemen flooding Williamsburg, the powers-that-be decided to reduce the Culpeper Minute Battalion into five companies, each containing approximately fifty men. So companies were consolidated and the men who were no longer needed, discharged. Colonel Taliaferro relinquished his command to Lt. Colonel Stevens and led these men home. The five Fauquier companies were reduced to two—those in Captain John Chilton's company and those in Captain William Blackwell's Company.[99]

The Committee of Safety, late in November, ordered Woodford to take his regiment and five companies of the Culpeper Minute Battalion to secure Norfolk. The plan was for minute companies under Josiah Parker and Captain Mathews of Princess Anne to join him. Woodford was free to call on any other minute men, militia or volunteers, if more aid was needed.

The Culpeper Minute Battalion, and its five companies, totaled approximately 150 men. They were under the command of Captains Buford, Jameson, Pickett, Chilton, and Spencer and formed a separate detachment of Woodford's forces. Woodford ordered these men, commanded by Lieutenant Colonel Stevens and Major Thomas Marshall, to Hampton to guard that town against another bombardment.[100]

Now that Colonel Woodford had enough troops to act against the British, he decided that the only way to stop Lord Dunmore's firing on the towns on the south shore was for his troops to cross the James. The British had been successful in eluding rifle fire from the shore by staying out of range on the south side of the channel. Woodford needed an effective crossfire which could only be accomplished by sending troops across into Suffolk. This would also have the effect of denying the British the use of the south bank to land supplies and troops.[101]

Lord Dunmore, getting wind of the impending crossing, realized that he did not have sufficient forces to either march on Williamsburg or defend Norfolk from an attack by land. He ordered instead the fortification of Great Bridge, a small village around twelve miles from Norfolk, as part of the defenses of Norfolk.[102]

Fortifying Great Bridge made strategic sense as well. It was a shipping point for shingles, barrel staves, lumber, tar, potash and turpentine from the Carolinas. The village was given this appellation because of a 120 foot long bridge over the southern branch of the Elizabeth River. On either side of the bridge were extensive marshes.

At the southern end of the bridge was an island with a few houses and a mill. North of the bridge was the British built stockade, called Fort Murray by the redcoats and the "hog-pen" by the rebel forces. Lieutenant Wallace, a sergeant, a corporal, some volunteers, a few negroes and twenty-five privates of the 14th Regiment of Foot were all left to defend this breastwork.[103] The stockade was intended to block the main road between Virginia and eastern North Carolina.[104]

Woodford's initial attempt to cross the James was prevented by a large armed British tender. He quickly moved upstream, out of range of the tender's cannons and prepared to cross at Sandy Point. When he heard that Dunmore was making raids into Suffolk, he sent Lieutenant Colonel Charles Scott and Major Thomas Marshall ahead of him with 200 mounted riflemen. By the 21 November 1775, Scott and Marshall had driven the British out of Suffolk.[105]

By the first week in December, Woodford and the Culpeper companies from Hampton had rejoined Scott. The 2 December 1775 *Virginia Gazette* reported a skirmish at Great Bridge:

> ... Since Lord Dunmore's proclamation [to free the slaves who fought for the British] made its appearance here, it is said he has recruited his army, in the counties of Princess Anne and Norfolk, to the amount of about 2000 men, including his black regiment, which is thought to be a considerable part, with this inscription on their breaths: Liberty to Slaves.
>
> However, as the rivers will henceforth be strictly watched, and every possible precaution taken, it is hoped others will be effectually prevented from joining those his Lordship has already collected.
>
> The army that went down last week, under command of Col. Woodford, to obstruct Dunmore's progress of enlisting men in the lower counties, fell in with a party of twelve or thirteen of Dunmore's friends, and made them all prisoners. Lieut. Col. Scott, with the advanced guard, upon his arrival at the Great Bridge, found the enemy entrenched there, and it is said a smart firing began by some of the riflemen, which was returned, and continued a considerable time on both sides, but to what effect we know not. It is also said, that Thursday last was fixed upon by our troops to begin a general attack; they were healthy in good spirits, and had great prospect of success.
>
> Some accounts from Norfolk are, that Dunmore's party has demolished several houses back of the town, and fortified themselves; also, that Col. Hutchings, and some other Gentlemen, their prisoners, had been removed to the ships on account of the gaol having been set on fire ...[106]

Seven: December 1775 – Great Bridge, December 1775

The 8 December 1775 *Virginia Gazette* enclosed part of a letter from Lieutenant Colonel Scott, written to Captain Southall, a friend in Williamsburg. The letter was dated Great Bridge, 4 December 1775.

In the letter, Lt. Colonel Scott described the attack by the British on Lieutenant Tibbs and the boat guard. The Lieutenant and some of his men were able to maintain their post, killing seven of the enemy forces including their commander. He held on until reinforced by Captain Nicholas[107] and fifty of his men, who had to pass through heavy fire from the British in order to reach the besieged troops.

Scott reported that his forces kept up a heavy fire from night fall to day light. Only two men had been lost and one, most recently wounded, shot through the arm, breaking a bone near his hand. He went on to say that

> Last night was the first of my pulling off my clothes for 12 nights successively. Believe me, my good friend, I never was so fatigued with duty in my whole life; but I set little value upon my health, when put in competition with my duty to my country, and the glorious cause we are engaged in.

Scott noted the arrival of Carolina forces under Lt. Colonel Howe and expected 800 to 900 more by the next day with much need artillery, ammunition and military stores.

> ...P.S. Since I finished my letter, we saw a large pile of buildings at the far end of this town all in flames, between which and the fort we had 4 sentinels, who can give no account how it happened. As I mentioned above, the fire was discovered when the gun fired; and by the time the

men got paraded a volley of small-arms was fired from the fort, mixed with now and then a cannon shot. About 11 at night it ceased for about half an hour, when, to our great surprise, we saw several other houses in a blaze, which are just now consumed. It is now 10 o'clock. I shall lie down till the next alarm.[108]

In another letter from Scott to Captain Southall, dated 5 December 1775, he described a skirmish at midnight between men in the Culpeper Minute Battalion, commanded by Colonel Stevens and a guard of 30 men, chiefly Negroes. The men of the minute battalion were able to move close enough to the British sentries before they were discovered. The sentry challenged, and when he was not answered, opened fire.

> Our people, being too eager, began the fire immediately, without orders, and kept it up very hot for near 15 minutes. We killed one, burnt another in the house, and took two prisoners (all blacks) with 4 exceeding fine muskets, and defeated the guard. There is hardly an hour in the day but we exchange a few shot…[109]

Very early Saturday morning well before daylight, on 9 December, the Virginia forces were awakened by a volley of gunfire from the British fortifications known as Fort Murray, or, as the Americans called it, the "hog-pens."

Astounded, they saw a line of British soldiers, with fixed bayonets, about to cross the bridge. The redcoats had hoped to take the rebel forces by surprise but replacing the planks on the bridge had taken them longer than they expected. While the rebel forces watched in astonishment, the cannons aboard the *Otter* opened up. Fewer than ninety Virginians were able to reach their breastwork before fighting began.

The British line was composed of sixty grenadiers from Captain Charles Fordyce's 14th Regiment, thirty men from Lieutenant John Battut's Queen's Loyalists, Norfolk volunteers under Captain Samuel Leslie and runaway (or freed, depending on your viewpoint!) slaves from the Dunmore's Royal Ethiopians.

Lieutenant Edward Travis who was in command of Captain Meade's company at the American breastworks, ordered his men to hold their fire until the British were within fifty yards of their fort.[110]

> Believing the redoubt to be deserted, Fordyce waved his hat over his head, shouted 'The day is our own!' and rushed forward toward the breast-work. The order of Lieutenant Travis was obeyed with terrible effect. His men… rose to their feet and discharged a full volley upon the enemy. The gallant Captain Fordyce, who was marked by the riflemen, fell, pierced by fourteen bullets, within fifteen steps of the breast-works. His followers, greatly terrified, retreated in confusion across the causeway, and were dreadfully galled in their rear.[111]

The first volley from the Americans also took down two of the 14th Regiment's Lieutenants, Napier and Leslie. The British began to pull back. By this time, Colonel Steven's men from the Culpeper Minute Battalion arrived at the breast-works. The Battalion attacked from trenches one hundred yards to the British right. Since the bridge was too narrow for the British to turn quickly, most of their regulars were killed. The entire engagement lasted less than half an hour.[112]

The Americans could not understand why Lord Dunmore had ordered his men to attack their breastwork in such a fashion. Only eleven of the Grenadiers of the 14th Regiment survived the attack. Lieutenant Battut, of the Queen's Loyalists, was wounded; he and seventeen of his company were made prisoners.[113]

The British pulled their dead back to their fortifications and buried them and then stole quietly out at the rear of the fort. They were gone before the rebel forces realized it. By the following morning when the Americans reached the stockade, only a deserted fort and mass burial ground greeted them.[114]

A graphic account of the Battle, by an unknown correspondent, appeared in the *Virginia Gazette* on 20 December 1775:

> As the scene of action is but little known to the generality of people, it may be necessary to give some description of it, that the relation may be more clear and satisfactory.
>
> ... The Great Bridge is built over what is called the Southern branch of Elizabeth river, twelve miles above Norfolk. The land on each side is marshy to a considerable distance from the river, except at the two extremities of the bridge, where are two pieces of firm land, which may not improperly be called islands, being surrounded entirely by water and marsh, and joined to the main land by causeways.
>
> On the little piece of firm ground on the farther, or Norfolk side, lord Dunmore had erected his fort, in such a manner that his cannon commanded the causeway on his own side, and the bridge between him and us, with the marshes around him.
>
> The island on this side of the river contained six or seven houses, some of which were burnt down (the nearest to the bridge) by the enemy, after the arrival of our troops; in the others, adjoining the causeway on each side, were stationed a guard every night by colonel Woodford, but withdrawn before day, that they might not be exposed to the fire of the enemy's fort in recrossing the causeway to our camp, this causeway being also commanded by their cannon.
>
> The causeway on our side was in length about one hundred and sixty yards, and on the hither extremity our breast- work was thrown up. From the breast work ran a street, gradually ascending, about the length of four hundred yards, to a church, where our main body were encamped.
>
> The great trade to Norfolk in shingles, tar, pitch and turpentine, from the country back of this, had occasioned so many houses to be built here, whence these articles were conveyed to Norfolk by water. But this by the bye. Such is the nature of the place as described to me, and such were our situation and that of the enemy.
>
> On Saturday the 9th instant, after reveille beating, two or three great guns, and some musquetry, were discharged from the enemy's fort, which, as it was not an unusual thing, was but little regarded by colonel Woodford. However, soon afterwards he heard a call to the soldiers to stand to their arms; upon which, with all expedition, he made the proper dispositions to reeve the enemy.
>
> In the mean time the enemy had crossed the bridge, fired the remaining houses upon the island, and some large piles of shingles, and attacked our guard in the breast-work. Our men returned the fire, and threw them into some confusion, but they were instantly rallied by captain Fordyce, and advanced along the cause way with great resolution, keeping up a constant and heavy fire as they approached. Two field pieces, which had been brought across the bridge; and planted on the edge of the island, facing the left of our breast-work, played briskly at the same time upon us. Lieutenant Travis, who commanded in the breast-work, ordered his men to reserve their fire till the enemy came within the distance of fifty years, and then they gave it to them with terrible execution.
>
> The brave Fordyce exerted himself to keep up their spirits, reminded them of their ancient glory, and waving his hat over his head, encouragingly told them *the day was their own.* Thus pressing forward, he fell within fifteen steps of the breastwork. His wounds were many, and his death would have been that of an hero had he met it in a better cause. The progress of the enemy was not at an end; they retreated over the causeway with precipitation, and were dreadfully galled in their rear.
>
> Hitherto, on our side only, the guard consisting of twenty five and some others, upon the whole, amounting to not more than ninety, had been engaged. Only the regulars of the 14th regiment, in number one hundred and twenty, had advanced upon the causeway; and about two hundred and thirty tories and negroes had, after crossing the bridge, continued upon the island.
>
> The regulars, after retreating along the causeway, were again rallied by captain Leslie, and the two field pieces continued to play upon our men. It was at this time that colonel Woodford was advancing down the street to the breast-work with the main body, and against him was not directed the whole fire of the enemy. Never were cannon better served; but yet in the face of them and the musquetry, which kept up a continual blaze, our men marched on with the utmost intrepidity.

Colonel Stevens, of the Culpeper battalion, was sent round to the left to flank the enemy, which was done with such activity and spirit that a rout immediately ensued. The enemy fled into their fort, leaving behind them the two field pieces, which, however, they took care to spike up with nails. Many were killed and wound in the flight, but colonel Woodford very prudently restrained his troops from urging their pursuit too far.

From the beginning of the attack till the repulse from the breast work might be about fourteen or fifteen minutes, till the total defeat upwards of half an hour. It si said that some of the enemy preferred death to captivity, from a fear of being scalped, which lord Dunmore inhumanly told them would be their fate should they be taken alive. Thirty one, killed and wounded, fell into our hands, and the number borne off was much greater.

Through the whole of the engagement every officer and soldier behaved with the greatest courage and calmness. The conduct of our centinels [sentinels] I cannot pass over in silence. Before they quitted their stations they fired at least three rounds as the enemy were crossing the bridge, and one of them, who was posted behind some shingles kept his ground till he had fired eight times; and after receiving a whole platoon, made his escape over the causeway into our breast work.

The scene was closed with as much humanity as it had been conducted with bravery. The work of death being over, every one's attention was directed to the succour of the unhappy sufferers, and it is an undoubted fact that captain Leslie was so affected with the tenderness of our troops towards those who were yet capable of assistance, that he gave signs from the fort of his thankfulness for it.

What is not to be paralleled in history, and will scarcely appear credible, except to such as acknowledge a providence over human affairs, this victory was gained at the expence of no more than a slight wound in a soldier's hand; and one circumstance, which renders it still more amazing is, that the field pieces raked the whole length of the street, and absolutely threw double headed shot as far as the church, and afterwards, as our troops approached, cannonaded them heavily with grapeshot.[115]

Colonel Woodford's report of the battle in a letter to Edmund Pendleton, the President of the Virginia Convention on 10 and 11 December 1775 gave a similar account of the defeat of the British troops at Great Bridge.

The Americans took possession of the fort and its stores and supplies that morning. The British had evidently left in a hurry leaving military stores behind. Among those supplies left behind were seven guns, a bayonet, twenty-nine spades, two shovels, six cannon, a few shot, some bedding, part of a hogshead of rum, two more barrels of what was believed to be rum, two barrels of bread, about twenty quarters of beef, half a box of candles, four or five dozen quart bottles, four or five iron pots, a few axes and old lumber and some spiked cannon.

> From the vast effusion of blood on the bridge, and in the fort, from the accounts of the centries [sentries], who saw many bodies carried out of the fort to be interred ... I conceive their loss to be much greater than I thought it yesterday, and the victory to be complete.

The Colonel also sent along an inventory of the captured arms, including two silver mounted fuzees[116] with bayonets, a steel bayonet, twenty-four "well-fixed muskets" with bayonets, two muskets without bayonets, twenty-eight cartouche boxes, and pouches, three silver mounted cartouche boxes, twenty-six bayonet belts, twenty-seven caps, two hats, one barrel with powder and cartridges; He also found among the leavings accoutrements of the officers and soldiers including two watches, a pair of gloves, four stocks and buckles, a pair of silver shoe buckles, three pair of silver knee buckles, two snuff boxes, twelve coats, twelve waistcoats, eleven pair of shoes, twelve pair of garters, a pair of breeches, a shirt, a pair of stockings, a parcel of old knee buckles, a parcel of old buttons and a black handkerchief.[117]

In the same letter, the American Colonel also reported that Lieutenant Battut, of the Queen's Loyalist troops, and his troops had been treated well by the Americans. Woodford noted the death of Captain Fordyce of the 14th Regiment, calling him "a gallant and brave officer." Fordyce was to be interred with all military honors "due to his great merit."

Included in this letter was a possible reason for Dunmore's dispatching the 14th Regiment and the Queen's Loyalist Regiment against the American breastworks at Great Bridge.

> I am just informed by lieutenant Battit that a servant of major Marshall, who was in the party with colonel Scott, and deserted, informed lord Dunmore that not more than 300 shirtmen were here; That imprudent man [Dunmore] caught at the bait, and dispatched captain Leslie, with all the regulars, who arrived at the fort about 4 in the morning.[118]

Colonel Woodford wrote the Virginia Convention, too, repeating the story about Marshall's body servant inducing the British to send all their troops against the American fortifications at Great Bridge. When Dunmore found he had been duped, he was furious. Dunmore "swore... that he would hang the boy who brought the information. [He] also blamed Captain Leslie for ordering the gunners of the *Otter* to fire too early."[119] From another unnamed correspondent, written 13 December 1775, came this report:

> Lord Dunmore raved like a madman, on hearing of the defeat of his forces, and swore he would hang the boy who had deserted to him and informed that there were by 300 shirtmen at the bridges, on whose information he had ordered the attack.
> ... We were well assured that there were but about 60 or 70 of our men at the breast-work; the rest were stationed at proper places, and intervals, to cover them, in case they had been forced from their entrenchments.[120]

Helen Maxwell, a Norfolk native, "credits Marshall's young body servant with an even more fertile imagination." He reported to Dunmore that "our men were out of ammunition, had no powder and had been obliged to melt up their shoe buckles for shot."[121] Major Spotswood[122] gave yet another account of the Battle to a friend in Williamsburg, in a letter published in the *Virginia Gazette* on 15 December 1775.

> We were alarmed this morning by the firing of some guns just after reveille beating, which, as the enemy had paid us the compliment several times before, we at first concluded to be nothing but a morning salute; but, in a short time after I heard adjutant Blackburn call out, *Boys, stand to your arms.*
> Col. Woodford and myself immediately got equipped, and ran out. The colonel pressed down to the breastwork, in our front; and my alarm post being 250 yards in another quarter, I ran to it as fast as I could, and by the time I had made all ready for engaging, a very heavy fire ensued at the breastwork, in which were not more than 60 men. It continued for about half an hour, when the king's troops gave way, after sustaining considerable loss, and behaving like true-born Englishmen.
> They marched up to our intrenchments with fixed bayonets; our young troops received them with firmness, and behaved as well as it was possible for soldiers to do. Capt. Leslie, of the regulars, commanded the fort on the other side of the bridge. Capt. Fordyce, of the grenadiers, led the van with his company, and lieutenant Battut commanded the advanced party. The former got killed within a few yards of the breastwork, with 12 privates. The lieutenant, with 16 soldiers, were taken prisoners, all wounded. Several others were carried into the fort, under cover of their cannon; and, from the blood on the bridge, they must have lost one half of the detachment. It would appear, that providence was on our side; for, during the whole engagement, we lost not a man, and only one was slightly wounded, in the hand.
> Col. Woodford is a brave officer, and a man I love. He had capt. Fordyce buried with the military honours due to his rank, and all the prisoners that fell into our hands taken the greatest care of. We have not, as yet, been able to ascertain the number killed and wounded on their side. Three officers fusees, with bayonets and cartouch boxes, fell into our hands, from which we judge that there were three commissioned officers killed. As soon as a general return can be made out, it will be sent to the Honourable Convention. I am at present in the greatest hurry, and can only give an account of what I have seen.[123]

While each of these accounts was similar, there were details of this engagement in each that were not found in the others. For that reason, they have all been included in this narrative.

After the Battle at Great Bridge, Colonel Woodford left Major Thomas Marshall in charge. He had orders to guard the village and keep the road to Norfolk open. Captain John Chilton and some of his men were part of the Culpeper Battalion that stayed at Great Bridge. This victory, however sweet it was to the patriot cause, must have proved bitter sweet to Chilton.

On 9 December 1775 while the British were retreating from the rifle fire on the causeway, Captain John Chilton's wife, Leticia died at their home "Rock Spring", near Baldwin's Ridge in Fauquier County. "Quietly he ordered his horse made ready. The way was long and treacherous in early winter, but, if he hurried, he would be home before Christmas. Then and only then, would he decide what to do next."[124]

Colonel Woodford, and his fresh minute men from Fincastle and Chesterfield and Colonel Robert Howe, with his newly arrived Carolina troops, marched on to Norfolk. By the time they arrived there, Dunmore, the remaining British troops not captured at Great Bridge and many of the loyalists from Norfolk were safely back aboard ships of the British fleet.[125]

Woodford's spirits no doubt were lifted with the arrival of even more troops. On 12 December, Colonel Woodford noted, in a letter to the Virginia Convention, the arrival of two more companies of "choice riflemen" at headquarters, "who are all well armed," commanded by Captain Campbell of Fincastle and Captain Gibson of West Augusta. Woodford also expected Captain Morgan Alexander,[126] with his rifle company, "as fine men, we hear, as ever were seen."[127]

Both sides spent the rest of December setting up some kind of winter quarters, the Americans in and around Norfolk, the British aboard their ships.[128] Almost in passing the Virginia Gazette noted the arrival in Williamsburg of the Prince William Minute Battalion on the day after Christmas. The battalion, commanded by Colonel William Grayson, was made up of "upwards of 350 minute-men."[129]

Eight: January 1776 – The British opened fire on Norfolk and American Forces under Woodford and Howe, January 1776

On New Year's Day, British guns erupted on the town of Norfolk. Colonel Woodford reported the British attack to the Virginia Convention.

> Between 3 and 4 o'clock a severe cannonade began from all the shipping, under cover of which they landed small parties, and set fire to the houses on the wharves. The wind favoured their design, and we believe the flames will be come general. In the confusion which they supposed would ensue, they frequently attempted to land; but this, by the bravery of our officers and men, we have hitherto prevented, with only a few men wounded on our side, and we persuade ourselves with a good deal of loss on theirs. Their efforts, and our opposition, still continue. We have stationed ourselves in such a manner as will, we believe, render everything but burning the houses ineffectual.[130]

Colonel Howe sent several reports to the President of the Convention, the first, on 2 January 1776.

> The burning of the town has made several avenues, which yesterday they had not, so that they may now fire with greater effect. The tide is now rising, and we expect at high water, another cannonade...
> I cannot enter into the melancholy consideration of the women and children running through a crowd of shot to get out of the town, some of them with children at their breast. A few have, I hear, been killed. Does it not call for vengeance, both from God and man! It is but justice to inform you, that I had the pleasure to execute orders at a moment's warning, and that the men behaved with steadiness and spirit.
> Col. Stevens went down at my command, and had some men near the water, where he engaged a party who had landed, with spirit and conduct of a good officer. Of my friend col. Woodford, it is almost needless to speak; but I cannot avoid expressing, that I received from him, every assistance which conduct and spirit could give me ...[131]

Colonel Howe's second report was written on 4 January 1776 from Norfolk. "At about a quarter past 3 on Monday afternoon, the whole fleet began a heavy cannonade" he told the Convention. It lasted for seven hours without stopping and continued off and on until last night.

Under fire of their ships, the British effected widely spread out landings and set fire to all the houses on the wharves. Each attempt to land was beaten off by the Americans. "We had not a man killed, and only 5 or 6 wounded, one supposed mortally ... They once landed and got into the streets with field-pieces, but were beat back with loss, and no execution done by their fire. Nine tenths of the town are destroyed, but the fire is now out."

He reported, too, the arrival of Lieutenant 16, and five grenadiers of the 14th Regiment, wounded at Great Bridge, with seventeen tories and eleven Negroes. The wounded soldiers were sent to the hospital; most of the Tories and Negroes were lodged in the jail.[132]

In the general confusion and panic that ensued, both the British and Americans set fires which soon spread out of control.[133] The forces under Colonel Howe took their ire out on the Scottish merchants and frequently took shots at shipping in the harbour.[134] A number of court-martials from the American side seemed to help to restore some control in the city as Howe tried to restore order.[135]

The net effect of the British firing on the town was apparent two days later. Four-fifths of Virginia's largest city was in ashes. Both sides blamed the other. The Mayor and Council of Norfolk acknowledged that Dunmore had burned fifty-one houses. The political leadership also blamed the forces under Colonels Woodford and Howe for their destruction of 863 buildings, 416 by orders of the Virginia Convention as a preventive measure. The Convention did not want the British to use the town as a landing stage for supplies or troops.

It is worth noting that Major Marshall and fully half of the Culpeper minute battalion were still at Great Bridge and thus did not take part in the rebel response to the two British attacks on Norfolk.[136]

Howe's efforts to restore order were further jeopardized by a second bombardment of Norfolk on 21 January. Colonel Woodford reported this battle to Edmund Pendleton, the President of the Virginia Convention:

> We have had a party, these ten days, upon Tanner's creek, who yesterday had a brush with a tender's boat attempting to land at Sprowle's plantation; they beat her off, and killed one man.
>
> 8 *o'clock at night*. About 4 this afternoon, another heavy cannonading began from the Liverpool and Otter, during which the enemy landed and set fire to some houses that remained unhurt, near to what is called Town Point wharf.
>
> I sent strong parties to reinforce our water guards. We had three fine men killed with cannon shot, and one wounded, who, it is thought, will lose his arm.[137] We have found one sailor and two negroes dead, and suppose many others were killed and wounded, that were carried off in their boats. Capts. Green and Markham arrived in the height of the fire...
>
> SATURDAY, Jan. 27. By capt. Green, just arrived from Norfolk, we learn that the day after the latest cannonading, from the Liverpool and Otter, two sailors were taken prisoners a little below the new distillery, in search of water (of which the fleet is greatly in want) who informed, that a number of men were wounded in the fray at the Town Point wharf, and carried off in the boats.
>
> And capt. Green tells us, that the enemy appear as solicitous to conceal their dead and wounded as their *brother savages* the Indians who have been always remarkable for that piece of *finesse*.[138]

Satisfied at the turmoil and disorder this attack had created, Dunmore withdrew, moving his ships up the Chesapeake out of Virginia waters.

While these events were taking place, more and more companies were being raised and sent to Norfolk and Williamsburg. This occasioned a general shortage of arms and precipitated the discharge of some of the troops involved in the struggle with Dunmore. On 14 February 1776, the Committee of Safety transmitted a note of thanks to the Culpeper Battalion and ordered Colonel Howe to discharge the companies on guard at Norfolk and Hampton.[139]

Nine: December 1775 to March 1776 – Transition from colonial "provincial" forces to Continental forces

On 28 December 1775 the Continental Congress, sitting in Philadelphia, authorized the raising of six continental battalions when they resolved that six battalions were necessary and to be immediately raised in Virginia. These regiments were to be raised and paid according to the terms as the continental forces in Cambridge were paid "unless the convention...can raised them on better terms."[140]

On 12 January 1776 sandwiched between the first and second attack on Norfolk, the Virginia Convention met to select the field officers of the new battalions, authorized by the Continental Congress in late December 1775 and raised for the defence and protection of the colony. Six of these battalions were to be made up of ten companies of sixty-eight men each, rank and file; the seventh battalion was to have seven companies of sixty-eight men each. This battalion was to be raised for the protection of the Virginia counties on the eastern shore.

The 1st and 2nd Virginia regiments, formerly raised to see action against Lord Dunmore were to be increased by 382 men. These men were to be placed into five companies, two to belong to the 1st Virginia and three to the 2nd Virginia.[141]

The Convention selected Hugh Mercer, as the commanding Colonel of the 3rd Virginia; George Weedon, as the Lieutenant Colonel; and Thomas Marshall as the Major of this Regiment.[142] Each of these field officers of the 3rd Virginia had already had prior military experience with either independent companies or Minute Battalions in the colony's response to Lord Dunmore's attacks on Hampton, Great Bridge and Norfolk.

On Tuesday, 13 February 1776 Congress, in two resolutions, confirmed the convention's recommendation for field officers in the six Virginia regiments or battalions. Hugh Mercer was elected as the Colonel of the 3rd battalion, George Weedon, as Lieutenant Colonel and Thomas Marshall as the major of the regiment. The President of the Continental Congress was directed to fill these officer's commissions and sent blank commissions to the Virginia convention for them to fill for the officers under the rank of major.[143]

The captains and subalterns commissioned in to the 3rd Virginia also had been battle-hardened as members of independent companies or minute battalions. Some of the soldiers followed their captains into continental service. In October 1776, Congress selected officers for the Virginia regiments, with commissions back dated to the previous spring. Captain John Ashby, 1st Lieutenant William Nelson, 2nd Lieutenant Isham Keith, and Ensign Nathaniel Ashby were all commissioned from 18 March 1776.[144]

Captain Ashby "may have taken part in Lord Dunmore's War in western Virginia in which a 'Captain Ashby', is mentioned in reports but not otherwise identified."[145] There is reliable evidence that he was in Williamsburg in October 1775 when he signed a receipt for goods from Armistead's Store, the regimental store for the Culpeper Battalion.[146] He may have served at Great Bridge although there is no record of him as a Captain in that Minute Battalion.[147]

It had been thought that John Ashby took over the company which had served under Captain William Pickett at Great Bridge.[148] However, from recently published lists of Captain William Pickett's Company in the Culpeper Minute Battalion,[149] it appeared that only seven men joined as privates in Ashby's 3rd Virginia company from Captain Pickett's company of minute men: Spencer Anderson,[150] John Dulin,[151] Charles Jones,[152] John Jones,[153] Henry Moffett,[154] Andrew O'Bannon,[155] and William Winkfield.[156] Congress confirmed Captain John Chilton, along with 1st Lieutenant John Blackwell and 2nd Lieutenant Joseph Blackwell, with commissions to date from 18 March 1776.[157]

John Chilton left the Culpeper Minute Battalion after Great Bridge, and returned home to Fauquier, His wife had died leaving him with five children and a growing sense of responsibility for his extended family. His brother William Chilton had died in 1774 and John was the administrator of that estate. He had also been appointed as guardian to William's young children. Six months after William's death, John's younger brother, Stephen, a captain of a merchant ship, died in London. Stephen Chilton was unmarried and left a large estate in Prince William for which some disposition had to be made.[158]

While all of these family responsibilities kept him busy, Chilton still found time to recruit the required quota of men to warrant his commission as a Captain in the 3rd Virginia.[159] Lieutenants John Blackwell and Joseph Blackwell were brothers, both in their early twenties, when they were granted commissions in the 3rd Virginia.[160] John Blackwell had the added advantage of previous experience with the Culpeper Minute Battalion. He had captained his own company[161] there and was happy to accept a lieutenant's commission in the Continental Army.

These two young men followed deep seated traditions of *noblesse oblige* within their families. Their uncles, cousins and male in-laws had all served in a public capacity, as part of the local political hierarchy, either as Sheriffs, militia officers or Justices in Fauquier and Prince William Counties.[162]

While the 3rd Virginia had been organized in December 1775, the delays in establishing rendezvous spots caused a delay in recruitment until February 1776.[163] Another factor in the delay resulted from the challenges some of the officers had in obtaining discharges from minute or independent companies so they could accept a commission into this Continental regiment. It all took time.

The Prince William Minute Battalion provided three Captains for the 3rd Virginia.[164] **Captain Andrew Leitch**, received his commission on 5 February 1776. He recruited men from Prince William. **Captain John Fitzgerald** accepted a commission on 8 February 1776. He raised his men from Fairfax or Prince William. Captain Fitzgerald had been one of those young men serving as a 2nd lieutenant in the Independent Company of Fairfax in 1774–1775.[165] **Captain Charles West**, another former officer of the Prince William Minute Battalion, acquired his commission on 9 February 1776. He raised his company in Loudoun.[166]

Captain John Thornton's commission was dated 12 February 1776. He recruited his men from Culpeper County[167] although he was not an officer of the Culpeper Minute Battalion.[168]

Gustavus Brown Wallace raised his company in King George. He was commissioned as a captain in the 3rd Virginia on 20 February 1776.

William Washington, a distant cousin of George Washington, and former Captain of a Stafford Minute company, was commissioned as a captain in the 3rd Virginia on 26 February 1776.[169] Captain Washington was wounded at Harlem, not Long Island as previously thought, and at Trenton, in December 1776. He was promoted out of the regiment, serving as a major in the 4th Continental Dragoons. He was one of the cavalry leaders at Cowpens in January 1781.[170]

Captain William McWilliams was commissioned in February 1776;[171] although he recruited men from Spotsylvania County, he did not appear to be an officer in the Caroline Minute Battalion.[172]

Captain Philip Richard Francis Lee received his Captain's commission on 8 March 1776. He raised troops from Prince William.[173] He had previously served as a Captain in the Independent Company of Prince William. This company took part in the planned march on Williamsburg in April after Lord Dunmore emptied the Williamsburg Magazine. George Washington, in command of this and other northern Virginia companies requested them to return to the homes and they did.[174]

Captain Thomas Johnson Jr was commissioned on 21 March 1776. He recruited men from Louisa County.[175] He resigned his commission 10 October 1776.[176]

Captain John Peyton was commissioned 29 April 1776.[177] He had begun his 3rd Virginia service as a 1st lieutenant, commissioned 5 February 1776. Captain Peyton was wounded at Brandywine in September 1777. He retired in September 1778 and later served as Clothier-General from 1780–1781. He died in 1790.[178]

David Arell began his 3rd Virginia service as a 1st lieutenant, commissioned 8 February 1776. He was promoted to captain after the Battle of Harlem Heights in September 1776. He resigned his commission 14 February 1778.[179]

Robert Powell Sr was commissioned as a Captain in the 3rd Virginia 18 October 1776.[180] Like John Peyton and David Arell, Powell began as a 1st lieutenant in the 3rd Virginia, commissioned 12 February 1776. He resigned his commission as captain in July 1779 and later served as a major in the Virginia Militia in 1781. He died in 1829.[181]

Many of these early officers of the 3rd Virginia had already been toughened by battles with Lord Dunmore in the Virginia campaigns of October 1775 through January 1776. This was also true of the field and staff officers of the 3rd Virginia. Hugh Mercer, George Weedon, and Thomas Marshall were all experienced military leaders as seen from their earlier service with independent companies or minute battalions. David Griffith, the surgeon and chaplain of the 3rd Virginia began his service as a surgeon with the Prince William Minute Battalion.[182]

The recruitment of men by these early officers in February took place "only a week before the regiment was taken over by Congress."[183]

While the 3rd Virginia had other prominent captains, most were either not commissioned or promoted until sometime in 1777. Captain John Francis Mercer, Lieutenant Robert Beale, Captain Reuben Briscoe, Captain Valentine Peyton, Captain John E. Blackwell, Captain David Miller all received commissions well into the war for independence. For that reason, these men have not considered here as part of the early group of men who led the 3rd Virginia during the first year of the battles in the struggle for American independence.

It was not until the last of February 1776 that the 3rd Virginia became an official part of the Continental establishment. Initially, they were placed the Southern Department, along with Continental regiments from the two Carolinas and Georgia.[184]

Then, in March, Congress authorized the establishment of three more Virginia battalions to be added to the six established ones. They agreed to pay the three new battalions as Continentals as soon as they are armed, fit for service and mustered. The Committee of safety for Virginia, Congress was informed, has contracted for the subsistence of the Virginia battalions, among them third battalion, [i.e. the 3rd Virginia] at 6 ½ pence per ration. Congress then passed a resolution that these contracts be confirmed.[185]

At least ten of the men who made up the ranks and file and non-commissioned positions in the 3rd Virginia had some military experience already, having fought against Lord Dunmore between October 1775 and January 1776.

While this number did not represent a large number of men who enlisted in the regiment, it has demonstrated the difficulty in discovering the identities of private soldiers in independent companies and minute battalions. It may also served to illustrate the difficulties Captains had in the recruitment of experienced soldiers when there were five other regiments also competing for the same qualified veterans.

Littleton Adams was a private in Captain James Scott's Company of the Culpeper Minute Men.[186] He served as a private under Captain John Ashby from 8 October 1776 to 12 February 1778. He enlisted until 18 March 1778. He evidently served as a substitute for John Davis in September 1778, according to Captain Ashby's muster roll for that month. He appeared on company muster rolls from October to December 1777 without remark. He spent January to 3 February 1778, sick in the hospital and was discharged 12 February 1778 at Valley Forge.[187]

Spencer Anderson was a private in Captain Wm. Pickett's Company of the Culpeper Minute Battalion in 1775.[188] He served as a private in Captain Philip Richard Francis Lee's company, on payrolls for April 1777 and December 1777. He joined the Light Horse according to a note on his reference envelope in the Compiled Service Records for the 3rd Virginia. He was discharged, according to an undated list of absentees by regimental pay master William Mountjoy.[189]

John Dulin was not found in the Compiled Service Records of the 3rd Virginia.[190] He served as a private in Captain William Picket's Company in the Culpeper Minute Battalion in 1775 and enlisted in April 1776 in Captain John Chilton's Company of the 3rd Virginia.[191]

Charles Jones was a private in Captain William Pickett's Company of the Culpeper Minute Battalion, 1775.[192] He served as a soldier in Captain John Chilton's company from October 1776 to February 1777. He was listed as dead in company payrolls from 7 December 1776 to March, 1777. His service was given as twenty-five days, meaning he died early in February 1777.[193]

Henry Moffett, a private in William Pickett's company of the Culpeper Minute Battalion,[194] served as a sergeant in Captain John Ashby's Company from February to September 1777. In October 1777, Sergeant Moffett was promoted into the wagon service. He later served as a wagon conductor with the 1st Pennsylvania Brigade from August 1780 to November 1781.[195]

Andrew O'Bannon, a private in Captain William Pickett's Company, was not found in the 3rd Virginia Compiled Service Records[196] although it appeared he enlisted in Captain John Chilton's Company in 1777 and served as the regimental wagon master in the 3rd Virginia. He fought at Brandywine, Germantown and Monmouth.[197]

Daniel O'Rear was another Culpeper Minute Battalion private who was not found in the Virginia compiled service records for the regiment.[198] He enlisted as a Private in Captain William Pickett's Company in 1775. He then enlisted in Captain John Ashby's Company of the 3rd Virginia.[199]

John Riley was a private in James Scott's Fauquier Independent Company in 1777. He enlisted in February 1778 for a year in Captain John Blackwell's 3rd Virginia Company. He served from 18 February 1778 until his discharge on 28 February 1779.[200]

William Winkfield was a private in Capt. William Pickett's Company in the Culpeper Minute Battalion.[201] He served as a soldier in Captain John Chilton's 3rd Virginia Company in February 1777. The company payroll for February credited him with service for twenty-seven days.[202]

Another soldier serving as a corporal under Captain Pickett who saw service in the 3rd Virginia was Moses Allen.[203] Allen served as a corporal in Captain John Chilton's company from 7 October 1776 to September 1777. He served in the came capacity in Captain John Blackwell's company from November 1777 to April 1778. He was listed as a sergeant in Captain Blackwell's company, serving in that position until November 1779.[204]

CONCLUSIONS

The 3rd Virginia Regiment of Foot, Continental Line, as it evolved from independent companies and Minute Battalions, was a blend of experienced officers interspersed with seasoned veterans and untested rank and file. The field staff and officers proved to be a steadying influence on their men especially in the 1776 New York and 1777 Philadelphia campaign.

There were no mutinies in the 3rd Virginia, even when soldiers lacked shoes, pants and blankets during the winter months in 1777 and 1778. No soldiers in the 3rd Virginia companies led precipitate, panicked retreats that degenerated into headlong flight from the redcoat's raking artillery fire. Neither did they run from a threat of a British advance with fixed bayonets. They stood their ground; they gave as good as they got. Their bravery was noted in General Orders. Even when 3rd Virginia companies were decimated at Brandywine and Germantown, and captains were killed or badly wounded, the remaining officers rallied their men and managed to survive.

The reputation of this regiment for pride, courage, valor, gallantry, bravery, and sheer nerve was no doubt due to this combination of experience and coolness under fire, by both veterans and raw recruits. The officer corps, for the most part were battle-hardened veterans. Twelve of the seventeen staff officers and captains had seen previous action against Lord Dunmore and his forces.

The evolution of the 3rd Virginia took place between April and December 1775 and matured in January 1776 as independent companies and minute battalions grew used to facing the British regulars and American Loyalists of Lord Dunmore.

Once Dunmore had been forced out of Virginia and the battles were over, officers and men alike realized that the fighting had not ended, it had just begun. The organization of the Virginia battalions for Continental defense gave these men an opportunity for further service against a well-organized, disciplined armed force.

END NOTES
CHAPTER 1
THE EVOLUTION OF THE 3RD VIRGINIA

1. Fred A. Berg, *Encyclopedia of Continental Army Units* (Harrisburg: Stackpole Books, 1972), 125. See also Paul Smith, *Letters of Delegates to Congress 1774–1789* (Washington, D.C: Library of Congress, 1977), "Virginia Delegate to Unknown, December 29, 1775", 2, 88.
2. Michael Cecere, *They Behaved Like Soldiers: Captain John Chilton & The Third Virginia Regiment, 1775–1778* (Bowie, Maryland: Heritage Books, 2004), 8. See also Robert Wright Jr, *The Continental Army* (Washington, D.C.: Center of Military History, U.S. Army, 1989), 285–286.
3. E. M. Sanchez-Saavedra, *A Guide to Virginia Military Organizations in the American Revolution 1774–1787* (Richmond: Virginia State Library, 1978), 39.
4. John Gott & Triplett Russell, *Fauquier in the Revolution* (Warrenton: Warrenton Printing & Publishing Company, 1977), 54.
5. Ibid., 58 and Colonial Williamsburg Foundation, "Proceedings of the 2nd Virginia Convention," *Virginia Gazette*, (Pinkney) 30 March 1775, 2, col. 2–3 (http://research.history.org/JDRLibrary/Online_Resources/Virginia Gazette). Hereafter, Colonial Williamsburg Foundation, *Virginia Gazette* (http://research.history.org).
6. Gott and Russell, 64.
7. Cecere, 1.
8. Gott and Russell, 64. The footnote to the text cites the *Journals of the House of Burgesses of Virginia 1773 – 1776, 231* for this quote.
9. M. Lee Minis, *The First Virginia Regiment of Foot 1775–1783* (Westminster, Maryland: Willow Bend Books, 1998), 3. See also Sanchez-Saavedra: 6–7.
10. Gott & Russell, 64–65.
11. *Journals of Continental Congress*, A Century of Lawmaking for a New Nation: U.S. Congressional Documents and Debates, 1774–1875, 3, image 403 (http://www.loc.gov/ammem/amlaw/lwjclink.html. Hereafter, *JCC*, (http://www.loc.gov/ammem). The circumstances surrounding Lord Dunmore's proclamation, along with the text of the document and Virginia's response can be found on the *Black Loyalist Home Page*, (http://www.collections.ic.gc.ca/blackloyalists/documents/official/dunmore.htm) .See also Gott and Russell, 67.
12. Minis, 3. Gott and Russell, 72.
13. Gott and Russell, 72. See note 14 on page 72 for the 3rd Virginia Convention's organization of the Virginia military system.
14. Joan W. Peters, *The Tax Man Cometh: Land & Property in Colonial Fauquier County Virginia 1759–1782* (Westminster: Willow Bend Books, 1999), iii. See also Colonial Williamsburg Foundation, "Proceedings of the 3rd Virginia Convention," *Virginia Gazette*, (Purdie) 24 August, 1775: 1–6, http://research.history.org and Wright, 67–68.
15. Jones, 15.
16. William Waller Hening, *The Statutes at Large, Being a Collection of all the Laws of Virginia from the First Session of the Legislature in the Year 1619*, Volumes 1–13 CD 0878 (Bowie, Maryland: Heritage Archives, 2003), 9, 16. Hereafter, Hening. See also Stuart Reid & Marko Zladich, *Soldiers of the Revolutionary War* (Oxford: Osprey Publishing Company, 2002), 8.
17. Henings 9, 27. For the organization of the county militia, see Henings 9, 27–33. See also Jones, 16 and Gott and Russell, 73–74.
18. Jones, 16. John Marshall went on to serve as a 1st Lieutenant in the 3rd Virginia for a very brief time. He was commissioned July 30, 1776. He was promoted out of the regiment in December 1776 as a Captain-Lieutenant in the 15th Virginia. He was a Deputy Judge Advocate in November 1777, a captain, commissioned 1 July 1778. He transferred to the 7th Virginia in September 1778 and retired from the Continental service in February 1781. He died on 6 July 1835. See Heitman, 381 and *Culpeper Minute Battalion 1775*.
19. Gott and Russell, 66.
20. Ibid.
21. Ibid., 74–76.
22. Gott and Russell, 69. See also Don Higginbotham, *Daniel Morgan, Revolutionary Rifleman* (Chapel Hill: University of North Carolina Press, 1961), 22–26.
23. Various historians have written about Morgan and his riflemen at Saratoga. See Chapter 7 for details of the part he played in this decisive victory.
24. Sanchez-Saavedra, 7.
25. Ibid.

26. Library of Congress, *The George Washington Papers 1741–1799. Series 4: General Correspondence 1697–1799 Prince William County, Virginia Independent Cadet's Company*, 11 November 1774 Resolutions (http://www.memory.loc.gov/cgi=bin/query/r?ammem/ngw). Hereafter, Library of Congress (www.memory.loc.gov).

27. Library of Congress, *George Washington Papers, 1741–1799: Diaries of George Washington 3, 1774 – 1775; 1780–1781.* Donald Jackson and Dorothy Twohig, eds. (Charlottesville, Virginia: University of Virginia Press, 1978) III: 291 (http://www.memory.loc.gov).

28. Ibid. This is a note explaining the formation of the Prince William independent company and Washington's response to this and other independent companies who requested that he take command of their companies as their field officer.

29. National Archives and Records Administration, Philip Richard Francis Lee's service records, Officers, 3rd Virginia, on an undated List of Officers who served in the 3rd Virginia from 1 January 1776 to 28 August 1778. "P.R.F. Lee, Capt. Commissioned March 19, 1776. Death: Jan. 29, 1778."

30. Gott and Russell, 198, 205. The authors refer to Captain Lee as "Philip Francis Lee" and as being "badly wounded."

31. Sanchez-Saavedra, 8–9.

32. Ibid., 38. See also *Journals of Continental Congress 1774–1789* (Washington: Government Printing Office, 1906) 5: 418, 420, 424. Hereafter, *JCC*.

33. Bernard Lossing, *Pictorial Field Book of the Revolution* CD 3261 (Bowie: Heritage Books, 2004) 2, 28–30.

34. Francis B. Heitman, *Historical Register of Officers of the Continental Army during the War of the Revolution, April 1775 to December 1783.* 1914; Reprint, (Baltimore: Clearfield, 1982), 512.

35. Ibid., 598.

36. Sanchez-Saavedra, 9.

37. Ibid.

38. Ibid., 30, 34.

39. National Archives, *Revolutionary War Rolls* M246 MR 137 *Returns of the Army under General Washington 1775-1782.* November 10, 1777 General *Return of the Continental Army encamped at White Marsh.* This return shows the 3rd Virginia, under the command of Colonel Marshall, was part of Woodford's Brigade. Other Virginia regiments in this brigade were the 7th and 15th Virginia. The comments for Woodford's Brigade reveal that two dozen men of the 3rd Virginia were unfit for duty, lacking clothes. Hereafter, NARA, *Returns of the Army*.

40. Sanchez-Saavedra, 10.

41. NARA, *Morning Return, 3rd Virginia at Harlem Heights,* September 13, 1776, M246 MR 97 *Returns of the Army.* Captain Fitzgerald's return showed a captain, lieutenant, ensign, four sergeants, a drum major, a fife major, a drummer and an artificer in his company. Thirty-four of the rank and file were fit for duty; thirteen were sick, three were sick and absent. Two men were on command.

42. Arthur S. Lefkowitz, *George Washington's Indispensable Men* (Mechanicsburg, Pennsylvania: Stackpole Books, 2003), 81–82. Captain John Fitzgerald, of the 3rd Virginia Regiment, was promoted to Major in October 1776 and joined Washington's staff in November as an aide de camp.

43. Sanchez-Saavedra, 11.

44. Ibid., 29, 34.

45. Ibid., 30.

46. Ibid. 35.

47. See note 39.

48. Sanchez-Saavedra, 15.

49. Heitman, 389. John Francis Mercer was commissioned a 1st Lieutenant in the 3rd Virginia, 26 February 1776. He was wounded at Brandywine in September 1777. He was promoted to a captaincy in the same month. In June 1778, Captain Mercer became an aide de camp to General Lee. He resigned his commission in July 1779. He later became a Lieutenant Colonel in the Virginia militia from October 1780 to November 1781. He died 3 August 1821.

50. Stephen E. Haller, *William Washington: Cavalryman of the Revolution* (Bowie: Heritage Books, 2001), 6. See also Mark Boatner III, *Encyclopedia of the American Revolution,* (Mechanicsburg: Stackpole Books, 1994), 1169. See also Colonial Williamsburg Foundation, "Election of Officers of Spotsylvania Minute Battalion," *Virginia Gazette* (Purdie), 22 September 1775, 1, col.1 (http://research.history.org).

51. Colonial Williamsburg Foundation, "Election of Officers ..." *Virginia Gazette* (Purdie), 22 September 1775, 1, col. 2 (http://research.history.org).

52. Jones, 16. See also Heitman, 381. Thomas Marshall had already enjoyed a distinguished career in Fauquier County, as Sheriff and as a vestryman for Leeds parish. He also served in the House of Burgesses from 1761–1767. His military experience also came before the hostilities occasioned by Lord Dunmore's attacks in late 1775 and early 1776 in Norfolk, Hampton and Great Bridge. Marshall served in the Indian wars as an ensign, lieutenant and captain of the militia. When the Culpeper Minute Battalion was discharged, he received a transfer to the 3rd Virginia. See Friends of the Hollow, *Thomas Marshall's Biography* (www.geocities.com/thehollow.geo/hollow.htm).

53. Jones, 15.

54. Heitman, 154. See also NARA, *John Chilton's compiled service records*, Officers, 3rd Virginia.

55. Ibid., 105. John E. Blackwell was commissioned a 1st Lieutenant in the 3rd Virginia in April 1776.

56. Ibid. Blackwell was wounded at Brandywine in September 1777. He was promoted to Captain when his Captain, John Chilton, was killed at Brandywine. He was made a prisoner of war at the fall of Charleston in May 1780. See also NARA, *John Blackwell's compiled service records*, Officers, 3rd Virginia.

57. Sanchez-Saavedra, 22.

58. Heitman, 263.

59. Ibid., 582. Charles West was commissioned as a Captain in the 3rd Virginia on 9 February 1776. He was promoted to Major in January 1777. He resigned his commission on 6 July 1778.

60. Ibid., 346. Andrew Leitch was commissioned as a Captain in the 3rd Virginia on 5 February 1776. He was promoted out of the regiment to be a Major in the 1st Virginia in March 1776. He died in October 1776 of wounds suffered at Harlem Heights in the previous month.

61. See note 42.

62. Wikipedia, the Free Encyclopedia, *Hugh Mercer's Biography* (http://www.en.wikipedia.org/wike/Hugh Mercer). See also *George Weedon's Biography* and *William Woodford's Biography* on this web site.

63. Gott and Russell, 73. The footnote on this page states that John Marshall noted the rendezvous took place on September 1, 1775. See note 32 above.

64. Ibid.

65. Philip Slaughter's diary entries are found in Jones, 16 and Gott & Russell, 73.

66. Colonial Williamsburg Foundation, "Expected Arrival of Culpeper County Minute Battalion," *Virginia Gazette Supplement* (Purdie), 20 October 1775, 2, col. 3 (http://research.history.org).

67. Raleigh Travers Green, *Genealogical and Historical Notes on Culpeper County, Virginia* (1900, Reprint, Bowie: Heritage Books, 1995), 47.

68. Cecere, 3.

69. Paul Drake, *What Did They Mean By That? A Dictionary of Historical Terms for Genealogists* (Bowie: Heritage Books, 1994), 155.

70. Cecere, 4.

71. Drake, 21. See also Cecere, 4 note 10.

72. Gott and Russell, 77.

73. Colonial Williamsburg Foundation, "Minute-men and regulars received and reviewed in Williamsburg," *Virginia Gazette Supplement* (Purdie), 7 October 1775: 2, col. 3 (http://research.history.org).

74. Ibid., "Minute-men to Williamsburg," *Virginia Gazette* (Dixon), 21 October 1775: 2, col. 3.

75. Gott and Russell, 77.

76. Random House, *Webster's College Dictionary*. (New York: Random House, 1991), 1214.

77. Colonial Williamsburg Foundation, "Hampton's Refusal to return confiscated English Goods," *Virginia Gazette*, (Pinkney) 15 September 1775: 3, col. 2 (http://research.history.org).

78. Ibid.

79. Ibid. "Terms offered to Captain Squires," *Virginia Gazette* (Purdie), 22 September 1775, 3, col. 1 & 2.

80. Ibid., "Hampton's request for troops to defend Town," *Virginia Gazette* (Purdie) 15 September 1775, 3, col. 1.

81. James Innes was the Captain of the Williamsburg Volunteers, an independent company. He later became a member of the Virginia Board of War and the Navy board. See Sanchez-Saavedra, 8. Innes became a Lt. Colonel of the 15th Virginia, commissioned in November 1776. He retired in September 1778. From July to September 1782, he served as Judge Advocate of the Army. See Heitman, 313.

82. Colonial Williamsburg Foundation, "Hampton's thanks to Officers who responded to defend the City," *Virginia Gazette* (Purdie), 22 September 1775: 3, col. 2 (http://research.history.org).

83. Ibid., "British skirmish at Kemp's Landing to retrieve military stores," *Virginia Gazette Supplement* (Purdie) 20 October 1775, 2, col. 2.

84. Gott and Russell, 77.

85. Jones, 18.

86. Captain Lynn was George Lyne of the Gloucester Minute Battalion. His name was spelled as either *Lynn* or *Lyne*. See text for note 91 below. Captain Lyne was from King & Queen County. See Sanchez-Saavedra, 17–18. George Lyne became a captain of Virginia State forces, commissioned in March 1776. He was promoted to major of the 13th Virginia in November 1776 and lieutenant colonel of the 9th Virginia in September 1777. He resigned his commission in November 1777. See Heitman, 361.

87. Colonial Williamsburg Foundation, "Description of Battle at Hampton," *Virginia Gazette* (Purdie), 26 October 1776: 3, col. 2.

88. Ibid.

89. Gott and Russell: 77.

90. Jones: 18.

91. Colonial Williamsburg Foundation, "Description of Battle at Hampton," *Virginia Gazette* (Purdie), 26 October 1775, 3, col. 2, and *Virginia Gazette* (Dixon), 27 October 1775, 3, col. 3.

92. Ibid. "Description of Battle of Hampton," *Virginia Gazette* (Pinkney), 2 November 1775, 2, col. 2–3.

93. Jones., 18.

94. Black Loyalists, *Lord Dunmore Proclamation,* November 7, 1775 (http:// www.collections.ic.gc.ca/black loyalists/documents/official/Dunmore.htm).

95. Paul Smith, *Letters of Delegates to Congress 1774-1789* (Washington: Library of Congress, 1977) 2, 227–228. Hereafter, *Letters.*

96. *Letters* 2: 406–407.

97. Captain Fontaine was probably William Fontaine, a Captain in the 2nd Virginia. His troops were raised in Amelia County. See note 98 below.

98. Colonial Williamsburg Foundation, "New troops arrive in Williamsburg," *Virginia Gazette* (Purdie), 10 November 10, 1775, 2, col. 3

99. Gott and Russell, 80–81.

100. Ibid., 82. See also Jones, 19.

101. Gott and Russell, 82.

102. Ibid.

103. Ibid.

104. Ibid: Cecere, 5 and Jones, 18–19.

105. Gott and Russell, 83.

106. Colonial Williamsburg Foundation, "Skirmish at Great Bridge," *Virginia Gazette* (Dixon), 2 December 1775, 2, col. 1

107. Captain Nicholas may have been George Nicholas, a captain in the 2nd Virginia Regiment, raised in Hanover County. See Sanchez-Saavedra, 36. There was also a Captain Nicholas who captained a company raised in Williamsburg. He served in the Elizabeth City District Minute Service. See Sanchez-Saavedra, 17.

108. Colonial Williamsburg Foundation, "Skirmish at Great Bridge," *Virginia Gazette* (Purdie), 8 December 1775, 3, col. 1, (http://research.history.org).

109. Ibid. The action described in this letter concerned that of the Culpeper Minute Battalion. Colonel Stevens was Edward Stevens of the Culpeper minute battalion. See Sanchez-Saavedra, 16–17.

110. Gott and Russell, 85.

111. Lossing, 329.

112. Gott and Russell, 85. See also Jones, 4 and Cecere, 6–7.

113. Gott and Russell, 85–86.

114. Jones, 20.

115. Colonial Williamsburg Foundation, "An Account of the Battle of Great Bridge," *Virginia Gazette* (Pinkney), 20 December 1775: 2, col. 2; 3, col. 1 (http:/ research.history.org).

116. A "fuzee" or "fusil" was a light musket designed for artillery or light infantry. British officers and, occasionally non-commissioned officers, carried these weapons. Fuzees were distinguished from artillery muskets by their superior workmanship. The mounting of these muskets were often engraved or decorated in some way. See Harold L. Peterson, *The Book of the Continental Soldier* (Harrisburg: The Stackpole Company, 1968), 29.

117. See note 115.

118. Ibid.

119. Ibid: See also Gott and Russell, 86.

120. See note 117.

121. Gott and Russell, 86.

122. Major Spotswood was Alexander Spotswood of the 2nd Virginia, commissioned in July 1775. See Sanchez-Saavedra, 35.

123. Colonial Williamsburg, "An Account of the Battle at Great Bridge," *Virginia Gazette* (Purdie), 15 December 1775, 2, col. 2 and 3, col.1 (http://research.history.org).

124. Gott and Russell, 88–89 and Cecere, 7.

125. Jones, 20.
126. Morgan Alexander was a Captain in the 2nd Virginia, whose company was made up of riflemen from Frederick County, Virginia. See Sanchez-Saavedra, 36.
127. See note 123.
128. Jones, 20.
129. Colonial Williamsburg Foundation, "Minute men from Prince William County arrive in Williamsburg," *Virginia Gazette Supplement* (Purdie) 29 December 1775, 2, col. 3.
130. Ibid., "British Attack & Burn Norfolk," *Virginia Gazette Supplement* (Purdie), 5 January 1776: 2, col. 1–2.
131. Ibid.
132. Ibid.
133. Jones: 20.
134. Gott and Russell, 89–90.
135. See note 133.
136. Gott and Russell, 90.
137. Among the men killed, two were from Captain Abraham Buford's company of the Culpeper Minute Battalion. The wounded soldier who, "it was thought, will lose his arm" was also one of Captain Buford's men. See Jones, 20. See Colonial Williamsburg Foundation, "Minute-men killed at Norfolk," *Virginia Gazette* (Dixon), 27 January 1776, 3 (http://research.history.org).
138. Ibid. "British Attack Norfolk," *Virginia Gazette* (Purdie) 26 January 1776: 3, col. 1.
139. Jones, 20–21 and Gott and Russell, 93.
140. *JCC* 3: 463.
141. Colonial Williamsburg Foundation, "Officers Chosen for Virginia Continental Regiments," *Virginia Gazette* (Purdie), 12 January 1776, 3, col. 2 (http://research.history.org).
142. Ibid., *Virginia Gazette* (Pinkney), 13 January 1776: 2, col. 2.
143. *JCC* 4: 131–132.
144. *JCC* 6: 864. Isham Keith had also served with the Culpeper Minute Battalion. See *Culpeper Minute Men Battalion 1775*, http://www.ccmsar.com. Hereafter, *Culpeper Minute Men Battalion, 1775*. For William Nelson's service in the 3rd Virginia, see Heitman, 411. See also NARA, *William Nelson, on List of Captains and Subalterns in the Virginia Service*, compiled *service records*, 3rd Virginia.
145. NARA, *Henry Moffett's compiled service records*, 3rd Virginia.
146. Andrew Obannon was not found in the compiled service records of the 3rd Virginia. The information relating to his 3rd Virginia service was found in the *Culpeper Minute Men Battalion, 1775*.
147. NARA, *William Winkfield's compiled service records*, 3rd Virginia.
148. Gott and Russell, 99.
149. *Culpeper Minute Men Battalion, 1775*.
150. NARA, *Spencer Anderson's compiled service records*, 3rd Virginia.
151. *Culpeper Minute Men Battalion, 1775*.
152. NARA, *Charles Jones's compiled service records*.
153. Ibid., *John Jones's compiled service records*.
154. Ibid., Henry *Moffett's compiled service records*.
155. See note 146.
156. NARA, *William Winkfield's compiled service records*.
157. *JCC* 6: 684. See also Gott and Russell, 100 and Sanchez-Saavedra, 40.
158. Gott and Russell, 100.
159. Cecere, 8.
160. Gott and Russell, 100.
161. *Culpeper Minute Men Battalion*.
162. Gott and Russell, 101.
163. Sanchez-Saavedra: 39.
164. Ibid., 22.
165. Ibid., 10.
166. Ibid., 39.
167. Ibid., 22.
168. See Note 161.
169. Sanchez-Saavedra, 39.
170. Heitman, 574.
171. Sanchez-Saavedra, 39.
172. Ibid., 12, 15.
173. Ibid., 39.
174. Ibid., 9, 11.

175. Ibid., 39.
176. Heitman, 321.
177. Sanchez-Saavedra, 40.
178. Heitman, 438.
179. Ibid., 73.
180. Sanchez-Saavedra, 40.
181. Heitman, 450.
182. Sanchez-Saavedra: 22.
183. Ibid., 39.
184. *JCC* 4: 74. Although the department is not specified, other regiments had been placed in the Northern Department—New England—and the Middle Department which consisted of regiments from New Jersey, Delaware, New York, and Maryland.
185. Ibid 4: 234–236.
186. Gott and Russell, 448.
187. NARA, *Littleton Adams compiled service records*, 3rd Virginia.
188. Gott and Russell, 448.
189. NARA, *Spencer Anderson's compiled service records*.
190. There was no service record found for John Dulin in the compiled service records of the 3rd Virginia.. Information about Dulin's Culpeper Minute Service was found in Gott and Russell, 456 and *Culpeper Minute Men Battalion 1775*.
192. Gott and Russell, 463.
193. NARA, *Charles Jones's compiled service records*.
194. Gott and Russell, 468.
195. NARA, *Henry Moffett's compiled service records*.
196. See note 146.
197. Gott and Russell, 470.
198. There were no compiled service records for Daniel O'Rear in the compiled service records of the 3rd Virginia..
199. Gott and Russell, 471.
200. NARA, *John Riley's compiled service records*.
201. Gott and Russell, 479.
202. NARA, *William Winkfield's compiled service records*.
203. Gott and Russell, 99.
204. NARA, *Moses Allen's compiled service record,* 3rd and 4th Virginia, M 881 MR 957.

Chapter 2

Structure & Organization of the 3RD Virginia

Field Officers and Staff 1776–1778

COLONEL HUGH MERCER was commissioned as the first colonel of the 3rd Virginia on 13 February 1776 and served in that capacity until his promotion 6 June 1776 to brigadier general of the Continental Army. He died of wounds suffered at Princeton in January 1777.[1]

LIEUTENANT COLONEL GEORGE WEEDON was originally commissioned on 13 February 1776. He was promoted to colonel of the 3rd Virginia in August 1776 some two months after colonel Mercer had been promoted out of the regiment. He served as the second colonel of the regiment from 13 August 1776 to 21 February 1777. In February 1777, Weedon became an acting Adjutant-General to Washington and a week later, a Brigadier in the Continental Army. He resigned his commission on 11 June 1783 and died in November 1793.[2]

MAJOR THOMAS MARSHALL, was commissioned on 13 February 1776;[3] then as lieutenant colonel, on 21 February 1776[4] and finally as colonel of the regiment, on 21 February 1777.[5] He served as the commanding officer of the 3rd Virginia from 21 February until 4 December 1777 when he officially resigned to become a Colonel of a Virginia State Artillery Regiment.[6]

COLONEL WILLIAM HETH began his career as a lieutenant in Captain Daniel Morgan's company of Virginia riflemen. He was taken prisoner at Quebec in the last part of December 1775. He was promoted to Major of the 11th Virginia in November 1776 and promoted to Lieutenant Colonel of the 3rd Virginia in April 1777. He became the colonel of the 3rd Virginia in late April 1778.[7] He was taken prisoner at Charleston in May 1780.[8]

LIEUTENANT COLONEL CHARLES FLEMING served in the 3rd Virginia from 14 June to 14 September 1778. He was promoted out of the regiment, to a colonelcy in the 8th Virginia Regiment.[9] He had formerly served as a captain in the 7th Virginia, commissioned on 29 February 1776 and was promoted to major of the 4th Virginia in June 1777.[10]

LIEUTENANT COLONEL THOMAS GASKINS began his service as a captain in the 5th Virginia, commissioned in February 1776. He was promoted to major in November 1777 in the same regiment. In May 1778 he was promoted out of the 5th Virginia to serve as a lieutenant colonel in the 4th Virginia. He transferred to the 3rd Virginia as a result of the September 1778 reorganization of the Virginia line and served until the end of the war.[11]

MAJOR WILLIAM TALIAFERRO is another 3rd Virginia staff officer with a varied career in the Virginia line. He began as a captain of the 2nd Virginia, commissioned in September 1775. He was promoted to major in the 3rd Virginia in August 1776 and served in that capacity until his promotion to lieutenant colonel in the 4th Virginia in February 1777.[12]

MAJOR CHARLES WEST was a former 3rd Virginia captain, commissioned on 9 February 1776. He was promoted within the regiment to major on 30 January 1777. He resigned his commission on 6 July 1778.[13]

MAJOR JOHN HAYS was Captain John Hays of the 9th Virginia, when he was taken prisoner at Germantown on October 4, 1777. He was promoted to major in the 3rd Virginia in April 1778[14] while a prisoner of the British. He remained a prisoner of war until his retirement in February 1781.[15]

MAJOR JAMES LUCAS transferred into the 3rd Virginia in September 1778[16] and served with the 3rd Virginia until his retirement in May 1779.[17]

Regimental Arrangement of the 3RD Virginia

August 1776 to October 1776

The 3rd Virginia was a separate regiment, under the command of George Weedon and attached to the main army from August 1776 until 17 October 1776.[18] While a separate regiment, Weedon's officers and men took part in the Battles of Harlem Heights, in September 1776; and White Plains, in October 1776.

October 1776 to May 1777

The 3rd Virginia served as part of Lord Stirling's Brigade from 17 October 1776 until 11 May 1777.[19] Lord Stirling's Brigade was composed of the 1st Virginia, under Isaac Reade; the 3rd Virginia, under George Weedon; a Delaware Regiment commanded by John Haslet; two Pennsylvania battalions from the Flying Camp, and the 1st and 2nd Battalion of Miles Pennsylvania rifle regiment.[20] In December 1776, Stirling's Brigade had been reorganized to comprise the 1st Virginia under Isaac Reade; the 3rd Virginia, under George Weedon; a Delaware Regiment, commanded by John Haslet; and the 6th Maryland commanded by Otho Holland Williams.[21]

As part of Stirling's Brigade the 3rd Virginia took part in a skirmish at New Rochelle, in November 1777, spent the winter at Valley Forge and saw action at Trenton and Princeton.

May 1777 to July 1778

In May 1777, the 3rd Virginia was relieved from Stirling's Brigade and assigned to the 3rd Virginia Brigade,[22] under the command of Brigadier General William Woodford.[23] In a 21 May 1777 general return of the Continental Forces under General Washington in New Jersey the Virginia regiments were all listed as separate entities. The 3rd Virginia, now commanded by Colonel Thomas Marshall, was comprised of sixteen commissioned officers, twenty-four non-coms, four staff members, and 123 rank and file, a total of 167 men. When the forty-eight men who were sick and present were added, the 3rd Virginia regiment totaled 194 men.[24]

In a 28 May 1777 general return of Continental Forces in New Jersey, the 3rd Virginia Regiment was composed of a colonel, a lieutenant colonel, five captains, eight lieutenants, and an ensign, along with a chaplain and surgeon, an adjutant and a quartermaster. The non-comms include one sergeant major, one quartermaster sergeant, nineteen sergeants, two drummers and three fifers. There were 123 rank and file fit for duty; thirteen were sick and present and fourteen were sick and absent. The 3rd Virginia totaled 169 men.[25]

The first return showing the arrangement of Brigadier General William Woodford's Brigade was a weekly return for 3 November 1777 of the Continental Army in Pennsylvania. Woodford's Brigade was comprised of the 3rd Virginia under Colonel Marshall, along with the 7th, 11th, and 15th Virginia Regiments and the Fauquier Militia.[26]

The brigade returned a colonel, four lieutenant colonels, two majors, eighteen captains, thirty-seven lieutenants and twenty-two ensigns as commissioned officers, along with two chaplains, five adjutants, four surgeons and a surgeon's mate. There were ninety-five sergeants and thirty-two drum and fife corps among the non-comms. Eight hundred six men made up the rank and file, with eighty-six sick and present; there were 406 men who were sick and absent; twenty-six were on furlough and 234 were on command. The brigade totaled 1558 men. One private had joined the brigade. General Woodford noted that his brigade also included Fauquier Militia, amounting to ninety-nine privates fit for duty.[27]

On 10 November 1777, in a general return of the Continental Army at White Marsh, Woodford's Brigade included the 3rd Virginia under Colonel Marshall, along with the 7th, 11th, and 15th Virginia.[28] As a result of losses inflicted at Brandywine and Germantown, in November 1777 the 3rd Virginia companies had been reorganized downward, from ten companies to eight.[29]

This November return broke down the 3rd Virginia's organization precisely. The regiment consisted of a colonel, a lieutenant colonel, a major, five captains, eleven lieutenants and five ensigns. An adjutant, a quartermaster, a paymaster, a chaplain and surgeon, and surgeon's mate filled out the officers. There were nineteen sergeants and seven drum and fifes among the non-comms. One hundred eighty-eight men were present and fit for duty. Twenty-nine were sick and present. sixty were sick and absent. One man was on furlough and fifty-two were on command. The Regiment totaled 300 men. One man had deserted and twenty-two privates had joined the regiment. It was noted that "in the 3rd Virginia Regiment, twenty-four men [were] wanting clothes [and] unfit for duty."[30]

While part of Woodford's Brigade, the regiment saw action, in September and October 1777, at Brandywine and Germantown, and in May and June 1778, in the skirmish at Barren Hills and Monmouth Court House.

July to December 1778

In July 1778, after the battle of Monmouth Courthouse, the 3rd Virginia was relieved from the 3rd Virginia Battalion and assigned, instead, to both the 1st and 2nd Virginia Battalion,[31] still part of Woodford's Brigade and still part of the main army. The 1st Virginia Battalion was made up of Captain Robert Powell's 3rd and 7th Virginia companies, selected from Captain John Francis Mercer's 3rd Virginia company and Captain Crockett's 7th Virginia company. The remainder of the regiment made up the 2nd Virginia Battalion. During this time, from July to September, 1778 the brigade was at White Plains.[32]

CAPTAINS OF THE 3RD VIRGINIA REGIMENT OF FOOT, 1776–1778

Historical Overview: February 1776 to September 1778

Between February 1776 and January 1777, there were ten captains in the 3rd Virginia. Andrew Leitch, John Fitzgerald, Charles West, John Thornton, Gustavus Brown Wallace, William Washington, Philip Richard Francis Lee, John Ashby, and Thomas Johnson Jr, and William McWilliams all received continental commissions as captains in the 3rd Virginia.

In addition, four more captains, John Chilton, John Peyton, David Arell and Robert Powell, were commissioned in 1776 "to replace captains who had been promoted or who were serving on detached duty."[33]

Between January 1777 and September 1778, captains of 3rd Virginia companies were shuffled around. John Chilton became the captain of John Thornton's 4th company; John Thornton in turn replaced Gustavus Brown Wallace of the 5th company[34] when Wallace was promoted out of the regiment.[35]

Reuben Briscoe was promoted to captain in January 1777[36] and became captain of Charles West's old company.[37] Captain Briscoe served in the 3rd Virginia until the last of September 1778 when he resigned his commission.[38]

John Francis Mercer, a 1st lieutenant in Captain Wallace's Company, was promoted to captain after Brandywine and initially replaced Phil Lee who died of wounds suffered at Brandywine.[39] He went on to become the captain of his old company when John Thornton was promoted out of the regiment.[40]

Valentine Peyton, a lieutenant in the 3rd Virginia, was promoted to captain after Brandywine, in September 1777.[41] He took over John Ashby's Company.[42] Captain Ashby had been wounded at Germantown, and resigned his commission on 30 October 1777.[43]

John E. Blackwell, a lieutenant in the 3rd Virginia wounded at Brandywine, was promoted to captain four days after that battle.[44] He became captain of John Chilton's company.[45]

Some of these promotions reflected the casualties suffered by the 3rd Virginia at Brandywine and Germantown. Captain Chilton was killed at Brandywine on September 11, 1777. Captain John Peyton was wounded in this Battle. Captain John Ashby was wounded at Germantown. Captain Phill Lee died in January 1778 as a result of wounds suffered at Brandywine the previous autumn. Captain Washington had been wounded in 1776 at Harlem Heights and then, again in January 1777 at Trenton.[46]

David Arell, a lieutenant in Captain John Fitzgerald's Company, was promoted to captain when John Fitzgerald was promoted out of the Regiment.[47]

3RD VIRGINIA CAPTAINS AND COMPANY RETURNS

Company returns, filed by Captains of the 3rd Virginia between 13 September and 5 November 1777, proved to be excellent sources for the structure and organization of the regiment before the action at Harlem Heights on a company level. These returns showed the strength and fitness of each company, They gave details relating to the numbers of commissioned officers, captains, lieutenants and ensigns; non-commissioned officers, sergeants and drum and fife; and the rank and file, the private soldiers in the company.

These returns also showed the number of men who were sick and present as well as those who were sick and absent. Two other important pieces of information in these returns included the number of men on furlough and the number on command. Artificers were also mentioned, if present in the company at the time the return was made.

All of the 3rd Virginia Captains filed returns beginning in September 1778. These returns, presented here, offer a fascinating glimpse into the inner workings of the regiment, especially when a captain's weekly returns were compared and contrasted against one another.

Colonel Weedon filed three regimental returns in October and December which showed the collective strength of the 3rd Virginia. These returns showed the ability of the regiment to respond to the enemy. He returned numbers for his commissioned officers, a colonel, lieutenant colonel, major, captains and lieutenants; his field staff, including an adjutant, quartermaster, surgeon, surgeon's mates; his non-commissioned officers which were sergeants and members of the drum and fife corps.

Finally, his rank and file numbers were posted for the regiment as a whole. He delineated the regiments' sick and present and sick and absent as well as those on furlough and command. Some of his returns gave numbers for sergeants, rank and file and drum and fife needed to bring the regiment up to full strength.[48] These returns, coupled with the company returns, show the structure and organization of the regiment in the fall of 1776 on the eve of battle.

Captain David Arell's Company, October 1776.

David Arell became captain of John Fitzgerald's old company in October 1776.[49] He resigned his commission on 14 February 1778.[50] He filed two returns, both in October 1776.

He filed his first return as a captain of this company on 4 October 1776. His officer corps included a 1st lieutenant, a 2nd lieutenant, an ensign and a captain. He had four sergeants and two drum and fife among his non-comms. He reported forty of his rank and file who were fit for duty. Six men were present and sick, two were absent and sick while four others were on command. He had fifty-two men and officers and needed sixteen privates to complete his company. One man had deserted.[51]

His next return was filed two days later. His officer corps remained unchanged while he added a sergeant to his non-commissioned officers. He had thirty-eight of his rank and file fit for duty, two less than in his 4 October 1776 return. Eight men were present and sick, none were absent and sick and seven were on command. He reported a total of fifty-three men and officers and needed fifteen privates to complete his company. He reported one more desertion since his 4 October return.[52]

Captain John Ashby's Company, September to October 1777
Valentine Peyton's Company, October 1777 to June 1778
Captain John Peyton, June to September 1778
Captain Val Peyton's Company, after September 1778.

Captain Ashby and his rifle company filed morning returns on their arrival in New York. Their first return was filed 13 September 1776. He reported an ensign, two lieutenants and a captain among his officers and four sergeants and two drum and fife among his non-comms. Captain Ashby reported sixty-two men and officers present. Forty-two of his rank and file were fit for duty, five were sick and nine were absent, sick. Four men were on command.[53]

His next return occurred five days after Harlem Heights on 21 September 1776. His officer corps remained intact and he now had a quartermaster sergeant along with three sergeants and two drum and fife among his non-commissioned officers. In this return, only thirty-three of his rank and file were fit for duty versus the forty-two reported on his earlier September return. He had twelve sick, nine absent who were sick, four on command and one man missing. He reported sixty-one men and officers present on this date.[54]

Two days later he filed a morning return, while his company was stationed on Morris Heights. His return did not change except there was no one missing and he had sixty men and officers present.[55] On 28 September 1776 he filed another morning return, still at Morris Heights. It was identical to his 23 September 1776 return.[56]

His first October return was reported on 6 October 1776 showing an ensign, a 1st lieutenant a 2nd lieutenant and a captain. He had four sergeants (no quartermaster sergeant in this return) and two drum and fife. Thirty-seven of his rank and file were fit for duty. Nine were sick and present, nine were also sick and absent. Six were on command. He had a total of sixty-one men present and needed seven privates to complete the company.[57]

His next return was filed on 11 October 1776. This showed an officer corps and non-comms with the same number, as his previous return. Six men were still on command. Twelve men were sick and present while nine continued to be sick, absent. He had a total of fifty-nine men and officers present and needed nine privates to complete his company.[58]

His last return was filed on 5 November 1776. His officers and non-comms remained the same as his last October return. However he had only twenty-nine of his rank and file fit for duty, down from thirty-seven on his 11 October 1776 return. While two were sick but present with the company, twenty-one men were sick and absent. Seven were on command. There were a total of fifty-nine men and officers present in November 1776 in his company.[59]

Captain John Ashby was wounded at Germantown and resigned in late October[60] and Valentine Peyton, who was promoted to captain on 12 September 1777, a day after Brandywine,[61] became the company's second captain, serving until June 1778.[62]

In June 1778, Captain John Peyton apparently took over this company,[63] melding it with Captain Phil Lee's late company.[64] The resulting company bore little resemblance to John Ashby's rifle company when Peyton took over control of the company in June 1778 from Val Peyton. Most of the men in Captain Ashby's original rifle company had already been discharged between January and March 1778.

The remaining company had been cobbled together with men from Captain John Thornton's rifle company and men from the late Phill Lee's company. John Peyton served as the company's captain until September 1778. In the September 1778 reorganization at White Plains, Captain Valentine Peyton was to become the Captain again of this 3rd Virginia company, slated to begin his duties in October of that year.[65]

It was necessary to follow the men and officers in these companies in order to understand the organization of the companies in the summer and fall of 1778. Many of the men who were caught up in the September 1778 reorganization at White Plains had enlisted in 1777 and were not due to be discharged until early 1779.[66]

The compiled service records for men in Captains Ashby and Val Peyton's companies from September 1776 through February and March 1778 revealed that quite a few men had enlisted in February and March 1776 for two years. These men were discharged in the late winter and early spring of 1778.[67]

Captain Ashby's company was further altered when Colonel Daniel Morgan selected eighteen men from the two rifle companies in the 3rd Virginia, his and Captain John Thornton's company, for his light infantry rifle corps in June 1777. These men went on to serve at Saratoga. When that service was finished, these veterans returned their 3rd Virginia Company, now commanded by Captain Val Peyton.[68]

Captain John Chilton's Company, September 1776 to September 1777
Captain John Blackwell's Company, October 1777 to April 1779.

Captain John Chilton had been commissioned as a Captain in the 3rd Virginia in late April 1776.[69] He had arrived in New York by 13 September 1776 when he wrote to his father-in-law, Joseph Blackwell about

> ...our Marches up and down the Country. I have not thought it worth writing to you as nothing of moment have happened; at the end of the Fatiguing one we have had I embrace the opportunity of informing You, our Regiment have reached this place in good Spirits and generally speaking healthy; tho not quite full, however great joy was expressed at our arrival and great things are expected from the Virginians and of consequence we must go through great fatigue & danger.[70]

Captain Chilton filed returns upon his arrival in New York on four September returns: 13 September 1776 at Massasinio Camp, and two returns from Morris Heights on the 21, and 23 September 1776 His October returns were reported on 6 October 1776 and 11 October 1776. His November return was filed on 5 November 1776 from the camp at John Fushee's. These returns were filed while the 3rd Virginia was under the command of Col. George Weedon.

Captain Chilton's first September return, filed on 13 September 1776 reported a lieutenant, an ensign and captain. He had four sergeants and a drummer among his non-comms. Forty-five of his rank and file were fit for duty with four sick and present, ten sick and absent, and two on command. He returned sixty-two men and officers present on this date.[71]

His next return, filed 21 September 1776 on Morris Heights, was just five days after Harlem Heights. His company did not suffer any damage, according to this return. He had gained a lieutenant, while all other numbers for his officers and non-comms remained the same. Forty-five of his rank and file were still fit for duty although he had fifteen present who were sick and two on command. He reported sixty-three men and officers present.[72]

Two days later, on 23 September 1776 Captain Chilton filed another morning return. His company was still at Morris Heights. In those two days he was back to one lieutenant, an ensign, and a captain. He continued to have four sergeants and a drummer. Now forty-six were fit for duty, one more than his 21 September return indicated. He still had twenty men who were sick. There were a total of sixty-six men present in his company.[73]

Captain Chilton's next return was dated 6 October 1776. In this return, he had a 1st lieutenant, a 2nd lieutenant, an ensign, and a captain. His non-comms had not changed: still four sergeants and a drummer. However his men fit for duty were down—from forty-five on his last September return—to thirty-nine on this return. He had fourteen men sick and present and ten who were sick but absent. Only one man was listed as being on command in this return. He had a total of sixty-four men present but needed four privates to complete his company.[74]

On 11 October 1776 Captain Chilton filed another return He still had his ensign, 1st lieutenant, and 2nd lieutenant. He was the captain listed in the return. He continued with four sergeants and one drum and fife. He had a total of sixty-four men present. Thirty-nine of his rank and file were fit for duty. Twenty-three were sick, though present with the company. Two men were on command.[75]

His last return was filed 5 November 1776 in camp at John Fushee's. His officers consisted of a captain, a 1st lieutenant and 2nd lieutenant. He had four sergeants and one drum and fife. In this return, there were thirty-three rank and file fit for duty. Two were sick and present while another twenty-three were sick and absent. Six were on command. He reported sixty-four men and officers present in his company.[76]

Captain Chilton continued to serve in the 3rd Virginia through the dark days of winter and the attack on Trenton in December 1776, and Princeton in January 1777. He was with the regiment when the army went into winter quarters at Morristown. In a February 1777 letter to his brother Charles, Chilton talked about the spread of cholera through the camp. He had advised his men

> to go into the Country to good Farmers houses and anoint for it, but by some strange infatuation, tho contrary to my orders as well as advice, they would immediately push for Philadelphia where Death in every kind of disorder lay in ambush for them, first the small pox, Jail fever, Yellow & Spotted fever, Jaundice and several other ailments and this I told them and warned them…
>
> [W]hen I heard of their being Sick and some dying, who had gone before and sent for those who were well enough to come up, either they never got my orders or did not chuse to leave a place that fate seems to favor them not. M[r] John Blackwell went home to recruit. Jo[s] [Blackwell] and Isham Keith [being] sick, …were not able to join till middle of Jany.[77]

In the same letter, Chilton spoke of himself, Lieutenant Alvin Mountjoy, Lieutenant Joseph Blackwell, and Ensign Peyton as having been "under a strict Regiment for the Small Pox".[78] While there were no returns extant for January and February 1777 it was likely that these two diseases accounted for much of the sickness and deaths that swept through the regiment.[79]

Captain Chilton served through 1777 until the Battle of Brandywine when his company and the 3rd Virginia sustained heavy casualties. He was killed in the action and his 1st lieutenant, John Blackwell was promoted to take over his old friend's company. Blackwell and Chilton had served together since their days in the Culpeper Minute Battalion.[80]

While many of the original men in this company were discharged in February and March 1778, new recruits during 1777 enlisted with their discharges scheduled to occur between January and April 1779.[81]

Captain John Fitzgerald's Company, September 1776
David Arell's Company, October 1776 to February 1778.

John Fitzgerald was commissioned on 8 February 1776 as a captain in the 3rd Virginia. In November 1776, Fitzgerald was promoted out of the regiment. He served as an aide-de-camp to General Washington, holding the rank of a lieutenant colonel.[82]

While there were no compiled service records for the men who served in Captain John Fitzgerald's 3rd Virginia Company in NARA's M 881 MR 951–956 *CSR, 3rd Virginia 1776–1778*, there were morning returns. These were filed by Captain Fitzgerald on 13 September, 21 September, and 28 September, all in 1776.

The 13 September 1776 morning return was filed from Camp Massasinio and showed an under-strength company. There were fifty-two officers and men present, including a captain, a lieutenant, an ensign, three sergeants, a drum Major, a fife major, and a drummer. Thirty-four men were fit for duty. Eleven were sick and one man was on furlough. Two were sick, absent and two men were on command.[83]

The 21 September 1776 morning return was the first filed after Harlem Heights, fought five days earlier on 16 September 1776. He still retained a captain, lieutenant, ensign, drum major, fife major and drummer in his company. He had increased his sergeants to four and now had an artificer along with thirty-four men fit for duty. Thirteen were sick but present with the company, while three were sick and absent; two were on command. He still showed fifty-two officers and men present.[84]

The 28 September 1776 morning return was filed at Morris Heights. His company showed a captain, lieutenant, ensign, four sergeants, a drum major, a fife major, and a drummer. Forty-two men were fit for duty. Five were sick and present, two were sick and absent and two were on command. He reported a total of fifty-three men and officers present.[85]

While there were no muster rolls or payrolls extant for Captain Fitzgerald's company,[86] it appeared that David Arell, his 1st lieutenant, took over the company in October 1776.[87]

Captain Thomas Johnson's Company, September to November 1776.

Captain Thomas Johnson was commissioned on 21 March 1776. He resigned 18 October 1776.[88] There were no service records of Captain Johnson's men in the compiled service records of the 3rd Virginia on NARA's M 881 MR 951–956 *CSR 3rd Virginia 1776–1778*. However there were six returns filed between September and October 1776 and one for 5 November 1776, that recorded his resignation.

His first return, filed on 13 September 1776 at Massasinio Camp returned an ensign, a lieutenant and a captain He had four sergeants and a drummer among his non-comms. He reported sixty-four men and officers present, with forty-two of his rank and file fit for duty. Sixteen were sick and present, while two were sick but absent. One man was on furlough and there were two artificers in the company.[89]

His return filed 21 September 1776 at Morris Heights showed his officers and non-comms with the same numbers as found in his earlier September return. He had sixty-five men and officers present. However, he had only thirty-four rank and file fit for duty, down from forty-two in his previous return. Twenty-three were sick and present, while two remained sick but absent from the company. He still had his two artificers and showed one man on command and one man wounded, probably at Harlem Heights.[90]

He filed his third return on 23 September 1776, while his company was on Morris Heights. His numbers remained almost the same as his return filed two days previously. The only difference was in the rank and file totals fit for duty and the numbers sick and present. In this return he had thirty-nine of his privates fit for duty versus the thirty-four previously stated. He also had less sick who were present with his company: eighteen instead of twenty-three in the 21 September 1776 return. He continued to have two artificers, one man on command and one man wounded.[91]

Captain Johnson's last September 1776 return was filed on 28 September, at Morris Heights. Here too, he had the same numbers as his earlier return except for rank and file fit for duty and those sick and present with the company. On this date, Captain Johnson reported thirty-seven rank and file fit for duty, down two from his earlier return. He had nineteen sick in this return, one more than stated on his 23 September report. He continued to carry two artificers. One man was still on furlough and one man was still wounded. He reported a total of sixty-five present in his company.[92]

Captain Johnson filed two October returns. His 6 October 1776 return showed an ensign, a 2nd lieutenant and a captain. He had four sergeants and one drum and fife among his non-comms. His company totaled sixty-four men and officers. Thirty-six of his rank and file were fit for duty while twenty-five were sick but present. Three were on command. He needed four privates and a drum and fife member to complete the company.[93]

His last return was filed 11 October 1776 a week before he submitted his resignation. He returned an ensign, a 2nd lieutenant and a captain as officers in his company. Four sergeants and a drum and fife made up his non-comms. He had a total of sixty-four men and officers present. Twenty-six of his rank and file were fit for duty, thirty-three were sick but present and two were sick and absent. He had three men on command. Captain Johnson needed one drum and fife and four privates to bring his company up to full strength.[94]

The 5 November 1776 return for this company stated that "Capt. Johnson resigned and No Capt. [was] appointed to his Company."[95]

Captain Philip Richard Francis Lee's Company, August 1776 to January 1778
Captain John Peyton's company June to September 1778
Captain Val Peyton after September 1778.

Phill Lee received a continental commission as a Captain in the 3rd Virginia on 8 March 1776.[96] He was severely wounded at Brandywine in September 1777 and died of his wounds on 29 January 1778.[97] His company was eventually absorbed, in June 1778, into John Peyton's old company[98] which had not fully recovered from the loss of men who died the year before,[99] probably from diseases prevalent then in camp, and from small pox.

Upon his arrival in New York, Captain Lee filed a morning return for 13 September 1776 three days before the Battle at Harlem Heights. He had thirty-four rank and file fit for duty; eight were sick, and three were on command.[100]

Another morning return filed 21 September 1776, showed thirty-five fit for duty, nine sick and three on command;[101] a similar return, filed 23 September 1776 at Morris Heights, showed thirty-one fit for duty, twelve sick, three on command and one man confined.[102] A morning return filed on 28 September 1776 showed thirty-six fit for duty, while ten were sick, and three were on command.[103]

Captain Lee's first return for October, on 6 October 1776, showed his company with thirty-two rank and file fit for duty, ten sick, and five on command. Two sergeants, twenty-one privates and a drummer were needed to bring the company up to full strength.[104] On his 11 October 1776 return, there were thirty-five of his rank and file fit for duty, nine sick, and four on command. He still needed twenty privates, a sergeant, and a drummer to fill out his company's numbers. His return reported that he was "absent, sick."[105]

His last return was filed 5 November 1776. On that date, his company had thirty rank and file fit for duty, six who were sick and present with his company, and sixteen who were sick but absent. Five were on command. Captain Lee was listed as "sick on the Jersey side of the river."[106]

Captain Lee served throughout the 1776 and 1777 campaigns. After his death in January 1778, his old company lost all its identity with its original captain. The men who were not discharged in February and March 1778 were those who enlisted during 1777. They went on to serve with Captain John Peyton until September 1778 and Captain Val Peyton from October 1778 to March 1779.[107]

Captain Andrew Leitch's Company, September 1776.

Andrew Leitch of Prince William County was an early Captain in the 3rd Virginia. He was commissioned on 5 February 1776[108] and promoted out of the regiment to be a major in the 1st Virginia Regiment in June 1776.[109] He died on 28 September 1776, from wounds suffered at Harlem Heights on 16 September 1776.[110]

There were two morning returns filed for Captain Leitch's company in September 1776. The returns, filed on the 21 and 23 September 1776 both stated that "Major Leitch" was "wounded. There was no information on the return about this company's strength or numbers in the officers, non-comms, or rank and file.[111]

An undated List of Captains in the Virginia Service for Andrew Leitch, Captain, 3rd Virginia, commissioned 5 February 1776, stated "Capt. Leitch is dead."[112] It is not known who took command of his company in June 1776 upon his promotion to major.

Captain William McWilliams' Company

Captain McWilliams was commissioned in February 1776 as a Captain in the 3rd Virginia Regiment.[113] Between October 1777 and May 1778, McWilliams was promoted to major and served as an aide-de-camp to General Alexander, Lord Stirling. He became the brigade major to General Weedon in October 1778.[114]

His name did *not* appear in the compiled service records for the 3rd Virginia. Nor did Captain McWilliams file returns in the 3rd Virginia muster rolls. However, he did appear as adjutant to the regiment in Colonel Weedon's morning returns for September and October 1776.[115]

Captain John Peyton's Company September 1776 to February 1778
Men and officers from Captain Phill Lee's company, Captain John Thornton's company, and Captain John Ashby's rifle company had been consolidated into this company by June 1778.
Captain Val Peyton's company after September 1778

Captain John Peyton was commissioned as a 1st lieutenant in the 3rd Virginia on 5 February 1776. He was promoted to Captain on 19 June 1776.[116]

Captain Peyton filed seven returns from September to November 1776. His first return was filed on his arrival to New York at Massasinio camp on 13 September 1777. He showed an ensign, two lieutenants and a captain along with four sergeants, a drummer and a fifer among his officers and non-comms. He reported sixty-two men and officers present. Forty-four of his rank and file were present and fit for duty, fourteen were sick and three were on command.[117]

His second return was filed on 21 September 1776, at Morris Heights. This return may have reflected the action at Harlem Heights on 16 September. His count for officers and non-comms remained as found in his earlier September return. He had sixty-two men and officers present. However, in this return, he reported thirty-nine rank and file fit for duty versus the forty-four reported on his 13 September return. Seventeen of his men were sick and one man was confined. Three were on command.[118]

In a return filed two days later, still at Morris Heights, he reported only two lieutenants and a captain. No ensign appeared on this return. His non-comms still numbered four sergeants and a drummer and a fifer. There were sixty-two men and officers present, although in this return there were thirty-three fit for duty, down from thirty-nine just two days earlier. Twenty-four were sick, up from the seventeen reported in the earlier return. One man was still confined and three were on command.[119]

His last return for September was filed 28 September 1776, at Morris Heights. Captain Peyton reported two lieutenants and a captain along with four sergeants, a drummer and a fifer among his officers and non-comms. He returned sixty-three men and officers present in his company with forty-two rank and file fit for duty. This was an improvement over his last return September return. So, too, were the numbers of sick. He reported seventeen sick in this return, an improvement of seven men. Two were on command and Captain Peyton had an artificer in his company for the first time.[120]

His first return for October 1776, was filed on 6 October. He showed an ensign, a 1st lieutenant a 2nd lieutenant and a captain along with the four sergeants and two drum and fife members. Sixty-three men and officers were present. Forty-three of his rank and file were fit for duty, while seventeen remained sick and three were on command. He noted that he needed five more privates to complete his company.[121]

His return on 11 October 1776, noted that he had only a 1st and 2nd lieutenant among his officers. He listed himself as present, but sick and did not count himself in the officers. He continued with four sergeants and two drum and fife. Forty-five of his rank and file were fit for duty, while twelve remained sick and four were on command.[122]

His last return was filed 5 November 1776, at the Camp at John Fushee's. In this return, he had gotten back an ensign and a captain, which means he was healthy in this return. He also reported a 1st lieutenant and a 2nd lieutenant in the company. There were only two sergeants in this return along with his two drum and fife. Captain Peyton reported sixty-one men and officers present. However only thirty-five rank and file were fit for duty, down ten from his 11 October return. Seven were sick but present. Twelve were sick and absent. Seven men were on command.[123]

His company took part in the 1776 New York campaign in the fall of 1776, the incursion over the Delaware at Trenton, New Jersey in December 1777, and the successful attack on Princeton in early January 1777.

Twenty-five of his men, including some of his non-commissioned officers, died between January and April 1777, perhaps from small pox, or perhaps from cholera, then prevalent in the 3rd Virginia.[124] These men included three sergeants, and five corporals. The remaining men were private soldiers.[125] Some may also have succumbed to wounds taken at Trenton and Princeton. A lieutenant had been killed at Brandywine while a corporal and a private soldier had died after Germantown.[126]

Captain Peyton showed a total loss of thirty-eight men in his company, the majority of these listed from January to March 1777. Two of his men deserted, early on, a drummer in August 1777 and a private in November of the same year. Two sergeants, a corporal and a private reenlisted in the Light Horse in December 1777. Eight of his men, including a sergeant, were discharged in January and February 1777.[127]

Captain Robert Powell's Company December 1776 to March 1779

Robert Powell began his military career as a 1st lieutenant, commissioned on 12 February 1776. He was promoted to captain on 18 October 1776.[128] In a 5 November 1776 return of the 3rd Virginia, Lieutenant Powell was listed as "sick at North Castle."[129] He resigned his Captain's commission in July 1779.[130]

There were no extant returns for Captain Powell's company for October or November 1776. He may have taken over either Captain Leitch's company or Captain Thomas Johnson's company as Leitch was dead in late September and Johnson's resignation took effect on the same day as Powell's promotion.[131]

The compiled service records of some of Captain Powell's company date from as early as December 1776 through early 1777 while others date from May and June 1778.

Between May and September 1778 the men in his company were selected from Captain Mercer's 3rd Virginia and Captain Joseph Crockett's 7th Virginia companies and designated as 3rd and 7th Virginia, part of Brigadier General William Woodford's Brigade.[132] This arrangement lasted until the September 1778 reorganization when the 3rd and 5th Virginia were consolidated and redesignated the 3rd Virginia Regiment.

Captain John Thornton's Company, September to March 1777
John Ashby's company June 1777 to October 1777
Val Peyton's company October 1777 to June 1778
John Peyton's company, June to September 1778
Val Peyton's company, after Septermber 1778

John Thornton received a continental commission as a captain in the 3rd Virginia on 12 February 1776. He was promoted out of the regiment on 20 March 1777.[133]

Captain Thornton filed returns for his rifle company from September to November 1776 while his company was in New York. His first return was filed 13 September 1776, at Massasinio Camp where he reported sixty-six men and officers present. Forty-two were fit for duty, Nine were present and sick; five were sick but absent. He reported a captain, two lieutenants, and an ensign along with four sergeants, a fifer and a drummer, present in the company.[134]

His next return was filed five days after the Battle at Harlem Heights, on 21 September, when his company was at Morris Heights. This return reflected the damage done at Harlem. One of his sergeants had been wounded. One of his men had been killed, eleven were sick and absent; two were on command, two were on furlough. Thirty-seven men were fit for duty. His officers remained the same as in the 13 September 1776 return although he showed one less sergeant in the 21 September return.[135]

On his 23 September 1776 return, still at Morris Heights, he showed sixty-five men present of which thirty-seven of his rank and file were fit for duty. Fifteen were sick, but well enough to be present while eleven were sick but absent. His officer corps remained intact while he had four sergeants and a drummer and a fifer among his non-comms.[136]

Captain Thornton filed another return on 28 September 1776, still at Morris Heights. He had sixty-five men and officers present. Thirty-six were fit for duty. Fifteen were sick and present, eleven were sick and absent. He carried an artificer with the company in all of his September returns.[137]

His 6 October 1776 return showed officers and non-comms remaining the same while forty of his rank and file were fit for duty. Eleven were sick and present with the company and a further eleven were sick and absent. One man had been killed since his return on 28 September 1776.[138]

His 11 October 1776 showed another man had died since his last return. Again his officers and non-comms remained intact. However he had only thirty-three of his rank and file now fit for duty with twenty-two sick who were sick and present; a further six sick but absent. No artificer was reported on this return. He needed six more privates to complete his company.[139]

In late October 1776, Captain Thornton and his company were involved in an unsuccessful attempt to capture Major Robert Rogers, an officer who had previously served as a captain of an independent company of New Hampshire rangers in the French and Indian War.[140]

Now a Major, Rogers with some 500 Tories in his command, advanced toward Mamaroneck, about three miles from New Rochelle. It was decided that American forces should cut off Major Rogers when 160 men from the 1st and 3rd Virginia, led by Major Green and 400 more under Colonel John Haslet of the Delaware Battalion attacked Rogers and his Tory regiment.

When Major Green fell, wounded in the shoulder, the command was transferred to Captain Thornton, who, "by the light of the moon, attacked and left twenty of the enemy dead and brought off thirty-six prisoners, without the loss of a man."[141]

Captain Thornton's morning return of 5 November 1777 was filed after this skirmish. He reported, in this return, that sixty-two men and officers were present in his company. Thirty-four of his rank and file were fit for duty with one sick and present and twenty sick and absent. Six men were on command and two men were on furlough. He showed a captain, 2nd lieutenant, an ensign, three sergeants, and two drum and fife. This return reported one less lieutenant and sergeant than found on the 11 October return.[142]

Captain Thornton served in the 3rd Virginia through the New York campaign in the fall and early winter of 1776 and the New Jersey campaign resulting in successful forays against Trenton in December 1776 and Princeton in early January 1777. When he was promoted out of the regiment in March 1777, his company languished without a captain until June when ten of the men were selected by Colonel Daniel Morgan for his independent rifle regiment.[143] The remaining men went into the other 3rd Virginia rifle company commanded by Captain John Ashby.[144]

Captain Gustavus Brown Wallace's Company, September 1776 to October 1777
Captain John Francis Mercer's Company, November 1777 to April 1779

Gustavus Brown Wallace was commissioned as a Captain in the 3rd Virginia 20 February 1776. He was promoted out of the regiment on 4 October 1777, to be a major in the 15th Virginia.[145] Captain Wallace served in the 1776 and 1777 campaigns until his promotion in October 1777.

Captain Wallace was another 3rd Virginia captain who filed returns upon his arrival in New York. He filed six returns between September and October 1776.

His first return was recorded on 13 September 1776 at Massasinio Camp. He showed a captain, two lieutenants, an ensign, along with four sergeants and a drummer among the officers and non-comms. He reported fifty-nine men present. Forty-one of his rank and file were fit for duty. Eleven were sick and present while four were sick and absent. He had an artificer in his company.[146]

His next return was filed five days after the Battle at Harlem Heights, on 21 September 1776, at Morris Heights. He showed a captain, two lieutenants and an ensign among the commissioned officers. He had one less sergeant than in the return a week earlier, while listing three sergeants and a drummer.

He reported fifty-nine men and officers present, just as he had in his previous return. Forty-one were again fit for duty with twelve sick and present versus the eleven reported on 13 September. He still had four men sick and absent and continued to carry an artificer. It was likely that one of the sergeants was sick, accounting for the increase by one in those sick and present and loss of a sergeant among the non-comms between the two September returns.[147]

Captain Wallace filed another return two days later, on 23 September 1776. While he reported fifty-nine men present in this return, only thirty-four rank and file were fit for duty. Nineteen were sick and present and four continued to be sick but absent. His non-comms were back up to four sergeants and a drummer while his officer corps remained the same as the 21 September return.[148]

His last September return was filed on 28 September 1776, at Morris Heights. He continued to report that fifty-nine of his men and officers were present. Thirty-nine of his rank and file were fit for duty, an increase of five from his last return It is likely these were men who were sick and present as that number dropped five to fourteen men. Four of his men continued to be sick and absent. He did not return an artificer in this return.[149]

He filed his next return on 6 October 1776. He reported a captain, a 1st lieutenant, a 2nd lieutenant and an ensign as his officers. The company had four sergeants and a drummer. In this return, fifty-five men and officers were present, down from the fifty-nine reported in September. Forty-four of his rank and file were fit for duty, while nine were sick and present. Apparently those who had been absent and sick had returned. One man was on command. Captain Wallace also reported that one man had deserted. He needed thirteen privates to bring his company up to full strength.[150]

His last return was filed on 11 October. He reported that fifty-nine men and officers were present in his company. His officers and non-commissioned officer numbers remained the same as found in his 6 October 1776 return. He had forty-five rank and file fit for duty. Five were sick and present; three were sick and absent. Six men were on command. He now needed nine privates to fill out his company, down four from his previous return.[151]

After Wallace's promotion to Major in the 15th Virginia in October, 1777,[152] his 1st lieutenant, John Francis Mercer, took command of this company. Mercer, who had been commissioned as a 1st lieutenant on 26 February 1776, was promoted to captain in September 1777, with his commission back-dated to June 1777.[153]

Lieutenant Mercer had served as a lieutenant in Captain William Washington's company from April to September 1777. He was wounded at Brandywine in September 1777. In October, he transferred to Captain Wallace's company. He took over the company in November, upon Captain Wallace's promotion, serving as Captain until May 1778 and from November 1778 until April 1779.[154] In June 1778, Captain Mercer became aide-de-camp to General Lee.[155] Field and staff muster rolls for the 3rd Virginia showed Captain Mercer as an aide to General Lee from July to November 1778 and from January to April 1779.[156]

Captain William Washington's Company, September 1776 to January 1777
Captain Gustavus Brown Wallace's company July to October 1777
Captain John Francis Mercer's company, November to February 1778

William Washington was commissioned on 25 February 1776 as a captain in the 3rd Virginia Regiment. It is now thought that Captain Washington did not arrive in New York until September 1776 rather than in August of that year. He is now believed to have been wounded at Harlem Heights and not at Long Island as other historians have reported.[157] He served through the 1776 campaign and was wounded again at Trenton in January 1777. He was promoted out of the regiment in January 1777 to be a major in the 4th Continental Dragoons.[158]

Captain Washington filed seven returns for his company between 13 September 1776 and 5 November 1776. His first return was filed 13 September 1776 at Camp Massasinio, near King's Bridge in New York. He returned an ensign, two lieutenants and a captain, along with four sergeants and a drummer from his non-commissioned officers.

He had fifty-nine men and officers present in his company. Forty-three of his rank and file were fit for duty, ten were sick and present, while a further eleven were sick but absent. He also reported an artificer in his company.[159]

Captain Washington filed his next return five days after Harlem Heights, on 21 September 1776, at Morris Heights. His officer and non-commissioned officer corps remained the same, as found in his previous returns. While he reported sixty-seven men and officers present, only thirty-three were fit for duty. Eighteen were sick and present, another eleven were sick but absent. One man was on command and one was wounded, probably at Harlem Heights. He continued to report an artificer in his company.[160]

In a morning return filed on 23 September 1776, he reported the same numbers as found in his return two days before. However there were differences in the number of rank and file fit for duty in this return. He had recovered four of his men—there were thirty-seven now fit for duty. Fourteen were sick and present, so those four came from the eighteen sick and present on the earlier September return. Eleven men continued to be sick and absent from the company. One was on command; Captain Washington reported one man still wounded. The artificer was still in the company.[161]

In his 28 September 1776 return at Morris Heights, there were some additions to his non-comms. He had added a fifer to those ranks. He continued with the same number of commissioned officers as his earlier return. He still had sixty-seven present and now forty of his rank and file were fit for duty. Twelve were sick and present, while ten were still sick and absent. His artificer was still there and he had one man on command and one man wounded.[162]

Washington filed another return 6 October 1776 which broke down his company in more detail. He showed a captain, a 1st lieutenant, a 2nd lieutenant, and an ensign in this return. He continued with four sergeants and two drum and fife. He still had sixty-seven men and officers present with thirty-three fit for duty. This was a decrease of seven from his previous return.

It was noted in this return that nineteen of his men were sick. This was up seven from his 28 September return. He now had eleven men sick and absent, instead of the ten reported in his last return. One man was on command. There was no mention of anyone wounded; nor was their mention of an artificer. He reported that he needed one private to complete the company.[163]

His next return was filed on 11 October 1776. His numbers remained the same for his officers and non-comms as found in his earlier October return. He returned sixty-seven men present, with thirty-five of his rank and file fit for duty. Seventeen were sick, ten were sick and absent and five were on command. He still needed a private and a drum and fife to complete his company.[164]

Captain Washington's last return was filed on 5 November 1776. There appeared to have been two returns filed for this date with somewhat contradictory information. In one return, he listed only a captain and a 2nd lieutenant among his officers. His non-comms consisted of four sergeants and one drum and fife. Sixty-five of his men and officers were present. Twenty-five of his rank and file were fit for duty, two were sick and twenty-nine were sick and absent. Nine of his men were on command.[165]

Another 5 November 1776 return, at the Camp at John Fushee's had different numbers associated with all the categories. In this return, Captain Washington returned an ensign, 1st lieutenant, 2nd lieutenant and captain. His non-comms were four sergeants and one drum and fife. Only fifty-seven were present in this return. Thirty-two were fit for duty, three were sick, and eighteen were sick and absent from his company. Four men were on command.[166]

As can be seen by the second return, there were differences in the number of his rank and file fit for duty and a significant difference in the number of men he reported sick and absent. There were four on command in contrast to the nine he reported in the first 5 November return

In August 1777, twenty of Captain Washington's men, including officers and sergeants, transferred into Captain Gustavus Brown Wallace's company. These men finished their tour of duty with Captain Mercer's company in January and February 1778.[167]

Captain Charles West's Company, September 1776 to July 1777
Captain Reuben Briscoe's Company, July 1777 to September 1778
Captain-Lieutenant John Tebbs, October 1778
Captain Robert Powell November 1778 to April 1779.

This company had three captains between September 1776 and December 1778. Charles West was the original captain, commissioned in the 3rd Virginia, on 9 February 1776. He was promoted to major in the 3rd Virginia on 30 January 1777,[168] at the death of Colonel Fleming. He was later promoted to a lieutenant colonelcy[169] outside the regiment when Lieutenant Colonel Lewis Willis of the 15th Virginia resigned in March 1778.[170] Lieutenant Colonel West resigned his commission on 6 July 1778.[171]

Reuben Briscoe, his replacement, had been commissioned a captain in the 3rd Virginia on 27 January 1777. Captain Briscoe continued with this company until he resigned in September 1778.[172]

John Tebbs, a lieutenant in Captain Briscoe's company took over the unit upon the resignation of Briscoe in September 1778, with a rank of Captain. He served in that capacity in October and November 1778. Briscoe remarked in his October return that Lieutenant Tebbs was "commanding the company at present, being indebted to a command from March 1, 1778."[173]

By December 1778 Tebbs was a supernumerary. He "never acted as a Captain but...acquitted himself with credit as a Sub. [He] has been in service since '75 and now left out, being a Jr. Officer."[174]

Captain West arrived in New York in mid September with the rest of the 3rd Virginia captains. He filed seven returns between September and November 1776. He filed his first return 13 September 1776, at Camp Massasinio near King's Bridge. He reported an ensign, two lieutenants and a captain. His non-comms consisted of four sergeants, a drummer and a fifer. There were sixty-two of his men and officers present, with forty-one of his rank and file fit for duty. Six were sick and present, thirteen were sick but absent, while one man was on command and one was on furlough.[175]

His next return, dated 21 September 1776 at Morris Heights, was filed five days after the Battle at Harlem Heights. This return reflected losses suffered at that battle. His officers consisted of an ensign, one lieutenant (one less than the return filed on 13 September) and a captain. He still had four sergeants and a drum and fife among his non-comms. However, he reported fifty-nine men present, a drop of three from his previous return. Only thirty-one of his rank and file were fit for duty (down ten from the 13 September return). Nine were sick and present; thirteen were sick and absent. One man was on command. Captain West reported four men wounded and one had been killed since the last return.[176]

Two days later, on 23 September 1776, Captain West filed another return. His numbers for his officers and non-comms remained the same as his 21 September return. He reported sixty present, with thirty-one of his rank and file fit for duty. Ten were sick and present while thirteen remained sick and absent from his company. One man was on command. Four of his men remained wounded.[177]

Captain West filed his last September return on 28 September 1776 at Morris Heights. His numbers for his officers and non-comms again remained the same as his two previous September returns. He had sixty-four men and officers present, with thirty-one still fit for duty. However he now had fifteen sick while others continued sick and absent from the company. One man was on command and there were still four men who were wounded.[178]

Captain West's first October return was filed on 6 October 1776, as a return of the 3rd Virginia in service of the United Colonies. He reported an ensign, a 1st lieutenant, a 2nd lieutenant and a captain. His non-comms were four sergeants and two drum and fife. Sixty-four men and officers were present. However, his rank and file fit for duty took a significant dip to twenty-two, down nine men from his 28 September return. Twenty men were sick, though present with the company, up five from his previous return; twelve continued sick and absent and now ten men were on command. He needed four privates to complete his company.[179]

Five days later, on 11 October 1776, he filed another return of his company in the service of the United Colonies. His numbers for officers and non-comms remained constant. Sixty-four men and officers were still present. Now, though, Captain West had forty-one of his rank and file fit for duty, up eleven men from his earlier October return. Nine were sick and present while twelve men were still sick and absent. Two were on command. Captain West reported that he still need four privates to bring his company up to full strength.[180]

Captain West filed his last return on 5 November 1776 at Camp at John Fushee's. He reported an ensign, a 1st lieutenant and a 2nd lieutenant as his officers and two sergeants, a drummer, and a fifer among his non-comms. He was down two sergeants and he, as captain was "sick at North Castle." He had a total of sixty-six men and officers present, with thirty-one rank and file fit for duty. Four were sick and present. Twenty two were sick and absent. Nine men were on command. This return showed an increase in the sick and those on command. He had also lost two sergeants from his previous October return.[181]

Reuben Briscoe had been promoted to captain in January 1777 and was awaiting a company, when finally assigned to command his old company some six months later. He took over Captain West's company in July 1777 and continued as the company's Captain until his retirement at the end of September 1778.[182] During this time, his company had nine men who were 3rd and 7th Virginia soldiers. Three of the these men came into Captain Briscoe's company from other 3rd Virginia companies: Lieutenant Thomas Hungerford transferred from Capt Thornton's old company while privates William Kent and George Jeffrey came from David Arell's old company.[183] Captain Briscoe's company was part of the 2nd Virginia Battalion of Woodford's Brigade.[184]

Captain Briscoe's 1st lieutenant, John Tebbs, then took over the company for a month. It appeared that Captain Robert Powell then absorbed this company in November 1778 as a result of the September 1778 reorganization of the Virginia Line.[185]

3RD VIRGINIA REGIMENTAL RETURNS 1776–1778.

George Weedon's Regimental Returns, October to December 1776

Regimental and Brigade returns have offered an insightful glimpse into the organization of the regiment and the general health and fitness of the men and officers of the 3rd Virginia. There were two returns filed in October, none in November and two in December 1776. When Colonel Weedon was promoted out of the regiment in February 1777, Thomas Marshall was promoted to Colonel. He filed his first return in May 1777.

Colonel Weedon's first two returns were filed in October 1776 both on 5 October . The first return showed a colonel, a lieutenant colonel, a major, ten captains, nineteen lieutenants and ten ensigns as commissioned officers. His field staff included an adjutant, a quartermaster and a surgeon's mate. There were nineteen sergeants among the non-commissioned officers. Weedon returned 134 rank and file present and fit for duty within his regiment. Nineteen were sick and present while 360 were sick and absent from the regiment. Eleven men were on furlough. Sixty-two others were on command. He reported one death and four discharges.[186]

The second return was a weekly return. Colonel Weedon's numbers for commissioned officers remained the same as in the general return although his field staff showed additions of a chaplain and surgeon and a surgeon's mate to the General return which had omitted these officers. There were still nineteen Sergeants in the weekly return. Weedon reported 365 fit for duty (an increase over the 134 reported in the General return) with 142 sick and present and only fifty-three now sick and absent. Forty-three were on command which was down from the sixty-two recorded in the above general return.

His regiment totaled 603 men and officers. Colonel Weedon still needed two sergeants, four drum and fife and seventy-seven rank and file to bring his regiment up to full strength. He reported one dead and two desertions on this weekly return.[187]

Weedon filed two more returns in December, 1776, one on 1 December 1776 at Trenton, and one on 22 December 1776 in Pennsylvania.

His 1 December 1776 return showed the regiment with a colonel, a lieutenant colonel, a major, five captains, thirteen lieutenants and eight ensigns among his commissioned officers. His field staff included an adjutant, a quartermaster and a surgeon. He had 290 rank and file fit for duty. Thirty of them were sick and present with the regiment at Trenton. He reported 217 men who were sick and absent. Two were on furlough and sixty-four were on command.[188]

His 22 December 1776 return was made a few days before the army attacked enemy forces at Trenton. This return showed a different picture of the 3rd Virginia. Weedon reported a colonel, a major, six captains, five lieutenants and five ensigns among his commissioned officers. These numbers showed some reduction among his officers when compared to his earlier December return. His captains were down in numbers as were his lieutenants and ensigns. His lieutenant colonel was missing in this return, perhaps one of the eleven men on furlough or one of the sixty-two on command. His field staff also showed a reduction since there was now no surgeon counted among his regimental numbers.[189]

Surgeon David Griffith was in Philadelphia on 8 December 1776 to "see the sick lodged in hospitals, & to send all the well back to the Army." He had left the regiment at Princeton on 6 December.[190] It is likely that Dr. Griffith was still in Philadelphia tending to the sick on 22 December since a surgeon was not listed on this return.

Colonel Weedon reported nineteen sergeants among his non-comms on the 22 December 1776 return. However, only 134 men were present and fit for duty. While nineteen were sick and present, Colonel Weedon reported that 360 men were sick and absent from the regiment. Eleven men continued to be on furlough and sixty-two were on command. He reported one death and four discharges on this return. Colonel Weedon reported that his regiment totaled 586 men and officers. A note on his return stated that the 3rd Virginia was in Stirling's Brigade, along with regiments commanded by Colonels Read and Haslett and Major Williams.[191]

In February 1777, Colonel Weedon was promoted out of the 3rd Virginia and Lieutenant Colonel Thomas Marshall became the colonel of the regiment.[192] In May, the 3rd Virginia was transferred to Brigadier General William Woodford's Brigade.[193]

Thomas Marshall's Regimental Returns, May 1777

Colonel Marshall filed a return for the 3rd Virginia on 21 May 1777, as part of the general return of Continental Forces under the command of General Washington. He reported sixteen commissioned officers, four field staff, twenty four non-comms and 123 rank and file, totaling 167 men. Thirteen were sick and present and fourteen were sick and absent from the regiment. The regiment's men and officers totaled 376.[194]

Another 3rd Virginia Regiment return, was filed on 28 May 1777, while the regiment was with the Continental forces in New Jersey. While the regiment suffered massive reductions in numbers, the figures for commissioned officers, field staff and non-commissioned officers remained fairly constant when compared to the December 1776 numbers. A colonel, lieutenant colonel, five captains, eight lieutenants, and an ensign made up the commissioned officers; a chaplain, adjutant, quartermaster, and surgeon were found among the field staff. Non-comms numbers showed a sergeant major, a quartermaster sergeant, nineteen sergeants, 2 drummers, and three fifers.

It was the rank and file that suffered the largest losses in numbers. There were only 123 men present and fit for duty. Thirteen were sick and present, while fourteen were sick but absent. The entire regiment totaled only 169 men and officers.[195]

Captains Ashby, Chilton, and John Peyton all sustained significant losses in their officers and soldiers who died between January and March 1777. Captains Ashby lost ten men who either had died or had service on payrolls that suggested their death; Captain Chilton lost twenty-two men; so did Captain John Peyton. To a lesser degree, Captains Wallace, West, and Powell also recorded deaths in these months. Captain Wallace reported eight dead; Captains West and Powell had two dead.[196]

Some of these deaths could have been attributed to disease. John Chilton talked about cholera and smallpox in the regiment in his February 1777 letter from Morristown to his brother Charles Chilton.[197] Some of the men may have died from wounds suffered at Trenton or Princeton. Some may have perished from the cold and a lack of winter clothing or housing. Whatever the reasons, it was obvious from the May 1777 return that the 3rd Virginia was far from full strength.

BRIGADE RETURNS, NOVEMBER 1777 TO APRIL 1778.

Colonel Weedon's Brigade Returns September to October 1776.

Brigade returns have also proved useful in determining changes in the organization and structure of the regiments belonging to them. The returns have provided a "big picture" look at the organization. They have been helpful in establishing the brigade's general fitness and strength that of the regiment itself.

The most interesting figures relating to the organizational health of the regiment were those dealing with the number of soldiers and officers present and fit for duty as compared to the grand total of men in the regiment, deaths, desertions, and the numbers recorded for the sick. Often there were comments at the end of the return, especially those for January through April 1778 which contained graphic depictions of brigade shortages as they related to clothing and shoes.

By late September 1776, Colonel Weedon had charge of his regiment along with Colonel Read's 1st Virginia and Colonel Chester's regiment. He filed a general return for these units on the last day of September 1776.

While these figures were inclusive for the three regiments, they may have reflected their collective strength after the battle at Harlem Heights. While the three regiments totaled 1663 men and officers, only 1011 rank and file were actually present and fit for duty; some 394 were sick and present. Seventy-six were sick and absent from the brigade. Six men in these regiments were reported dead and three had been discharged. Colonel Weedon reported that he still needed a sergeant, a drum and fife, and 118 rank and file to bring the regiments in his brigade up to full strength.[198]

Colonel Weedon's 5 October 1776 weekly and general return showed a total of 603 men and officers. His weekly return reported 365 rank and file present and fit for duty; 142 were sick and present while fifty-three were sick and absent. There was one death and two desertions.[199]

His general return, filed the same day, presented a different picture of the regiment's organization. In this return, there were only 134 present and fit for duty. Nineteen were sick and present while 360 were sick and absent. He reported one death, four discharges and no desertions.[200]

William Alexander, Lord Stirling's Brigade Returns October 1776 to May 1777

By late October 1776, the 3rd Virginia, under Colonel Weedon, had been transferred into Lord Stirling's Brigade. In an October return, dated 3 November 1776, at White Plains, Stirling's brigade consisted of the 1st Virginia, under Colonel Isaac Reed; the 3rd Virginia, under Weedon; a Delaware regiment, commanded by John Haslet; and two Pennsylvania battalions, part of the flying camp and the 1st and 2nd Battalion of Miles' Pennsylvania Rifle regiment.[201]

While each regiment formed an integral part of the brigade, their returns were filed separately. Thus it was possible to gauge the 3rd Virginia's relative strength within the brigade structure. In this return, the 3rd Virginia totaled 368 men and officers. Two hundred ninety were rank and file, bringing the grand total of the regiment to 681. Thirty were sick and present, 228 were sick and absent. Deaths, desertions, and discharges were not recorded on this return.[202]

Isaac Read's regiment contained a total of 586 men, Haslet's Delaware regiment numbered 586. The Pennsylvania Battalions from the flying camp contained 352 and 502 men and officers respectively. The two Pennsylvania rifle battalions totaled 310 and 238 men and officers.[203] It appeared from just these figures that the 3rd Virginia totals showed the regiment to be in good shape relative to the 1st Virginia and the Delaware and Pennsylvania units.

The next return for Stirling's Brigade was not filed until 22 December 1776 when the forces were in Pennsylvania under General Washington. Colonel Weedon's return was part of the brigade return. Stirling's brigade had changed its composition somewhat. While the 1st Virginia, 3rd Virginia, and Haslet's Delaware regiment were still part of the brigade, the 6th Maryland replaced the Pennsylvania regiments.[204]

Colonel Weedon reported 586 men and officers in the regiment. One hundred thirty-four were rank and file present and fit for duty. Nineteen were sick and present while 360 men were sick and absent. Weedon reported one death and four discharges.[205] While these numbers remained fairly constant when compared with the earlier October return, there was still an increase in the numbers of sick and absent troops.

William Woodford's Brigade Returns, November 1777 to April 1778.

The 28 May 1777 return of the 3rd Virginia, now under the command of Colonel Thomas Marshall, and part of William Woodford's Brigade, has already been discussed in relation to its strength and fitness.

It was not until November 1777, that Woodford's Brigade, consisting of the 3rd, 7th, 11th, and 15th Virginia, provided details about the lack of clothing and shoes. In this return, numbers were reported for the brigade collectively. Numbers for the officers in the brigade were down... considerably. There were only five captains, eleven lieutenants and five ensigns reported for the whole brigade. There was a total of 330 men and officers, with 188 rank and file present and fit for duty. Twenty-nine were sick and present; sixty were sick and absent. The brigade reported no dead, no discharges and only one desertion. However, there were twenty-four men in the 3rd Virginia wanting clothes and unfit for duty.

The 11th and 12th Virginia shared the same fate, with four sergeants and thirty-four men wanting clothes and unfit for duty in the 11th Virginia, and two sergeants, two drum and fife and thirty privates, wanting clothes and blankets who were unfit for duty in the 12th Virginia. All of these men were still considered present and fit for duty according to this return.[206]

Returns filed for William Woodford's Brigade in December also showed that men in the brigade suffered for lack of clothes.[207] A field return, filed two days before Christmas, reported 257 men "unfit for want of clothes."[208] On New Year's Eve, 1777, Woodford's Brigade reported a total of 285 men and officers. One man was dead, there was one discharge and one desertion. Seventy men in the brigade were unfit for "want of shoes and Cloathes."

Adjutant General Timothy Pickering observed that "some brigades have distinguished the men unfit for duty from the want of cloathes, from the sick, present, others include them, with the sick, present and some have ret^d all those fit for duty who were well, although barefooted ..."[209]

All through the winter months of January, February, March and into April 1778, this Brigade suffered from a serious lack of clothes and shoes. The information in Table 1 below was extracted from these returns.

Table 1. Woodford's Brigade Returns January 12, 1778 to April 18, 1778 [210]
Abbreviations: all dates abbreviated; n.g. =not given; R&F=Rank & File; D&F=Drum & Fife; Sgts=Sergeants

Date of Return	Unfit for want of clothes Shoes, etc.	Desertions	Dead	Discharges	Newly Joined
1/12/78	267	2	14	5	1 R&F
1/19/78	263	3	6	0	33 R&F
1/24/78	273	1	9	1	n.g.
NB: 23 Sgts, 2 D&F, 329 R&F enlistments shortly set to expire.					
1/31/78	282	0	6	17	0
2/9/78	276	1	5	76	25 R&F
2/14/78	248	3	2	53	n.g.
2/12/78	244	2	8	84	n.g.
2/29/78	246	9	20	273	26 R&F
3/1/78	198	2	13	46	n.g.
3/14/78	141	0	2	32	2 R&F
3/21/78	157	8	1	5	1 R&F
3/30/78	124	6	16	83	2 R&F
4/4/78	115	0	6	0	9 R&F
4/11/78	76	0	8	0	22 R&F
4/18/78	n.g.	0	5	1	107 R&F; 6 Sgts, 2 D&F

This table has amply illustrated the plight of Woodford's Brigade, which included the 3rd, 7th, 11th, and 15th Virginia, during their winter encampment at Valley Forge. In the return filed 24 January 1778, the total for the brigade amounted to 1255 men and officers. Thus, the brigade was about to lose more than one quarter of its manpower, through discharges in January February and March.

There were 107 rank and file and non-commissioned officers discharged from the 3rd Virginia between January and March 1778. Six men were discharged from Captain Arell's company, ten from Captain Valentine Peyton's company, twelve from Captain Blackwell's company, fourteen from Captain Lee's company, six from Captain John Peyton's company, fifteen from Captain Powell, six from Captain Thornton, eighteen from Captain Wallace, fourteen from Captain Washington, and eight from Captain West's company.[211]

Unidentified Officers in the 3rd Virginia

There were eighteen commissioned officers whose companies were not identified in the compiled service records of the 3rd Virginia. Six of these officers died while in service. Two died in August 1776, two died in December 1776, and two died in January 1777. Five resigned, two were promoted, one was superseded and one was sick.[212] These officers have been included in the biographies found in volume two.

The 3rd Virginia September 1778 to 1780.

In September 1778, the Virginia line was reorganized. On 14 September 1778, the 3rd Virginia and the 5th Virginia Regiments were combined and designated as the 3rd Virginia. These Captains from the old 3rd Virginia remained: John Blackwell, Robert Powell, Val Peyton, and John Francis Mercer. Captains William Fowler, John Anderson, and William Bentley came in from the 5th Virginia. David Miller, Leroy Edwards, Robert Beale, John H. Fitzgerald, and John Hawkins were also added to the Captains of this reconstituted Regiment.[213] This regiment bore little resemblance to the old 3rd Virginia.

For this reason, the officers and men from the 5th Virginia who became part of the 3rd Virginia in September 1778 have not been included here or in the biographies found in Chapters 7 and 8. Neither have the captains who were added to the regiments from other commands.

In May 1779, the regiment, already a combination of 3rd and 5th Virginia men and officers, was further augmented with the temporary addition of the enlisted men of the 4th Virginia to its ranks. Later that year, the regiment was combined with the 2nd and 4th Virginia and redesignated as the 2nd Virginia. By the end of the year, the identity of the old 3rd Virginia of 1776–1778 had disappeared.

It was, for all intents and purposes an entirely new Virginia Line regiment, with some officers and men of the old 3rd Virginia added to officers and men of the 2nd, 4th, and 5th Virginia regiments. It was this regiment which went south with Woodford's Brigade and was captured at Charleston in May 1780.[214]

END NOTES
CHAPTER 2
STRUCTURE AND ORGANIZATION OF THE 3RD VIRGINIA

1. Heitman, 388. See also Sanchez-Saavedra, 38.
2. Ibid., 479. See also Sanchez-Saavedra, 38.
3. Heitman, 381.
4. Ibid.
5. Ibid.
6. Sanchez-Saavedra, 38.
7. Heitman, 287.
8. Sanchez-Saavedra, 38.
9. Ibid.
10. Heitman, 229.
11. Heitman, 242, and Sanchez-Saavedra, 38.
12. Heitman, 530, and Sanchez-Saavedra, 38.
13. Heitman, 582.

14. Heitman, 282.
15. Sanchez-Saavedra, 39.
16. Heitman, 359.
17. Sanchez-Saavedra, 39.
18. Ibid.
19. Robert K. Wright, Jr. *The Continental Army* (Washington: Center of Military History, 1985), 285. See also Charles H. Lesser, ed, *The Sinews of Independence: Monthly Strength Reports of the Continental Army* (Chicago: University of Chicago Press, 1976), 32.
20. Lesser, 37.
21. Ibid., 48.
22. Wright, 285.
23. See NARA, No. 51. 3 November 1777, *Weekly Return of Continental Army in Pennsylvania*, M 246 MR 137 *Returns of the Army under General Washington, 1775–1782*. Colonel Woodford's Brigade was made up of the 3rd, 7th, 11th, and 15th Virginia, with an attachment of Fauquier Militia. Hereafter NARA, M 246 MR 137, *Returns of the Army*.
24. Lesser, 46–47.
25. NARA, No. 46. 28 May 1777, *General Return of Continental Forces in New Jersey: the 3rd Virginia*, M 246 MR 137, *Returns of the Army*.
26. NARA, No. 51. 3 November 1777, *Weekly Returns of Continental Army in Pennsylvania*.
27. Ibid.
28. NARA, No. 47. 10 November 1777, *General Return of Continental Army encamped at White Marsh, Pennsylvania, 3rd Virginia Returns*.
29. Wright, 285.
30. See Note 28.
31. Wright, 285.
32. NARA, No. 76–77; 83–88. July to August 1777, *Weekly & Monthly General Returns of the Army at White Plains, 3rd Virginia Returns*, M 246 MR 137.
33. Sanchez-Saavedra, 39–40.
34. Ibid., 38–39.
35. Heitman, 566.
36. Ibid., 121.
37. Charles West's company was known at various times as Captain Charles West and Reuben Briscoe's company. See service records for men in Captain West and Briscoe's companies, NARA, *Compiled Service Records*, M 881 MR 951–956, *CSR, 3rd Virginia*.
38. Heitman, 121.
39. Sanchez-Saavedra, 39–40.
40. Heitman, 542. John Thornton was promoted to Major in March 1777 and Lt. Colonel in November 1778 in Grayson's Additional Continental Regiment.
41. Ibid., 438.
42. Sanchez-Saavedra, 39–40.
43. Heitman, 76.
44. Ibid., 105.
45. Captain John Chilton's company was known at various times as Captain Chilton's company and as Captain John Blackwell's company. See service records for men in Captain Chilton and Blackwell's companies, NARA, *Compiled Service Records*, M 881 MR 951–956, *CSR, 3rd Virginia*.
46. Sanchez-Saavedra, 40.
47. NARA, *Edward Abbey's Pension file No. 34621*, M 804 MR 1, *Revolutionary War Pension &Bounty Land Warrant Pension Applications 1800–1900*. Hereafter NARA M 804.
48. See No. 36, 44–45. 5 October 1776 and 1 December 1776, *Colonel Weedon's General Returns under General Washington at Harlem Heights*, M 246 MR 137.
49. Sanchez-Saavedra, 39–40.
50. Heitman, 73.
51. NARA, 4 October 1776, *Captain Arell's company return of 3rd Virginia in the service of the United Colonies, commanded by Colonel George Weedon*, Officers, 3rd Virginia.
52. Ibid., 6 October 1776, *Captain Arell's Morning Return*, Officers, 3rd Virginia.
53. Ibid., 13 September 1776, *Captain Ashby's Morning Return*, 3rd Virginia.
54. Ibid., 21 September 1776, *Captain Ashby's Morning Return*.
55. Ibid.,23 September 1776, *Captain Ashby's Morning Return*.
56. Ibid., 28 September 1776, *Captain Ashby's Morning Return*.
57. Ibid., 6 October 1776, *Captain Ashby's Morning Return*.

58. Ibid., 11 October 1776, *Captain Ashby's Morning Return*.
59. Ibid., 5 November 1776, *Captain Ashby's Morning Return*.
60. Heitman, 76.
61. Ibid., 438.
62. The service records for Captain John Ashby's company show that this company was designated at various times as Captain Ashby's company and as Captain Valentine Peyton's company. See NARA, *Compiled Service Records*, 3rd Virginia, M 881 MR 951–956.
63. See the service records for men in Captain Valentine Peyton's company which show that this company at various times was known as Captain Valentine Peyton's company and Captain John Peyton's company. NARA, *Compiled service records*, 3rd Virginia.
64. See the service records for men in Captain Philip Francis Lee's Company who show up on Captain John Peyton's Company after June 1778, NARA *Compiled service records*, 3rd Virginia.
65. Ibid. See the service records for John Peyton's company June to September 1778 whose men appear in Captain Valentine Peyton's company after the September 1778 reorganization of the Virginia Line.
66. Ibid.
67. See the service records for men in Captain John Ashby's company, NARA, *Compiled service records*, 3rd Virginia.
68. Ibid. See also Chapter 7 for details relating to the twenty-three men chosen by Morgan from Captains Ashby and Thornton's' rifle companies.
69. Cecere, 8. See also Sanchez-Saavedra, 39.
70. VHS, *Captain John Chilton to Joseph Blackwell*, September 13, 1776, Mss2c4395a1, *John Chilton Papers*, VHS, Richmond, Virginia.
71. NARA, 13 September 1776, *Captain Chilton's Morning Return*, Officers, 3rd Virginia.
72. Ibid., 21 September 1776, *Captain Chilton's Morning Return*.
73. Ibid., 23 September 1776, *Captain Chilton's Morning Return*.
74. Ibid., 6 October 1776, *Captain Chilton's Morning Return*.
75. Ibid., 11 October 1776, *Captain Chilton's Morning Return*.
76. Ibid., 6 November 1776, *Captain Chilton's Morning Return*.
77. VHS, *Captain John Chilton to his brother Charles Chilton, in Fauquier*, February 11, 1777, Morristown, New Jersey, Mss2c4395a1-11, VHS, Richmond, Virginia.
78. Ibid.
79. See the service records for men in Captain John Peyton's company, NARA *Compiled service records*, 3rd Virginia.
80. See Chapter 1 for details of Captains Blackwell and Chiltons' service in the Culpeper Minute Battalion in 1775–1776.
81. See the service records for men in Captain John Blackwell's company, NARA, *Compiled service records*, 3rd Virginia.
82. Heitman, 229.
83. NARA, 13 September 1776, *Captain Fitzgerald's Morning Return*, Officers, 3rd Virginia.
84. Ibid., 21 September 1776, *Captain John Fitzgerald's Morning Return*.
85. Ibid., 23 September 1776, *Captain John Fitzgerald's Morning Return*.
86. NARA, *Revolutionary War Rolls*, M 246, MR 97 *Muster Rolls*, 3rd Virginia.
87. NARA, *Edward Abbey's Pension File No. 435621*, M 804 MR 1. Edward Abbey stated, in his pension declaration, that he "enlisted for eighteen months in Alexandria, Fairfax County in Captain John Fitzgerald's Company. Capt. David Earl [Arell] was the Lt …"
88. Sanchez-Saavedra, 39. See also Heitman, 321.
89. NARA, 13 September 1776, *Captain Johnson's Morning Return*, Officers, 3rd Virginia.
90. Ibid., 21 September 1776, *Captain Johnson's Morning Return*.
91. Ibid., 23 September 1776, *Captain Johnson's Morning Return*.
92. Ibid., 28 September 1776, *Captain Johnson's Morning Return*.
93. Ibid., 6 October 1776, *Captain Johnson's Morning Return*.
94. Ibid., 11 October 1776, *Captain Johnson's Morning Return*.
95. Ibid., 5 November 1776, *Captain Johnson's Morning Return*.
96. Sanchez-Saavedra, 39.
97. Heitman, 345–346. See also NARA, *List of Officers in 3rd Virginia*, 1 January1776 to 8 August 1778, Officers, 3rd Virginia.
98. See the service records for men in Captain Phill Lee's company and their consolidation into Captain John Peyton's company in June 1778, NARA, *Compiled service records*, 3rd Virginia.
99. See Chapter 4 for a full accounting of the mortality rates in Capt John Peyton's Company for January through April 1777.

100. NARA, 13 September 1776, *Captain Lee's Morning Return*, Officers, 3rd Virginia.
101. Ibid., 21 September 1776, *Captain Lee's Morning Return*.
102. Ibid., 23 September 1776, *Captain Lee's Morning Return*.
103. Ibid., 28 September 1776, *Captain Lee's Morning Return*.
104. Ibid., 6 October 1776, *Captain Lee's Morning Return*.
105. Ibid., 11 October 1776, *Captain Lee's Morning Return*.
106. Ibid., 5 November 1776, *Captain Lee's Morning Return*.
107. See note 98 above.
108. Sanchez-Saavedra, 39–40. See also Heitman, 346.
109. Heitman, 346.
110. Ibid. See also NARA, *List of Officers in 3rd Virginia from January 1, 1776 to August 8, 1778*, Officers, 3rd Virginia.
111. Ibid., 21 September 1776 and 23 September 1776, *Morning Return of 3rd Virginia*. "NB: Major Leitch wounded."
112. Ibid., *Undated List of Captains & Subaltern Officers in Virginia Service with dates of Commission, etc.*
113. Sanchez-Saavedra, 39–40.
114. Heitman, 376.
115. Captain McWilliams was not found in NARA's *Revolutionary War Rolls*, M 246 MR 97, *Muster Rolls, 3rd Virginia* or on MR 137 *Returns of the Army*. See the compiled service records for the officers of the 3rd Virginia for *Morning Returns* of the 3rd Virginia on 2 September, 13 September, 21 September 1776, 6 October, and 11 October 1776 for information relating to William McWilliams as the adjutant of the regiment.
116. Heitman, 438.
117. NARA, 13 September 1776, *Captain Peyton's Morning Return*, Officers, 3rd Virginia.
118. Ibid., 21 September 1776, *Captain Peyton's Morning Return*.
119. Ibid., 23 September 1776, *Captain Peyton's Morning Return*.
120. Ibid., 28 September 1776, *Captain Peyton's Morning Return*.
121. Ibid., 6 October 1776, *Captain Peyton's Morning Return*.
122. Ibid., 11 October 1776, *Captain Peyton's Morning Return*.
123. Ibid., 5 November 1776, *Captain Peyton's Morning Return*.
124. VHS, *Captain John Chilton to his brother Charles Chilton, in Fauquier*, February 11, 1777, Morristown, New Jersey, Mss2c4395a1-11, VHS, Richmond, Virginia. John Chilton talked about the pervasiveness of cholera and small pox in the regiment and nearby Philadelphia in this letter.
125. See biographies of men and officers in volume two, along with the compiled service records, for the 3rd Virginia, M881 MR 951–956; and the 3rd and 4th Virginia on M 881 MR 957–970 for details about the resignations, deaths, discharges, desertions and reenlistment of men in Captain John Peyton's company.
126. Ibid.
127. Ibid.
128. NARA, *List of Officers in 3rd Virginia from January 1, 1776 to August 8, 1778*, Officers, 3rd Virginia.
129. Ibid., 5 November 1776, *Return of 3rd Virginia in service of the United Colonies, commanded by Colonel George Weedon*.
130. Heitman, 450.
131. Sanchez-Saavedra, 39–40.
132. See the service records for men in Captain Robert Powell's company in the compiled service records for the 3rd Virginia
133. Ibid., *List of Officers in 3rd Virginia from January 1, 1776 to August 8, 1778*.
134. Ibid., 13 September 1776, *Captain Thornton's Morning Return*, Officers, 3rd Virginia.
135. Ibid., 21 September 1776, *Captain Thornton's Morning Return*.
136. Ibid., 23 September 1776, *Captain Thornton's Morning Return*.
137. Ibid., 28 September 1776, *Captain Thornton's Morning Return*.
138. Ibid., 6 October 1776, *Captain Thornton's Morning Return*.
139. Ibid., 11 October 1776, *Captain Thornton's Morning Return*.
140. William A. Fowler, *Empires at War: The French & Indian War and the Struggle for North America 1754–1763* (New York: Walker & Co, 2005), 111–112, 217–219.
141. Colonial Williamsburg Foundation, "Account of October 22, 1776 Skirmish near New Rochelle," *Virginia Gazette* (Purdie), 15 November 1776, 3, col. 1, http://research.history.org. (Accessed July 15, 2006).
142. NARA, 5 November 1776, *Captain Thornton's Morning Return*, Officers, 3rd Virginia.
143. Ibid., Service records for 3rd Virginia men in Colonel Morgan's rifle command thoughout the compiled service records of the 3rd Virginia.
144. Ibid. See service records for the men in Captain John Thornton's company in the compiled service records of the 3rd Virginia.

145. Heitman, 566.
146. NARA, 13 September 1776, *Captain Wallace's Morning Return*, Officers, 3rd Virginia.
147. Ibid., 21 September 1776, *Captain Wallace's Morning Return*.
148. Ibid., 23 September 1776, *Captain Wallace's Morning Return*.
149. Ibid., 28 September 1776, *Captain Wallace's Morning Return*.
150. Ibid., 6 October 1776, *Captain Wallace's Morning Return*.
151. Ibid., 11 October 1776, *Captain Wallace's Morning Return*.
152. Ibid., 5 November 1776, *Captain Wallace's Morning Return*.
153. Heitman, 389.
154. NARA, *John Francis Mercer's compiled service records*, 3rd Virginia.
155. Heitman, 389.
156. See note 154 above.
157. Haller, 11, 13, 24, note 14; See also Heitman, 574.
158. Heitman, 574.
159. NARA, *Captain Washington's Morning Return*, 13 September 1776, Officers, 3rd Virginia.
160. Ibid., 21 September 1776, *Captain Washington's Morning Return*.
161. Ibid., 23 September 1776, *Captain Washington's Morning Return*.
162. Ibid., 28 September 1776, *Captain Washington's Morning Return*.
163. Ibid., 6 October 1776, *Captain Washington's Morning Return*.
164. Ibid., 11 October 1776, *Captain Washington's Morning Return*.
165. Ibid., 5 November 1776, *Captain Washington's Morning Return*.
166. Ibid.
167. Ibid. See service records for Lieutenant John Francis Mercer, Lieutenant Allen Mountjoy, Quartermaster Sergeant James Primm, Quartermaster Sergeant James Hansborough, Sergeant/Ensign William Bunberry, James Arrowsmith, Moses Baker, Edmond Bowling, George Boyle, Richard Green, Jeremiah Kendall, Peter Kendall, John King, Valentine King, William McCullough, Colbert McDaniel, Richard Simms, James Smith, Elijah Taylor, and William Williams on M 881 MR 951–956.
168. Ibid., *List of Arrangement of Officers of Virginia Line*, December 1, 1777. See also *Schedule of Promotions in General Weedon & Woodford Brigade*, Officers, 3rd Virginia.
169. Ibid.
170. Ibid.
171. Heitman, 598.
172. Ibid., 120.
173. See General Woodford's remarks relating to John Tebbs in NARA, *List of Arrangement of Several Regiments in the 1st Virginia Brigade*, December 78, in his compiled service records of the 3rd Virginia.
174. Ibid. See Reuben Briscoe's remarks on his September 1778 muster roll.
175. NARA, 13 September 1776, *Captain Charles West's Morning Return*, Officers, 3rd Virginia.
176. Ibid., 21 September 1776, *Captain Charles West's Morning Return*.
177. Ibid., 23 September 1776, *Captain Charles West's Morning Return*.
178. Ibid., 28 September 1776, *Captain Charles West's Morning Return*.
179. Ibid., 6 October 1776, *Captain Charles West's Morning Return*.
180. Ibid., 11, October 1776, *Captain Charles West's Morning Return*.
181. Ibid., 5 November 1776, *Captain Charles West's Morning Return*.
182. Heitman, 121.
183. Service records for Ensign Beverly Roy, Lieutenant John Tebbs, Lieutenant Thomas Hungerford, Fife Abram Hamsley, Charles Bettisworth, Luke Huse, George Jeffrey, William Kent, and James Pollock were listed as 3rd and 7th Virginia officers and men, on reference envelopes in the compiled service records of the 3rd Virginia.
184. Ibid. See service records for Reuben Briscoe's 3rd Virginia men and officers for months of July through September 1778, in the compiled service records for this regiment. Some of these records stated that Briscoe's company consisted of 3rd and 7th Virginia soldiers from July to September while other records noted that, in August 1778, Briscoe's company was made up of just 3rd Virginia soldiers.
185. Ibid. See service records for men and officers in Captain Robert Powell's company in the compiled service records for the 3rd Virginia.
186. NARA, No. 44. 5 October 1776, *Colonel Weedon's Regiment, General Return of Brigades under General Washington at Harlem Heights*, M 246 MR 137 *Returns of the Army*.
187. Ibid., No. 45. 5 October 1776, *Colonel Weedon's Weekly Return under General Washington at Harlem Heights*.
188. Ibid., No. 36. 1 December 1776, *Colonel Weedon's Regiment, Return of the Army under General Washington at Trenton*.

189. Ibid., 22 December 1776, *Colonel Weedon's Regiment, Return of Forces under General Washington in Pennsylvania.*
190. VHS, *David Griffith to his wife Hannah,* Philadelphia, 8 December 1776, Mss2G8755b, *David Griffith Papers, 1776–1778.* VHS, Richmond, Virginia.
191. See note 189 above.
192. NARA, *Schedule of Promotions re Thomas Marshall,* M 881 MR 951 *Officers, 3rd Virginia.*
193. Wright, 285.
194. Lesser, 46.
195. NARA, No. 47. 28 May 1777, *3rd Virginia Return, General Returns of Continental Forces in New Jersey,* M 246 MR 137 *Returns of the Army.*
196. These numbers are taken from an analysis of the deaths recorded by 3rd Virginia Captains from January to March 1777 in the compiled service records for the 3rd Virginia. See Chapter 4 for the names of the men who died in the 3rd Virginia in January, February and March 1777.
197. VHS, *Captain John Chilton to his brother Charles Chilton,* Morristown, February 11, 1777, Mss2c4396a1-11 *Keith Family Papers,* VHS, Richmond, Virginia.
198. NARA, No. 42. *Colonels Read, Weedon & Chester's Regiment, General Returns under General Washington at Harlem Heights,* September 30, 1776, M 246 MR 137 *Returns of the Army.*
199. Ibid., No. 45. *Colonel Weedon's Weekly Return,* October 5, 1776.
200. Ibid., No. 44. *Colonel Weedon's General Return,* October 5, 1776.
201. Lesser, 36.
202. Ibid.
203. Ibid.
204. Ibid., 42.
205. NARA, 22 December 1776, *Colonel Weedon's Return for Forces under General Washington in Pennsylvania,* M 246 MR 137, *Returns of the Army.*
206. Ibid., No. 47. 10 November 1777, *William Woodford's Brigade Return, General Return of Continental Army at White Marsh.*
207. Ibid., No. 48 and 49. 3 December 1777 at White Marsh and 22 December 1777 at Valley Forge, *William Woodford's Brigade Return.*
208. Ibid., No. 52. *Field Return of William Woodford's Brigade.*
209. Ibid., No. 50. *Woodford's Brigade Return, General Return at Valley Forge.*
210. Ibid., No. 48–64, 74–75. *Woodford's Brigade Returns.*
211. See biographies of men and officers in volume two and the compiled service records for the 3rd Virginia on for of the names of men discharged from the regiment from January to March 1778.
212. NARA, *Compiled Service Records,* Officers, 3rd Virginia.
213. Sanchez-Saavedra, 40–41.
214. Ibid.

Plate 14

M 881 MR 137 Field Return of Troops
under Washington at Coryell's Ferry, 22 June 1778

22

Field Return of the Troops under the Command of His Excellency General Washington at Coryell's Ferry June 22nd 78

95

Brigades	Officers present fit for duty							Rank & File present fit for action
	Field			Commiss'd		Non Commiss'd		
	Colonels	Lt. Colonels	Majors	Captns.	Subs.	Serjts.	Drums & Fifers	
Woodford's		3	2	11	33	61	25	562
Scott's	1	2	1	19	37	81	42	518
1st Pennsylvania	.	.	1	15	29	58	51	514
2nd Pennsylva.a	3	4	3	17	26	66	45	664
Poor's	2	4	1	18	46	76	46	871
Glover's	2	4	1	26	51	83	50	781
Larned's	2	2	2	13	32	55	36	561
Paterson's	3	2	2	21	45	85	41	570
Weedon's	4	3	5	20	46	81	42	664
Muhlenberg's	3	5	4	19	49	80	55	752
Late Conway's	1	3	4	12	28	88	54	541
Huntington's	2	2	2	18	40	94	56	755
Varnum's	.	1	3	16	24	73	48	674
N. Carolina	2	2	1	11	27	47	34	728
1st Maryland	1	.	2	11	49	92	40	1000
2nd Maryland	2	2	1	11	21	52	26	542
Total	28	39	35	258	583	1172	691	10697

PLATE 15

M 246 MR 97 Field & Staff Muster Roll,
Officers of 3rd Virginia, July 1777

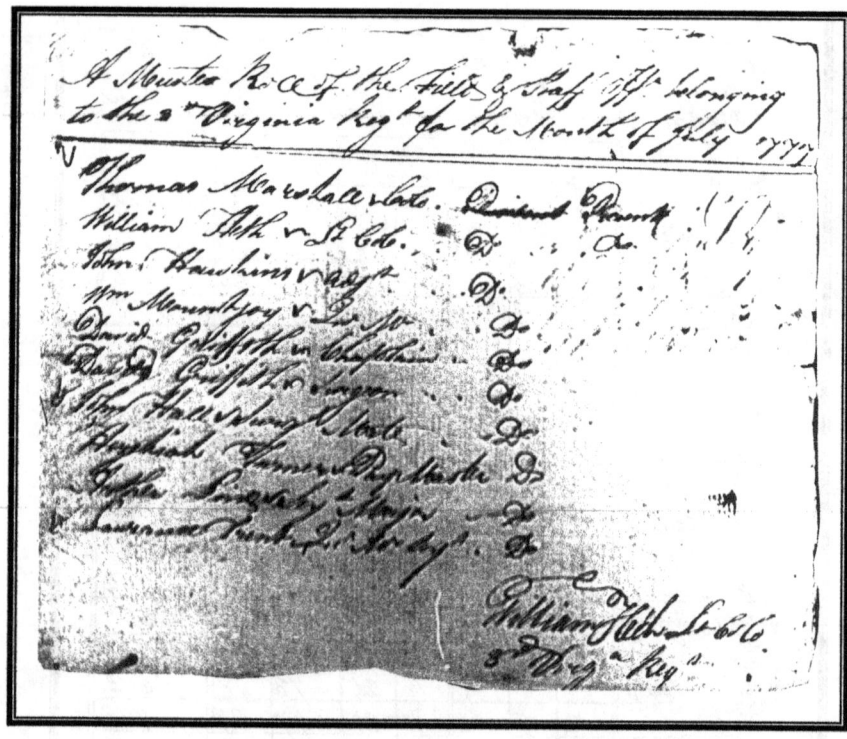

CHAPTER 3

TRACKING THE 3RD VIRGINIA REGIMENT

The importance of the primary record base in tracing the movements of companies of the 3rd Virginia Regiment

It has been possible to trace the movement of companies in the 3rd Virginia Regiment between February 1776 and December 1778 by using a variety of original sources from Army returns from the National Archives to diaries, letters, and battle accounts from universities, libraries, historical societies, and on-line newspaper collections.

These sources included the Captains' morning returns found on NARA's M 881 MR 951 *Compiled Service Records, 3rd Virginia Regiment* and M 246 MR 97, *Revolutionary War Rolls for 3rd Virginia Brigade and 3rd Virginia Regiment 1776–1778* and the General Returns on M 246 MR 136 *Returns of Brigades, Divisions, Armies &c* and MR 246 MR137 *General Returns of the Army Under General Washington 1775–1782*. Pension records of 3rd Virginia veterans also helped to locate companies of the 3rd Virginia in the 1776 campaign, as found on *M 804 Revolutionary War Pension and Bounty land Warrant Application Files 1800–1900*.

Copies of Surgeon and Chaplain David Griffith's letters to his wife, which contained family information and a poignant letter that described the death of Major Andrew Leitch, are at the Virginia Historical Society.[1]

So were Captain John Chilton's letters and diary. His letters, written between 13 September 1776 and 14 August 1777, were helpful in pinpointing his company's whereabouts. They also gave interesting tidbits about soldiers and officers in his company.[2] His diary, which began in January 1777, ended on 8 September 1777, three days before his death on 11 September 1777 at Brandywine.[3] The information here also helped to pin down the location of his company and members of the 3rd Virginia during the first eight and a half months of 1777.

Gustavus Brown Wallace's letters were found at the University of Virginia.[4] Three of his letters, written between September 1776 and January 1777, have been useful in establishing his whereabouts after the Battle of Brandywine on 11 September 1777 and before the Battle of Germantown in October. A January 1777 letter spoke, among other things, of the death of Hugh Mercer.

George Weedon's letters were also found at the University of Virginia.[5] Many of these messages contained first hand accounts of battles and skirmishes in which the 3rd Virginia participated. They proved to be both eloquent and graphic in their detail. Several of the letters described actions performed by 3rd Virginia officers—Major Andrew Leitch, Captains John Thornton, William Washington, John Chilton, and Colonel Thomas Marshall.

In addition, there were letters from members of Congress to George Weedon[6] as the commanding officer of the 3rd Virginia, during the summer of 1776 which helped place the regiment's position before their arrival in New York. Finally articles in the *Virginia Gazette* provided clues as to the whereabouts of the regiment between January and September 1776.[7]

The 3rd Virginia served in a brigade in the Continental establishment under the command of Colonel George Weedon, from August 1776 to mid October 1776 when they were placed in Lord Stirling's Brigade. They were part of this brigade until May 1777 when the regiment became part of Col. William Woodford's Brigade.[8]

December 1775 to August 1776: The formation and organization of the 3rd Virginia regiment,

The 3rd Virginia Regiment had its official beginnings as a Continental Regiment in December 1775 when Congress authorized the creation of six Virginia continental battalions. The men were to be paid as the continental forces at Cambridge, unless the Virginia convention could raise them on better terms.[9]

In January 1776, Congress confirmed the selection of field and staff officers for the Virginia Battalions, made by the Virginia Convention. Hugh Mercer became the first colonel of the 3rd Virginia. George Weedon, the lieutenant colonel and Thomas Marshall, the major or the regiment.[10]

Throughout February 1776, Congress granted continental commissions to captains for companies in the 3rd Virginia: on 5 February, to Andrew Leitch; on 8 February, to John Fitzgerald; on 9 February, to Charles West; on 12 February, to John Thornton; on 20 February, to Gustavus Brown Wallace; and on 26 February, to William Washington and William Mc Williams.[11]

In March 1776, two more commissions were handed out for 3rd Virginia Captains: to Philip Richard Francis Lee on 8 March; and to Thomas Johnson Jr on 21 March.[12]

On 29 April 1776, John Peyton, who had been commissioned as a 1st lieutenant in the 3rd Virginia in February,[13] was promoted to captain.[14]

It was not until October 1776 that Congress confirmed John Ashby's commission and back dated it to 18 March 1776. His subalterns, 1st Lieutenant William Nelson, 2nd Lieutenant Isham Keith and Ensign Nathaniel Ashby's commissions carried the same date. Likewise, Congress confirmed commissions for Captain John Chilton's and his subalterns, 1st Lieutenant John Blackwell and 2nd Lieutenant Joseph Blackwell which were to take effect from 29 April 1776.[15]

In June 1776, Hugh Mercer was promoted from his Colonelcy of the 3rd Virginia to a Brigadier of Virginia troops.[16] Congress ordered him to immediately "repair to headquarters in New York."[17] This left a vacancy in the 3rd Virginia and George Weedon as the Lt. Colonel became the de facto commanding officer of the regiment.

On 20 July 1776, the 3rd Virginia was relieved from the southern department and assigned to the main army.[18]

On 23 July 1776 Congress resolved that Dr. David Griffith be appointed as chaplain and surgeon in the 3rd Virginia, "he being a person of uncommon merit, and there being very few surgeons of abilities who will enter into the army in that state; this appointment not to be drawn into precedent." Dr. Griffith was to be paid in both capacities for time served in the regiment.[19]

On 13 August 1776, Congress promoted George Weedon to Colonel and Thomas Marshall to Lieutenant Colonel of the 3rd Virginia.[20]

July to August 1776: Congress ordered two Virginia battalions to New Jersey and diverted the 3rd Virginia to New York.

In a letter dated 2 July 1776 Surgeon and Chaplain David Griffith wrote his wife Hannah, to report that he and other 3rd Virginia companies were still in Williamsburg, awaiting the arrival of 3rd Virginia companies from Alexandria, along with necessaries and arms.[21]

Nearly three weeks later, on Saturday, 20 July 1776 Congress passed a resolution to send two Virginia battalions to march "with all dispatch" to the flying camp in New Jersey, under the command of General Mercer.[22] Since the colonelcy of the 3rd Virginia had been left vacant since June, it was not until mid August, after Congress had confirmed the promotions of George Weedon to be the commanding officer and Thomas Marshall to act as his second in command that the regiment was ready to march. They left Dumfries three days later, on 16 August.[23]

> The route they followed is not absolutely certain but there were sufficient clues dropped along the way to approximate it in general. From Dumfries, they took the Dumfries Road to Red House [in] Haymarket in Prince William County. Here they joined the Old Carolina Road which took them east of the Bull Run Mountains, past West's ordinary and through Leesburg to cross the Potomac at Noland's Ferry. Passing through Frederick, Maryland, they crossed into Pennsylvania and stopped near Hanover.[24]

On 5 August 1776, David Griffith, in a letter to Major Levin Powell of Loudoun County, reported that his regiment expected to march north towards New York. "Congress," he told Major Powell, "has certainly ordered two Regts from this Colony & have agreed to pay as many of our militia in their absence."[25]

On 18 August 1776, a delegate to Congress, one John Morton, wrote to Persifor Frazer that "two Battalions of Regulars [were] also on their march from Virginia to New York."[26] On 20 August 1776, Thomas Jefferson informed John Page that he had enclosed the requested commissions except for Weedon's and Marshall's who were on the road "hither. Would to god they were in N. York," he concluded.[27]

Eight days later, on 28 August 1776, information was given to Congress that one of the Virginia battalions was on their march to New Jersey, with the intention of passing through Yorktown and Philadelphia. Congress resolved that the commanding officer be directed to "continue their march from York Town, by the nearest route to New Jersey, there to be subject to the orders of General Washington."[28]

In a letter written from Philadelphia on the same day from John Hancock, President of the Continental Congress, to George Weedon, Hancock declared that

> The Congress being informed that you are on your March to New Jersey with Intention to pass through York Town & Philada., I have it in Charge to direct, that you continue your March from York Town [in Pennsylvania] by the nearest Route to New Jersey (avoiding Philada. on Acct. of the Small Pox) where on your Arrival you will execute such Orders as Genl. Washington shall think proper to give you.[29]

This correspondence took place a day *after* the Battle of Long Island. On 30 August 1776, Hancock sent a letter to the commanding officer of the 3rd Virginia:

> You are directed notwithstanding a former order to March to New Jersey & wait the orders of General Washington, to march your Battalion immediately on receipt of this to New York & inform the General of your arrival.[30]

General Mercer, who had also heard that his old regiment was on the march, sent similar orders to Weedon. Washington had apparently asked Mercer for the use of the 3rd Virginia in the defense of New York.[31]

August to September 1776: Did Captain Washington arrive in New York, to take part in the Battle of Long Island while the rest of the regiment appeared in September in time for the Battle at Harlem Heights?

There seems to be a controversy surrounding the presence of Captain William Washington at the Battle of Long Island in late August where he was believed to have been wounded. It is now thought that he did not appear in New York until mid-September, with the rest of the 3rd Virginia captains and was wounded, instead, at the Battle of Harlem Heights.[32] A 2nd lieutenant, Robert Dade, whose captain has not been identified, was also reported as having died in August 1776.[33] Lieutenant Dade may have died on the march to New York.

Captain John Chilton's company arrived at King's Bridge on 13 September 1776, according to a letter he wrote to Joseph Blackwell on that date.[34] Two days later, Captain Gustavus Brown Wallace, was in a camp on the North River, ten miles from New York. "General Washington was rejoiced to see us" he told his brother Michael, in a letter dated 15 September 1776.[35]

All ten Captains of the 3rd Virginia had arrived in New York by 13 September 1776 and filed morning returns on that date, at Massasinio Camp: Captains John Chilton, John Fitzgerald, Thomas Johnson, Phill Lee, John Ashby, John Peyton, John Thornton, Gustavus Brown Wallace, William Washington, and Charles West all filed returns for their companies.[36]

From Captain Chilton's letter written to Joseph Blackwell on the same date, it is possible to pinpoint this camp as being in the vicinity of King's Bridge.[37]

The first general return for the 3rd was filed at King's Bridge on 21 September 1776, five days after the Battle of Harlem Heights. The regiment's field staff consisted of a colonel, a lieutenant colonel, and a major. Officers and subalterns listed were ten captains, eight 1st lieutenants, eight 2nd lieutenants, ten ensigns, a chaplain and surgeon, an adjutant, a quartermaster, a paymaster, and a surgeon's mate; there were thirty-seven sergeants and 383 of the regiment were fit for duty, 147, were sick and present; Fifty-three were sick and absent; and seventeen men were on command. The regiment totaled 602.[38]

Thus, it appeared, from this return, that the Regiment's full compliment of Captains had arrived and the 3rd Virginia was close to full strength.

They had made good speed, covering well over 400 miles in twenty-six days. Their route took them from York to Lancaster, then avoiding the highlands, they passed north of Norristown. They crossed the Delaware near New Hope, moving through New Jersey and passed by Plainfield, Montclair and Hackensack. They crossed over the Hudson at Dobbs Ferry. After making a safe passage there, the regiment proceeded south through Yonkers where they crossed the Harlem River at King's Bridge and encamped at Hell's Gate about fourteen miles above New York.[39] John Coppage, a private in Captain John Ashby's company, remembered his company having operated from Fort Washington.[39a]

The route through the Jerseys and New York had been made in the intense heat of late August. John Chilton, in his letter to his father in law, Joseph Blackwell, reported that the regiment was "in good spirits, and, generally speaking, healthy, tho' not quite full."[40]

During the month of September 1776, the 3rd Virginia returns were filed on the 13 September, near King's Bridge; on the 16 September, at Harlem Heights; on the 21 September at Kingsbridge, and on the 23 and 30 September at Harlem Heights.

In late September 1776, Captain Gus Wallace wrote his brother Michael, from Harlem Heights, ten mile above New York. In a letter dated September 28th, he reported, among other things,

> ...The Virg^a officers here seem to talk of resigning and coming home, but god knows when I shall come, not before my men's time's up. If it was not for leaving the men I shou'd most certainly see you this winter if I escaped the ravage of war—for you may depend, this is the most disagreeable place I ever saw. There is nothing to eat here but Beef & Beef ...
>
> I don't recollect that I informed you ... that the two thirds of the city of Newyork is in ashes. This is a fact. I saw the smoke ... but how it was fired, I cannot say ... There was a skirmish the other night which happened by our men's attempting to land on Montzure's Island where the Enemy had a Guard ...[41]

The 30 September 1776 general return of Colonels Read, Weedon and Chester's regiments revealed the losses inflicted on the regiment in the September 1776 campaign. The colonels listed six dead, and reported twenty-five Captains, twenty-three 1st lieutenants, twenty-four 2nd lieutenants, twenty-three ensigns, a chaplain, three Adjutants, three quarter masters, four surgeons, four surgeon's mates, and 102 sergeants among their officers and non-comms. Forty-four of their rank and file were fit for duty. The colonels needed 118 rank and file, a sergeant, and a drum and fife to bring their regiments up to full strength.[42]

October 1776: The 3rd Virginia remained in New York at Harlem Heights through the Battle at White Plains and the skirmish at New Rochelle where Captain Thornton was part of an unsuccessful attempt to capture Major Rogers and his Tory regiment.

On 5 October 1776, Colonel Weedon filed a weekly return at Harlem Heights for the 3rd Virginia. His regiment contained ten captains, nine 1st lieutenants, ten 2nd lieutenants, and ten ensigns among his commissioned officers, along with a major, lieutenant colonel and colonel.

He reported a staff consisting of a chaplain, an adjutant, a quarter master, a surgeon, and two surgeon's mates. His non-commissioned officers were thirty-nine sergeants. He had 364 rank and file present and fit for duty. 142 were sick and present while fifty-three were sick and absent. Forty-five men were on command. He reported a total of 603 men and officers present. Colonel Weedon still needed two sergeants, four drum and fife, and seventy-seven rank and file to bring the regiment up to full strength. He also reported one dead and two desertions since his last return.[43]

The 3rd Virginia remained in New York throughout the month of October as the regiment took part in the Battle at White Plains. The companies of at least three Captains, Fitzgerald, Thornton and Lee, were in this engagement, on 26 October 1776.[44]

David Baker, a private in Captain Thornton's company remembered enlisting in February 1776 and marching from Dumfries to Alexandria and then northward, crossing the Delaware at Trenton. His company then joined the main army at White Plains. They fought at White Plains and retreated, recrossing the Delaware.[45] Spencer Anderson, a private in Captain Phillip Richard Francis Lee's company, also remembered having fought at White Plains.[46]

Edward Abbey, a private in Capt John Fitzgerald's company recalled that the "American Army was over powered" at White Plains and forced to retreat. "We marched through New Jersey and crossed the Delaware", he stated in his pension file "and remained there until Christmas."[47]

A letter from a "field officer" in the 3rd Virginia appeared in the Purdie's Virginia Gazette on 15 November 1776. This letter gave details of the battle at White Plains and the attempt by the 1st and 3rd Virginia to capture Major Rogers and his Tory regiment at New Rochelle.[48]

The regiment, still under Weedon's command, was now part of Lord Stirling's Brigade, having been transferred to this unit in mid October 1776 before the battle of White Plains. Along with the 3rd Virginia, Stirling's brigade consisted of the 1st Virginia, John Haslet's Delaware Regiment, two Pennsylvania battalions from the Flying camp, and the 1st and 2nd Battalion of Miles' Pennsylvania rifles.[49]

November 1776 through January 1777: the 3rd Virginia moved from North Castle, New York into New Jersey, thence into Pennsylvania, with engagements at Trenton and Princeton, New Jersey. After the attack on Princeton, the army made their winter quarters at Morristown.

On November 9th, the 3rd Virginia, along with the rest of the army, occupied the heights of North Castle, in New York, about five miles from the White Plains.[50]

Between 9 November and 30 November 1776, it appeared that the regiment moved into New Jersey. Captain John Chilton's company had progressed through New Jersey to Elizabeth town, Hackinsack to Brunswick, New Jersey. Captain Chilton wrote his brother Charles, on that date

> I wrote from this place [Brunswick] by Capt Ashby at which time I expected to have been in Winter Quarters before this. The day after his Departure, we were ordered up to Elizabeth Town, about 20 miles, hearing the enemy had crossed the N° River and got to a small town called Hack&Sack; by the time we got there, they [the British] had proceeded to Aquakinac Bridge, 4 or 5 Miles nearer.[51]

On 26 November 1776 Chilton's company forded the Aquakinac river while the rest of the troops were at Newark; the regiment came through Elizabeth the next day, on their way to Brunswick.

> [O]ur Regiment brought up the rear. This was a melancholy day, a deep Miry road and so many Men to tread it, made it very disagreeable marching. [W]e came 8 or 10 miles & encamped. Yesterday, we reached this place, how long we shall stay I cant say but expect we shall make a stand near this place, if not at it, but no certainty where the enemy are and are advancing on and an engagement may happen before Tomorrow Night ... I have pretty well got over my jaundice & the comp^y are healthy except three or four who are not dangerous I hope ...[52]

On 1 December 1776 the 3rd Virginia was with the army under General Washington at Trenton, New Jersey. On that date, Colonel Weedon made a general return of men and officers: 290 men and officers were fit for duty; thirty were sick, present, 217 were sick and absent. Two men were on furlough and sixty-four men were on command.

Weedon had five captains, and thirteen lieutenants, eight ensigns, a major and a lieutenant colonel, along with himself as the colonel among his staff. An adjutant, a quarter master, a surgeon, and fourteen rank and file rounded out the regiment.[53]

On 7 December 1776, Washington began an advance towards Princeton when he received information that the British were advancing with the idea of attacking the American's rear. Whereupon Washington decided to retreat, crossing the Delaware, the next day, into Pennsylvania.[54]

While on the Pennsylvania side of the Delaware, between 10 and 17 December, Washington was "distressed by a number of perplexing complexities." In a letter to Lund Washington, his manager at Mount Vernon, the General was concerned about the state of his army.

> I have no Idea of being able to make a stand, as My numbers, till joined by the Philadelphia Militia did not exceed 3000 Men fit for duty—now we may be about 5000 to oppose Howes whole army… We have brought over and destroyed, all the Boats we could lay our hands on, upon the Jersey Shore for many miles above and below … it is next to impossible to guard a Shore for 60 miles with less than half the Enemys numbers; when by force or stratagem they may suddenly attempt a passage in many different places …[55]

Washington was concerned, too, with the health of his men. He worried constantly about the sickness that afflicted so many of his men.[56] David Griffith, the Surgeon of the 3rd Virginia echoed this concern, in his 8 December 1776 letter to wife Hannah back in Loudoun County.

> I arrived in this Town [Philadelphia] yesterday Evening – my business here to see the Sick lodged in hospitals, & to send all the well back to the army. I left the army two days ago at Prince Town, where I thought we shoud have remained some time; But the enemy have been reinforced & have advanced from Brunswick. Genl Washington, not being strong enough to repel them, is again retreating. [57]

Washington's strongest regiment appeared to be the 3rd Virginia, which on paper provided him with 586 men.[58] Colonel Weedon's return, filed 22 December 1776 reported a grand total of 586 men and officers; in reality only 134 of them were fit for duty.

This return, filed as part of the Army under General Washington at Trenton, included six captains, five lieutenants, five ensigns, a major and a colonel. The return also included an adjutant, a quarter master, a surgeon's mate, nineteen sergeants, and seven rank and file. Nineteen men were sick and present; 360 were sick and absent, eleven were on furlough and sixty-two were on command. He reported one dead and four discharged since his last return. Remarks on this return showed that the 3rd Virginia was part of Stirling's Brigade, along with the regiments of Colonels Read and Haslet and Major Williams.[59]

The regiment took part in the attack on Trenton in late December and capture of the Hessian forces there. In a 29 December 1776 letter from Colonel Weedon to John Page, President of the Continental Congress, he gave an account of this battle and the part his regiment played in it.[60]

On 2 January 1777, the Americans attacked Princeton. David Baker, a private in Captain John Thornton's company remembered guarding the baggage during this battle. This was the battle where his old 3rd Virginia colonel now General, Mercer was killed. So was Baker's brother, Richard.[61] After the attack on Princeton, the army went into winter quarters at Morristown, New Jersey.[62]

Captain John Chilton's diary gave an account of the regiment's movements after Princeton. His diary began on 3 January 1777, with his first entry for that date entered at four in the morning. According to his diary, the regiment left off their pursuit of the British very early before daybreak on 3 January and marched to Somerset Courthouse; on the 4th of January, they're arrived in Pluckemin; on the 5th they marched to Morristown, where they remained until the 9th or 10th of that month.

> … Our whole force did not amount to 2500, Pennsylvania Militia included, therefore [we] were obliged to stop pursuit [of the enemy] & gather our Men and march with expedition towards the Mountains, got to Somerset Courthouse that night, from Trenton 26 Miles; next morn^g early marched got to a small Town called Pluckimin where we got plenty of beef, pork &c which we had been starving for a day or two, not having time to draw and dress victuals. We staid here a day to refresh about 14 miles from Somerset Court house to this place, from Pluckimin. [M]arched to Morris Town, where the 3^d Virg^a Reg^t was stationed 4 or 5 days on side of a Mountain, without tents. Ground covered with snow.[63]

While Captain Chilton and the 3rd Virginia were on the march to Pluckamin, their Colonel was busy transporting the Hessian officers captured at Trenton to Philadelphia. He and his prisoners arrived in that city on 4 January 1777.

> Last Tuesday night col. George Weedon, of Virginia, arrived in this city with the Hessian officers taken at Trenton, in the action of the 26th; he this day delivered them to the Council of Safety, with six standards. They are allowed their parole of honour, and declare themselves perfectly satisfied with their fate. We hear the colonel sets off again, in a day or two, for the continental army in Jersey.[64]

Once Weedon had delivered his prisoners, he went back to Morristown where, on 9 January 1777, he received orders from Washington to return to Virginia on a recruiting expedition to fill the ranks of his regiment.

> Sir: You are to leave proper Officers with the Men of your Regiment at the several posts where they are, including the sick. You are also to use every means in your power, to collect the Straglers of your regiment, and then, with such Officers as can be spared, you are to repair to Virginia immediately and facilitate the recruiting of your Regiment with all possible expedition, upon the Terms prescribed by Congress, and agreeable to the instruction given by me.
> The Straglers properly officer'd as before mentioned, are to be assembled at Newtown or Philadelphia; the Officer commanding them is to report their numbers to the General or Officer commanding where they assemble, as also to me, without delay, and to see that they are regularly exercised and well instructed in the Manoeuvres. The recruits are to be sent forward by fiftys or upwards, as raised, to Philadelphia, which is to be considered as your place of Rendezvous.
> P.S. Your Major is to remain with such of your Regiment as you leave at Philadelphia, for the purpose of receiving the recruits as they come, providing for 'me, and forming and disciplining of them in a proper manner.[65]

About the time that Colonel Weedon received his orders to go on a recruiting trip to Virginia, the 3rd Virginia was leaving Morristown, where they had been stationed on a mountain side without tents for four or five days. The regiment then proceeded to Samuel Robert's house, some two miles outside Morristown. They settled in at Robert's house for a fortnight and then returned to winter quarters at Morristown, where they remained until sometime in February.[66]

On 17 January 1777, General Mercer's body was brought to Philadelphia and interred with military honours.[67] Captain Chilton had recorded his death in his diary on 3 January: "As we were obliged to retreat at the beginning of the Battle," Chilton said, "the much lamented Genl. Mercer had his horse shot under him ... and was inhumanly murdered with Bayonets ..."[68] The 3rd Virginia, stationed at Morristown, undoubtedly made the trip with others of the army to Philadelphia to witness the burial of their esteemed first regimental officer.

February, 1777: In February, the 3rd Virginia encountered smallpox in Morristown and was ordered to Hanover for inoculations; in March and April they were in Chatham, Newark and at the Metuchen Lines.

In a letter to his brother Charles Chilton written from Morristown on February 11, 1777, Captain Chilton reported that

> Lieut. Alvin Mountjoy, Lieut. Jos Blackwell, Ensgn B. Peyton and myself have been under a strict Regimen for the Small Pox ... we expected we had taken it from a man who broke out in our Room ... I hope to obtain leave tomorrow to get Innoculated in a day or so if no Symptoms appear. Joseph we though was taken with it on Sunday, he was unwell yesterday and very ill all this day and not symptoms appearing, the Doctr gave him Some just before night. [I]t has worked him and he is easier. [W]e should see in a day or two whether it is the Small pox. [W]e are well prepared for it I hope ...[69]

Captain Chilton also noted the presence of small pox among 3rd Virginia men in his diary in February 1777 with the note that the regiment had been ordered to Hanover township to be inoculated since some of the men had small pox, although "very lightly generally".[70]

March to April 1777: Chilton and the 3rd Virginia marched to Chatham, then to Newark with the hopes of crossing the river at Bergen to engage Tory forces there; unfortunately there were no boats available, so the regiment marched instead to the Metuchen lines.

After their inoculation at Hanover, Chilton observed in his journal that the regiment went seven miles further to Chatham, located on the Passaic River. Chilton called the river "a smart River, [but] not navigable." They remained in Chatham until sometime in April when they marched to Newark with

> an intent to cross over to Bergen where we heard 4 or 500 Tories were assembled, but being disappointed in Boats, did not cross; [we] staid at Newark 2 or 3 day[s], then marched to the Matuchin Lines where we staid till [the] 4th of May when we were ordered to join the Grand Army at Middle Brook.[71]

While the 3rd Virginia was on the march during March, Weedon, now acting Adjutant General of the Army, with the rank of a Brigadier, was urged by Washington "to call upon every Colonel within your reach and order him to march whatever Men he may have raised, to join the Army immediately." He implored Weedon to "endeavour to procure me the returns of all the regiments, that I may form some judgment of the time in which a force may be drawn together, a matter that I am presently intirely [entirely] ignorant..."[72]

Washington spent the winter and early spring of 1777 directing operations to harass the enemy since he did not have enough of an effective force to risk a battle. At the same time, he worked on his officers to bring in new recruits to replenish the army as the forces recruited during the heady days of 1776 had largely disappeared. The general had gone into winter quarters at Morristown with less than 1400 men. Small pox had rendered many of his troops unfit for duty and desertions by militia men attached to the main force and a lack of reenlistments had further reduced its size.

Washington's army was in disarray. Enlistments were up, soldiers were deserting and smallpox had moved through the army, since its arrival at Morristown, filling the hospitals and sharply cutting the troops fit for duty. The disease even spread to nearby Philadelphia; the disease was the primary reason for Washington's order for a mass inoculation of the troops [73] that John Chilton talked about in his earlier diary entries. To make matters worse, food and clothing were in short supply. Lack of shoes and tents plagued both officers and men.[74] It is not surprising that men deserted or returned home when their enlistments were up, given the chronic shortages in basic supplies, food, clothing, and shoes.

There were serious problems in manpower. Washington wrote the governor of Connecticut that by 15 March,

> I shall be left with the remains of five Virginia Regiments, not amounting to more than as many hundred men, and parts of two or three more Continental Battalions—all very week. The remainder of the army will be composed of small parties of militia from this state and Pennsylvania, on whom little dependence can be put, as they com and go when they please." [75]

In another letter to John Hancock, dated 14 March 1777, Washington thought his troops numbered less than 3000 throughout New Jersey. The balance of these numbers was militia who were supposed to go home at the end of March. Washington told Hancock he had only 981 Continentals.[76]

In a 15 March 1777 return of Continental Troops in New Jersey under Washington's command, these troops now numbered 2543; these numbers were somewhat misleading as 571 men of the six Virginia regiments had been inoculated and not yet ready to return to duty. There were 976 militia attached to the continental forces. Two hundred forty of these men were scheduled to leave when their service expired in April. There was another 300 or 400 militia whose service expired in two weeks.[77]

This was borne out by a letter John Chilton wrote, on 19 March 1777, to Major Martin Pickett from Hanover Township, informing him

> ... I had just got out of the small pox for which I had been innoculated and had it favourably. [O]ur Brother Joseph [Blackwell]was not so lucky, he had it pretty severely, the laurels that he was reaping... was whelts and carbuncles on his nose and face... [H]e is very sullen occasioned by a weakness in one of his eyes that was a little infected with the S. Pox, tho not to injure it... [A]s soon as innoculation is over and a few more troops arrive, I expect [Howe] will be closely invested and I hope his retreat cut off. They now scarce dare creep out of their lines and when they do forage a little, our scouting parties precipitate them into their Lines again like hares before a hound. [The British troops] have the small Pox among them worse than we have...[78]

It is likely that John Chilton's company and perhaps the rest of the 3rd Virginia were still at Hanover Township as late as 19 March 1777.

On 27 March 1777, Washington, still in winter quarters at Morristown, wrote General Weedon about the impending promotion of two 3rd Virginia captains, Thornton and Washington. He also stated that he had "not yet seen any of the recovered soldiers of the third Regiment, spoken of as ordered to this place by you;"[79] It appeared, that the 3rd Virginia was still recuperating from their inoculation for small pox while on the march to the Metuchen lines.

An April 1777 return of troops under command of Major General Lincoln at Bound Brook, New Jersey appears to bear this out. The 3rd Virginia was one of six Virginia Regiments which did *not* show up in the return. The 2nd, 7th, 8th, 10th, 11th, and 12th Virginia were at Bound Brook.[80] The 1st, 3rd, 4th, 5th 6th, and 9th Virginia were not. These units were still among the missing.

There were at least two reasons to explain their absence. Some of the officers and men were undoubtedly still recuperating from small pox. It is also possible that they could have been one of the regiments on the way to Newark with the 3rd Virginia, to attempt a river crossing into Bergen County to engage the Tory regiment there.

At any rate, John Chilton's company found they could not pass over the Passaic due to a lack of boats and did not receive orders to march to Middlebrook and join the main army until 4 May 1777.[81]

May 1777: The 3rd Virginia remained with the main army at Middlebrook, New Jersey. In mid-May, the regiment transferred from Stirling's Brigade to Brigadier General William Woodford's Brigade.

With the advent of spring and much warmer weather, some 8,000 new Continental troops dribbled into Morristown to strengthen the nucleus of regulars and Jersey militia men. The recruitment of these troops was undeniably made easier by Congress's authorization for the states to raise 75,000 men.

It also helped that that body also gave Washington virtual dictatorial powers for six months, beginning in December 1776. This allowed Washington to deal with the civilian population who were not particularly cooperative in providing his army with goods and services. He commandeered provisions, food and services when civilians balked accepting paper currency for their sale. He placed the sick and wounded in private homes around Morristown, over the objections of the householders.

The spring brought about a change in his attitude as secret aid from France began to trickle in—thousands of muskets, tons of powder and quantities of clothing and shoes made their way into Army depots.[82]

On 10 May 1777, Washington wrote to Brigadier General William Woodford, offering him the command of a new brigade consisting of the 3rd, 7th, 11th, and 15th Virginia Regiments. He quickly accepted.[83]

At the end of May, on 28 May 1777, a general return was filed of Continental Forces in New Jersey. The regiments reported a total of 10,003 men and officers on Continental duty. The report also noted that "No accurate returns are yet received of the light Corps & artillery, being very much dispersed. There are about 500 Jersey Militia under the Command of General Heard."[84]

The 3rd Virginia, along with the other Virginia regiments missing on the March return, was in New Jersey. The regiment was now under the command of Thomas Marshall.[85] There were sixteen commissioned officers including a colonel, lieutenant colonel, five captains, eight 1st lieutenants, and one ensign. A chaplain, surgeon, adjutant, and a quartermaster made up the field staff, while twenty six non-comms were present—a sergeant major, a quarter master sergeant, nineteen sergeants, two drummers, and three fifes.

There were 123 rank and file present and fit for duty, with thirteen sick but present and fourteen sick and absent. This brought the 3rd Virginia totals to 169 men and officers.[86]

The May 1777 return for Captains reflected the promotion of Captains Thornton and Washington out of the regiment.[87] These totals were a far cry from the 3rd Virginia's total in December 1776 before Trenton. Colonel Weedon's regiment in May totaled 586 men and officers although only 134 were fit for duty.[88]

On the last day of May 1777, George Weedon gave an update on the Virginia troops in a letter from Camp Middle Brook, to John Page.

> ... The army is now drawn together at at this place, at least that part of it which have been castomed [accustomed] all winter in this state. The whole of them now Encamped in Comfortable Tents on a vally covered in front and rear by ridges, which afford us serenity. His excellency, our good old General, has also spread his Tent, and lives amongst us... Our men all happily over the small pox and remarkable healthy, well Armed, well Cloathed and from our Commander in Chief down, to the priv^t Contin[ent]al in the highest Spirits ... For Heaven's sake, expedite the Completion of your Quota's of men for the operations of this Campaign does in a great measure defend the American Cause ... let me know what is doing in my Country and what prospect there is of Getting our Reg^{ts} Completed ...[89]

June 25 to June 29, 1777: The 3rd Virginia was at Piscataway, which was abandoned by the enemy a few days before; Captain Chilton's company guarded the pass at Steel's Gap while Colonel Morgan's riflemen skirmished with the British on the Metuchen lines; After this battle, Colonel Marshall and the regiment received orders to move on to Bound Brook.

In a letter written 29 June 1777 to his brother Charles, John Chilton explains his whereabouts in relation to the rest of the regiment.

> I am at this time stationed with 50 Men to Guard this pass; came here [the] 27th in the night. Mr Blackwell and my own Comp^y with me, except a few who stay in Camp with the Baggage. Our station is pretty agreeable ... only 2 Mile[s] from Camp. [On] the 26th [of June] our Reg^t was at Piscataway which place the enemy had abandoned a few days before.[90]

Colonel Morgan, with his Rifle Regiment was on the Metuchen Lines at the same time the Army came down into the Plains. The British, on 25 June 1777, unexpectedly "stole a March in the night" and nearly caught Morgan and his troops unawares. With some difficulty, Morgan was able to save his men and baggage and retreated. "There were but few Virginians except Morgans in this battle,"[91] Chilton reported to his brother.

> Two thirds of our Army was not in Action. I was in 4 Miles of this engagement and heard it all. Just as the battle ended, Col^o Marshall received orders to leave Piscataway and march up by the way of Bound Brooke. A Party of the enemy had advanced within 2 Miles of us, about 2000, and had set down to refresh themselves. We marched on with Colours flying and Drums beating, which they hearing and expect^s we were coming to attack them, made the best of their way to P. Amboy [Perth Amboy] ...[92]

3 July to 31 July 1777: John Chilton's diary recorded the passage of his company through New Jersey to the Delaware River.

Friday, 3 July. The army marched from Middle Brook to Morris town by way of White's Tavern, about 10 miles from Middlebrook. They then went 18 miles further where they stayed until the 12th of July.

Saturday, 12 July. The whole army marched and encamped at the western end of Pumpton Plains, crossing the Whippany. They took the Troy road and passed Hanover Township, then crossed the Rockaway River which ran into the Passaic. The Rockaway ran nearly southwest until it was near the junction with the Passaic and then nearly east 3 miles further. The army encamped there, 16 miles from Morristown.

Sunday, 13 July. Captain Chilton lost his Journal entries from April 15, 1777 to this date.

Monday, 14 July. The regiment beat to quarters at day break and crossed Beaver Dam Brook and marched to a "regular built fort, just below Mount Holly." They crossed the Long Pond River, also known as the Pumpton River and then crossed another "considerable" river. They marched fifteen miles altogether.

Tuesday, 15 July. The 3rd Virginia proceeded up the river for eleven miles to The Clove. The river here was known as the Ramepo, Chilton recorded, winding through large and barren mountains.

Friday, 18 July. "At 9 in [the] forenoon, [we] marched about 2 Miles back, encamped in the Dutch Valley… part of our encampment at the Clove was in N. York state, part in Jersey." The rest of the 3rd Virginia, according to his diary, was still in New Jersey.

Sunday, 20 July. His company's tents were struck at the Morning Gun and the troops marched by the Clove. They followed the Ramepo River since a road could not be made due to the mountainous terrain. Chilton recorded in his diary that there were very few houses for sixteen miles. The reason for this was the narrowness of the valley. The soil was so stony, he noted, that few people could live there. There were deer (some say wild goats) and an abundance of rattlesnakes.

It was very late in the evening before the army made camp on the western side of the Haverstraw Mountains, within fourteen miles of New Windsor. The countryside was barren.

Monday and Tuesday, 21 July and 22 July. Captain Chilton remained here; about 1 ½ miles further, on the Haverstraw Mountains, was "a beautiful Lake" which he described as being "in Length & 400 Yd^s broad, clear and transparent, said to be 30 or 40 feet deep, abounding with various kinds [of] fishes; near this Lake on the Mountain are Garden Gooseberries, Currans & Rasberries…"

Wednesday, 23 July. At nine in the morning, the 3rd Virginia marched two miles to Smith's Tavern. From there they crossed the Mountains and traveled seven miles to Oxford, where they stopped to refresh themselves. They went four miles further to Chester, passed through this town and made camp.

Thursday, 24 July. Captain Chilton remained here in camp. He called it a "lay by" in his diary.

Friday, 25 July. The regiment then marched from Chester for fifteen miles and, on the way, breakfasted with a family named Wickham. Eight miles further on, they encamped at a place called "Warwiendah, about a Mile & [a] half in Jersey …"

Early Saturday morning, on 26 July 1777, Captain Chilton related an unpleasant incident in his diary. It is recounted here in its entirety.

> Before we Marched, Capt. Wallace, Capt. Powel, myself, Lt. Mercer, Lieut. Tebbs, Lieut Baynham & Ens^n Payton were denied our Posts in [the] Battalion, for this reason—there was a Genl Order for every Officer to attend Roll Call at Retreat. I had not seen my chest for near a week. I was consequently very dirty with a long beard. I had embraced this $opport^y$ of Shaving & shifting and was about ½ shaved at beat. I saw the Men turn out and also saw Mr Blackwell go to hear the Roll call. [F]or this I was arrested—the other Gent. no doubt had their reasons or at least ought to have had, tho' to say truth, this order has been too much neglected but to bring in those who had not neglected their duty indiscriminately with those who had, argues a New raised officer grasping a superiority and power.
>
> [I]n 15 Minutes our Swords were ordered to be given us again, which all refused to receive but myself. I knew that Col^o Marshall had been urged to this piece of strict, tho' ill timed discipline, that he would act when it came to the pinch as it really turned out, and that it would end in a manner that would do neither party honour. [B]esides, we were on a forced March where I knew we could have not trial until a battle should be fought as there was at that time the greatest prospect, the report being that the enemy were some distance up the Delaware; and I was very averse to giving my command up to men of their $chose^g$ to command my $Comp^y$.

After noting this confrontation Chilton continued the entry for the day. The regiment was up very early and by nine in the morning had already marched eleven miles. They breakfasted in a meadow by a fine spring. After breakfast, they went by three lakes all on the right hand side of the road.

Sunday, 27 July. The regiment did not get an early start due to rain the night before. They passed another lake when they crossed the mountains. Three miles further, at Hackitt's town, the regiment was ordered to sit down, although there was no water nearby to drink and no food to eat.

The regiment marched so late into the night before that nothing could be cooked. No wagons were allowed to carry our cooking utensils and soldiers had to carry their kettles and pains in their hands and their provisions on their backs.

Since it was hot out and the march was a forced one, the food turned putrid from the heat of the sun and the sweat from the men. Many of the men were entirely barefoot. At a rest stop, an inspection was made of the regiment to see what articles could be discarded. The regiment finally encamped at Musconconk Brook.

Monday, 28 July. The army, along with the 3rd Virginia, was up early and on the march, crossing the brook four or five miles below their previous encampment. The reached Pitts town at noon and stayed there until four in the afternoon to refresh and draw provision. They then moved on to Quakers town and encamped there.

Tuesday, 29 July. They were up at sunrise and marched nine miles when they were ordered to pitch their tents. They stayed in this place for a day, about a mile from the road.

Wednesday, 30 July. The regiment, along with the army, marched to Howell's Ferry on the Delaware.

Thursday, 31 July. At Howell's ferry, misfortune struck Captain Chilton. In fording the river, his wagon overturned. A horse drowned and the wagon and tents were lost. "[T]his scheme of fording," Chilton said, "had like to have proved fatal to several soldiers, two were drowned a day or two before."

Fortunately Captain Chilton's bed clothes were wrapped up in Lieutenant Mountjoy's tent and their bulk kept the water from soaking through the clothing so these garments, at least were saved. However the regiment was forced to sleep in the woods since their tents were lost to the river.[93]

August 1777: Chilton's diary continued relating the march into Pennsylvania with arrival at Germantown; from thence to Sandy Brook and then to Philadelphia. The 3rd Virginia encamped at Darby and then went on into Newcastle County, Delaware. By the end of the month they had stayed briefly in Wilmington and then returned to Pennsylvania to Brandywine.

Friday, 1 August. The regiment overtook General Conway's brigade and encamped at the forks of the Fall road.

Saturday, 2 August. The 3rd Virginia stopped for about an hour at Germantown then camped near the Schuylkill River, about five miles from Philadelphia. The remained here until Friday, 8 August 1777.

Friday, 8 August. A general review of the regiments was held early in the morning, with orders to be under way at two in the afternoon. Although the men were told they weren't going to march more than five miles, in reality they marched until nine in the evening. Their pace was slow and they were put into a stubble field "as uneven as a Plough could make [the] Ground" with water a half mile away from their camp.

Saturday, 9 August. The regiment moved a mile or so to be closer to water and encamped at Sandy Brook.

Sunday, 10 August. They camped at the Cross Road where they remained for the next thirteen days.[94]

On *14 August 1777*, Captain Chilton wrote to his brother Charles and the other to his sisters, from a camp at the Cross Roads, Pennsylvania. Among the topics discussed in this letter, was the news of his whereabouts.

> From 10th July we have been continually Marching. [W]e have made a compleat Tour of the Jerseys, went into the N. York State to a small town Chester, where we staid one day. [T]he next [day we received] Marching orders, this was a forced March, from Chester in N. York to Browns ferry, [on the] Delaware, [a total of] 95 Miles. This we marched in 4 days and had many impediments on the way. Horses dying in the Waggons, shoeng [shoeing] of horses, mending Waggons &c.
>
> We went the Western Road ... we staid at the Delaware part [of the road] 2 days, had the misfortune of losing our Baggage Waggon [while] fording the River ... From Delaware [we] marched and encamped on the Schuylkill within 5 miles of Philadelphia where we [stayed] until [the] 8th Augt when we marched again. We are now stopt about 20 miles from Philadel^a, near Newtown ...[95]

Captain Chilton did not continue his diary until 23 August 1777.[96]

Saturday, 23 August. Up and out before sunrise, the regiment camped five or six miles from Philadelphia, where they received orders "for every Man to have clean clothes ready for the morning, the arms to be furbished & bright."

Sunday, 24 August. The entire army was on the march by four in the morning. Just as they entered Philadelphia, a rain storm broke. They crossed the Schuylkill River on a floating bridge and made it down the River to Darby, a small town on a river navigable only be small craft.

Monday 25 August. The regiment again was up early and marched eight miles to Chester and from there to Marcus Hook. They camped within two and a half miles of Wilmington, Delaware. Captain Chilton commented on the good quality of the land, meadows and cattle there.

Tuesday, 26 August. The army marched through Wilmington two miles to the northwest, where they heard that the British had landed about 3000 troops the night before, within twelve miles of the American army, taking possession of Iron Hill. The Americans remained where they were for a day, enduring more rain.

Thursday, 28 August. Generals Stevens and Greens' division returned to Brandywine, a small town consisting of Mills and Taverns. "A navigable Creek runs up to the Mills [and] the Water is brought in canals from Brandywine Creek." On this day, Captain Chilton was Captain of the rear guard where he observed Colonel Hollingsworth come by the rear guard, wounded in the cheek and neck. After stopping for an hour or two, Chilton marched again, stopping just after sunset where the rear guard was relieved. Chilton returned to the regiment which lay in the woods without pitching tents.

Friday 29 August. The 3rd Virginia moved about a half mile and pitched their tents to dry them at four in the afternoon; They moved on another three miles to the east where they pitched their tents, now dry, and stayed there for the night.

Saturday, 30 August. Captain Chilton was made officer of the day. The regiment stayed in place through the weekend.

Sunday, 31 August. Captain Chilton identified the camp as being in "Christeen Hundred." Colonel Heth, who had been out with the advance detachment, came in for provisions.

September 1777: According to Captain Chilton's diary, the 3rd Virginia, along with the rest of the Army, now held itself in readiness for an expected battle with the British. His diary ended September 9th, two days before his death at Brandywine.

Monday 1 September. Rain prevented a detachment from moving out to observe the enemy.

Tuesday, 2 September. Captain John Ashby, Lieutenant William White,[97] and Lieutenant Val Peyton all set out, on a "close cloudy morn^g" with the detachment under Colonel Heth.

Wednesday, 3 September. The enemy was met by an advanced party under the command of Colonel Crawford in a "pretty hot" engagement. General Stephen's division, under whom the 3rd Virginia served, was sent to their alarm posts and stayed there. When they returned to camp, they pitched their tents and "slept heartily."

Thursday, 4 September. Captain Chilton was on guard duty at a bridge over the Red Clay Creek, along with two subalterns, two sergeants, two corporals and forty privates, commenting that it was "a peaceable" guard that night. Troops from Pennsylvania and Ensign Cornelius Westfall of the 8th Virginia regiment,[98] both in General Scott's Brigade, shared guard duty with Captain Chilton.

Friday, 5 September. Early in the morning more troops came in, laden with entrenching tools and wagons loaded with axes. These men felled trees and, forming a long line, made them into a hedge.[99] In the afternoon, Sullivan's division took possession of these lines. That night Sullivan's men were relieved by Captain Stephen Ashby.

Saturday, 6 September. The 3rd Virginia marched with their division commander, General Stephens and camped near Newport where they expected an attack by the British early on Sunday morning.

Sunday, 7 September. "Every necessary order was given to be in readiness."

Monday, 8 September. "The enemy approached as near as Newark. We all lay at our alarm posts."

Tuesday, 9 September. General Stephen's division, which included the 3rd Virginia, received orders to march at two in the morning. The division took the road from Newport to Wilmington, then crossed Brandywine Creek and encamped on the heights of the Creek.

September 1777: The 3rd Virginia took part in the Battle of Brandywine, Pennsylvania September 11, 1777. The regiment remained in Pennsylvania through out the month with Washington's main army.

11 September 1777. Battle of Brandywine.
14 September 1777. Americans retreated to Germantown.[100]
15 September 1777. Washington's army arrived at White Horse, where he placed his soldiers squarely between the British and the Schuylkill fords.[101]
16 September 1777. The Battle of the Clouds involved Pennsylvania troops and heavy rain eventually caused the Americans to retreat.[102] With rain coming down in torrents, miring cannons in mud and obscuring the field of view, the Americans retreated, pulling back to Yellow Springs, thus leaving the upper fords of the Schuylkill to the British. With all the rain, the Americans faced enormous problems in supply: their cartridge boxes became waterlogged, making their ammunition useless, cannon had to be hauled in relays in deep mud, and troops were tired and hungry, having marched for nearly twelve hours.[103] They made camp at Yellow Springs.
18 September 1777. The bulk of the American army, including the 3rd Virginia, was at Reading Furnace, in northern Chester County, Pennsylvania.
19 September 1777. The 3rd Virginia was on the move with Washington's main army, crossing the rain-swollen Schuylkill River at Parker's Ford.
20 September 1777. The American army rested for a few hours on the eastern banks of the Schuylkill and then were on the move again. They pressed forward to occupy a position stretching from the river to Swedes Ford. The line was nearly eight miles long. Washington had nearly 10,000 troops along the river to block any British advance over the Schuylkill.[104]
21 September 1777. **Paoli Massacre** – General Wayne's Pennsylvania forces had been left behind on the 19th September to harass the British. Unfortunately his plans to ambush the British two miles southwest of Paoli Tavern became known to the enemy and his forces were massacred.[105] Wayne and some of his troops escaped, retreating to the Cross Roads.[106] The 3rd Virginia was not involved in this battle as they were with Washington's army on the east bank of the Schuylkill.
23 September 1777. By this date, Washington had moved his army back from the Schuylkill towards Reading, fearing a British attack on his flanks and the capture of military stores at Reading. On the 23rd September he had reached Pottsgrove, Pennsylvania, leaving only a small picket of forces to keep an eye on the Hessians. This guard consisted of Pennsylvania militia who fled when approached by the Hessians, thus leaving Philadelphia open to the British. The British captured the stores at Valley Forge and on September 26th marched triumphantly into Philadelphia.[107]
28 September 1777. The American army shifted its camp to Pennypacker Mills, about 30 miles southwest of Philadelphia. Over the next several days, the main army, including the 3rd Virginia, inched closer and closer to the British camp at Germantown.[108]

October 1777: The 3rd Virginia took part in the Battle of Germantown in early October 1777 and was still in Pennsylvania a little more than two weeks later according to David Griffith, the Surgeon and Chaplain of the regiment.[109] Meanwhile the riflemen selected from the 3rd Virginia by Colonel Daniel Morgan were busy at Saratoga hemming in the British under General John Burgoyne.

On 19 October 1777 David Griffith wrote his wife Hannah from camp in North Wales. This letter gave details of the victory at Saratoga and the storming of Fort Montgomery by the British.[110]

November 1777; The 3rd Virginia, as part of Woodford's Brigade, were part of the Continental Army in Pennsylvania on November 3rd and encamped at White Marsh on November 10th. They remained at White Marsh through the rest of November. Meanwhile, Morgan's rifle unit rejoined the Continental army in Pennsylvania during the second week of November.

It was possible to follow the 3rd Virginia through the returns of the Army from November 1777 to September 1778. On 3 November 1777, Woodford's Brigade, consisting of the 3rd, 7th, 11th, and 15th Virginia and the Fauquier County, Virginia Militia; the brigade and attached militia were in Pennsylvania with the main army.

This November brigade return included the totals for the four regiments. A colonel, four lieutenant colonels, two majors, eighteen captains, thirty-seven lieutenants, and twenty-two ensigns made up the commissioned officers. Two chaplains, five adjutants, five quarter masters, four surgeons, and one surgeon's mate made up the staff while there were ninety-five Sergeants and thirty-two drum and fife in the regiment.

The rank and file, present and fit for duty, totaled 806 men. Eighty-six of them were sick and present and 406 were sick and absent. Twenty-six men were on furlough and 234 were on command. The brigade totaled 1558 men and officers. One private had since joined and it was noted that the Woodford's unit "include[d] Farquhar Militia, amounting to 99 privates fit for duty."[111]

The 10 November 1777 return for Woodford's brigade, showed much lower numbers. The brigade reported a colonel, a lieutenant colonel, a major, five captains, eleven lieutenants and five ensigns. An adjutant, a quartermaster, a paymaster, a chaplain, and surgeon and a surgeon's mate made up the staff while nineteen sergeants and seven drum and fifes made up the non-commissioned officers.

There were 188 rank and file, present and fit for duty. Twenty-nine were sick and present; sixty were sick and absent. One man was on furlough and fifty two were on command. The regiment numbered 300 men and officers. There were no men who had died or who had been discharged. One man had deserted and twenty two privates had lately joined.

Under the comments for this return, the following note was made: "In the 3rd Virginia Regiment, [there are] 24 men wanting clothes, [and] unfit for duty." In the 11th Virginia, there were four sergeants and thirty-four men wanting cloths and unfit for duty. In the 15th Virginia, two sergeants, two drum and fife and thirty privates needed clothes and blankets and were thus unfit for duty even though they were returned as being fit for duty.[112]

It is clear from this return that the Brigade was not well clothed or supplied which did not bode well when winter arrived.

On 18 November 1777, Colonel Daniel Morgan and his elite rifle unit rejoined the main army under Washington.[113] The men from the 3rd Virginia remained with Morgan and did not rejoin their old companies although they continued to be carried on paper in their 3rd Virginia companies.[114]

December 1777: Woodford's Brigade remained at White Marsh and then moved into winter quarters at Valley Forge.

On 3 December 1777, General Woodford's brigade made a general return of forces under his command. His commissioned officers included a colonel, three lieutenant colonels, two majors, eighteen captains, twenty-eight lieutenants, and sixteen ensigns. His staff consisted of four adjutants, a quartermaster, and a paymaster, two chaplains, four surgeons, and a surgeon's mate.

His non-comms consisted of seventy-nine sergeants and thirty four drum and fife. There were 726 rank and file present, fit for duty. Eighty-four men were sick and present and 329 were sick and absent. Twenty-nine men were on furlough and 229 were on command. His brigade totaled 1397 men and officers.

It was noted that "among those returned fit for duty are included several hundred really unfit form the want of shoes and clothing and some returned sick, present are only unfit for duty as wanting clothing and shoes ..."[115] It is obvious from this return that the clothing and supply situation in the Brigade had not improved. Indeed, it had worsened dramatically.

By 22 December 1777, the brigade had moved into winter quarters at Valley Forge. This return reported the brigade's commissioned officers as two lieutenant colonels, two majors, nine captains, twenty lieutenants and two ensigns. Two adjutants, four quartermasters, two paymasters, two chaplains, four surgeons, and a surgeon's mate made up the brigade staff.

Sixty-eight sergeants and twenty-one drum and fife made up the non-comms. There were 319 rank and file, present and fit for duty while eighty-five were sick and present and 333 were sick and absent. There were 212 men on furlough and 179 on command. Those unfit for want of clothes numbered 180. The brigade had a total of 1308 men and officers present.[116]

There can be no doubt that the 333 men who were sick and absent were those without proper clothing, shoes or blankets. While the Brigade numbered 1308 men, on paper, it is doubtful that the 319 rank and file present and fit for duty could have been anywhere near battle-ready.

The next day, on 23 December, the Brigade filed a field return showing forty-four Sergeants (out of sixty eight the day before) and eleven drum and fife, (out of twenty-one the previous day) were actually fit for duty. Only 149 privates were ready while another 257 were unfit, needing cloths and shoes. There were 261 men on guard and on detached duty.[117]

On New Year's Eve, 1777, General Woodford filed his last return for December. A lieutenant colonel, a major, four captains, two lieutenants and three ensigns made up his commissioned officers. A quartermaster, paymaster, chaplain, surgeon, and surgeon's mate were his staff while only seven sergeants and one drum and fife made up his non-commissioned officers.

Only forty-seven rank and file were present and fit for duty. Sixteen were sick and present; fifty-nine were sick and absent. Fifty-three men were on furlough and forty were on command. One man had died, one had deserted and one had been discharged. There were seventy men unfit for duty for want of clothes and shoes. "Some brigades have distinguished the men unfit for duty from the want of cloathes, from the sick, present, others include them, with the sick, present and some have ret'd all those fit for duty who were well, although barefooted..."[118]

January to 30 May 1778: Weekly, monthly and General Returns revealed that General Woodford's Brigade stayed at Valley Forge,[119] for the most part ill-clothed and ill-supplied— without sufficient food, blankets, clothes or shoes.

Included here are the returns that show the physical and mental effects of the winter on the men in the brigade. These returns show that the death rate was mounting in the brigade as the winter no doubt began to take its toll on the men's strength, general health, morale and will.

The 12 January 1778 return revealed only 199 men present and fit for duty. Three hundred twenty-seven men were sick and absent, 210 on furlough, 155 on command. There were 276 men unfit for duty for want of shoes and clothes. Fourteen had died. Five were discharged and two men had deserted since the last return.[120]

The 19 January 1778 return showed 201 present, and fit for duty. Sixty-four were sick and present, 301 were sick and absent. There were 212 men on furlough and 154 on command. Six were dead. Three deserted. However, thirty-three privates had joined since the brigade since the 12 January 1778 return.[121]

The 24 January 1778 return showed 217 present and fit for duty. Sixty-nine men were sick and present and 290 were sick and absent. Another 209 were on furlough and 167 were on command. Two hundred seventy-three men were unfit for duty for want of shoes and other clothes. Nine men had died and one had deserted.

Twenty three sergeants, two drum and fife and 329 rank and file were due for discharge from the army. This return noted that the terms of service of the Virginia troops would expire at different times between 24 January and the middle of March 1778.[122] These men were those who enlisted in the February and March 1776 for two years. There is not much doubt that the organization of the 3rd Virginia, along with the other regiments comprising this Brigade, would be dramatically altered after March. New men and non-comms would take their place and the brigade would lose their seasoned veteran and non-commissioned officers.

The last January return for the brigade was filed on 31 January 1778. Only 147 rank and file were present and fit for duty. Ninety were sick and present while 277 were sick and absent. Two hundred eight men were on furlough and 199 were on command. Two hundred eighty-two men were unfit for duty for want of shoes and clothes. Another six had died since the week before. Seventeen had been discharged, indicating that the original enlistees were returning home. No sergeants, rank and file or drum and fife had joined the brigade since the last return on 24 January 1778.[123]

The death toll continued to mount throughout February as returns were made on 9 February, 14 February, 21 February, and 29 February 1778. By the end of the month, the brigade showed a total of forty-eight dead, twenty having died on the leap year date of 29 February 1778. Fifteen men had deserted during February 1778. Discharges for the month totaled 586 with 273 discharged on the last day of February.[124]

In March, returns were filed on 7 March, 14 March, 21 March, and 30 March 1778. The death toll in this month had decreased somewhat to thirty-two dead. Sixteen men had deserted, showing an increase of one. One hundred sixty-six more men had been discharged. Only five rank and file had joined since February. During the month, the men unfit for duty for want of clothing and shoes varied from a high of 198 on 7 March 1778 to 141 wanting clothes on the 14 March 1778 return and back up to 157 in need of cloths on the 21March return. By the end of March, the number had dropped to 124.[125]

In April, returns were filed on 4 April, 11 April, 18 April, and 25 April, 1778. The death toll continued to decrease, with twenty-three reported dead. Desertions also decreased from the March returns to five. Only two were discharged. One hundred fifteen men needed clothes in the 4 April 1778 return which dropped to seventy six on the 11April 1778 return.[126] These returns probably reflected a change in the weather as temperatures warmed up and supplies of clothing began to arrive.

May returns were reported on 2 May, 9 May, 16 May, 23 May, and 30 May 1778. The dead had increased from twenty-three in April to seventy five by the end of May. Desertions were up from five in April to twenty-five in May. In addition twenty-three men had been discharged. The brigade began to show some success in recruiting non-comms and rank and file as nine sergeants, sixteen drum and fife, and 331 rank and file had joined the regiment in May.[127] However, the 2 May 1778 return showed that the brigade wanted forty-two sergeants, thirty-three drum and fife and 1550 rank and file to bring the regiment up to full strength.[128]

The 30 May 1778 return for Woodford's brigade commented that "23 Rank & File [were] killed and missing since the last [return]. 1263 Rank & File [were] unfit for duty for want of arms, clothing and Accoutrements."[129]

While Washington had ordered harassing parties out to harry the British and isolate Philadelphia,[130] the only action that might account for the above comment on the May 30th return of Woodford's brigade was the skirmish at Barren Hill on May 18th under Lafayette.[131] Lafayette's division consisted of the Virginia brigades of Woodford and Scott and the North Carolina brigades.[132]

June 1778: The British evacuated Philadelphia, leaving it in American hands in mid June; Washington left Valley Forge to pursue the British, crossing the Delaware at Coryell's Ferry, north of Trenton and moving on to halt briefly within five miles of Princeton. The Americans finally caught up and engaged the British, in the last week of June, at Monmouth Courthouse.

On 6 June 1778, William Woodford filed a return of his brigade from an unidentified place. This June return may have shown some of the effects of the skirmish at Barren Hill, although he did not report anyone missing; he did note seven deaths in the return.

The brigade still had no colonels, although he returned two lieutenant colonels, a major, twelve captains, twenty-eight lieutenants, and seven ensigns as his commissioned officers.

Four adjutants, three quartermasters, three paymasters, two chaplains, three surgeons, and two surgeon's mates made up his field staff. Four sergeant majors, and four quartermaster sergeants, along with two drum majors and a fife major, fifty five sergeants, and twenty-four s drum and fife comprised his non-comms.

Four hundred seventy-two of his rank and file were present, fit for duty; 276 were sick and present and ninety-two were sick and absent. He reported twenty men on furlough and 171 on command. The brigade totaled 1031 men and officers. He reported five desertions. He needed forty sergeants, twenty-nine drum and fife, and 1529 rank and file to bring his brigade to full strength. In addition, he noted 805 men "destitute of clothes and necessaries [were] included [among those] 'fit for duty.' "[133]

His brigade numbers, shown above, on paper looked all right although in actuality the regiments in his brigade were far from full strength and appeared to be plagued still from a lack of clothes and accoutrements.

15 June 1778. Washington learned of the British intentions to evacuate Philadelphia.

17 June 1778. General Washington met with his Generals, including Woodford and Lafayette to discuss the impending British evacuation. He ordered a detachment under Colonel Henry Jackson to take possession of the city.[134] The order of march into Philadelphia was determined as early as June 1st and Lafayette's 3rd division was to be part of the march. Woodford's brigade, which included the 3rd, 7th, 11th, and 15th Virginia, was part of this division.[135]

20 June to 23 June 1778. Washington left Valley Forge and forded the Delaware at Coryell's Ferry north of Trenton. 11,000 soldiers eventually crossed the river.

24 June to 25 June 1778. The American army halted at Hopewell, five miles from Princeton while Washington and his generals met to determine a course of action against the British. It did not appear that Lafayette was present at this counsel as he wrote Washington urging aggressive action against the redcoats.

Washington responded by sending Daniel Morgan and his rifle regiment and Charles Scott after the British. At the same time he added the advance corps under Maxwell, Morgan, Scott, and Anthony Wayne to Lafayette's command.[136]

28 June 1778. Woodford's Brigade took part in the Battle of Monmouth Courthouse.[137]

July 1778: The American Army remained in New Jersey, at New Brunswick and Paramus until mid July when Woodford's brigade stayed behind; the brigade rejoined the main Army at White Plains, New York at the end of July.

General Woodford filed returns for his brigade on 4 July and 12 July 1778 from New Brunswick and Paramus and on 25 July 1778 from White Plains.

His 4 July 1778 return showed a total of 1023 men and officers present in his brigade. Four hundred eighty-five of his rank and file were present, fit for duty while eighteen were sick and present and 324 were sick and absent. There were no deaths or desertions on this return, suggesting that the brigade did not lose anyone immediately after Monmouth. Thirteen men were on furlough and 183 were on command. His commissioned officers comprised three lieutenant colonels, two majors, eleven captains, twenty-four lieutenants, and eleven ensigns.

These numbers were up from his 6 June 1778 return and there were no comments about a lack of clothes or weapons. He was able to increase his commissioned officers, his field staff and his non-comms. While more men were sick and absent in July, those who were sick and present in July showed a remarkable decrease.[138]

General Woodford's 12 July 1778 return showed 1009 men and officers present with two dead, one desertion and three discharges. He had only one lieutenant colonel and no majors, seven captains, and twelve lieutenants. His also showed a decrease of two ensigns reported the week before. Adjustments were also made in his field staff as he lost an adjutant, a quartermaster, a paymaster, and a surgeon's mate relative to the 4 July 1778 return.

He also lost a sergeant major, a drum major, and five sergeants among his non-comms. He showed an increase in the number of rank and file to 504 fit for duty, with the same number, eighteen, sick and present as found in the earlier return. His number of sick and absent men increased from 324 on the 4 July 1778 return to 369 on this return. Eleven men were on furlough versus the thirteen reported the previous week and 107 were on command, a decrease from the 183 in the earlier return. Two new rank and file joined the brigade. There were no numbers for men or officers to bring his brigade to full strength. The comments noted that his brigade was left at Paramus.[139]

By the time General Woodford filed his 25 July 1778 return, he had rejoined the Continental Army at White Plains. His brigade then numbered 1214 officers and men. He had 649 rank and file present, fit for duty. He still had a large number of sick and absent men—369 of them and a slight increase in men who were sick and present: thirty-six.

Nine men were on furlough and 151 were on command. The brigade continued to be led by two lieutenant colonels. A major and fourteen captains (an increase from his July 12th return) twenty-three lieutenants and twelve ensigns completed his commissioned officers. This part of the return also showed an increase over his earlier July report. He once again had four paymasters and now had three fife majors, seventy-four sergeants and thirty-three drum and fife. Three rank and file joined the brigade while one man was discharged. There were no deaths or desertions reported in this return.[140]

August to September 1778: Woodford's Brigade remained at White Plains throughout August and September. The 3rd Virginia was reorganized in mid September and completed the transition begun in the spring into a regiment quite different from the one organized in February and March 1776.

General Woodford filed five returns in August, 1778 on 1 August, 9 August, 15 August, 22 August, and the 30 August. A synopsis of these returns show that the number of men and officers in the brigade generally increased from 1215 men on the 1 August 1778 return to 1263 men on the 30 August 1778 return.

By the end of August, twenty men had been reported dead, sixteen men had been discharged and twelve men had deserted. Six men had transferred out of the brigade while a lieutenant colonel had been promoted to colonel by 15 August 1778. Twenty-two new recruits joined the brigade in August. The men fit for duty increased from 625 on 1 August 1778 to 673 by 30 August 1778. The amount of men sick and present went from sixty at the beginning of August to 136 by the end of the month. At the same time, the number of men sick and absent decreased from 314 at the beginning of the month to 239 by the end of August. Eight men were on furlough for the first two weeks in the month and then decreased to seven men for the remaining returns. There were 208 men on command at the beginning of August, increasing to a high of 282 men on the 15 August return and then decreasing to 203 by the end of the month.[141]

These August returns show that the brigade's numbers were more stable although the men sick and present and sick and absent showed fluctuations as some of the rank and file returned to health and other became sick. The brigade showed a slight increase in new recruits.

There were just two September 1778 returns filed for the brigade: one filed on 5 September and the other on 12 September.[142] The reorganization of the Virginia line took place two days later on 14 September 1778. The 3rd Virginia was combined with the 5th Virginia, thus dramatically changing the composition of the regiment.[143]

These two returns in early September before the reorganization of the Virginia line offer the last glimpse of the 3rd Virginia before its identity altered dramatically. The number of men and officers present at the beginning of September decreased by six by 12 September 1778, from 1240 to 1234. Woodford reported twenty-one dead in these two returns, along with five desertions and six discharges. He gained four new recruits among his rank and file. In the first week in September, there were 680 men fit for duty; by the second week there were 691, an increase of eleven men. Likewise, 144 men were sick and present on 5 September, increasing by twelve men to 156 a week later. His sick and absent decreased from 213 to 190 in those first two weeks. There were only four men on furlough while the number of men on command decreased from 199 on the 5 September return to 193 on the 12 September 1777 return.[144]

CONCLUSIONS

There are four conclusions that may be drawn from tracking the regiment from its formation until the September 1778 reorganization at White Plains.

1) The primary record base has demonstrated the importance in tracking the whereabouts of a Continental Line Regiment. In this instance, there was an abundance of records that made it possible to trace the 3rd Virginia's whereabouts on a consistent basis from its formation in December 1776 until its reorganization in September 1778.

2) Several points emerged that underscored the trials, tribulations, endurance and perseverance of the regiment when tracing its locations from December 1776 to September 1778:

> Small pox was so widespread in American army the winter months of January through March 1777 that it was necessary to inoculate regiments against a further onslaught of the disease. Its prevalence may explain why so many men in John Peyton's company died in January and February 1777. There were other reasons as well that could explain his company's large loss of men—some could have died of wounds from Princeton, other could have died from the cumulative effects of winter weather and lack of provisions needed for life in a winter army camp.

> The returns from winter encampment at Valley Forge from December 1777 to May 1778 revealed that Woodford's brigade, of which the 3rd Virginia was a part, was without the most basic necessities of life—clothes, shoes, blankets, tents.

> It is not surprising, once these figures are known, that so many men in William Woodford's brigade died or deserted. One wonders where the brigades would have been without Baron von Steuben and his drill tactics which were given credit for turning this ragtag Army into a disciplined fighting force.

3) By the beginning of April 1778, the men who had first enlisted in the 3rd Virginia in February and March 1776 had been discharged. The men and non-comms that were left were those who had joined the army after August 1777. Some of these new enlistees fought at Brandywine and Germantown so there was at least a mix of men who were battle hardened from the Philadelphia campaign in 1777 to go along with the new recruits who were to join after March 1778.

4) Thus the transition to entirely new 3rd Virginia began in March and was finally completed six months later in the September 1778 reorganization. In that reorganization, the 3rd and the 5th Virginia were combined. While there were still some 3rd Virginia Captains still around from the 1776–1777 campaigns, the merging of these regiments so distorted the identity of the old 3rd Virginia that it was, for all intents and purposes, a completely new regiment.

END NOTES
CHAPTER 3
TRACKING THE 3RD VIRGINIA

1. For David Griffith's letters to his wife Hannah, see Virginia Historical Society, Mss 2G 8755a1 and Mss 2G 8755b *Letters &c of David Griffith, 1776–1778* at the Virginia Historical Society, Richmond, Virginia.
2. For John Chilton's Letters, see Virginia Historical Society, Mss 2c 4395a1, *John Chilton Letters* and Mss K 2694 a 1-11, *John Chilton Letters* from the *Keith Family Papers*, VHS, Richmond.
3. John Chilton's diary is transcribed in L.G. Tyler, ed. "Diary of John Chilton, 3rd Virginia Regiment" *Tyler's Quarterly Historical and Genealogical Magazine* (Richmond: Richmond Press, 1931), XII: 283–289. Hereafter "Diary of John Chilton, *Tyler's Quarterly*, XII: 283–289. Diary entries are also found in Cecere, Appendix II, 113–123.
4. University of Virginia, *Papers of the Wallace Family 1750–1888*, Accession 38150, Albert H. Small Special Collections Library, University of Virginia, Charlottesville.
5. Library of Virginia, *George Weedon Papers, 1776–1789*, Accession 22954a, Personal Papers Collection, The Library of Virginia, Richmond. Hereafter, Library of Virginia, *George Weedon Papers*.
6. There are several letters from members of Congress to George Weedon in *Letters* 5: 34, 78. See also *JCC* 5: 649, 711 for Congressional orders to Colonel Weedon to move his regiment in August 1776.
7. The selection of field staff for the 3rd Virginia Regiment occurred 12 January 1776 and was published in the *Virginia Gazette*. See Colonial Williamsburg Foundation, "Selection of Officers for the 3rd Virginia," *Virginia Gazette*, (Pinkney) 13 January 1776, 2, col. 3 (http://research.history.org). In August 1776, the 3rd Virginia was ordered to New York and had "already gone forward." See Colonial Williamsburg Foundation, "3rd Virginia Ordered to New York," *Virginia Gazette* (Purdie), 9 August 1776, 3, col. 2 (http://research.history.org).
8. See NARA, no. 33, 36, 44, 45. September to December 1776, *Colonel Weedon's Returns*, M246 MR 137 *Returns of The Army*. See also Wright, 285.
9. *JCC*, December 28, 1775, 2: 463, www.memory.loc.gov See also *Letters*, 2: 533.
10. Colonial Williamsburg Foundation, "Officers Chosen for the 3rd Virginia," *Virginia Gazette* (Purdie), 12 January 1776, 3, col. 2 (http://research.history.org). See also *Virginia Gazette* (Dixon), 12 January 1776, 3, col. 2.
11. Sanchez-Saavedra, 39.
12. Ibid.
13. Heitman, 438.
14. Sanchez-Saavedra, 39.
15. *JCC* 5: 863-864.
16. Ibid. 5., 418, 420.
17. Ibid. 5., 424.
18. Wright, 283.
19. *JCC* 5: 502-503.
20. Ibid. 5: 649.
21. VHS, *David Griffith to his wife Hannah*, 2 July 1776, Mss 2G8755b *Letters of David Griffith*, VHS, Richmond, Virginia.
22. See *JCC* 5: 595; 596; 597 ff. Although the 3rd Virginia was not specifically identified here, Gott and Russell stated that the 3rd Virginia was the first regiment to march northward and that the 1st Virginia, commanded by Colonel Isaac Reade left Williamsburg about two weeks after the departure of the 3rd Virginia.
23. Gott and Russell, 109.
24. Ibid., 111.
25. VHS, *David Griffith to Major Levin Powell*, 5 August 1776, Mss2G8755b, *Letters of David Griffith*.
26. *Letters* 5: 21-22.
27. Ibid. 5: 34.
28. *JCC* 5: 711.
29. *Letters* 5: 78.
30. Ibid. A footnote in this letter stated that George Weedon was in command of the 3rd Virginia Battalion and goes on to say that "At the time this letter was written Hancock was uncertain about the identity of the Virginia unit that was on the march to New Jersey. This uncertainty stemmed from the fact that on August 22 Congress had read a letter from Gen. Andrew Lewis stating that he had ordered the 2nd and 3rd Virginia Battalions to proceed to New Jersey, but saying that the 3rd "may be expected before the other" and describing Weedon as commander of the 3rd only "for the present ... " See also *JCC* 5: 696.
31. Gott and Russell, 111.

32. Heitman, 574. Heitman stated that Captain Washington was wounded at the Battle of Long Island. For a differing view, see Haller, 11. This author states unequivocally that "the 3rd Virginia missed the Battle of Long Island ..." See also Haller, 13. "William [Washington] may well have been wounded at the Battle of Harlem Heights, and not, as some historian have claimed, in the previous Battle of Long Island. The 3rd Virginia was not in the American order of battle until September 10, *after* the August Battle of Long Island." For the historians who subscribed to Captain Washington's being wounded at Long Island, see Haller, note 14, 24.

33. NARA, *Officers of the 3rd Virginia (1776)* and *Compiled Service Records*, 3rd Virginia.

34. VHS, *Captain John Chilton to Joseph Blackwell*, 13 September 1776, MSS2c 4395a1, *Keith Family Papers*, Virginia Historical Society, Richmond, Virginia. Hereafter, VHS, *Keith Family Papers*, VHS, Richmond.

35. University of Virginia, *G. B. Wallace to his brother Michael Wallace*, 15 September 1776, Accession # 38150 *Papers of the Wallace Family 1750–1888*, Albert M. Small Special Collections, University of Virginia, Charlottesville, Va. Hereafter, University of Virginia, *Papers of the Wallace Family*.

36. See Chapter 2 for details of these September through November 1776 returns of the 3rd Virginia.

37. See note 34 above.

38. NARA, no. 33. 21 September 1776, *Return of 3rd Virginia at King's Bridge under Colonel Weedon*, M 246 MR 137 *Returns of the Army*.

39. Gott and Russell, 111–112.

39a. NARA, *John Coppage's Pension* S 39363, M 804 MR 652.

40. See note 34 above.

41. University of Virginia, *G.B. Wallace to his brother Michael Wallace*, 28 September 1776, Accession 38150, *Papers of the Wallace Family*.

42. NARA, no. 42, 30. September 1776, *General Return of the Army at Harlem Heights*, Returns of the Army.

43. Ibid., no. 45. 5 October 1776, *Weekly Returns of Regiments under General Washington at Harlem Heights*.

44. NARA, *William Berry's Pension* S 39187, M 804, MR 228.

45. Ibid., *David Baker's Pension* W 1802, M 804 MR 115.

46. Ibid., *Spencer Anderson's Pension* S 37672, M 804 MR 58.

47. Ibid., *Edward Abbey's Pension* S 34621, M 804 MR 1.

48. Colonial Williamsburg Foundation, "Battle of White Plains described," *Virginia Gazette* (Purdie) 15 November 1776, 2, cols 1 & 2 (http://research.history.org).

49. Wright, 285. See also Lesser, 32, 37, 48.

50. Colonial Williamsburg Foundation, "Extract of a letter from Philadelphia, November 9th," *Virginia Gazette* (Dixon) 29 November 1776, 3, col. 2 (http://research.history.org).

51. VHS, *Captain John Chilton to his Brother Charles Chilton*, 20 November 1776, *Keith Family Papers*, Mss K 2694 a 1-11, VHS, Richmond, Virginia.

52. Ibid.

53. NARA, no. 36. 1 December 1776, *Colonel Weedon's Regiment, Return of the Army at Trenton*, Returns of the Army.

54. John Buchanan, *The Road to Valley Forge* (New York: John Wiley & Sons, Inc, 2004), 139.

55. Ibid., 145.

56. Ibid., 146.

57. VHS, *David Griffith to his wife Hannah*, 8 December 1776, Mss 2 G 8755b, *Letters &c of David Griffith*, VHS, Richmond.

58. Buchanan, 145.

59. NARA, 22, December 1776, *Colonel Weedon's Regiment under General Washington in Pennsylvania*.

60. Library of Virginia, *George Weedon to John Page*, 29 December 1776, Accession 22954a, *George Weedon Papers*, Library of Virginia, Richmond, Virginia. Hereafter, LVA ... *George Weedon Papers*. See Chapter 4 for details of this battle.

61. NARA, *David Baker's Pension* W 1802, M 804 MR 115.

62. Ibid.

63. "Diary of John Chilton," *Tyler's Quarterly*, XII: 283–289.

64. Colonial Williamsburg Foundation, "Hessian Prisoners delivered to Philadelphia," *Virginia Gazette* (Purdie) 24 January 1777, 1, col. 2 (http://research.history.org).

65. Electronic Text Center, University of Virginia, *George Washington to George Weedon*, Morristown, 9 January 1777, *Writings of George Washington from the Original Manuscript Sources* (Fitzpatrick), 6, pg. n.g (http://www.etext.virginia.edu). Hereafter University of Virginia, *WW;* For the digital image of this letter, see the Library of Congress, *George Washington to George Weedon*, 9 January 1777, image 664, *George Washington Papers at the Library of Congress, 1741–1799 Series 4, General Correspondence 1697–1799* (www.memory.loc.gov).

66. "Diary of John Chilton," *Tyler's Quarterly*, XII: 283–289.

67. Colonial Williamsburg Foundation, "An Extract of a Letter from Philadelphia, January 17th," *Virginia Gazette* (Dixon) 31 January 1777, 6, col. 2; 7, col. 1(http://research.history.org).
68. "Diary of John Chilton," *Tyler's Quarterly*, XII: 283–289.
69. Ibid.
70. Ibid.
71. Ibid.
72. University of Virginia, *George Washington to Brigadier General George Weedon*, Headquarters, Morris Town, 8 March 1777, *WW*, 7, pg n.g (http:www.etext.virginia.edu).
73. Ibid., *WW, George Washington to Dr. William Shippen, Jr,* Headquarters, Morristown, 26 March 1777.
74. Buchanan, 192. See also George F. Scheer & Hugh F. Rankin, *Rebels & Redcoats: The American Revolution Though the Eyes of Those Who Fought and Lived It* (New York: DaCapo Books, 1957), 215, 220.
75. Buchanan, 201.
76. Ibid.
77. Ibid., 201–202. This return was found in the volume 8 of the Papers of George Washington according to a footnote in this text. The return was *not* found in the General Returns of the Army on NARA's M 246 MR 137.
78. VHS, *Captain John Chilton to Major Martin Pickett & others from Hanover Township, New Jersey, March 19, 1777,* Mss K2694a1-11, *Keith Family Papers*.
79. University of Virginia, *George Washington to Brigadier General George Weedon*, Morristown, 27 March 1777, *WW*, 7, pg .n.g (www.etext.lib.virginia.edu).
80. Lesser, 45.
81. "Diary of John Chilton," *Tyler's Quarterly*, XII: 283–289.
82. Don Higginbotham, *The War of American Independence: Military Attitudes, Policies & Practice 1763–1789* (Boston: Northeastern University Press, 1983), 181–182.
83. Cecere, 41.
84. Lesser, 47.
85. Ibid.
86. NARA, No 46. May 28, 1777, *General Return of Continental Forces in New Jersey*, M 246 MR 137, *Returns of the Army*.
87. University of Virginia, *George Washington to Brigadier General George Weedon*, from Morristown, 27 March 1777, *WW*, 7: pg n.g (http://www.etext.virginia.edu). John Thornton was promoted to Major of a regiment raised in Virginia by Colonel Thruston with the chance of being a Lieutenant Colonel if Angus McDonald refused the position. Captain Washington was promoted to be a major in Moylan's Light Dragoons.
88. NARA, 22 December 1776, *Return of Forces under General Washington in Pennsylvania,* M 246 MR 137 *Returns of the Army*.
89. LVA, *George Weedon to John Page*, 31 *May* 1777, Accession 22954a *George Weedon Papers.*
90. "Diary of John Chilton," *Tyler's Quarterly*, XII: 283–289.
91. Ibid. This entry is here to demonstrate the location of the 3rd Virginia in June. Morgan's men included riflemen from Captains Thornton and Ashby's rifle companies. See Chapters 7 for a description of Morgan's rifle regiment chosen from the 3rd Virginia regiment in June 1777.
92. Ibid.
93. Ibid. See also Cecere, 47–49.
94. "Diary of John Chilton," *Tyler's Quarterly*, XII: 283–289.
95. VHS, *Captain John Chilton to his Brother Charles Chilton in Fauquier,* Mss K2694a1-11, *Keith Family Papers.*
96. "Diary of John Chilton," *Tyler's Quarterly*, XII: 283–289.
97. Heitman, 588. William White was commissioned as a 1st Lieutenant in the 3rd Virginia on 21 March1776. He died 16 September 1777 from wounds suffered at Brandywine.
98. Ibid., 583.
99. Random House, *Webster's College Dictionary* (New York: Random House, 1991), 1033. See the second meaning of "plash".
100. Stephen R. Taafe, *The Philadelphia Campaign* (Lawrence, Kansas: University of Kansas Press, 2003), 77.
101. Ibid., 81.
102. Thomas J. McGuire, *The Battle of Paoli* (Mechanicsburg, Pennsylvania: Stackpole Books, 2000), 31–37.
103. Taafe, 82–84.
104. McGuire, 79–80.
105. Mark M. Boatner III, *Encyclopedia of the American Revolution* (Mechanicsburg, Pennsylvania: Stackpole Books, 2000), 31–37.
106. McGuire, 141.
107. *Ibid.*, 159–162.
108. *Ibid.*, 167.

109. *JCC:* 602–603. Dr. David Griffith was appointed both surgeon and chaplain to the 3rd Virginia in a Continental Congress resolution on 12 July 1776. He was appointed because he was "a person of uncommon merit, and there being very few surgeons of abilities who will enter into the army in that state; this appointment not to be drawn into precedent."

110. VHS, *David Griffith to his wife Hannah from Camp in North Wales,* 19 October 1777, Mss 2G 8755b, *Letters of David Griffith.*

111. NARA no. 51. 3 November 1777, *Return of Woodford's Brigade in Continental Army in Pennsylvania,* M 246 MR 137 *Returns of the Army.*

112. *Ibid,* no. 47. 10 November 1777, *Return of Woodford's Brigade in Continental Army at White Marsh.*

113. Boatner, 736.

114. See Chapter 7 for the names of Morgan's riflemen chosen from the 3rd Virginia rifle companies. See also the compiled service for the 3rd Virginia for further information about these men.

115. NARA, No 48. 3 December 1777, *Return of Woodford's Brigade in Continental Army at White Marsh,* M 246 MR 137, *Returns of the Army.*

116. Ibid., no. 49. 22 December 1777, *Return of Woodford's Brigade at Valley Forge.*

117. Ibid., no. 52. 23 December 1777, *Field Return, Woodford's Brigade.*

118. Ibid., no. 50. *Return of Woodford's Brigade at Valley Forge.*

119. Ibid., See no. 53–75, 89. *Returns of Woodford's Brigade.*

120. Ibid., no. 53. *Return of Woodford's Brigade.*

121. Ibid., no. 55. 19 January 1778 *Woodford's Brigade Return, Valley Forge.*

122. Ibid., no.54. 24 January 1778, *Woodford's Brigade Return, Valley Forge.*

123. Ibid., no. 89. 31 January 1778, *Woodford's Brigade Return, Valley Forge.*

124. Ibid., no. 56–58, 74. February 1778, *Woodford's Brigade Return, Valley Forge.*

125. Ibid., no. 59–61. March 1778, *Woodford's Brigade Return, Valley Forge.*

126. Ibid., no. 62–65. April 1778, *Woodford's Brigade Return, Valley Forge.*

127. Ibid., no. 66–70. May 1778, *Woodford's Brigade Return, Valley Forge.*

128. Ibid., no. 66. 2 May 1778, *Woodford's Brigade Return, Valley Forge.*

129. Ibid., no. 70. 30 May 1778, Woodford's *Brigade Return, Valley Forge.*

130. Taafe, 187–188.

131. Colonial Williamsburg Foundation, "Skirmish at Barren Hill," *Virginia Gazette* (Purdie), 12 June 1778, 2 col. 1 (http://research.history.org).

132. Ibid., "British Evacuation of Philadelphia," *Virginia Gazette* (Purdie), 19 June 1778, 2, col. 1 (http://research.history.org). Lafayette's division in the plan of march was the third division, comprising Woodford's Virginia Brigade, Scott's Virginia Brigade and the North Carolina Brigades.

133. NARA, no. 71. 6 June 1778, *Woodford's Brigade Return,* M 246 MR 137 *Returns of the Army.*

134. Taafe, 208.

135. Colonial Williamsburg Foundation, "British Evacuation of Philadelphia," *Virginia Gazette* (Purdie), 19 June 1778, 2, col. 1 (http://research.history.org).

136. Taafe, 208–209.

137. Ibid., 219–220.

138. NARA, no. 72. 4 July 1778, *Woodford's Brigade Return, New Brunswick.*

139. Ibid., no. 90. 12 July 1778, *Woodford's Brigade Return, Paramus.*

140. Ibid., no. 83. 25 July 1778, *Woodford's Brigade Return, Continental Army at White Plains.*

141. Ibid., no.76–77, 84–86. August 1778 *Woodford's Brigade Return as part of Continental Army at White Plains.*

142. Ibid., no. 87–88. September 1778 *Woodford's Brigade Return as part of Continental Army at White Plains.*

143. See Chapter 2 for a brief description of the composition of the 3rd Virginia after its reorganization on 14 September 1778.

144. NARA, no. 87–88. September 1778, *Woodford's Brigade Return as part of Continental Army at White Plains,* M 246 MR 137, *Returns of the Army.*

Chapter 4

Skirmishes & Battles: 1
September 1776 – April 1777

Historical Overview

The 3rd Virginia Regiment was involved in the skirmishes at Harlem Heights in September 1776, and New Rochelle and the Battle of White Plains in October 1776. While some of the men may have been stationed at Fort Washington, the regiment had left the fort before its surrender in November. The 3rd Virginia spent most of November with Washington's army as it retreated in New Jersey, first to Hackinsack [1] and later to Newark, and Brunswick.[2] The Americans reached Brunswick on noon on 29 November 1776. They stayed there for two days.

> The army was melting away. When it left Newark, Lieutenant James Monroe [of the 3rd Virginia] stood by the side of the road and counted the men as they passed by. He was shocked to discover that the army was reduced to three thousand men. At Brunswick it grew smaller, as many units came to the end of their service and went home.[3]

As part of Stirling's brigade, the regiment no doubt had the opportunity to observe the artillery battle between the American and British artillery as the Americans crossed the Raritan River. The army had made its way to Princeton by 6 December 1776. "Enoch Anderson, a captain in Haslet's Delaware Regiment which was part of Stirling's brigade, recalled that there were comfortable lodgings for the troops at the college. However, the army had shrunk, to "about twenty-five hundred men, and as their enlistments expired, they went off by the hundreds."[4]

The American forces took up positions along the Delaware River in December and later that month took part in the now-famous 26 December 1776 strike on Trenton. In January 1777, the 3rd Virginia took part in the assault on Princeton. After the successful attack on Princeton the army took up winter quarters at Morristown.

In the fall of 1777, the 3rd Virginia was heavily involved in the defense of Philadelphia. They took heavy losses at Brandywine in September and Germantown in October. A detachment of men from the rifle companies of Captains John Thornton and John Ashby had been chosen in June 1777 by Daniel Morgan for his independent light infantry and fought at Saratoga.

The regiment went with the main army into winter quarters in 1777–1778, at Valley Forge and suffered appallingly that winter from a lack of clothing and shoes and from desertions. They were further weakened when many of the non-commissioned officers and enlisted men were discharged in February and March 1778. Those remaining were those who had enlisted in 1777 and were scheduled to be discharged in the spring of 1779. It was these men with their officers who fought in the skirmish at Barren Hills under Lafayette in late May and Monmouth Court House in June.

A detailed account of these engagements as shown below, underscore the importance of the regiment's involvement and sacrifices into perspective vis-à-vis the larger picture of the war as fought in the middle states.

1776 Defense of New York
Harlem Heights, 16 September 1776

The 3rd Virginia was still on the march in late August and did not take part in the 28 August 1776 Battle of Long Island.[5] It was not until 13 September 1776 that all twelve captains in the regiment had assembled in New York as part of Colonel Weedon's brigade.[6]

The British Landing at Kip's Bay

The regiment barely had time to get settled in when, two days later, news came of the landing of British troops on the eastern shore of New York near Turtle Bay. Fortunately, Washington had already ordered the evacuation of New York City fearing that the British would pass from Long Island and land in the rear of the American army, thus cutting off all communication with the countryside. His assessment proved to be accurate. In a letter dated 17 September 1776, from his headquarters at Colonel Morris's house, Washington wrote Governor Cooke of Connecticut,

> [The evacuation] was set about with greatest industry and as to the sick was completely effected; but on *Sunday* morning before we had accomplished the removal of all our cannon, provision and baggage, [the British] sent three ships of war up the *North River*, whereby the water carriage was totally stopped, the ships anchoring not far above the city and about eleven o'clock those that were lying at *Turtle Bay* or rather below it in the *East River*, being six or seven in number, besides some transports, began and continued for some time a most severe and heavy cannonade, to scour the grounds and cover the landing of their troops.[7]

The Flight of Connecticut Militia

Washington described his "mortification" at the action of the Connecticut troops posted to stop the British advance in a letter to his brother John Augustine on 22 September 1776.

> I had gone the Evening before to the main body of our army which was posted about these Heights & the Plains of Harlem, where it seemed probable from the movements, and disposition of the Enemy they meant to land & make an attack the next morning. However, the event did not happen. Immediately on hearing the cannonade I rode with all possible expedition towards the place of landing, and where breast works had been thrown up to secure our men, & found the troops that had been posted there to my great surprize & Mortification, and those ordered to their support (consisting of eight regiments) notwithstanding the exertions of their Generals to form them, running away in the most shameful and disgraceful manner—I used every possible effort to rally them but to no purpose, & on the appearance of a small part of the enemy (not more than 60 or 70) they ran off without firing a single gun—Many of our heavy cannon wd [would] have fallen into the enemy's hands as they landed so soon, but this scandalous conduct occasioned a loss of many tents, baggage & camp equipage, which would have been easily secured had they made the least opposition.

Washington then went on to describe the retreat of the American forces in greater detail.

> The retreat was made with the loss of a few men only—We incamp'd and stare are on, the Heights of Harlem which are well calculated for defence against their approaches. On Monday morning they advanced in sight in several large bodys but attempted nothing of a general nature tho' there were smart skirmishes between their advancd parties and some detachments from our lines which I sent out—In these our Troops behaved well, putting the enemy to flight in open ground, and forcing them from posts they had seized two or three times—A sergeant who deserted from them says they had, as he was told, 89 wounded and missing besides slain, but other accts make the wounded much greater.
>
> Our loss in killed and wounded was about 60—but the greatest loss we sustaind was in the death of Lt Colo. Knolton, a brave and gallant officer—Majr Leitch of Weedons Regiment had three balls through his side, & behaved exceedingly well—he is in a fair way of recovery—Nothing material has happened since this—the Enemy, it is said, are bringing up their heavy cannon, so that we are to expect another attack soon—both by land & water, as we are upon the Hudson (or North River) at the place where we have attempted to stop the Navigation by sinking obstructions in the River & erecting batteries.[8]

Two Virginia views of the skirmish at Harlem Heights

Captain John Chilton described the skirmish at Harlem Heights from the 3rd Virginia's perspective in a letter dated 17 September 1776 to his friends in Fauquier.

> ... On Friday last the enemy's cannon played the greater part of the day from their forts & shipping. Friday night, we discovered a body of the enemy were landing on a small island in the East River, our Regimt was ordered to march at 3 o'clock in the morning, after marching, countermarching till about 7, then returned to our camps. Saturday, about midnight, we were ordered out and paraded as the day before, returned to camp. Sunday, we had scarce time to get our breakfast, being informed of the enemy's having taken possession of N. York, and our troops who were chiefly from Connecticut had shamefully abandoned their posts below us without exchanging a fire.
>
> Our soldiers were greatly exasperated and being drawn up for battle it was very discoverable that they were determined to fight to the last for their County, every soldier encouraging and animating his fellow; this night our Regt was on guard, posted on an eminence over against the enemy. Monday morn^g we marched down toward them and posted ourselves near a meadow having that in our front, [the] N^o River to our right, a body of woods in our rear & on our left, we discovered the enemy peeping from their heights over the fencings & rocks & running backwd & forwards, we did not alter our position.
>
> I believe they expected we should have ascended the hill to them, but finding us still, they imputed it to fear & came skipping down towards us in small parties, at the distance of about 250 or 300 years they began their fire; our orders were not to fire till they came near, but a y7oung officer (of whom we have too many) on the right fired and it was taken from the right to left. We made about 4 fires.
>
> I had fired twice & loaded again, determined to keep for a better chance but Colo. Weedon calling to keep up our fire (he meant for us to reserve it but we misunderstood him) I fire once more. We then all wiped & loaded and sat down in our ranks and let the enemy fire on us near an hour. Our men observed the best order, not quitting their ranks tho' exposed to a constant & warm fire, I cant say enough in their praise. He behaved like soldiers who fought from principle alone.
>
> During this, three companies of riflemen from our regt, West's, Thorntons & Ashby's with other Compys of riflemen were flanking the enemy and had begun a brisk fire on the right of them. [O]n this, they began to retreat up the hill, carrying off their dead & wounded, for we had galled them a little;
>
> And then let me not forget the brave Marylanders who were below us and sustained the hottest of the fire and must have done the greatest execution as they kept a constant fire after we were ordered to reserve ours. The enemy retreated about a quarter & half q^r when they were reinforced with men & cannon. We had but one field piece in the battle, they had several. The battle began between 8 & 9 in the morn^g and lasted till about 2.
>
> It was rather a skirmish than a battle, however, it has taught our enemy that we are not all Connecticut troops and they seem more peaceably inclined than before. Their task was to have marched through our camp to Kings Bridge four miles above us the day of the battle, but they are deceived for once & I hop—will be ever so...
>
> We had three killed & 8 wounded in our Regt.... Maj^r Leitch was also wounded badly, he rec^d three ball, one just above the groin, the other two in the side of his belly just above the one in his groin; he is a man of spirit and bears it such; it is dangerous but hope, not mortal ...[9]

Perhaps one of the best descriptions of this engagement was one by the 3rd Virginia's colonel. George Weedon wrote to John Lee from headquarters at Morris Heights, eighteen miles above New York on 20 September 1776.

> Since my last, we have evacuated N. York, a step that was found absolutely necessary for the preservation of the Army... We should have got of[f] all the stores & troops on Sunday night but believe the enemy suspected a thing or the sort, and early on Sunday morning sent several frigates up the East & North Rivers, and landed two considerable armies near the same time on the shores of the east river, Genl Putnam commanded in York, and had time to bring the troops...
>
> Two brigades of northern troops were to oppose their landing, and engage them. They run of[f] without firing a gun... Genl Washington was himself present, and [with] all he, his aide de camps, & other gen^l officers could do, they were not to be rallied till they had got some miles.

> The General was so exasperated that he struck several officers in their flight; three times [he] dashed his hatt on the ground, and at last exclaimed 'Good God, have I got such troops as those'. [I]t was with difficulty his friends could get him to quit the field, so great was his emotions. He got of[f] safe, and all the troops, as you may think...
>
> The enemy, elated at this piece of success, formed next morning and advanced in three columns; a disposition was made at this place to check them, in which your 3rd Virginia Regiment made part. I was ordered to defend or fight at a valley that divides those heights from N. York and the country below. The brave Major Leitch was detached with 3 rifle companies, commanded by Captains Thornton, West and Ashby, to flank the enemy that were then making for it [the valley].
>
> I even got engaged, as did the Major of his party. How we behaved, it does not become me to say, let it suffice to tell you that we had the Generals thanks in publick orders for our conduct ... The poor Major received three balls through his body before he quitted the field, and so lucky are their direction, that I am in hopes he will do well; at present, he is in a fair way. Also with his party, and my own, three killed & 12 wounded; the other corps that joind us, lost in proportion. The enemies loss was at first supposed to be 97 but a deserter that came in today made them to have lost between 2 & 3 hundred...
>
> We are now very near Neighbors [with the enemy] and view each other ever y hour in the day; the two armies lay within two miles of each other and a general action is every hour expected. I ma more easy in my mind since we have got elbow room, and had the army first thrown up lines... it would have saved vast labour & expense; indeed, I could wish we were three miles further back yet without... run[ning] any risqué of being surrounded...
>
> Our regiment has had exceeding hard duty since they have been here, being kept in constant alarm...[10]

General Washington, from his headquarters on Harlem Heights on 17 September 1776 issued the following statement.

> The General most heartily thanks the troop commanded yesterday by Major Leitch, who first advanced upon the enemy, and the others who so resolutely supported them. The behaviour of yesterday was such a contrast to that of some troops the day before, as must show what may be done, when officers and soldiers will exert themselves ...[11]

3rd Virginia casualties: Major Andrew Leitch

Andrew Leitch was one of the original captains in the 3rd Virginia. He was promoted to major in the 1st Virginia in March 1776[12] but continued to have close ties with his old regiment. It is thought he may have ridden north with his old regiment rather than waiting for the 1st Virginia which left two weeks after the 3rd Virginia. In one of the great ironies of history, had he waited for the 1st Virginia, he would not have been at this skirmish at all since the 1st Virginia did not arrive in New York until after 27 September 1776.[13]

Washington described the involvement of Major Leitch and the three rifle companies of the 3rd Virginia in a letter to the President of Congress on 18 September 1776 from his headquarters at Colonel Roger Morris's house.

> About the time of the post's departure of my letter the enemy appeared in several large bodies upon the plains, about two and a half miles from hence. I rode down to our advance posts, to put matters in a proper situation, if they should attempt to come on. When I arrived there, I heard a firing, which I was informed was between a party of our rangers under the command of Lieutenant-Colonel Knowlton, and an advanced party of the enemy. Our men came in and told me, that the body of the enemy, who kept themselves concealed, consisted of about three hundred, as near as they could guess.
>
> I immediately ordered three companies of Colonel Weedon's regiment from Virginia, under the command of Major Leitch and Colonel Knowlton, with his rangers, composed of volunteers from different New England regiments, to try to get in their rear, while a disposition was making as if to attack them in front, and thereby draw their whole attention that way.

This took effect as I wished on the part of the enemy. On the appearance of our party in front, they immediately ran down the hill, took possession of some fences and bushes, and a smart firing began, but at too great a distance to do much execution on either side.

The parties under Colonel Knowlton and Major Leitch unluckily began their attack too soon, as it was rather in flank than in rear. In a little time Major Leitch was brought off wounded, having received three balls through his side; and in a short time after, Colonel Knowlton got a wound, which proved mortal. Their men however, persevered and continued the engagements with the greatest resolution.

Finding that they wanted a support, I advanced part of Colonel Griffith's and Colonel Richardson's Maryland regiments, with some detachments from the Eastern regiments, who were nearest the place of action. These troops charged the enemy with great intrepidity, and drove them down from the wood into the plain and were pushing them from thence, having silenced their fire in a great measure, when I judged it prudent to order a retreat, fearing the enemy, as I have since found was really the case, were sending a large body to support their party.

Major Leitch, I am in hopes, will recover; but Colonel Knowlton's fall is much to be regretted, as that of a brave and good officer. We had about forty wounded; the number of slain is not yet ascertained; but it is very inconsiderable...[14]

In an extract of a letter, dated 17 September from Headquarters, to a gentleman in Annapolis, a more precise report described the action at Harlem Heights and the nature of Major Leitch's wounds.

Never did troops go to the field with more cheerfulness and alacrity; when there began a heavy fire on both sides. It continued about one hour, when our brave Southern troops dislodged them from their posts. The enemy rallied, and our men beat them the second time. They rallied again; our troops drove them the third time, and were rushing on them, but the enemy had gon on an eminence, and our troops were ordered to retreat, the General considering there might be a large number of the enemy behind the hill, concealed; which was the case. We were informed by a prisoner that our men too, there were about eight or ten thousand concealed.

From the number of the enemy that I saw lay on the field dead and wounded, I think their loss must be three or four times ours. I have not yet been able to get a full account of our loss, only of our brigade, which is as follows: Captain Low, wounded through both his thighs. Twelve privates wounded, and three missing. Major Leitch, of Colonel Weedon's regiment, received three balls through his body. More is the pity, for never was a braver hero. He stood the field, with ... great bravery, til the third shot, when he was obliged to fall. He appears to be in good spirits. The doctors are of opinion he will recover ...

From our present situation, it is firmly my opinion we shall give them a genteel drubbing, in case the Yankees will fight with as much spirit as the Southern troops. As near as I can collect, our loss, killed, wounded and taken, amounts to fifty men. We expect every hour when the general engagement will come one; and if we prove successful, the campaign will be settled for this present year. General Washington gave great applause to our Maryland troops, for their gallant behaviour yesterday.[15]

General George Clinton wrote the committee of the New York Convention from King's Bridge on 18 September, providing more details of the engagement at Harlem Heights and of the strength and disposition of the British forces there.

... On Sunday morning, the enemy landed a very considerable body of troops, principally consisting of their Light Infantry and Grenadiers, near Turtle Bay, under cover of a very cannonade from their shipping. Our lines were but thinly manned, as they were then intended only to secure a retreat to the rear of our army, and unfortunately by such troops as were so little disposed to stand in the way of grape–shot that the main body of them almost instantly retreated, nay fled, without a possibility of rallying them, though General Washington himself, (who rode to the spot on hearing the cannonade) with some other General Officers, exerted themselves to effect it.

The enemy on landing immediately formed a line across the Island. Most of our people were luckily north of it and joined the army. The few that were in the city crossed the river, chiefly to Paulus–Hook, so that our loss of men, artillery, or stores, is very inconsiderable; I don't believe it exceeds one hundred men, and I fancy most of them, from their conduct, staid out of choice. Before evening, the enemy landed the main body of their army, took possession of the city, and marched up the Island and encamped on the heights extending from McGown's and the Black–Horse to the North River.

On Monday morning, about ten o'clock, a party of the enemy, consisting of Highlanders, Hessians, the Light Infantry, Grenadiers and English troops, (number uncertain) attacked our advanced party, commanded by Colonel Knowlton... They were opposed with spirit, and soon made to retreat to a clear field, southwest of that about two hundred paces, where they lodged themselves behind a fence covered with bushes.

Our people attacked them in front, and caused them to retreat a second time, leaving five dead on the spot. We pursued them to a buckwheat field on the top of a high hill, distant about four hundred paces, where they received a considerable reinforcement, with several field–pieces, and there made a stand. A very brisk action ensued at this place, which continued about two hours.

Our people at length worsted them a third time, caused them to fall back into an orchard, from thence, across a hollow, and up another hill not far distant from their own lines. A large column of the enemy's army, being at this time discovered to be in motion, and the ground we then occupied being rather disadvantageous, a retreat likewise, without bringing on a general action, (which we did not think prudent to risk) rather insecure, our party was therefore ordered in, and the enemy was well contented to hold the last ground we drove them to.

We lost, on this occasion, Colonel Knowlton, a brave officer and sixteen privates, killed. Major Leitch, from Virginia, and about eight or ten subaltern officers and privates wounded. The loss of the enemy is uncertain. They carried their dead and wounded off, in and soon after the action; but we have good evidence of their having upwards of sixty killed; and violent presumption of one hundred. The action, in the whole, lasted about four hours.

I consider our success in this small affair, at this time, almost equal to a victory. It has animated our troops, gave them new spirits, and erased [a] very bad impression the retreat from Long Island, &c, had left on their minds. They find they are able, with inferior numbers, to drive their enemy, and think of nothing now but conquest...

Since the above affair, nothing material has happened. The enemy keep close to their lines. Our advance parties continue at their former station. We are daily throwing up works to prevent the enemy's advancing ...[16]

Four days after the battle, Major Leitch's prognosis for recovery still looked good. On 20 September 1776, General Washington wrote General Schuyler that although Major Leitch received "three balls through his body... he is likely to do well. Their parties behaved with great bravery, and being supported with fresh troops, beat the enemy fairly from the field...This little advantage has inspirited our troops prodigiously; they find that it only requires resolution and good officers to make the enemy (that they stood in too much dread of) give way ..."[17] In a letter written from Philadelphia by the Maryland delegates to the Maryland Council of Safety on the same day, they reported that "Maj^r Leach of the Virginians is wounded though it is hoped he will recover ..."[18]

By 21 September 1776, the outlook for Major Leitch's recovery began to dim somewhat. In a letter from Samuel Chase of Maryland [19] to Horatio Gates, written from Philadelphia, he reported that "Major Leitch of Maryland was wounded & despaired of."[20]

It was with considerable dismay that a crestfallen and chagrined David Griffith, the 3rd Virginia regimental surgeon, wrote about the circumstances surrounding Major Leitch's sudden demise the day before in a letter to Richard Henderson on 3 October 1776.

> ... as it may assuage much of its bitterness, if accompanied with this kind condolence & of a friend, I have [thought] it best to communicate the disagreeable intelligence immediately to you.
>
> The disagreeable duty of informing Mrs Leitch, through you, of the death of her husband is imposed upon me. He expired yesterday morning (2nd October) at Hackinsack Bridge where he had been removed for his better accommodation, & to relieve him from the anxiety of dread of a general attack which was then expected.
>
> You must long ago have been informed from his own hand that he had rec^d 3 wounds in the action on Monday 17th Ult. One through his hip & two through his belly: These, though exceedingly dangerous, I make no doubt he would have survived. The intestines were undoubtedly unhurt, and he continued for near a fortnight free from every bad symptom. His appetite was good, his spirits great, he slept well, & it was expected his wounds woud be healed in two or three weeks.

But on the 28th Sept' he was seized with a lock'd jaw—with spasms about his neck & throat so violent as to baffle every effort to [minister?] to him by medicine. Under the agonies attending such a situation, he laboured four days with fortitude & magnanimity equal to bravery in the field. His conduct, in short, through the whole of this unlucky catastrophe does him the highest Honour to his memory while it raised his character, [it] adds greatly to the regret his friends feel for his loss. His remains were this day interred with the honour of war.

I have the satisfaction to inform you that he [was?] comfortably accommodated through the whole of his [illness]...

The people about him were kind & obliging & he had—[letter is torn here]... the medical assistance which five experience practitioners—[letter is torn] afford. The care of the effects of the deceased become the duty of Major Fitzgerald,[21] who I make no doubt will account very faithfully for them.[22]

The *Virginia Gazette* presented this picture of the Battle at Harlem Plains on 4 October 1776.

> ...A gentleman from Dumfries writes, that by a letter just received from general Washington's headquarters from an officer of note, we took 89 prisoners in the late action, and killed a considerable number, with very moderate loss on our side. There were about 1000 of the enemy who engaged with our third regiment of Virginians, and draughts from several northern regiments. They all behaved with great bravery, and major Leitch is much extolled for his distinguished behaviour; in so much that the general, after having returned his thanks to the officers and soldiers, gave out as parole LEITCH, countersign VIRGINIA. The major is out of danger from his wounds...[23]

In a communication dated 20 September 1776 from Philadelphia, in the *Virginia Gazette*, the newspaper stated that "our 3d regiment (col. Weedon's) was in the action, and behaved gallantly; they have received the general's thanks in publick orders. Major Leitch had three balls through his body, but it is thought none are mortal. Col. Weedon's thigh was bruised, by a spent ball striking the guard of his sword. This regiment has one ensign wounded slightly, a serjeant and one private killed, 12 privates wounded, and two missing ..."[24]

The news of the Major's death was also slow in reaching the Virginia delegates to Congress. George Wythe did not learn of Leitch's death until 7 October 1776 when he wrote John Page from Philadelphia with the news: "Major Leitch [was] in this action wounded with no less than three balls [and] was thought to be in a way to recover," Wythe said. "But", he went on, "I am told he died last week."[25]

Captain Chilton informed his friends in Fauquier on 4 October 1776 that "the brave Maj' Leitch who died of the wounds received the 16th was interred yesterday ..."[26]

Colonel Weedon was even more explicit. In a letter to John Page, the President of the Virginia Council in Williamsburg, written on 10 October 1776, the colonel stated

> ... I have had the misfortune of loosing poor Major Leitch, he was unexpectedly attack'd with a locked jaw... Not only to this regiment in particular but to the states in general, in him, America has lost as brave & grand [an] officer as ever defended her rights, and a pattern to all military character who steps forth in her cause. We paid him our last tribute of respect on the 4th Ins' by interring him with all the honour of war, the [brigade?] to which he belongs is in mourning, to continue one month.[27]

The correspondence of General Washington, along with that of the Delegates of the Continental Congress, and of 3rd Virginia officers has shown the regard and admiration with which the American army regarded this officer. Colonel Weedon's sentiments summed up the feelings of loss that this skirmish at Harlem Heights had brought to the Virginia forces. It was obvious, too, that this officer was held in the highest esteem by the policy-makers in the Continental Congress and in the various states.

SKIRMISH AT NEW ROCHELLE
22 OCTOBER 1776

In October 1776, Washington realized that he must move his troops off Manhattan northward to White Plains in order to escape being trapped by British forces. In the general orders, issued by the His Excellency at his headquarters at Harlem Heights on 14 October 1776, he ordered Colonel Weedon's Virginia brigade to remain on Manhattan Island under the command of Major General Putnam.

Putnam's task was to pay special attention to "all the works, and necessary places of defence... particularly to the works about Mount Washington, and to the obstructions in the River ..."[28] Then, three days later, the "movements of the enemy [made] an alteration of [the American] position necessary and Washington had a change of heart. He ordered Colonel Weedon, then with Putnam at Fort Washington, along with Colonel Reed's regiment, to join Lord Stirling's brigade immediately.[29]

When Lord Stirling heard that Major Robert Rogers[30] and his Queen's American Rangers were at Mamaroneck, he decided to try to cut off Major Rogers and his men from the main body of British troops near Rye, New York. He chose Colonel John Haslet's Delaware regiment, along with some Marylanders and 160 men from the 1st and 3rd Virginia to attempt this.

He scheduled the attack to begin on 22 October 1776. The Virginia troops, under the command of Major John Green, took a crossroad leading into New Rochelle. The Americans entered the crossroads just below the Tory camp where they found an outpost guard of some sixty Tory rangers. The entry was contested thanks to the quick thinking of one of the British ranger captains and a melee ensued. This alerted the enemy's main camp and Colonel Haslet's Delaware regiment was forced to withdraw. When Major Green was wounded in the attack, Captain John Thornton of the 3rd Virginia, took command. Thornton successfully extricated the Major and the rest of the Virginians. In the process, the men of the regiment became the "heroes of the day with thirty-six prisoners, a pair of colours, sixty stand of arms and as many precious blankets."[31]

On 26 October 1776, a "field officer in the third Virginia regiment" (undoubtedly Colonel Weedon) sent to the *Virginia* Gazette a description of the action at New Rochelle.

> General Howe's head-quarters are at New Rochelle, his right wing extending towards Rye, and his left to East Chester and Frog's Point, with a large fleet before him; and has advanced four or five miles towards us, fortifying as he came. We are now about four miles asunder and skirmishing every day, in all of which we have had the advantage.
>
> Poor major Green was unfortunately wounded in one of these affairs; for having intelligence of the famous major Rogers being advanced with 500 Tories, who have embodied under him, towards Maroneck, three miles from Rochelle, a plan was concerted to cut him off in the night, when 160 men from the 1st and 3d Virginia regiments, led on by the brave old major, composed the advanced guard, covered by 400 more under the command of major Haslet or the Delaware battalion, fell in with the enemy's Tory regiment. The major got wounded in the shoulder the first fire, when the command devolved on capt. John Thornton of our regiment, who soon did the business, leaving, by the light of the moon, 20 of them dead on the spot, and bringing off 36 prisoners, without the loss of a man on our side.
>
> Col. Haslet, by this time getting up and finding he was discovered, and that his guide had left him, ordered a retreat; but the traitor Rogers narrowly escaped himself, and has never since dared to venture from the main body.[32]

BATTLE OF WHITE PLAINS
26 OCTOBER 1776

When the battle of White Plains took place four days after the abortive attempt to capture Major Rogers and his Tory regiment, Stirling's brigade was "well removed from the thrust of the attack. The Virginia troops were simply spectators, required only to hold their position while Washington withdrew to stronger ground at North Castle beyond the Croton River."[33]

Several of the men in the 3rd Virginia mentioned taking part in this battle in their pension applications. One such soldier was Samuel Cox, who was in Captain Ashby's company. He stated that he was in the Battle at White Plains, although this may have meant he was there when the battle was fought.[34] David Baker, a private in Captain Thornton's company also remembered having fought at White Plains, and was with the army when they retreated and recrossed the Delaware.[35] Edward Abbey was a private in Captain John Fitzgerald's company and remembered the retreat to White Plains in the fall of 1776.[36] Spencer Anderson, a private in Captain Phill Lee's company stated he participated in, among others, the battle at White Plains.[37] William Berry, another soldier in Captain Fitzgerald's company was at White Plains.[38] John Coppage, a soldier in Captain Ashby's company, was yet another person who mentioned being at this battle in his pension papers.[39]

Engagement between the two forces came about when the American brigade under the command of General Alexander McDougall, occupied an isolated position on the right flank. The British attacked and forced the brigade off the hill.[40] The *Virginia Gazette* carried a description of the battle in their 29 November 1776 newspaper, in a letter from a Marylander dated 29 October 1776.

> I now snatch an opportunity, by the post, of informing you that General McDougal's brigade, of which the Maryland regulars is a part, having laid in the woods for three nights, two miles from this place, and to the right of the main body, as a covering party, was ordered to advance along the road, about a mile, near a place called the Mile Stone, and there take place, which was accordingly done.
>
> The brigade was there joined by Hazlet's Delaware battalion, and a small regiment of militia from Connecticut; they were no sooner formed than the enemy began a heavy cannonade from a great number of field-pieces, advantageously disposed on several rising grounds, which was answered by the (only) two cannon which attended our brigade, little or no execution being done on either side, till Colonel Smallwood, with the Marylanders, was ordered to march down the hill and attack the enemy which they did, and a smart contest ensued, in which the enemy gave way, but rallying again, and attacking the right of the brigade, composed of the militia... they got the advantage, and their situation being such, and being drawn up in a heavy column, only our regiment and another (Ritzura's) could come in for any part of the action.
>
> Those two brave regiments stood a very heavy fire of their artillery and musketry for about half an hour, when the whole brigade, being vastly out-number, and cramped in respect of ground, was obliged to retreat, a reinforcement under General Putnam not being able to get up in time to give the necessary assistance; this reinforcement was General Beall's brigade.
>
> The enemy now occupy the ground where we took post yesterday, and are a mile from our lines at the White Plains. Colonel Smallwood staid upon the place of action some time after the retreat had begun, and received two wounds, one a flesh wound on his hip, the other through his arm; he is, however, in good spirits, and I hope will soon be in condition to take the field again.
>
> All our officers and men behaved with their usual bravery. We have lost of our regiment Captain Bracco, killed in the retreat; serjeants Belt and Westbay, killed. Captain Scott is mortally wounded, indeed I fear he is dead at this moment; Lieutenant Goldsmith badly wounded in the leg, and Lieutenant Water's leg broke to pieces. As near as I can guess, our regiment has nearly forty killed, wounded, and missing. The enemy form a considerable body near to our main body, and I expect every moment to see them attack.[41]

A few days later, Washington moved the army to the rear to a stronger position and awaited an attack that never came.[42] This was because General Howe decided to wait for reinforcements before attacking the rebel forces. Then, on the last day of October, heavy rain ruined the British gunpowder, thus preventing the attack altogether.[43]

Washington used the heavy rain to hide his evacuation of the army at White Plains to North Castle New York. Here the Americans made "piled-up cornstalks, with dirt still attached to their roots" look so like redoubts that the British were deceived and did not attack.[44]

Meanwhile, Washington had other problems to deal with. The continuing series of defeats was demoralizing; soldiers were deserting and others, whose enlistments were up, planned to go home.

> Almost all the Continental regiments were eligible to disband on November 30 or December 31; few fresh troops were arriving to take their place. Enlistments were slow, which was no surprise since the Americans had lost every major engagement in the New York campaign and were on the run. Washington was aware that his army was diminishing with each passing day and wrote Congress to say 'how essential it is to keep up some shew of force and shadow of an Army.'[45]

Added to these tribulations was the constant challenge of logistics and supply—food and equipment. Both were in short supply. The American forces had lost blankets and tents in the New York campaign and, by late October, the Americans were sleeping on frozen ground.[46] In October, John Chilton wrote his friends in Fauquier about the condition of his men and their diet.

> ...Our men have been sickly with fevers & agues but are now mending. We have plenty of good beef but no variety of other food, & tho we are between two Rivers we get no fish & very few oisters & clams or cockles. The oisters here are good & sell by the 100 at 3/ to pick. We sometimes get pork & pease, rum, brandy &c at 1/ Virg^a currency p^r Galln. It has sold at 32/.[47]

In late October, Colonel Weedon wrote John Page from the camp at White Plains about the deteriorating conditions of his regiment.

> ... Something of consequence must take place in a day or two, I wish it was over, for the sufferings of my poor men makes me feel exceedingly, for these five weeks we have been under arms every morning before day, exclusive of the other necessary duties of the Army, which has been uncommonly hard. They have been oblige[d] to engage it, entirely naked, some without shoes or stockings, several without blankets and almost all with out shirts ...[48]

While troop strength and the logistics of keeping an army clothed, housed, and fed on the move were constantly in the back of his mind, Washington was more concerned with the whereabouts of General Howe. In early November, the British had shifted their army from White Plains to Dobb's Ferry on the Hudson, where the Navy was waiting with the redcoats' supplies.

At a council of war, held in November 1776, Washington talked the situation over with his officers. They were divided. Some felt that Howe was planning to move either into New England or progress northward up the Hudson to Albany. Washington thought Howe would use part of his army to attack Fort Washington and another part to invade New Jersey. After much discussion, his officers agreed with their General's assessment. So, they decided to divide the American forces. Part of the army would be dispatched immediately into New Jersey. Another 3000 troops would be detached to defend the New York highlands.

Now, Washington mused, how to protect the Hudson and New England and still defend New Jersey? Reluctantly, he decided to divide his small army into three unequal parts. He would stay with the troops to defend New Jersey. General William Heath would lead the 3000 troops northward to Peekskill to defend the Hudson highlands. The remaining portion of his army, he placed under the command of General Charles Lee. These troops would remain at North Castle. Lee was to halt any British thrust into New England and act as a reserve until Howe's intentions were better known.

On 8 November 1776 Washington began to move his troops. Having heard from his spy network that the British were active at Dobb's Ferry, Washington felt that a British invasion of New Jersey was imminent.

He ordered part of the army—the Virginia,[49] Delaware, and Pennsylvania troops in Lord Stirling's Brigade—across the Hudson into New Jersey. Stirling's brigade was more precisely made up of 1st Virginia, the 3rd Virginia, John Haslet's Delaware Regiment, two Pennsylvania battalions from the Flying Camp— Colonel Henry Haller's Pennsylvania battalion and Colonel James Cunningham's 1st Pennsylvania battalion—along with the 1st and 2nd battalion of Miles' Pennsylvania Rifle regiment.[50] On paper, the brigade totaled 3229 men and officers although only 1683 of the rank and file were present and fit for duty.[51]

In a letter to the President of Congress from Peekskill, on 11 November 1776, Washington wrote that he left White Plains mid-day the day before.

> The enemy appeared to be preparing for their expedition to Jersey, according to every information. What their designs are, or whether their present conduct is not a feint I cannot determine. The Maryland and Virginia Troops under Lord Stirling have crossed the river as have part of those from Jersey, the remainder are now embarking.[52]

Once across the Hudson and in New Jersey, the brigade covered the crossing of 2,700 additional soldiers the next day. On 12 November, the brigade was at Hackensack, New Jersey. Washington, meanwhile, reached Fort Lee on 13 November and discussed the situation at Fort Washington at length with General Greene. He then rode on to Hackensack where he set up his headquarters at Peter Zabriskie's home.[53]

FALL OF FORT WASHINGTON
15 NOVEMBER 1776

Just as Washington suspected, Howe had begun to turn his attention to an assault on Fort Washington, whose position was untenable to the Americans, as much from a water supply retrieved from the Hudson River some 240 feet below its rocky crest as from the British fleet observing the fort above them.[54]

A description of the Fort appeared in the *Virginia Gazette* in an extract in a letter from Philadelphia, dated November 9, 1776.

> I must not forget to mention, that we have spared to the enemy a part of the province of New York, yet we still hold a part of York island.; on this portion are the lines of Harlem, Fort Washington... which are defended by a chosen body of volunteers, a band of brothers, from the several States who are determined to defend them to the last extremity. The whole under the command of Col. Magaw, a brave officer. The fort is admirably situated on a rocky height on the banks of the North river, and is a commanding situation on every side. It is supplied with every thing necessary for a long siege.[55]

Just the day before, the *Virginia Gazette* reported that the "garrison at Fort Washington are in high spirits, and go a Hessian-hunting every day ..."[56] Two days later, on November 10, 1776 the *Gazette* reported, in an extract of a letter from Fort Lee that "Colonel Magaw's men killed 13 Hessians and an officers, and stripped them. This little enterprise gives spirit to our men, and insensibly reduces the number of the enemy."[57]

A little more than a week later, the mood had changed considerably. In an extract of a letter from Philadelphia on November 19, the *Gazette* reported

> This moment an express arrived to Congress with advice that the enemy's whole army, passing down to New York, attacked Fort Washington by storm, and carried it, but with what expense we cannot yet tell, as we have not the particulars; but as the firing continued long and heavy, it is supposed they met with great loss ...[58]

There *was* a great loss—Colonel Magaw[59] and 2,800 Americans—captured by the British.[60]

In a letter from White Plains to his brother John Augustine, the General echoed his shock and dismay at the loss of so many troops.

> ...By a letter wch I have just receivd from Genl Green at Fort Lee (wch is opposite to Fort Washington) I am informd that 'one of the train of artillery came across the river last night on a raft—by his Acct the Enemy have suffered greatly on the North side of Fort Washington—Colo. Rawling's regiment (late Hugh Stephenson's) was posted there, and behaved with great spirit—Colo. Magaw could not get the men to man the lines, otherwise he would not have given up the fort.'
> This is a most unfortunate affair and has given me great mortification as we have lost not only two thousand men that were there, but a good deal of artillery, & some of the best arms we had. And what adds to my mortification, is, that this post after the last ships went by it, was held contrary to my wishes & opinion; as I conceived it to be a dangerous one: but being determind on by a full Council of General Officers, & receiving a resolution of Congress strongly expressive of their desires, that the Channel; of the river (which we had been labouring to stop a long while at this place) might be obstructed, if possible; & knowing that this could not be done unless there were batteries to protect the obstruction I did not care to give an absolute order for withdrawing

the garrison till I could get round & see the situation of things... then it became too late as the fort was invested ...[61]

Although the 3rd Virginia did not appear to have men or officers in this contingent captured by the British,[62] at least one soldier in Captain John Ashby's company remembered having served at Fort Washington in his pension application. This was John Coppage, a private in Captain John Ashby's rifle company. He recalled marching to New York to Fort Washington where he joined Woodford's brigade. Coppage was in the battle at York Island when the Major of his regiment, named Leitch, was wounded and died of his wounds. After Harlem Heights, his company marched to King's Bridge and then went back to Fort Washington.[63]

NEW JERSEY CAMPAIGN
NOVEMBER 1776 TO JANUARY 1777

November 1776: The evacuation of Fort Lee.

In the aftermath of the loss Fort Washington to the British, Washington quickly decided that he would not lose Fort Lee. To prevent an anticipated attack on this fort, he ordered the removal of the equipment and food stores there. However, he was hampered by not having the proper transportation to remove these from the fort to the interior of New Jersey. Five days after the loss of Fort Washington, on 20 November, the British invaded New Jersey.

Washington responded immediately. He "gave instructions for troops from his skeleton force at Hackensack to secure the strategic points between the crossroads of Liberty Pole (modern Englewood) and Fort Lee, especially the New Bridge." He knew that the garrison at Fort Lee could only be evacuated across the Hackensack River at New Bridge. If the British managed to capture the Bridge or the crossroads at Liberty Pole, the Fort Lee troops would be trapped.[64]

Among those skeleton troops that were to secure these strategic points in New Jersey were Stirling's Brigade and the 2700 troops that had crossed into New Jersey on 11 November 1776. Lord Stirling's brigade were at Hackensack on 12 November.[65]

General Washington had written the President of Congress from Hackensack, the day before the British landed in New Jersey, on 19 November 1776, explaining his position on holding Fort Lee.

> ... Fort Lee was always considered, as only necessary in conjunction with that on the East side of the River, to preserve the Communication across, and to prevent the Enemy from a free Navigation. It has become of no importance by the loss of the other, or not so material, as to employ a force for its defence. Being viewed in this light and apprehending that the stores there would be precariously situated, their removal has been determined on to Boundbrook above Brunswick, Prince Town, Springfield and Acquackinac Bridge, as places that will not be subject ot sudden danger in case the enemy should pass the river...The troops belonging to the Flying Camp under Genls. Heard and Beal, with what remains of Genl. Ewing's Brigade, are now at Fort Lee, where they will continue till the stores are got away.
> By the time that is effected, their term of inlistment will be near expiring, and if the enemy should make a push in this quarter, the only troops that there will be to opposed them, will be Hand's,[66] Hazlet's, the [five] regiments from Virginia ...[67] [Those troops which were] lately Smallwood's [have been] greatly reduced by losses ... and sickness ...[68]

Although Washington managed to evacuate the Fort successfully, it was not without danger. The retreating garrison force was made up of "poorly trained troops of the Flying Camp," amounting to around 2000 men and officers. The retreat became tumultuous as the troops crossed over the Hackensack at New Bridge. Inexplicably, the British did not follow.[69]

November 1776: The American Retreat through New Jersey.

During the night of 20 November, American entered the village of Hackensack. A resident remembered the army's bedraggled appearance as they marched through the village.

> The night was dark, cold, and rainy, but I had a fair view of them from the light of the windows as they passed on our side of the street. They marched two abreast, looked ragged, some without a shoe to their feet, and most of them wrapped in their blankets.[70]

General Washington posted guards at crossing points over the Hackensack and then went to his headquarters, set up at Peter Zabriskie's.[71] The troops were without tents "and cramped into houses and barns along the main road from New Bridge to the Hackensack village green."[72]

The British were close on the retreating army's heels. The next morning British troops were at the New Bridge, just two miles north of the village. The American troops fought a rear-guard action with the British and managed to hold their own.[73]

Washington explained his actions to evacuate Fort Lee to Major General Charles Lee in a letter from Hackensack on 21 November and directed him to cross at Kings Ferry with his division; Generals Heath, Lord Stirling and Stephen were "to hold themselves in readiness to follow."[74]

> It must be painful to you as well as to us to have no news to send you, but of a melancholy nature. Yesterday morning the enemy landed a large body of troops below Dobb's Ferry, and advanced very rapidly to the Fort called by your name. I immediately went over and, as the fort was not tenable on this side, directed the troops consisting of Beall's, Heard's, the reminder of Ewing's Brigades, and some other parts of broken regiments, to move over to the west side of Hackensack River.
>
> A considerable quantity of stores and some artillery have fallen into their hands. We have no account of their movements this morning, but as this country is almost a dead flat, we have not an intrenching tool, and not above 3000 men, and they much broken and dispirited, not only with our ill success, but the loss of their tents and baggage; I have resolved to avoid any attack, tho' by so doing I must leave a very fine country open to their [the British] ravages, or a plentiful store house, from which they will draw voluntary supplies.[75]

By 21 November, Washington and his exhausted troops had reached the Aquackinack Bridge with the Fort Lee brigades of Generals Beall[76], Heard,[77] and Ewing.[78] "Three other regiments, left to guard the passes upon Hackensack River, and to serve as covering parties, are expected up this evening," he explained in a letter describing the retreat from Fort Lee to Governor William Livingston.

> ... the enemy landed yesterday morning, in very considerable numbers, about six miles above the fort; Their intent evidently was to form a line across, from the place of their landing to Hackensack Bridge, and thereby hem in the whole garrison between the North and Hackensack Rivers. However, we were lucky enough to gain the Bridge before them; by which means we saved all our men, but were obliged to leave some hundred barrels of flour, most of our cannon, and a considerable parcel of tents and baggage.
>
> Finding we were in the same danger of being pent up between Hackensack and Passaic Rivers, that we have been between the North and Hackensack, and also finding the country, from its levelness and openness, unfit for making a stand; it was determined to draw the whole of our force over this side of the River, where we can watch the operations of the enemy, without danger of their surrounding us, or making a lodgment in our rear. But as our numbers are still very inadequate to that of the enemy, I imagine I shall be obliged to fall down toward Brunswick, and form a junction with the troops, already in that quarter, under the command of Lord Stirling ...[79]

John Chilton wrote his brother Charles, from Brunswick, New Jersey on 30 November 1776. He had thought he would be in winter quarters before now. His company had been ordered to Elizabeth when the British were entering Hackensack. On 26 November, he noted that the British had forded the Aquackinack above the bridge. The Americans were "mostly at Newark" and did not oppose them. On the 27 November, he declared, the American army passed through Elizabeth on their way to Brunswick.

> Our regiment brought up the rear. This was a melancholy day, a deep miry road and so many men to tread it, made it very disagreeable marching. [W]e came 8 or 10 miles & encamped. Yesterday, we reached this place, how long we shall stay I cant say but expect we shall make a stand near this place, if not at it, but no certainty where the enemy are and are advancing on and an engagement may happened before tomorrow night.
> We must fight to a disadvantage. They exceed us in Numbers greatly. You will wonder what is become of the great Army of Americans you have been told we had—I really cant tell. They were in some degree imaginary militia, s some enlisted for 2, some 4 & some 5 months, their times were mostly out before the battle for the white Plains (if I may call it a battle) and I suspect that the thinness of our troops was one reason why we were not allowed fight them that day. The same reason prevents us now...until we get them to a place advantageous to us and we daily expect a reinforcement. [B]ut as I told you before I do not know where this stand will be--- It is conjectured by some that Burgoyne from Quebec is to join Howe & make a push for Philadel^a but this is not known.
> You may guess we are in some confusion and yet let me tell you not so much as you may imagine— I just hear the enemy are making to cross this River about 8 miles above her, upon certain intelligence we shall move up I suppose—O God that our congress should raise men just for an expence till time for them to fight & then their time to be out. Howe must have known of this. [T]here are many Tories all over the Continent. The very Time of his Landing first was about the time of whole Regim^{ts} time being up.
> Genl Lee is yet in N. York Gov^{mt} with 10 or 12000 but fear he can't join us in time and indeed I dont know whether it is intended he should come over to our assistance. [I]f he should & we could get them a little further in the Country we could shortly give a good acct of ourselves & them too I trust, but if the militia joins us in day or two, I hope they will repent their bold step. Our men are very willing to fight them on any terms but our Generals are the best judges when it is best to be done.[80]

The Americans had reached Brunswick on noon on 29 November and remained there until 1 December.

December 1776: The American Retreat into Pennsylvania.

The American army, whose ranks had been already depleted by soldiers whose enlistments were up at the end of November,[81] crossed the Delaware River into Pennsylvania during the first week in December. A projected line of march for Washington's main army would have included the advance parties of Connecticut militia, Maryland and Virginia riflemen and some infantrymen detached from the three Continental regiments still under Washington. Then, among the infantry regiments, came Stirling's brigade.

> After the advance party were infantry regiments, marching according to their place in the order of battle. First was Sterling's brigade, consisting of Isaac Read's 1st Virginia Regiment followed by the remnants of Colonel John Haslet's 1st Delaware Regiment. Better known as 'The Delaware Blues,' Haslet's corps had formed on the Green in Dover, Delaware, in the summer of 1776, and marched off in high spirits to join Washington's army for the defense of New York City. The Delaware troops had suffered so many battle casualties and deaths from disease that by December 1776, they ceased to exist as a fighting unit. Next came the 3rd Virginia (181 officers and men fit for duty) commanded by George Weedon ... Weedon was followed by the 6th Marylanders (199 officers and men), whose commanding officer, Otho Holland Williams, had been wounded and captured at Fort Washington.[82]

While the Virginia regiments in Stirling's brigade may have set out with the army, Washington detached these troops and the Virginia regiments under Adam Stephens to other duties: to watch the enemy and report their movements back to Washington and to act as a covering force until the baggage and stores of the army could be moved across the Delaware. In a letter to the President of Congress on 3 December from his headquarters at Trenton, Washington gave his reasons for this.

> I arrived here myself yesterday morning with the main body of the army, having left Lord Stirling with two Brigades at Princeton and that neighbourhood to watch the motions of the enemy and give notice of their approach.
>
> I am informed that they had not entered Brunswick yesterday morning at 9 o'clock, but were on the opposite side of the Raritan. Immediately on my arrival here, I ordered the removal of all the military and other stores and baggage over the Delaware, a great quantity are already got over, and as soon as the boats come up from Philadelphia, we shall load them, by which means I hope to have every thing secured this night and tomorrow if we are not disturbed. After being disencumbered of my baggage and stores, my future situation will depend intirely upon circumstances.
>
> I have not heard a word from General Lee, since the 26th last month, which surprises me a little, as I have dispatched daily expresses to him, desiring to know when I might look for him...
>
> I look out earnestly for the reinforcement from Philadelphia, I am in hopes, if we can draw a good head of men together, it will give spirits to the militia of this State who have as yet afforded me little or no assistance, no can I find they are likely to do much ...[83]

On 5 December 1776, in a letter to John Hancock, Washington further explained his reasoning for leaving Lord Stirling at Princeton.

> As nothing but necessity obliged me to retire before the enemy, & leave so much of the Jerseys unprotected, I conceive it my duty, and it corresponds with my inclination to make head against them so soon as there shall be the least probability of doing it with propriety. That the country in some measure be covered, I left two brigades consisting of the five Virginia Regiments and that of Delaware, containing in the whole about 1200 men fit for duty, under the command of Lord Stirling & Genl Stephen at Princeton, till the baggage & stores could cross the Delaware, or the troops under their respective commands should be forced from thence.[84]

After the baggage and stores were moved across the river, Washington planned to return to Princeton, "with such troops as are here fit for service ..." He planned to "reinforce Lord Stirling with about 1200 men which will make his numbers about 2400" and added "tomorrow, I mean to repair to Princeton myself & shall order the Pensylvania troops (who are not yet arrived, except part of the German Batallion & a company of Light Infantry) to the same place." As far as he knew, the British were still at Brunswick.[85]

On 7 December, Washington ordered Colonel John Cadwalader's Pennsylvania troops to Trenton.[86] On the same day, he sent orders to Major General Heath to cross the North River with his troops and move towards Morristown.[87]

Washington was obviously gathering these outlying brigades into New Jersey. On the same day, Stirling's brigade evacuated Princeton.

> To slow any pursuit, his troops tore apart the wooden bridge across Stony Brook, a stream a few miles south of the village. As they retreated towards Trenton, the troops skirmished with some of the British advance guards, killing at least one light dragoon. Stirling's brigade arrived at Trenton that night and started crossing the Delaware. However, some of his men must have stayed behind because Ewald [the Hessian commander] wrote in his diary that rebels roamed around Princeton all night, and sporadic fighting continued.[88]

On 8 December, he received word that the British were "advancing by different rout[e]s by one of which it appear they were attempting to get in the rear of the [American] troops at Princeton." The forces at Princeton, decided, since their numbers were so small, it would be prudent to retreat to Trenton and from there to the Pennsylvania side of the Delaware River."[89] Among those forces were the Virginia and Delaware regiments of Lord Stirling's brigade.[90]

On 9 December, Washington reported more news to the President of Congress from his headquarters at Trenton Falls. The British entered Trenton, he said, just as the American rear guard left. Washington believed that the redcoats had one part of their army around Trenton and the other "some miles higher up and inclining towards Delaware." He wasn't sure whether the enemy intended to cross there or whether they were going to "throw themselves between General Lee and me."

That morning, the general had detached Lord Stirling and his brigade and posted them at various prospective landing places which he hoped would prevent the enemy from "stealing a march upon us from above." If, on the other hand, the British should at Coryell's ferry they would be as close to Philadelphia as the Americans.

> In the meantime, every step should be taken to collect force[s] not only from Pennsylvania but from the most neighbourly states; if we can keep the enemy from entering Philadelphia and keep the communication by water open, for supplies, we may yet make a stand, if the country will come to our assistance, till our new levies can be collected.[91]

In a postscript, Washington relayed news that all of the army's military stores still remained in Philadelphia. "This makes the immediate fortifying of the city so necessary, that I have desired Genl Mifflin to return, to take charge of the stores and have ordered Major Genl Putnam immediately down to superintend the works ..."[92]

On 10 December 1776 Washington wrote Major General Charles Lee, entreating him to bring his army to the defense of Philadelphia. Without these troops, Washington held out little hope that Philadelphia could be saved. He also requested Lee to "exert [his] influence and bring... all the Jersey Militia" he possibly could.[93]

A distressed and worried commander in chief wrote to Lund Washington from the south side of the falls of Delaware, 10 December 1776.

> I wish to Heaven it was in my power to give you a more favourable acct of our situation than it is—our numbers, quite inadequate to the task of opposing that part of the Army under the command of Genl Howe, being reduced by sickness, desertion, & political deaths (on & before the first instt, & having no assistance from the militia) were obliged to retire before the enemy, who were perfectly well informed of our situation till we came to this place, where I have no idea of being able to make a stand, as my numbers, till joind by the Philadelphia militia did not exceed 3000 men fit for duty—now we may be about 5000 to oppose Howes whole Army, that part of it excepted which sail'd under the comd of General Clinton.
>
> I tremble for Philadelphia, nothing in my opinion but General Lee's speedy arrival, who has been long expected, tho still at a distance (with about 3000 men) can save it.[94]

In the same letter, he appended an explanation of his whereabouts on 17 December, where he was now ten miles above the falls. He had, he said, moved to where he could more conveniently defend the river. The American destruction of transport to cross the river and their vigilance in watching the fords above the falls had so far prevented the British from moving across the Delaware. He talked of the impossibility of defending Philadelphia with his present numbers and spoke specifically of Colonel Weedon's regiment which was the strongest of his remaining troops.

> How long we shall be able to do it [i.e. prevent the British from crossing the river], God only knows, as they are still hovering about the river, and if every thing else fails will wait till the first of Jany where their will be no other men to oppose them but militia, none of which but those from Philadelphia... are yet come (tho I am told some are expected from the back counties) when I say none but militia, I am to except the Virginia regiments & the shatterd remains of Smallwoods which by fatigue, want of cloaths &c, &c are reduced to nothing;
>
> Weedons which was the strongest, not having more than between one hundd & thirty & 40 men fit for duty; the rest being in hospitals. The unhappy policy of short inlistments, and a dependence upon militia will, I fear, prove the downfall of our cause, tho early pointed out with an almost prophetick spirit.[95]

While Washington was worried about the fate of Philadelphia, the British were taking Princeton and Trenton. Trenton was almost entirely deserted when the British arrived there on 8 December. Howe sent out light infantry to probe the American defenses. These forces came under heavy artillery fire from the other side of the Delaware. The light infantry and German troops were forced to retreat. The redcoats lost thirteen men from the American cannonading.

On 10 December, Washington began to deploy his army along the Delaware. He was explicit in his directions in the General Orders for that date.

> The General desires that Brigadiers Lord Stirling, Mercer, Stephen and de Fermoy, do, respectively, quarter their brigades in houses or hutts as compactly as possibly, that they may be soon form'd and ready for action at the shortest notice of the approach of the enemy. Each Brigadier is to take care of his own front, and keep strong guards at all the convenient passing places; the intermediate spaces between the brigades, are to be attended to by the Brigadiers next adjoining ...
>
> The Brigadiers are to use their utmost endeavours to have the men got under the best cover they can, consistent with the above order for quartering them compactly, and as it does not admit of a doubt but that the enemys attempt to cross the river will be conducted with the utmost secrecy and expedition, they cannot possible [sic] use too much vigilance and caution with their guards.
>
> That no intelligence may be conveyed to the enemy that can be avoided, no person is to pass the River but by written leave from the Brigadier in the district he commands, or a verbal message from him by an officer to the guard who has charge of the boats ...[96]

On 11 December, Washington wrote the President of Congress from his headquarters at the Falls of the Delaware. He had received information that the British had repaired the Crosswicks Bridge and an advance party was headed to Bordentown. Washington was convinced that they were moving on Philadelphia.

He reported that he had ridden up the Delaware to Lord Stirling's post the day before. There he found a prisoner from the 42nd Highland regiment who told the general that Cornwallis was at Pennington with two battalions of Grenadiers and three battalions of Light infantry, along with Hessian Grenadiers, the 42nd Highland regiment and two other battalions.

> He knew nothing of the reasons of their being assembled there, nor what were their future intentions; but I last night received information from my Lord Stirling, which had been brought in by his scouts, which in some measure accounted for their being there. They had made a forced march from Trenton on Sunday night to Coryell's Ferry, in hopes of surprising a sufficient number of boats to transport them, but finding themselves disappointed, had marched back to Penny Town where they remained yesterday.
>
> From their several attempts to seize boats, it does not look as if they had brought any with them, as I was at one time informed. I last night sent a person over to Trenton to learn whether there was any appearance of building any, but he could not perceive any preparations for a work of that kind ...[97]

On the same day, Washington wrote once again to Major General Lee saying "I shall only say that Philadelphia beyond all question, is the object of the enemy's movements and that nothing less than our utmost exertions, will be sufficient to prevent Genl Howe from possessing it. The force I have is weak and entirely incompetent to that end. I must therefore entreat you to push on with every possible succour you can bring ... You know the importance of the City of Philadelphia and the fatal consequences that must attend the loss of it."[98]

David Griffith, the regimental surgeon for the 3rd Virginia had been in Philadelphia attending the wounded since 8 December. He was also under orders to send the healthy men back to the army. He had left the army at Princeton on 6 December and heard of the British advance from Brunswick. He wrote his wife that "it is supposed that they mean to come to this place. If they succeed here, the dispute is at an end. I think there will not be much more opposition [that] Howe will [not be able to] terminate."[99]

On the 12 December, Washington described events to Governor Jonathan Trumbull of Connecticut, from his headquarters at Trenton Falls. He brought the Governor up to date on the happenings from the fall of Fort Washington, shared his concerns about the British intentions on Philadelphia, and gave him the most up-to-date information on the position of the two armies.

> The Delaware now parts the two armies; and nothing hinders the passage of the enemy, but the want of boats, which we have been lucky enough to secure. General Lee is still in the rear of the enemy, with about four thousand men, with whom he is on his march to join me; if he can effect this junction, our Army will again make a respectable appearance, and such as, I hope, will disappoint the enemy in their plan upon Philadelphia.[100]

On the same day, the members of the Continental Congress, perhaps bowing to the inevitable, left Philadelphia for Baltimore. At the same time, Washington wrote the President of Congress regarding his intelligence of British movements. It was "far from being so certain and satisfactory as I could wish," he said, "tho every probable means in my power and that I can devise are adopted for that purpose."

> The latest I have received was from Lord Stirling last night, he says that two Grenadiers of the Inniskilling Regiment who were taken and brought in by some countrymen, inform that Genls Howe, Cornwallis, Vaughan &c with about 6000 of the flying Army were at Penny Town waiting for pontoons to come up, with which they mean to pass the river near the Blue Mounts, or at Correls [Coryell's] Ferry, they believe the latter…the two Battalions of Guards were at Brunswick and the Hessian Grenadiers, Chasseurs and a regiment or two of British troops are at Trenton …[101]

On 13 December, Washington removed the army from Trenton Falls, fearing that the British had plans to land above and below the Trenton ferry. The general wanted to "throw them [his forces] into a different disposition on the River, whereby I hope not only to be more able to impede their passage, but also to avoid the danger of being inclosed in this angle of the river." In a letter to the President of Congress, written from the camp at Trenton Falls on the above date, he explained his actions further.

> … not withstanding the extended appearance of the enemy on the other side, made at least in part, to divert our attention from any particular pint, as well as to harrass us by fatigue, I cannot divest myself of the opinion that their principal design is to ford the river somewhere about Trenton; to which design I have had particular respect in the new arrangement, wherein I am so far happy to have the concurrence of all the General Officers at this place.
> Four brigades of the Army under Generals Lord Stirling, Mercer, Stephen and D'Fermoy extend from Yardley's up to Coryel's Ferry, posted in such a manner as to guard every suspicious part of the river and to afford assistance to each other, in case of attack. Genl Ewing with the Flying Camp of Pennsylvania and a few Jersey troops under General Dickinson, are posted from Yardley's Ferry down to the Ferry opposite Bordentown. Col. Cadwallader with the Pennsylvania Militia occupied the ground above and below the mouth of Neshaminy River, as far down as Dunks Ferry, at which place Colonel Nixon is posted with the 3d battalion of Philadelphia. A proper quantity of Artillery is appointed to each brigade, and I have ordered small redoubts to be thrown up opposite every place where there is a possibility of fording.[102]

Washington planned to remove "further up the river to be near the main body of my small Army, with which every possible opposition shall be given to any further approach of the enemy toward Philadelphia."[103]

In an earlier draft of this letter, Washington was even more explicit as to his placement of Lord Stirling's brigade. "As I cannot at present farther enter into the various motives of this alteration, I shall only add a copy of the arrangement itself. Generals Lord Sterling, Mercer, Stevens and La Roch De Fermoy's brigades are to take post at and below Corriels and McConkeys Ferrys. Lord Stirling's brigade to continue at and near where his head quarters are [at Blue Mount Ferry."[104]

On 14 December, Washington wrote Lord Stirling directly with a change in his orders.

> My Lord: Repair with all possible expedition to Genl Lee's Camp. Know his situation, numbers &ca. Send officers you can confide in to Genls Gates, and Heath, to be informd of their numbers, condition and when they may be expected at Pitts Town.
>
> Use very possible means without regard to expence, to come with certainty, at the enemys strength, situation and movements; without this we wander in a wilderness of uncertainties and difficulty, and no plan can be formd upon a rational plan. When you see Genl. Lee and converse with him as also (Gates and Heath if possible) what probable mode of attack can be attempted and give me the earliest advice of it; recollect that there is a difficulty in crossing from hence to the other side (on acct of boats) and that it will take some time to put the troops about Bristol in motion if a cooperation is necessary.
>
> Weigh every circumstance of attack, and retreat properly, that nothing that can be guarded against may be unprovided for. Give me the earliest and best advice of every matter; and do all in your power to inspirit the militia and bring them into use to the best advantage.
>
> Reposing the most implicit confidence in you and the officers before mentioned I do not mean to tie you down to any rule but leave you to the free exercise of your own judgments of wch as I before said I only want timely advice ...[105]

What an extraordinary letter! This letter, as no other in Washington's correspondence in December 1776, demonstrated the unswerving trust Washington had in the commander of the brigade in which the 3rd Virginia had been placed.

On the same day as the directive to Lord Stirling, Washington wrote Major General Lee, saying that there were still boats remaining at Tinnicum, under a strong guard, to transport him across the Delaware so he could proceed to Pittstown.

Washington noted that the British had advanced as far as Burlington while their main body was in the Trenton and Pennington vicinity. He informed Lee that although the Continental Congress had adjourned to Baltimore, he still planned to defend Philadelphia "to the utmost extremity." He appealed to Lee to move faster since his arrival "may be the means of saving" the city.[106]

At last on the move, Lee was in Basking Ridge at White's Tavern on 12–13 December with his aides and guards, several miles away from his army. On the morning of 14 December, the same day Washington was urging him to make haste, Lee was captured by members of the British dragoons. He was taken to Brunswick and "kept under close confinement."

> Lee sent word to Howe that he was ready to talk and offered unsolicited advice on how the Americans might be defeated. British leaders were appalled. Captain Munchausen wrote that Lee 'repeatedly asked to see general Howe, but Howe will not see him nor speak to him.' On infuriated British officer wrote of Lee, 'He is as perfect in treachery as if he had been an American born...They swallow their oaths of allegiance to the King and Congress alternately, with as much ease as your lordship does poached eggs ...[107]

Although the American army and Congress knew nothing of this perfidy and regarded Lee's capture as a loss to the American side, Washington finally lost patience with his general.[108] In a letter to his brother, John Augustine, written at the camp, near Trenton Falls, 18 December 1776, he gave full fury to his frustration over the capture.

> ... Before this reaches you, you will no doubt have heard of the captivity of Genl Lee; this is an additional misfortune, and the more vexatious, as it was by his own folly and imprudence (and without a view to answer any good) he was taken, going three miles out of his own camp [for the sake of a little better lodging] and with 20 of the enemy to lodge, a rascally Tory rid in the night to give notice of it to the enemy who sent a party of light Horse that seized and carried him with every mark of triumph and indignity.[109]

Mystified at the situation in which he found himself, he went on "You can form no idea of the perplexity of my situation. No man, I believe ever had a greater choice of difficulties and less means to extricate himself from them. However, under a full persuasion of the justice of our Cause I cannot [but think the prospect will brighten, although for a wise purpose it is, at present hid under a cloud] entertain an idea that it will finally sink tho' it may remain for some time under a cloud ..."[110]

TRENTON
25–26 DECEMBER 1776

Recap: British and American face–off across the Delaware.

The British went into winter quarters on 13 December in a string of outposts stretching from New York to Trenton.[111] Their invasion of New Jersey had been swift. They captured Brunswick on 2 December, and less than a week later, the redcoats were in Princeton, which they thoroughly plundered.[112] On 8 December they arrived at Trenton.

On that same day, the American army had made it safely across the Delaware into Pennsylvania. Washington's troops had destroyed bridges on the New Jersey roads as they went and Washington had added additional guards on all the ferry crossings into Pennsylvania.[113]

From the Pennsylvania side of the Delaware, the Americans spread out over a seventy mile section of the river. Four Brigades, including Stirling's, were set up to guard the river from Yardley's Ferry to Coryell's Ferry. Other units, mostly remnants of the Pennsylvania Flying Camp and some New Jersey militia, guarded the river from Yardley's Ferry to Bordentown. Pennsylvania troop extended the defensive line further south to Dunk's ferry while ships of the Pennsylvania Navy patrolled the river.[114]

Meanwhile, Howe, now in Trenton, ordered Lord Cornwallis, with four regiments, to requisition any boats at Coryell's Ferry for British use. Cornwallis left Maidenhead at one in the morning on 9 December with the Reserve and the 2nd Battalion of Light Infantry. They moved through Pennington to arrive at the Ferry only to find that the Americans had removed or destroyed all boats in the vicinity. He noted the presence of American troops directly across the river and returned to Pennington that afternoon. Then, a little less than a week later, on 13 December Howe announced that British troops were going into winter quarters.

Howe left scattered outposts of British troops in New Jersey. Two Hessian garrisons were in Bordentown and Trenton: Fifteen hundred in Bordentown and another fourteen hundred in Trenton. The remaining Jersey winter quarters were at Princeton, New Brunswick, Perth Amboy and Elizabethtown. Cornwallis took leave to return to England and Howe returned to New York, leaving the army in the hands of James Grant.[115]

Unaware that the British were through campaigning for the year and still worried that Philadelphia lay open to the redcoats, Washington issued orders to his generals on 14 December.

> ... I would advise you to examine the whole River from the upper to the lower Guard of your district; and after forming an opinion of the most probable crossing places, have those well watchd and direct the Regiments or companies most convenient to repair as they an be formed, immediately to the point of attack, and give the enemy all the opposition they possibly can, every thing in a manner depends upon the defence oat the water edge, in like manner one Brigade is to support another without loss of time, or waiting orders from me.
>
> I would also have you fix upon some central spot convenient to your Brigade, but in the rear a little and on some road leading into the back road to Philadelphia for your unnecessary baggage, waggons and stores, that in case your opposition should prove ineffectual these things may not fall but be got off and proceed over Neshamony Bridge towards German Town ...
>
> Let me entreat you to cast about to find some person who can be engaged to cross the River as a spy, that we may, if possible, obtain some knowledge of the enemy's situation, movements and intention; particular enquiry to be made by the person sent if any preparations are making to cross the River; whether any boats are building, and where; whether any are coming across land from Brunswick; whether any great collection of horses are made ... Expence must not be spared in procuring such Inteligence, and will readily be paid by me. We are in a neighbourhood of very disaffected people, equal care therefore should be taken that one of these persons do not undertake

the business in order to betray us … If possible get some person in to Trenton, and let him be satisfied if any boards are building at that place and on Croswicks Creek.[116]

In a letter to General Charles Lee,[117] Gates,[118] and Maxwell,[119] Washington issued orders to the three generals to proceed with their troops to meet up with Lord Stirling at Pittstown. His orders to Charles Lee came the day before his capture by the British dragoons, and noted that part of the British forces had advanced as far as Burlington; the rest were at Trenton and Pennington.[120]

In the letter to Major General Horatio Gates written on 14 December, Washington worried about Philadelphia and the small numbers of his army.

> … With a handful of men, compared to the Enemy's force, we have been pushed thro' the Jerseys, without being able to make the smallest opposition and to pass the Delaware. Genl Howe is now on the other side, and beyond all questions means, if possible, to possess himself of Philadelphia. His troops are extended from Penny Town to Burlington; the main body… within the neighbourhood of Trenton … few to the militia of this state have yet come out, except those belonging to the City, nor have I any great hope of their assistance, unless we can collect a respectable force … I have heard that you are coming on with seven regiments … and let me entreat you, not to delay a moment in hastening to Pitts Town.[121]

In a letter to his brother John Augustine, from the Camp near Trenton Falls on 18 December 1776, Washington noted the dwindling numbers of his army. He had expected "at least 5000 men of the Flying Campo and militia". Instead he found "less than one half and no disposition in the inhabitants to afford the least aid. This being perfectly well known by the enemy, they threw over a large body of troops, which pushed us from place to place till we were obliged to cross the Delaware with less than 3000 men fit for duty, owing to the dissolution of our force by short inlistments; the enemy's numbers, from the best accts exceeding ten and by some 12,000 men."

After removing to the Pennsylvania side of the Delaware, Washington continued, he had all the boats and vessels brought over or destroyed from Philadelphia "upwards for 70 miles" and having instituted guard posts along the river, "baffled all their attempts to cross". He was heartened by the augmentation to his forces of 2000 Philadelphia militia but had "no doubt that General Howe [would] still make an attempt on Philadelphia this winter."[122]

"A Stroke upon the forces of the enemy": Plans for an attack on Trenton.

Washington may have been laying plans for a counterattack on the British as early as 14 December when he wrote Gates to say "if we can draw our forces together, I trust … we may yet effect an important stroke, or at least prevent Genl Howe from executing his plans."[123]

In another letter to Governor Trumbull of Connecticut Washington stated he wanted to

> attempt a stroke upon the forces of the enemy, who lay a good deal scattered and to all appearance in a state of security. A lucky blow in this quarter would be fatal to them, and would most certainly raise the spirits of the people, which are quite sunk by our late misfortunes.[124]

The commander in chief knew that time was of the essence. He was going to lose all his troops, except his Virginians and Smallwood's Marylanders, by the end of the month when their enlistments expired.[124] So if he was to plan any kind of "stroke upon the forces of the enemy," it must be before then.

At the beginning of December, Washington had only 3765 troops who were fit for duty under his direct command.[125] Among these troops was Colonel Weedon's 3rd Virginia who numbered only 290 men and officers fit for duty. Weedon's 1 December 1776 return for the 3rd Virginia showed a colonel, lieutenant colonel, major, five captains 13 lieutenants, and eight ensigns. His staff consisted of an adjutant, a quartermaster, and a surgeon. There were 290 men and officers fit for duty. This figure did not include the 30 who were sick and present or the 217 who were sick and absent. Nor did it include the two men who were on furlough or the sixty-four who were on command.[126]

By 22 December, Washington's forces had increased somewhat. On paper, he had 11423 men and officers spread out among eight brigades. In reality, however, 6104 were fit for duty. Colonel Weedon's 3rd Virginia, in Lord Stirling's brigade, numbered only 181 "effectives" out of the total of 633 men in the regiment.[127]

Washington planned his attack on Trenton as a "secret expedition".[128] The broad plan of attack was for the general and his veteran continental troops to cross the Delaware at McConkey's and Johnson's ferries, some ten mile upstream from Trenton and attack the town from the north and west. James Ewing's brigade, numbering 800 Pennsylvania militia, was to cross the Delaware at the Trenton ferry and take and hold the bridge across Assunpink Creek. These troops were to block the only exit from Trenton to the southeast of town.

John Cadwallader's 1200 Philadelphia militia and Colonel Daniel Hitchcock's 600 New Englanders were to embark near Bristol, Pennsylvania and land in Burlington, New Jersey. They were to divert the attention of Colonel von Donop's Hessians and the Highland troops under Colonel Thomas Stirling from what was happening in Trenton. "I am determined, as the night is favourable, to cross the River and make the attack upon Trenton in the morning" Washington wrote Cadwallader. "If you can do nothing real, at least create as great a diversion as possible."[129]

Washington even had some hopes that Israel Putnam, now organizing the defense of Philadelphia, might cross the river and join the South Jersey militia south of Mount Holly.[130] That was the plan.

The specifics were a little more precise. A small detachment of infantry, of about forty men, under the command of Captain William Washington of the 3rd Virginia, was to operate as an advance party. Their orders were to set road blocks outside Trenton and detain anyone coming in or out of town. Another detachment under Captain John Flahaven of the 1st New Jersey was to block the lower River Road that ran beside the Delaware River to Trenton.

General Adam Stephen's brigade of Virginians, part of General Nathaniel Greene's left wing, was to attack the Hessian guards and sentries on the periphery of Trenton, seize the alarm posts and storm any house in the town that offered resistance. General Stephen was given the further responsibility to appoint a guard to form a chain of sentries around the landing-place at a sufficient distance from the river, to permit the troops to form. This force was not to allow anyone to go in or come out of Trenton and was ordered to detain anyone who attempted to do so. These men could rejoin their brigade only after all the troops were over the Delaware.

Washington divided the army into two divisions. The right wing of the army was to be under General John Sullivan's command. These troops were men from New England, composed of St. Clair's, Glover's, and Sargent's brigades. They were to advance along the River Road and enter Trenton from the southwest. General St. Clair's brigade was to form the reserve for this wing

The left wing Washington placed under the command of Nathaniel Greene. This division included three brigades, one of which was Stirling's. His brigade along with General Mercer's brigade was to act as a support for Adam Stephen. Stirling's brigade was also to form the reserve for the left wing. Greene's division was to approach Trenton by way of the Pennington road, moving inland and approaching the town from the northwest. In addition, one of the brigades in Greene's division was to march via the Princeton road and enter Trenton from the northeast. They were to block that road and encircle the town.[131]

> Nathanael Greene had the hardest task. He was to lead his division left at Birmingham crossroads to the upper Ferry Road. It ran uphill away from the river to the Scotch Road and the Pennington Road, which would bring Greene's division into Trenton on its northern side. The other division of the army under Sullivan had orders to continue on the River Road and 'enter the town by Water Street.' Greene's roundabout uphill route was the longer and slower of the two. He was ordered to start first and move quickly. Washington rode with him, to help spur the men forward. As Sullivan had the shorter distance and a down hill road, he was told to 'halt for a few minutes at the cross road which leads to Howell's Ferry' so that both divisions would reach Trenton at the same time ...[132]

Each brigadier was "to make the colonels acquainted with the posts of their respective regiments... and the major-generals will inform them of the posts of the brigades in the line." The artillery was split among the brigades—four pieces at the head of each column, three pieces at the head of the second brigade in each division and two pieces with each of the reserves.

The troops were to cross the Delaware at McConkey's Ferry as soon as it grew dark, in the following order: In Greene's 1st division, the left wing, General Stephen's brigade was to go first, then General Mercer followed by Lord Stirling. General Fermoy was to march in the rear of the Major General Sullivan's division. He was allowed to take two artillery pieces with him. His brigade was to file off from Pennington to the Princeton road in order to secure the passes between Princeton and Trenton. The rest of Sullivan's division was to embark in the following order: first, St. Clair, then Glover, followed by Sargent's brigade. Washington ordered "a profound silence and no man [was] to quit his ranks on pain of death."

Each brigadier was to appoint flanking parties while the reserve brigade, in this instance Stirling's brigade for Greene's left wing, and General St. Clair for Sullivan's right wing, could appoint their own rear guards of their columns. "The heads of the columns [were] to arrive at Trenton at five o'clock."[133]

FIGURE 1. On the March to Trenton

Virginia descriptions of the approach to Trenton: Lieutenant James Monroe's account of the advance party's advance toward Trenton.

James Monroe was a young lieutenant in Captain William Washington's company in December 1776. Captain Washington and his eighteen year old lieutenant led their company to the Pennington Road and the highway between Trenton and Princeton.[134]

> After crossing the Delaware, Captain Washington, Monroe, and their men, as Monroe would later recall had 'hastened to a point which led from Trenton to Princeton, for the purpose, in obedience to orders of cutting off all communication between them from the country to to Trenton. The night was tempestuous ... and made more severe by a heavy fall of snow.' Here they remained on guard until General Green's troops caught up with them ...[135]

Thankfully, they reached their destination without incident. "Captain Washington executed his orders faithfully. He soon took possession of the point to which he was ordered, and holding it through the night, intercepted and made prisoners of many who were passing in directions to and from Trenton."[136]

> Whilst occupying this position, the resident of a dwelling some distance up a lane, had his attention directed to some unusual commotion by the barking of dogs. He came out in the dark to learn the cause, and encountered my command, and supposing we were from the British camp, ordered us off. He was violent and determined in his manner and very profane and wanted to know what we were doing there on such a stormy night.[137]

The lieutenant ordered the man to return to his house and be quiet or be arrested. When the resident realized he was talking to American troops, his manner changed.

He invited the men into his house, out of the storm, and offered to give them something to eat. Orders were orders, Monroe told him, and they could not leave their post. The man hurried back to his house and in a short time returned from some food for the men. 'I know something is to be done,' he said to Monroe, 'and I'm going with you. I'm a doctor and I may be of help to some poor fellow.' This was agreeable to Monroe and Captain Washington. The man—he really was a doctor, it turned out, Dr. John Riker—waited with the soldiers for the rest of Washington's Continentals to appear. When they did, about dawn, Dr. Riker joined the march along with Captain Washington's party.[138]

Virginia descriptions of the approach to Trenton: Adam Stephen's unauthorized foray into Trenton.

A little after sunrise on 26 December, the main columns of the army were within two or three miles of Trenton when a group of fifty armed men were spotted coming from Trenton. Washington hastened to the front of the column and discovered, to his astonishment, that these were a party of Virginians from Adam Stephen's 4th Virginia regiment.

Since these troops were not in any advanced detachment, Washington asked Captain George Wallis, their commander, why they were coming from Trenton.

Wallis said that a few days before Christmas, Hessian Jaegers had killed one of his brigade commander's men in a boat on the river. Stephen, on Christmas Eve, before the army was informed on the Trenton mission, acted on his own and ordered a raiding party to cross the Delaware and "take revenge." So, as the sun was setting on Christmas day, Captain Wallis and his company crossed the river into New Jersey. The rest of the army, meanwhile, was mustering in Pennsylvania and Adam Stephen had not bothered to tell Washington of the raid.

As night fell on Christmas, Wallis's raiding company attacked a Hessian outpost at Trenton. He thought the American had killed four German soldiers and wounded eleven. The foray drew the attention of the Hessian forces in Trenton and an alarm was sounded which brought out the entire garrison, led by Colonel Rall himself. The Hessians quickly mounted their horses and took after the small force of Virginians. Fortunately Captain Wallis and his company eluded the Germans and remained on the outskirts of town until the next morning, when they met Washington's columns coming towards Trenton.

> George Washington listened to the story of Captain Wallis with growing dismay. He was convinced that all his attempts to achieve surprise and secrecy had been wrecked by one of his own officers. He summoned Adam Stephen from the column and asked if it was so. Stephen confirmed the truth of it. The general grew very angry. 'You, Sir!' he raged. 'You, Sir, may have ruined all my plans by having put them on their guard.' Others remembered that they had never seen Washington in such a fury. The more he thought about what Stephen had done, the more infuriated he became. Once again, the indiscipline of the American army and even of its high officers threatened his entire operation.[139]

Twentieth Century Historians[140] descriptions of Trenton involving Stirling's brigade or the 3rd Virginia.

Colonel George Weedon and his regiment were in the middle of Trenton in the vicinity of General Knox's artillery who was blasting away at the enemy.

> Henry Knox went over to [Weedon] and asked if he thought some of his men could get down the street and capture the Hessian cannon. [Weedon] turned and gave an order to Captain William Washington, who with young James Monroe and a Massachusetts sergeant named Joseph White and several other men, lit out along the west side of the street, keeping close to the houses and running for all they were worth in the direction of the guns.
>
> 'I hallowed as loud as I could scream to the men to run for their lives right up to the pieces,' White said, and he was the first soldier to reach them. There was only one Hessian left there when he raced up, and the man ran when White drew his sword back over his head to take a swipe at him.

The rebels swarmed around the cannon and began turning it towards the Hessians who were crowded into the alley' William Washington by this time was wounded in both hands, and Monroe's shoulder was bleeding profusely from a ball which had cut an artery.[141]

Another view of this encounter gave more detail about the New England and Virginia forces who stormed this Hessian battery. Joseph White was a New Englander, a sergeant whose artillery crew had worked their gun so hard they shattered its carriage. The gun crew was forced to stand idle while the Hessians fired away at them.

Colonel Knox rode up to Sergeant White's destroyed gun, looked towards the Hessian battery and said, " 'My brave lads, go up and take those two held pieces sword in hand. There is a party going [Captain Washington of Weedon's 3rd Virginia] and you must join them.' " The battery commander, Captain John Allen, repeated the order. " 'You heard what the colonel said, Sergeant White. Now take your men and join the others in the attack.' "

Sergeant White did so and found that the party consisted mostly of Virginias commanded by Captain Washington and Lieutenant James Monroe. "The Virginia infantry and New England gunners charged side by side straight towards the Hessian guns." Lieutenant Monroe remembered that "Captain Washington rushed forward, attacked and put the troops around the cannon to flight and took possession of [the guns]."

In the ensuing fight, Captain Washington went down, severely wounded in both hands. Lieutenant Monroe then took over and led the men. He was hit by a musket ball, which severed an artery and was carried from the field, bleeding profusely. "His life was saved by Doctor Riker, who had joined Monroe's company as a volunteer the night before. The New Jersey physician clamped Monroe's artery just in time to keep him from bleeding to death."[142]

Another description by the same historian illustrated the advantages of good intelligence and the rewards of catching an enemy unaware.

George Washington was well informed about the German dispositions in Trenton. His tactical intelligence was excellent this day. After hearing from his scouts, Washington halted the American left wing on the Pennington Road, behind a screen of woods. They were about eight hundred yards from the Hessian guard house, a small wood-frame cooper shop that belonged to Richard and Arthur Howell, a mile from the town center.

Senior American officers deployed their brigades in three attacking columns: Mercer's New Englanders and Maryland men on the right, Stephen's Virginians and Stirling's Delaware men in the center; and Fermoy's Pennsylvanians on the American left. The vanguard was Virginia infantry, led by Captain William Washington and Lieutenant James Monroe.

On command the three columns started forward in a thick flurry of snow. George Washington himself led the attack in the center. As the men emerged from the woods into open fields on both sides of the road, Washington picked up the pace. One soldier remembered that he led them forward t a "long trot" across the fields.

Peering ahead through dense clouds of swirling snow, they saw a door open at the cooper shop, and a Hessian emerged. An American raised his weapon, fired at long range, and missed. Other Hessians ran out of the cooper shop, pulling on their coats and equipment. The Americans managed to get of a ragged volley in the storm, then a second and a third. The Hessians formed and fired back.

The time was a little past eight o'clock. Three minutes later, the heavy boon of American artillery was heard from the lower River Road. In the center of the town, German kettledrums suddenly began to beat the urgent call to arms. George Washington could scarcely believe it. Both American wings attacked at nearly the same moment, thorough a heavy squall of snow that masked their approach. Against all expectation, they had taken the Hessians by surprise.[143]

Such was the stuff of legends.

George Washington, on 27 December 1776, wrote the president of the Continental Congress with a description of the battle. That description appeared in the *Virginia Gazette* on 10 January 1777. It appeared to have been the lone comprehensive account of this battle. None of the 3rd Virginia officers— Captain John Chilton, Captain Gustavus Brown Wallace, or regimental surgeon and chaplain David Griffith—whose letters remain extant, wrote of Trenton.

Colonel Weedon, who was always ready to sing the praises of the regiment he commanded, was also silent. There was no account in his extant letters at the Library of Virginia. Likewise, there was no letter to the *Virginia Gazette*, his usual platform for touting the prowess of his regiment at Trenton.

True, there *were* excerpts from James Monroe's autobiography on the part his company played at Trenton already quoted above. However, it appeared that the only complete account of the action which took place on Christmas and the day after, was the one sent by Washington to the President of the Continental Congress on 27 December and published in the *Gazette* on 10 January 1777.

> ...The evening of the 25th, I ordered the troops intended for this service to parade back of McKonky's ferry, that they might begin to pass as soon as it grew dark, imagining we should be able to throw them all over, with the necessary artillery, by 12 o'clock, and that we might easily arrive at Trenton by five in the morning, the distance being about nine miles. But the quantity of ice, made that night, impeded the passage of the boats so much, that it was three o'clock before the artillery could all be got over, and near four before the troops took up their line of march.
>
> I formed my detachment into two divisions, one to march up the lower or river road, the other by the upper or Pennington road. As the divisions had nearly the same distance to march, I ordered each of them immediately upon forcing the out guards, to push directly into the town, that they might charge the enemy before they had time to form. The upper division arrived at the enemy's advanced post exactly at 8 o'clock, and in three minutes after, I found, from the fire on the lower road that that division had also got up: The out guards made but a small opposition, though, for their numbers, they behaved very well, keeping up a constant retreating fire from behind houses.
>
> We presently saw their main body formed, but, from their motions, they seemed undetermined how to act. Being hard pressed by our troops, who had already got possession of part of their artillery, they attempted to file off by a road, on their right, leading to Princeton; but perceiving their intention, I threw a body of troops in their way, which immediately checked them; Finding, from our disposition, that they were surrounded, and they must inevitably be cut to pieces, if they made any further resistance, they agreed to lay down their arms. The number that submitted in this manner, was 23 officers, and 886 men. Col. Rohl, the commanding officers, and seven others, were found wounded in the town. I don't exactly know how many they had killed; but I fancy not above twenty or thirty, as they never made any regular stand. Our loss is very trifling indeed, only two officers [William Washington and James Monroe of the 3rd Virginia] and one or two privates wounded.[144]

Interestingly enough, the original letter contained more information. Washington related the difficulties imposed upon the troops by the formation of ice in the river and then went on to say

> this made me despair of surprising the Town, as I well knew we could not reach it before the day was fairly broke, but as I was certain there was no making a retreat without being discovered, and harassed on repassing the river, I determined to push on at all events.[145]

The original draft also contained information of interest relating to Stirling's brigade, which was later crossed out.

> [The enemy] first moved towards their left, but being briskly charged by Genl Sullivans division, they were drove into the Town again; they then filed off to their right and I suspected were attempting to gain a road leading to Princetown, upon which I ordered Colo Hands and the German Battalion to throw themselves before them, this they did with spirit and rapidity and immediately checked them. I then ordered Lord Stirling to advance his brigade upon their other flank which effectually prevented them from regaining the town, finding themselves in this situation and seeing our other troops advancing upon them from every quarter they in a very little time agreed to lay down their arms.[146]

Robert Morris, a delegate to Congress from Pennsylvania[147] wrote the commander-in-chief on 26 December from Philadelphia.

> We have just heard of your success at Trenton. The acct is but imperfect but we learn you are master of that place & of all the baggage & stores our enemies had there & of 300 prisoners and that your troops were still in pursuit of the flying enemy. I have just wrote to Congress & told

them thus much as the substance of an acct just come down & I told them further I had been informed that you had executed in this matter your part of a well concerted plan, that Genl Heath at Hackensack had orders from you & that Genl Ewing & Colo Cadwallader also had orders to cross [the] Delaware at the same time you did, but had been prevented by driving ice.[148]

Colonel Weedon and the Hessian prisoners

Immediately after the battle at Trenton, General Washington "gave the 3rd Virginia the honor of escorting several hundred Hessian prisoners to Philadelphia. Thus, the regiment did not participate in the subsequent and equally impressive victory at Princeton on January 3, 1777."[149]

That the 3rd Virginia did not participate in the victory at Princeton appears to have been contradicted by 3rd Virginia veterans who later filed for pensions. Edward Abbey, a soldier in Captain Fitzgerald's company, later David Arell's, relates the retreat through New Jersey when the army crossed the Delaware into Pennsylvania where they remained until Christmas.

> We then recrossed the Delaware to the Jersey side and attacked + took a body of Hessian troops in Trenton and crossed with the prisoners to the Pennsylvania side of the river, and then soon after, crossed back again to the Jersey side to keep possession of Trenton. There we were met in the evening by a reinforcement of the enemy under the command of Lord Cornwallace from Princetown; only a few rounds were fired + hostilities ceased for the night.
>
> The American army moved towards Princeton the next day and engaged a detachment of British troops near Princeton at day break. Our army entered Princeton victoriously ... It was this engagement where General Mercer was mortally wounded. We then marched to Morristown where we remained for the balance of the winter.[150]

It would appear, from Edward Abbey's statements above, that Captain Arell's company at least, recrossed the Delaware almost immediately after depositing their prisoners in Pennsylvania and met a reinforcement of British forces under Cornwallis. He specifically says "our army entered Princeton victoriously ... we then marched to Morristown ..."

Spencer Anderson, a private in Captain Phill Lee's company, stated, in his pension declaration, that he had been "wounded over his eye at Princeton." [151] David Baker, a private in Captain John Thornton's Company fought at Trenton, "guarding the baggage during this battle. His brother Richard was killed at Trenton. He fought at Princeton where General Mercer of Virginia was killed. He was with the army when they went into winter quarters at Morristown.[152] Isaac Barr, a private in Captain John Ashby's company stated he took part in both the battles of Trenton and Princeton.[153] It would seem, from this sampling of pension declarations of 3rd Virginia veterans that at least *some* of the men in the companies of Captains Ashby, Arell, Lee, and Thornton saw action at Princeton.

After the surrender at Trenton, the Hessian prisoners were quickly collected and marched off towards Johnson's Ferry, under guard. They crossed the Delaware with the American troops; the officers were separated from the enlisted men who were quartered at Newtown. The officers spent their first night as prisoners of the Americans at McKonkey's Ferry. They were housed in the ferry-house, all twenty-seven crammed into the small room. After that first night, their treatment improved. On signing a parole, they were taken to Newtown and "given considerable freedom of movement."[154]

Four days later, Colonel George Weedon, the commanding officer of the 3rd Virginia, escorted the Hessian officers to Philadelphia. He arrived, on New Year's Eve,[155] and delivered them to the Council of Safety, along with six captured flags. "We hear", the dispatch went on, "the Colonel sets off again, in a day or two, for the continental army in Jersey."[156]

It is likely that Colonel Weedon took an honor guard selected from his regiment's companies to accompany him. Since the above dispatch stated the Colonel was to leave Philadelphia, "in a day or two, for the continental army in Jersey," he and his detachment may not have arrived in time to take part in the action at Princeton. However, it does appear from the pension declarations of men in other 3rd Virginia companies that they did indeed take part in this engagement.

The "Ten Dollar Men"

Although Congress had granted "dictatorial powers" to Washington regarding army matters,[157] the General knew his time to plan any further action with the enemy was limited; his army, with the exception of his Virginia regiments, was due to be discharged at the end of the month. Among those troops were "some of his best regiments". Glover's Massachusetts troops were one such unit who had played such an important part in the Trenton operation, transporting the men over the ice-filled Delaware. Haslet's Delaware regiment which was part of Stirling's brigade was another. Their enlistments ended December 30th and they departed for home, leaving Colonel Haslet and six officers behind. "If Washington hoped to remain in the field, he had to persuade some of his veterans to stay with him." [158]

The general borrowed an idea from Thomas Mifflin, a Philadelphia merchant-turned-militia-general, who advanced a novel idea to the New England regiments at Crosswicks who were scheduled for discharge.

The militia general mustered the New England troops on horseback, clothed in a rose colored blanket overcoat and fur hat. He entreated them to think about why they were there and what they had been fighting for; he appealed to their conscience and, even more importantly, offered them a bounty of ten dollars to be paid in hard money, not in the all-but-worthless continental currency, if they would stay on for just six more weeks. He asked them to cock their firelocks if they were willing to stay. One of the members of the regiment remembered that everyone's firelock went up. Captain Stephen Olney's regiment " 'agreed to stay to men; as did also the others, except a few who made their escape by the enemy at Trenton...' "[159]

Washington decided to try the same approach with his continental troops in Greene's and Sullivan's division. He mustered the New England continentals and implored them to serve another six weeks. He spoke of the great need for troops, that they could do more for their country now than any future date. The regimental commanders asked the troops to step forward. The drums beat but no one made a move. They were worn out, they said, they wanted "to go home." Washington rode again to the front of the lines and addressed them again.

> My brave fellows, you have done all I asked you to do, and more than could be reasonably expected; but your country is at stake, your wives, your houses, and all that you hold dear. You have worn yourselves out with the fatigues and hardships, but we know not how to spare you. If you will consent to stay one month longer; you will render that service to the cause of liberty, and to your country, which you probably can never do under other circumstances.[160]

He then sweetened the pot by offering a ten dollar bounty, hard money, to every continental soldier who agreed to stay. It worked. In the end, nearly all of the troops fit for duty, stayed—some 200 veterans joined the Virginia regiments. One of the soldiers who stayed " 'remembered later that nearly half of the men who stepped forward would be killed in the fighting or [would be] dead of disease 'soon after.' "[161]

In a letter to the commanding officer at Morristown on 30 December 1776, Washington was pleased

> to acquaint you that the Continental Regiments from the eastern governments, have, to a man, agreed to stay six weeks beyond their term of inlistment, which was to have expired the last day of this month; for this extraordinary mark of their attachment to their country, I have agreed to give them a bounty of ten dollars pr man, besides their pay ... I hope this noble example will be followed by the four regiments under your command; promise them the same reward and endeavour to work upon them by every means in your power; let them know the militia are pouring in from all quarters and only want veteran troops to lead them on.[162]

Washington had his breathing space ... even though his forces were substantially reduced. The three New England brigades that numbered 2600 men on 22 December 1776 were reduced to 1400 men during the first weeks of January 1777. "Mercer's and Stirling's brigades, 1,500 men a week earlier, were now consolidated in one small unit of 325." Stephen's brigade contained approximately 400 men; Fermoy's Pennsylvania regiment numbered around 610 men. All told, Washington lost approximately 2600 of his veterans to illness and to the conclusion of their enlistments.

On the plus side, he still had 3300 veterans that he could use for another engagement with the British. Washington awaited the arrival of Mifflin's Pennsylvania militia, nearly 1500 men. General Mifflin had formed them into a brigade at Burlington. General Cadwalader's brigade of Philadelphia Associators was also on the march—between 1700 and 1800 men—to join the continental forces. General Ewing took the field with another militia brigade, the remnants of the old Flying camp. The Jersey militia, too, had risen to the occasion. So the general had augmented his forces considerably.[163]

After Trenton, Washington decided to move his troops to the more easily defended open knoll south of Assunpink Creek. It had a deep creek in front, the Delaware on its right flank and impassable swamps on the right flank. The Creek itself could only be crossed at a narrow stone bridge or several fords. The rising ground behind the creek "made a perfect glacis, with broad fields of fire for infantry and artillery. It was a natural fortress against an enemy who approached from the north."[164]

Skirmish at Assunpink: Prelude to Princeton, 2 January 1777

Thomas Rodney, a Delaware militia captain, described the action at Allentown on 2 January.

> Trenton stands upon the River Delaware, with a creek called the Assanpink passing through the town across which there is a bridge. The enemy came down on the upper side of this creek, through the town, and a number of our troops were posted with riflemen and artillery to oppose their approach.
> The main body of our army was drawn up on a plain below, or on the lower sided of the Assanpink, near the bridge, and the main force of our Artillery was posted on the banks and high ground along the creek in front of them ...
> The attack began about 2 o'clock and a heavy fire upon both sides, chiefly from the artillery continued until dark. At this time the enemy were left in possession of the upper part of the town but we kept6 possession of the bridge, altho' the enemy attempted several time to carry it but were repulsed each time with great slaughter.
> After sunset this afternoon the enemy came down in a very heavy column to force the bridge. The fire was very heavy and the Light troops were ordered to fly to the support of that important post ... The enemy were soon defeated and retired and the American army also retired to the woods, where they encamped and built up fires.[165]

Robert Morris, in a letter to Silas Deane on 8 January, gave more details of this skirmish and the part Washington assigned to Lord Stirling and his brigade.

> During this time, General Howe sent all the reinforcements he could from New York & whilst Genl Washington was collecting his whole force at Trenton [the] enemy were doing the same at Brunswick. On the 2d instant, our Army was collected and had concerted some plan of operations when intelligence was brought that the enemies main body were on their march [to] attack them at Trenton.
> Genl Washington [dispatched] a brigade under Ld. Stirling to amuse them... he drew the whole army (that Brigadier excepted) [over] the Bridge of Trenton & took post on the Heights [on] the side the creek that runs through that place. [He] posted his artillery advantageously and waited the return of Lord Stirling's brigade, which met [the] enemy & kept up a warm fire against them, retreating from about one oClock until Sunsett [when] they entered & marched through Trenton.
> The enemy pushed them very hard & killed near 100 of our [men] at the bridge which they attempted to cross, but [so soon] as our own people were over the compliment was [...] return and equal, if not a great slaughter, made amongst them. They were broke and retired, each army then mounted their guards within 100 yards of each other ... a bloody battle was expected the next day.[166]

PRINCETON
3 JANUARY 1777

As the morning of 3 January dawned, the Continental Congress voiced its anxiety in a letter from its Executive Committee to John Hancock.

> [We] have reason to think an engagement was commenced this morning the decision of which will have the most important consequences to all America. Cap James Nicholson (of the Frigate Virga.) came down from Trenton about an hour ago & says that Genl Mifflin & Genl Cadwallader joined Genl Washington yesterday in the forenoon, that he imagines a plan of attacking the enemy had been concerted & was to have been executed this day, that Ld Stirling's and Colo Hands Brigades had been sent from Trenton on the road to Prince Town yester forenoon and then about one oClock they fired the alarm guns, about three miles from Trenton where they met the enemy who pressed on them with superiour numbers ...
> [These] two brigades supported a retreating engagement from that time until sunset when they joined our main army which had taken post & was drawn up on the high grounds of this side Trenton Bridge. The loss of the two brigades Capt Nicholson thinks was inconsiderable, he saw but two or three wounded men come in & don't imagine the whole loss can amount to 100 men.[167]

Captain Nicholson went on to tell the executive committee that the American forces "must have suffered much from the severe cold" of the night. Because the two armies were so near to one another, the American forces probably did not sleep well. He thought the enemy numbered around 7000 troops.[168]

In an extract of a letter from Philadelphia, published in the *Virginia Gazette* on 24 January 1777,

> Glorious intelligence has this day arrived from Jersey. Every countenance, a few of the wretched [Tory] excepted, seems to sparkle with joy. The substance of the information I have received is, that our army, after a long conflict with ... the enemy, are in possession of Princeton, and driving them with the utmost precipitation, insomuch that it is not doubted but a total rout...
> I have great pleasure in informing you that troops from the country are continually coming into this city, on their way to join general Washington, and in such numbers as would really amaze you; that 3000 are, this day, to march to Bristol, headed by the gallant general Putnam; and col. Fleming's battalion of 6 or 700 continental troops, from the Eastern Shore of Virginia, it is expected, will be in town this evening ...[169]

Details of this "glorious intelligence" were soon forthcoming, provided for by a "gentleman of great worth, in the American army" in a dispatch to the *Virginia Gazette* dated 7 January 1776 near Princeton.

> On the 2^d instant intelligence was received, by express that the enemy's army was advancing from Princeton towards Trenton, where the main body of our forces was then stationed. Two brigades, under brigadier—generals Stephen and Fermoy, had been detached several days before, from the main body, to Maidenhead, and were ordered to skirmish with the enemy during their march, and to retreat to Trenton, as occasion should require.
> A body of men, under command of col. Hand were also ordered to meet the enemy, by which means their march was so much retarded as to give ample time for our forces to form, and prepare to give them a warm reception upon their arrival.
> Two field pieces, planted upon a hill, at a small distance above the town, were managed with great advantage, and did considerable execution for sometime; after which they were ordered to retire to the station occupied by our forces on the south side of the bridge, over the little [part?] which divides the town into two parts and opens at right angles into the Delaware.
> In their way through the town the enemy suffered much by an incessant fire of musketry, from behind the houses and barns. Their army had now arrived at the northern side of the bridge, whilst our army was drawn up, in order of battle, on the southern side. Our cannon played very briskly from this eminence, and were returned as briskly by the enemy. In a few minutes after the cannonade began a very heavy discharge of musketry ensued, and continued for 10 or 15 minutes.
> During the action a party of men were detached from our right wing, to secure a part of the river, which it was imagined, from the motions of the enemy, they intended to ford. This detachment arrived at the pass very opportunely, and effected their purpose. After this, the enemy

made a feeble and unsupported attempt to pass the bridge, but this likewise proved abortive. It was now near 6 o'clock in the evening, and night coming on, closed the engagement.

Our fires were built in due season, and very numerous, and whilst the enemy were amused by these appearances, and preparing for a general attack the ensuing morning, our army marched, about 1 in the morning, from Trenton, on the south side of the creek, to Princeton.

When they arrived near the hill, about one mile from Princeton, they found a body of the enemy formed upon it, and ready to receive them; upon which a spirited attack was made upon them, both with field pieces and musketry, and after an obstinate resistance, and losing a considerable number of their men upon the field, those of them who could not make their escape surrendered, [as] prisoners of war. We immediately marched on to the centre of the town, and there took another party of the enemy, near the college.

After tarrying a short time in the town, general Washington marched his army from thence towards Rocky Hill, and they are now at Morris town, in high spirits, and in expectation of a junction with the rest of our forces, sufficiently seasonable to make a general attack upon the enemy, and prevent, at least, a considerable part of them from reaching their asylum in New York.

It is difficult, precisely, to ascertain the loss we have sustained in the two engagements; but, as near as I can judge, I think we have lost about 40 men killed, and had near double the number wounded. In the list of the former are the brave col. Hazlett, cap. Shippen, and capt. Neal, who fell in the engagement upon the hill near Princeton ...

According to information from the inhabitants of Princeton, the number which marched out of it to attack our army amounted to 13,000 men, under command of general Cornwallis. This body, as soon as they discovered that they were out-generalled by the march of general Washington, being much chagrined at their disappointment (as it seems they intended to have cut our army to pieces, crossed the Delaware, and marched immediately, without any farther delay, to Philadelphia) pushed, with the greatest precipitation, towards Princeton, where they arrived about an hour after general Washington had left it; and imagining he would attempt to take Brunswick in the same manner, proceeded directly for that place.

Our soldiers were much fatigued, the greatest part of them having been deprived of their rest the two preceding nights, otherwise, we might, perhaps, have possessed ourselves of Brunswick. The enemy appear to be preparing to decamp, and retire to New York, as they are much disgusted with their late treatment in New Jersey, and have a great inclination to rest themselves a little in some secure winter quarters.[170]

Robert Morris's aforementioned letter to Silas Deane on 8 January also contained details of the battle at Princeton. He explained to Deane that Washington was concerned about the mood of the militia for if "he gave battle or waitd to be attackd he could not promise himself the least chance of success, [and] being beaten, his army would instantly disperse and leave this province to the enemy." Moreover, the boats used to cross the Delaware were now on the Pennsylvania side above Trenton so it was impossible to cross back over the river to the safety of the Pennsylvania countryside. If he retreated towards Bordentown, then his "raw troops would be totally dispirited." He decided, instead, to "strike a bold stork that might disconcert the enemy and gain him time to place himself in a better posture."

[Washington] knew there was at Prince [town] a party of not more than 2000 men with cloathing, [stores] & baggage, that at Brunswick was the Chief of [their] stores & baggage but badly guarded. He called a [Council] of the Genl officers, told them his situation and proposed decamping and by a forced march thro the woods round Trenton to surprise Prince Town in the morning. This was agreed to and orders given accordingly.

About 12 oClock the whole army was in motion, not knowing where they were going and a guard of about 500 men left at the bridge, totally ignorant of this movement (except the commanding officers). [The] fires had all been made up afresh before the march & the intire baggage of the army sent off for Burlington so that few of [the] soldiers took with them even their blankets. The [enemy] never discovered this movement nor did our own guards at the bridge, until the morning, when our army had passed Maidenhead on their march to Princetown ...

About a mile & a half of this side [of Princeton] the enemy had taken post very advantageously, consisting of three Regimts of British, some broke Hessians & highlanders & a small party of Light horse, a small action ensued between them & our advanced party, in which both sides exemplified great bravery ... [The] enemy were forced to give way to superior numbers, with the loss of 50 or 60 killed, as many wounded and 140 prisoners.

> Our army pushed on, took possession of Prince Town with some field pieces, 100 oxen, a number of sheep, a quantity of blankets, baggage & stores, killed here some more of the enemy & made more prisoners. Their whole loss on this occasion supposed to amount to about 600 in killed, wounded & prisoners. The general's original design was to surprise Brunswick also, but his troops were totally unfit either to undertake any new exploit or to sustain another action ...
>
> The enemy's army at Trenton under command of Lord Cornwallis, did not miss our army for some time as our guard at the bridge gave 'em a cannonade before they went off, but when they found Genl Washington had decamped and heard the firing towards Prince Town [they] were in the utmost consternation & immediately made hearty march after them.[171]

Washington, however, knew the British and Hessian forces were advancing towards Princeton and realizing that he was not in a position to defend the town adequately, had his troops destroy the bridges along their march. The army moved out and marched to Pluckemin and from there to Morristown where he set up winter quarters.[172]

Casualties at Princeton: Brigadier General Hugh Mercer, the first colonel of the 3rd Virginia

A nineteenth century historian described General Mercer's wounding by the British during the action at Princeton in this way.

> The action continued only about fifteen minutes, but was very severe. Washington was exposed to the hottest fire, while encouraging the militia by voice and example. General Mercer dismounted after the first fire, the gray horse he was riding having been disabled by a musket ball that wounded his fore leg; and while on foot, endeavoring to rally his broken troops, he was felled to the ground by a blow from a musket dealt by a British soldier.
>
> When his rank was discovered, the enemy, believing it to be Washington, raised an exulting shout and cried, 'The rebel general is taken!' Several rushed to the spot, exclaiming, 'Call for quarters, you d—d rebel!' 'I am no rebel,' cried Mercer, indignantly, while half a dozen bayonets were at his breast; and instead of calling for quarter, he determined to die fighting. He struck several blows at his enemies with his sword, when they bayoneted him and left him for dead.[173]

Captain John Chilton's diary entry for 3 January 1777 also addressed the demise of the former commanding officer of the 3rd Virginia at Princeton.

> 1777. January 3d at 4 in the Morng.
> The whole army marched from Trenton to Princeton, engaged a party of the enemy commanded by Major Leslie, defeated them. Leslie was slain in this battle with other[s] of his officers. As we were obliged to retreat at the beginning of the battle, the much lamented Genl Mercer had his horse shot under him as he staid too much behind to conduct our retreat and was inhumanly murdered with bayonets, &c...[174]

A 7 January 1777 dispatch to the *Virginia Gazette* reported the capture of General Mercer who "received seven wounds, five in his body, and two in his head, and was much bruised by the breech of a musket. His life was yesterday almost despaired of, but this morning I find him much relieved, and some of the most dangerous complaints removed, so that I still have hopes of his recovery... He is now a prisoner upon parole."[175]

After the British had retreated from the Princeton, General Mercer was taken to the house of Thomas Clark. There he was cared for by a Quaker, Sarah Clark and a female slave belonging to the family. "He languished in great pain until the 12th, when he expired in the arms of Major George Lewis, a nephew of Washington." Dr. Benjamin Rush was the attending physician.[176]

General Mercer's body was taken to Philadelphia, where it arrived on 17 January. "[The] body of the worthy and brave General Mercer was brought to this city, and interred with the military honours due his rank and merit. In the death, or rather murder of this gentleman, our country has lost a gallant and a virtuous citizen."[177]

His body, covered with wounds and mangled by our savage enemies, was exposed to public view. After he had surrendered himself, and had been carried into a house, he acquainted the enemy that he was a General in the service of the United States; deaf to the voice of humanity and the law of nations, they stabbed him with the bayonet, and with the butt end of a musket battered and disfigured his face. [178]

After the success at Princeton, General Washington moved the army to Morristown and into winter quarters.

Deaths in the 3rd Virginia: 31 December 1776 to April 1777

Captains Peyton, Chilton, Wallace, Ashby and West all had men in their company who died during this period. These death dates were determined by using the payrolls in the compiled service records. For example, Benjamin Basye was a soldier in Captain John Chilton's company. The compiled service records for this soldier showed two pay rolls: one from 7 October to 7 December 1776, for service for 2 months. The last payroll dated from 7 December 1776 to 1 March 1777, for service for two months and twenty-five days. Two months and twenty-five days from 7 December 1776 to 1 March provided a death date of 26 February 1777. There were no other records in the compiled service records for this soldier. Benjamin Basye's name can be found in Table 2 below.

Joshua Cage, a soldier in Captain John Peyton's company showed service from January 1777 to March 1777 for 15 days. The April payroll stated that he "was not to be accounted for." This information supplied his death date as 15 January 1777. There were no other records associated with this soldier in the compiled service records. George Calvert, another soldier in Captain Peyton's company, whose name appeared on Captain Peyton's payroll for the period 1 January to 1 March 1777 showed service for just fifteen days, with a further comment "dead." This furnished a death date of 15 January. The names of these two men appear in Table 3.

Ensign George Peyton, in Captain Wallace's company has two payrolls in the compiled service records: One, from 8 October to 7 December 1776; the other, from 7 December 1776 to 1 January 1777 with the comment "Name cancelled on roll." However, these records also contain another account for George Peyton, in a book of a List of Officers of the Virginia Line on Continental Establishment who received certificates for the balance of their full pay, agreeable to an Act of Assembly passed in November 1781. George Peyton, an ensign in the infantry, is listed as "decd". Elisha Price received his certificate. His name is found in Table 4.

Moses Carter, a soldier in Captain John Ashby's company, had only one payroll, found in the compiled service records for the 3rd Virginia. It was dated February 1777, with service for 14 days. The amount he earned for this month was $3.00 and eight pence. While there were no further records for this soldier, it appeared that he may have died on 14 February 1777. Since a full month's service would have earned him $ 6 1/3, and he was paid for only half the month, his name appears in Table 5 as having died on the above date.

Captains John Chilton and John Peyton suffered significant losses in their companies due to death of their rank and file and some non-commissioned officers. John Chilton had twenty-seven men in his company who died between 31 December 1776 and April 1777. With the exception of one death, all of these deaths took place after the army had arrived at winter quarters in early January. The names of the men who died in Captain Chilton's company are found in Table 2 below.

Table 2: Deaths in Captain John Chilton's 3rd Virginia company January to April 1777.[179]
Abbreviations: n.g. = not given

Name	Rank	Death date	Source
Benjamin Basye	Private	2/26/77	M 881 MR 951
William Bearmore	Rank n.g.	2.22.77	M 881 MR 951
Willoughby Brent	Sergeant	During 2/77	M 881 MR 951
William Bruin	Rank n.g.	Before 3/1/77	M 881 MR 952
John Clendenny	Soldier	2/1/77	M 881 MR 952
Eppa Cooke	Soldier	1/11/77	M 881 MR 952
Edward Durham	Rank n.g.	Before 3/1/77	M 881 MR 953
Henry Fewell	Rank n.g.	2/1/77	M 881 MR 953
Jeremiah Garner	Rank n.g.	2/1/77	M 881 MR 953
Uriah Hamrick	Soldier	1/21/77	M 881 MR 953
John Johnson	Private	1/1/77	M 881 MR 954
Charles Jones	Soldier	2/1/77	M 881 MR 954
Hilvy Linton	Rank n.g.	2/16/77	M 881 MR 954
Jesse Marmaduke	Rank n.g.	3/4/77	M 881 MR 955
Thomas Marr	Rank n.g.	2/1/77	M 881 MR 955
Benjamin Mason	Rank n.g.	2/1/77	M 881 MR 955
Dudley Matthews	Rank n.g.	2/1/77	M 881 MR 955
Willoughby Maxwell	Rank n.g.	3/3/77	M 881 MR 955
Andrew Morrison	Rank n.g.	2/15/77	M 881 MR 955
John Morrison	Rank n.g.	2/1/77	M 881 MR 955
John Rogers	Private	1/17/77	M 881 MR 955
Robert Smith	Private	2/17/77	M 881 MR 956
George Strong	Soldier	12/31/76	M 881 MR 956
Charles Taylor	Soldier	2/1/77	M 881 MR 956
John Thornbury	Soldier	2/14/77	M 881 MR 956
Isaac Williams	Private	2/1/77	M 881 MR 956
James Wilson	Soldier	2/1/77	M 881 MR 956

Captain Peyton's company experienced even more losses: thirty-five men died between 31 December 1776 and April 1777. Twenty-four of these men all died on the same day: 15 January 1777.

Table 3: Deaths in Captain John Peyton's 3rd Virginia company, January to April 1777.[180]

Name	Rank	Death date	Source
Peter Burn	Rank n.g.	1/15/77	M 881 MR 952
Joshua Cage	Rank n.g.	1/15/77	M 881 MR 952
George Calvert	Rank n.g.	1/15/77	M 881 MR 952
Reuben Calvert	Sergeant	1/15/77	M 881 MR 952
Isaac Carroll	Rank n.g.	1/15/77	M 881 MR 952
Rawleigh Chinn	Sergeant	1/15/77	M 881 MR 952
James Clark	Rank n.g.	1/15/77	M 881 MR 952
Douglas Conner	Corporal	1/15/77	M 881 MR 952
Zachary Crook	Corporal	1/15/77	M 881 MR 952
John Davis	Private	3/1/77	M 881 MR 953
Presley Davis	Sergeant	2/1/77	M 881 MR 953
Richard Gambrell	Rank n.g.	1/15/77	M 881 MR 954
William Kenny	Private	Before 4/1/77	M 881 MR 954
John Lankford	Rank n.g.	1/15/77	M 881 MR 954
William Laws	Rank n.g.	1/15/77	M 881 MR 954
John Learney	Rank n.g.	12/31/76	M 881 MR 954
James Lynch	Rank n.g.	During 3/77	M 881 MR 954
John Marloe	Private	1/15/77	M 881 MR 955

Table 3. (Continued) Deaths in Captain John Peyton's company, January to April 1777

Name	Rank	Death date	Source
John Matlow	Soldier	12/31/76	M 881 MR 955
James McComb	Rank n.g.	1/15/77	M 881 MR 955
William McKinney	Private	1/7/77	M 881 MR 955
Leonard Milstead	Private	1/15/77	M 881 MR 955
Jesse Murphy	Rank n.g.	By 4/1/77	M 881 MR 955
John Murray	Private	1/15/77	M 881 MR 955
Charles O'Bryan	Soldier	3/1/77	M 881 MR 955
Nathaniel Overall	Rank n.g.	1/15/77	M 881 MR 955
Emmanuel Pannell	Soldier	1/15/77	M 881 MR 955
Leonard Powell	Soldier	1/15/77	M 881 MR 955
Batt Rinde	Soldier	1/15/77	M 881 MR 955
William Smith	Soldier	3/1/77	M 881 MR 956
Alexander Spiller	Soldier	By 4/1/77	M 881 MR 956
Alexander Steele	Soldier	2/15/77	M 881 MR 956
Robert Stribling	Soldier	2/15/77	M 881 MR 956
James Vaughn	Private	2/15/77	M 881 MR 956
John Wickliffe	Private	2/15/77	M 881 MR 956

The only other captain whose company lost more than ten men in these months was Captain Gustavus Brown Wallace's company. The names of these soldiers appear in Table 4. Seven of the eleven men died on 1 January 1777; their deaths occurred before the attack on Princeton on 3 January.

Table 4: Deaths in Captain Wallace's company 31 December 1776 to 1 April 1777.[181]

Name	Rank	Death date	Source
George Peyton	Ensign	By 1/1/77	M 881 MR 955
Burdett Massey	Corporal	2/1/77	M 881 MR 955
Thomas Sharp	Corporal	2/15/77	M 881 MR 956
John Debuty	Private	2/1/77	M 881 MR 953
John Dansey	Private	2/15/77	M 881 MR 953
James Powers	Private	2/15/77	M 881 MR 955
William Putman	Private	2/1/77	M 881 MR 955
Peter Taylor	Private	2/1/77	M 881 MR 956
Thomas Turner	Private	2/1/77	M 881 MR 956
Adam White	Private	2/1/77	M 881 MR 956
Isaac Wilkinson	Private	2/1/77	M 881 MR 956

Captain John Ashby's company was also hit with nine deaths, all of which occurred in February 1777, after the regiment was in winter quarters at Morristown. Their names are found in Table 5. Four of these men died on 15 February 1777.

Table 5: Deaths in Captain John Ashby's company 31 December 1776 to 1 April 1777.[182]

Name	Rank	Death date	Source
Moses Carter	Soldier	2/15/77	M 881 MR 952
Elijah Ford	Soldier	2/15/77	M 881 MR 953
John Jones	Private	2/9/77	M 881 MR 954
Elijah McDaniel	Soldier	2/6/77	M 881 MR 955
Daniel Noble	Soldier	2/15/77	M 881 MR 955
Vincent Rust	Soldier	2/15/77	M 881 MR 955
Spencer Shoemake	Soldier	2/11/77	M 881 MR 956
William Stamps	Soldier	2/17/77	M 881 MR 956

Captain Charles West's company suffered three deaths, two in February and one in March. Daniel Holifield died on 15 February 1777[183] as did George Peart, both privates in his company. Another private, Thomas Milburn, died on 1 March 1777.[184] The remaining Captains—William Washington, David Arell, Robert Powell, and John Thornton—did not have any men who died during this period according to the compiled service records of the 3rd Virginia.[185]

So ... what happened to cause so many deaths in Captains Chilton, Peyton, Wallace, and to a lesser degree in Ashby's and West's companies during the winter months of 1777? A letter written by John Chilton on 11 February 1777 to his brother Charles may provide some answers—at least for the deaths of the men in his company.

He reported to his brother that when his company crossed over the Delaware into Pennsylvania in December, his "was the most healthy comp^y with the Reg^t." Then cholera hit and Chilton gave leave to some of his men, advising them to go to neighboring farms, in the healthier countryside, in order to avoid the sickness in camp.

> [By] some strange infatuation, tho contrary to my orders as well as advice, [the men] would immediately push for Philadelphia where death in every kind of disorder lay in ambush for them, first the small pox, jail fever, yellow & spotted fever, jaundice and several other aliments... I told them [this] and warned them ...
> When I hear of their being sick and some dying, who had gone before and sent for those who were well enough to come up, either they never got my orders or did not chuse to leave a place that fate seems to ordain them not to go to ...
> This to me has been a dreadful campaign. I pray God I may never experience the like. The loss of my men gives me the greatest uneasiness. I could have been with them, I could have seen them well used. I could bear it with greater resignation, but I know they must have suffered many wants. I sometimes blame myself for not going to them, for I had leave. But what could I do, the poor lads who had shared every danger with me begged I would not leave them in the very face of the enemy.
> The soldiers of other companies also chuse [that] I should stay if their own [officers] went. My own pride, and let me say, my reason told me it was not a time to take pleasure. So I left to those who went to take care of my sick. I hope they have done them best. I have not heard. I am told I have lost 18 men. I forbear to mention them because I am not sure who they are.[186]

The compiled service records for men in John Chilton's company in Table 2 list eighteen men who died in January and February before Chilton's 11 February 1777 letter to his brother. One of these men, Benjamin Basye, has been further identified by an affidavit establishing heirs at law in the Fauquier County Court Loose Papers.

In March 1818, John Deane, a Revolutionary War soldier, gave evidence that Benjamin was a soldier in Captain Chilton's company who died in the service of their country, without children.[187] John Deane, was another 3rd Virginia soldier in Captain Blackwell's company.[188] He also swore under oath to the death of Benjamin's brother Jesse although there was no date specified. The two brothers left Jeremiah Basye as the only surviving male heir-at- law.[189]

John Chilton also reported, in the 11 February 1777 letter to his brother that he, Lieutenants Alvin Mountjoy and Joseph Blackwell, and Ensign Peyton, "have been under a strict regimen for the small pox." He went on

> We expected we had taken it from a man who broke out in our room... I hope to obtain leave tomorrow to get inoculated in a day or so if no symptoms appears—Joseph, we though had taken with it on Sunday, he was unwell yesterday and very ill all this day ... no symptoms appearing, the Doct^r gave him oil just before night. It has worked him and he is easier. We should see in a day or two whether it is the small pox ...[190]

While there was no information in the *Virginia Gazette* regarding the cause of these deaths in the 3rd Virginia,[191] it *is* likely that smallpox was a source for at least *some* of these deaths. Since supplies were slow in arriving during this winter, no doubt the cold and a lack of warm clothing, stout winter boots, blankets, and proper lodging also proved to be a likely culprit for the demise of these men.

The first main encampment of the Continental Army in Morristown on January 6 presented a grim picture. Exhaustion, deplorable health conditions, lack of proper clothing and food, and insufficient pay plagued the soldiers. Many were billeted in private homes, public buildings, barns, and sheds in Morristown and surrounding villages. Others, according to eyewitnesses of the Revolutionary scene, built a village of log huts in the Valley of Loantaka Brook. Snow covered the ground everywhere ...

Soon after General Washington's arrival at Morristown, an epidemic of smallpox broke out so severely that it threatened the future of the army. As it ran rampant among the troops at Morristown and broke out in Philadelphia, Washington ordered the first mass inoculation against the disease in American history.[192]

Captain Chilton expressed other worries as well to his brother in the 11 February 1777 letter. He was concerned that "the trouble of the whole comp^y devolved on me as well as that of Capt Ashbys—and as if that had not been enough, marched up to this place [Morristown] where every officer but one went off so Col^o Weedon was appointed Adjut^t Genl so that I had the trouble and care of the Reg^t, which tho small, yet equally troublesome in many respects with the whole."[193]

Not only did he the responsibility of the regiment itself devolve upon his soldiers, with the promotion of Colonel Weedon, but Chilton was further distressed at the behavior of some of his fellow officers and the lack of regular payments from the regimental paymaster. He had, he said,

money for my own men and to spare (of those with me) yet I find it very insufficient for all and yet they look up to me for cash on every exigency; and indeed some of their Capt^s have wrote to me to furnish their men with money and they, at the same time are out at some town, living in luxury or capering away to Virg^a while I, many times, scarcely know how I am to pay for my next shirts being washed...[194]

Small wonder that the campaign had been "dreadful" and he "prayed God [he] might never experience the like!"

Sometime in February Captain Chilton's company was ordered to Hanover Township "to be inoculated; we had the small pox very lightly generally," he recorded in his diary.[195] He reported better details of this occurrence in a letter written from Hanover Township on 19 March to Major Martin Pickett and others. At the beginning of February, Chilton said "I had just got out of the small pox for which I had been inoculated and had it favourably. Our brother Joseph [Blackwell] was not so lucky, he had it pretty severely, the laurels that he was reaping when received... was whelts and carbuncles on his nose and face... I believe he wont bring many home with him as they begin to disappear fast, be this as it will, he is very sullen occasioned by a weakness in one of his eyes that was a little infected with the s. pox, tho not to injure it."[196]

Captain Chilton also was able to report some war news. He told of daily skirmishes with the enemy and described the American's near capture of General Howe to his friends.

Genl Howe the other day was out with a few light horsemen reconnoit'ring and had like to have fallen into our hands, his horse plunged into a mire which he was obliged to quit and mount the horse of one of his Guards and escaped narrowly, they [the Americans] could have killed him but wanted to take him alive. We were obliged to be content with the Guard and the Generals horse.[197]

Chilton was hopeful that once inoculation was over "and a few more troops arrive" that the British would be closely invested and their "retreat cut off. They now scarce dare creep out of their lines and when they do forage a little, our scouting parties precipitate them into their lines again like hares before a hound. They have small pox among them worse than we have ..."[198]

It was not until 11 April 1777 that the *Virginia Gazette* was able to report to its readers "that all the Virginia troops have recovered of the small pox."[199]

While small pox took its undoubted toll among the Americans, the weather conditions also added to the general misery of the army. John Peebles, a Captain in the British Army recorded weather conditions in the Jerseys for February in his diary entries from the 13 to 24 February 1777. The second half of the month was one of frost, sharp north and northwest winds and bitter cold. On the 24 February, "it came on to snow & blow ... which it continues to do very hard, the worst day of wr. [war] we have seen this winter."[200] These conditions would have contributed to the 3rd Virginia's death toll in February as the constant cold sapped the men's strength and energy, already depleted from a lack of warm clothes, shoes, blankets, and tents.

The promotion of Colonel Weedon to be Adjutant General Pro Tempore, 13 January 1777, and Brigadier-General, 21 February 1777.

In mid-January, the 3rd Virginia's commanding officer, Colonel George Weedon, was promoted to acting Adjutant General of the army.[201] This left the regiment without a commanding officer. During the interim, as reported by Captain Chilton, all of the regiment's officers except for him, "went off" and he "had the trouble and care of the Reg^t, which tho small, yet equally troublesome in many respects with the whole."[202] No doubt it was a much-relieved John Chilton when Lieutenant Colonel Thomas Marshall was promoted to the colonelcy of the regiment on 21 February 1777. His promotion took place when Weedon was promoted to Brigadier-General on the same date.[203]

CONCLUSIONS

The 3rd Virginia had had quite a year from their organization and enlistment in the winter months of 1776 through February and March of 1777. They were halfway through their tour of service and had become battle-hardened veterans, some of Washington's most reliable troops. They had fought bravely through out the New York campaign and the retreat through New Jersey.

The regiment felt the loss of their former Captain, now Major Leitch of the 1st Virginia, in the preceding autumn at Harlem Heights. They were proud of the part Captain Thornton took in the near capture of Major Robert Rogers and his Tory outfit. The regiment took part in both Trenton and Princeton. At Trenton, Lieutenant Monroe had his near-miss with history when his life was saved by a Doctor he allowed to accompany his men to Trenton. They mourned the loss of General Mercer at Princeton. Through all of the glory and all of the despair brought about by small pox, cholera, and other diseases associated with camp life, and the lack of supplies that hampered the army during the winter months of 1776 and 1777, the regiment persevered.

What was amazing was that during the winter months of 1777, only 3 men deserted. Two of those returned to the regiment. George Gregory, a private in Captain John Ashby's company deserted in January 1777 and returned. He went on to serve out his tour and was discharged 28 February 1778.[204]

Henry Harrison, a soldier in Captain Chilton's company, deserted on 1 March 1777 and returned in April 1777. Payrolls for Captain Chilton company listed him as further serving in April and May 1777.[205] Only one soldier, Alex Burk, a private in Captain Wallace's company, deserted and did not return. He left, while in Philadelphia, during the last part of April 1777.[206]

With the promotion of Colonel Weedon out of the regiment and the promotion of Lieutenant Colonel Marshall to the colonelcy of the 3rd Virginia, the regiment was set to leave Lord Stirling's brigade as well. In May 1777, the 3rd Virginia became part of Brigadier-General William Woodford's Brigade.

END NOTES
CHAPTER 4
SKIRMISHES & BATTLES: 1
SEPTEMBER 1776–APRIL 1777

1. David Hackett Fischer, *Washington's Crossing* (New York: Oxford University Press, 2004), 117.
2. Ibid., 127. The map showing the American retreat through New Jerseys explains the route Washington's army took through New Jersey.
3. Ibid., 129.
4. Ibid., 131.
5. The general returns of the Army for August and early September 1776 support this as the 3rd Virginia was not found on those returns. See NARA, No. 38 & 39. *General Returns of the Army under General Washington near New York City*, M 246 MR 137, Returns of the Army.
6. See the morning returns filed from September to November 1776 for Captains of the 3rd Virginia, NARA in Officers, 3rd Virginia, M 881 MR 961.
7. Peter Force, ed. *American Archives: A Collection of Authentick Records, State Papers, Debates and Letters and other Notices of Publick Affairs*, 5th Series (Washington: 1851) 3: 370. Hereafter, *Am. Archives*.
8. John Rhodehamel, *George Washington: Writings* (New York: Library of America, 1997), 246–247. Hereafter, Rhodehamel, *George Washington: Writings*.
9. VHS, *Captain John Chilton to his friends in Fauquier*, dated 17 September 1776, MssK2694a1–11, *Keith Family Papers*, VHS, Richmond.
10. LVA, *George Weedon to John Page*, Accession 22954a, *George Weedon Papers*.
11. *Am. Archives*, 5th series, 3: 382.
12. Ibid., 3: 844; Heitman, 346.
13. Gott and Russell, 109, 118.
14. *Am. Archives*, 5th series, 3: 382.
15. Ibid., 3: 371.
16. Ibid., 3: 384.
17. Ibid., 3: 417.
18. *Letters*, 5: 203.
19. Samuel Chase was a Maryland delegate to Congress. See Boatner, 218. Obviously the Major Leitch he referred to was not in a Maryland regiment involved at Harlem Heights but a Virginia one.
20. *Letters*, 5: 212.
21. On 2 October 1776, Captain Fitzgerald was appointed Major in Colonel Weedon's regiment until further notice, "instead of the brave Major Leitch who is dead of his wounds." See *Am. Archives*, 5th Series, 3: 844. Unfortunately, Congress overruled this promotion and gave it instead to Captain John Green. Washington then made Fitzgerald an aide de camp on his staff. See Gott and Russell, 120–121.
22. VHS, *Letter from David Griffith to Richard Henderson*, Mss 2G8755b, *David Griffith Papers*, VHS, Richmond.
23. Colonial Williamsburg Foundation, "Battle of Harlem Plains, Virginia", *Gazette* (Purdie's Series Supplement) October 4, 1776, 1, col. 2 (http://research.history.org).
24. Ibid.
25. *Letters*, 5: 317.
26. VHS, *Captain John Chilton to his friends in Fauquier*, Mss 2c 4359a1–11, *Keith Family Papers*, VHS, Richmond.
27. Library of Virginia, *George Weedon to John Page*, 10 October 1776, Accession 22954a, *George Weedon Papers*, LVA, Richmond.
28. University of Virginia, *General Orders from Headquarters at Harlem Heights* 14 October 1776, *WW*, 6, 206 (http://etext.lib.virginia.edu).
29. Ibid, 6, 214–216. Thankfully for the 3rd Virginia, who were now out of harm's way and *not* captured by the British when they took the fort by storm in November, 1776.
30. Boatner, 945–946. Major Rogers was a military officer of note in the French and Indian War.
31. Gott and Russell, 123–124.
32. Colonial Williamsburg Foundation, "Letter from a field officer of the third Virginia Regiment," *Virginia Gazette*, (Purdie) November 15, 1776, 3, col. 1 (http://research.history.org).
33. Gott and Russell, 124.
34. NARA, *Samuel Cox's Pension File* S 39343, M 804 MR 672.

35. Ibid., *David Baker's Pension File* W 1804, M 804 MR 115.
36. Ibid., *Edward Abbey's Pension File* S 34621, M 804 MR 1.
37. Ibid., *Spencer Anderson's Pension File* S 37672, M 804 MR 58.
38. Ibid., *William Berry's Pension* S 39187, M 804 MR 228.
39. Ibid., *John Coppage's Pension* S 39363, M 804 MR 652.
40. Mitchell, 68–69.
41. Colonial Williamsburg Foundation, "Battle of White Plains," *Virginia Gazette* (Dixon) 29 November 1776, 3, col. 1 (http://research.history.org).
42. Mitchell, 69.
43. Ian Barnes, *The Historical Atlas of the American Revolution* (New York: Routledge, 2000), 84.
44. Arthur S. Lefkowitz, *The Long Retreat: The Calamitous American Defense of New Jersey 1776* (New Brunswick: Rutgers University Press, 1999), 20.
45. Ibid., 21.
46. Ibid.
47. VHS, *Captain John Chilton to his friends in Fauquier, from Camp at Morris Heights,* 4 October 1776, Mss11c2694a1–11, *Keith Family Papers.*
48. LVA, *Colonel George Weedon to John Page from Camp at White Plains,* 26 October 1776, Accession 22954a, *George Weedon Papers.*
49. Colonel George Weedon and his 3rd Virginia had been ordered to join Lord Stirling's brigade on 17 October 1776. See. University of Virginia, *General Orders, Headquarters Harlem Heights,* 17 October 1776, *WW,* 6: 216 (http://extext.lib.virginia.edu).
50. Lesser, 36. See also Heitman, 181, 269.
51. Ibid.
52. University of Virginia, *George Washington to the President of Congress,* 11 November 1776, *WW,* 6, pg n.g (http://extext.virginia.edu).
53. Lefkowitz, 23–24.
54. Ibid.
55. Colonial Williamsburg Foundation, "Description of Fort Washington," *Virginia Gazette* (Dixon) 29 November 1776, 3, col. 2 (http://research.history.org).
56. Ibid.
57. Ibid.
58. Ibid., "Battle of Fort Washington," (Purdie) 29 November 1776, 2, col. 3.
59. Colonel Robert Magaw was the commanding officer of the 5th Pennsylvania Battalion and was taken prisoner at For Washington on 16 November 1776. He was not exchanged until 25 October 1780 and did not reenter service. He died 7 January 1790. See Heitman, 376.
60. Barnes, 84.
61. Rhodehamel, *George Washington: Writings*, 254.
62. There were no prisoners taken at Fort Washington in the 3rd Virginia recorded in the regiment's compiled service records.
63. NARA, *John Coppage's Pension* S 39363, M 804 MR 652.
64. Lefkowitz, 40–41.
65. See note 53.
66. Edward Hand of Pennsylvania was the colonel of the 1st Pennsylvania in November 1776. See Heitman, 272.
67. Haslett's Delaware battalion and the five Virginia regiments were part of two different Virginia brigades. The 1st and 3rd Virginia were part of Stirling's brigade. The 4th, 5th, and 6th Virginia were part of General Adam Stephen's brigade. See the October 1776 return in Lesser, 36–37. The November 1776 return of troops in New Jersey does *not* show either Stirling's or Stephen's brigades. See Lesser, 40–41. Apparently the 2nd Virginia was "originally attached to Weedon's brigade [and] became a part of Woodford's brigade following [his] promotion to brigadier general." See Sanchez-Saavedra, 36.
68. University of Virginia, *George Washington to President of Congress,* Hackensack, 19 November 1776, *WW,* 6, 293–294 (http://etext.lib.virginia.edu)
69. Lefkowitz, 49–52.
70. Fischer, 125.
71. Ibid.
72. Lefkowitz, 52–53.

73. Fischer, 126.
74. Adrian C. Leiby, *The Revolutionary War in the Hackensack Valley* (New Brunswick: Rutgers University Press, 1992), 63, See also University of Virginia, *George Washington to Major General Charles Lee*, Hackensack, 21 November 1776, *WW*, 6, 298–299 (http://etext.lib.virginia.edu).
75. Ibid, George *Washington to Major General Charles Lee*, Hackensack, 21 November 1776, *WW*, 6, 297–298.
76. Reazin Beall began his military career as a captain in an independent Maryland company in January 1776. He served as a brigadier-general of the Maryland contingent of the Flying Camp from 17 August to 1 December 1776. See Heitman, 94.
77. Nathaniel Heard of New Jersey served as a brigadier-general of the New Jersey militia from February 1776 to the close of the war. See Heitman, 283.
78. See Heitman, 220.
79. University of Virginia, *George Washington to Governor William Livingston*, Aquackinack Bridge, 21 November 1776, *WW*, 6, 301–302 (http://etext.lib.virginia.edu).
80. VHS, *Captain John Chilton to his brother Charles Chilton*, dated 30 November, 1776 from Brunswick, Mss K2694a1–11, *Keith Family Papers*.
81. Fischer, 129.
82. Lefkowitz, 99–100.
83. University of Virginia, *George Washington to the President of Congress*, Trenton, 3 December 1776, *WW*, 6, pg n.g (http://etext.virginia.edu).
84. Rhodehamel, *George Washington: Writings*, 256.
85. Ibid., 258.
86 University of Virginia, *George Washington to Colonel John Cadwallader*, Trenton, 7 December 1776, *WW*, 6, pg n.g (http://etext.virginia.edu).
87. Ibid., *George Washington to Major General William Heath*, Trenton, 7 December 1776.
88. Lefkowitz, 119.
89. University of Virginia, *George Washington to the President of Congress*, 3 December 1776, *WW*, 6, pg n.g (http://etext.virginia.edu).
90. See note 88.
91. University of Virginia, *George Washington to the President of Congress*, Headquarters at Trenton Falls, 9 December 1776, *WW*, 6, pg n.g (http://etext.virginia.edu).
92. Ibid,, *George Washington to Major General Charles Lee*, Trenton Falls, 10 December 1776.
93. Ibid.
94. John Rhodehamel, *The American Revolution: Writings from the War of Independence* (New York: Library of America, 2001), 235. Hereafter, Rhodehamel, *The American Revolution: Writings*.
95. Ibid.
96. University of Virginia, *General Orders*, [Trenton, December 1776], *WW*, 6, pg n.g (http://etext.virginia.edu).
97. Ibid., *Washington to the President of Congress*, Headquarters at Falls of Delaware, 11 December 1776.
98. Ibid., *Washington to Major General Charles Lee*, Trenton Falls, 11 December 1776.
99. VHS, *David Griffith to his wife Hannah*, Philadelphia, 8 December 1776, Mss 2G8755b, *Letters &c of David Griffith*.
100. University of Virginia, *Washington to Governor Jonathan Trumbull*, Headquarters, Trenton Falls, 12 December 1776, *WW*, 6, pg n.g (http://etext.virginia.edu).
101. Ibid., *Washington to the President of Congress*, Trenton Falls, 12 December 1776.
102. Ibid., *Washington to the President of Congress*, Trenton Falls 13 December 1776.
103. Ibid.
104. Ibid. See note in online version.
105. Ibid., *Washington to Lord Stirling*, 14 December 1776, *WW*, 6, pg n.g (http://etext.virginia.edu).
106. Ibid., *Washington to Major General Lee*, Headquarters at Keith's, 14 December 1776.
107. Fischer, 149, 507, note 32.
108. Ibid., 150.
109. University of Virginia, *Washington to John Augustine Washington*, Camp near Trenton Falls, 18 December 1776, *WW*, 6, pg n.g (http://etext.virginia.edu).
110. Ibid.
111. Craig L. Symonds, *A Battlefield Atlas of the American Revolution* (Baltimore: The Nautical & Aviation Publishing Company of America, 1986), 31.

112. Lefkowitz, 113–119.
113. Ibid., 120.
114. Ibid., 122–123.
115. Ibid., 124–125.
116. University of Virginia, *George Washington to the General Officers*, Headquarters at Keith's 14 December 1776, *WW*, 6, pg n.g (http://etext.virginia.edu).
117. Ibid., *George Washington to General Lee*, Headquarters at Keith's, 14 December 1776.
118. Ibid., *George Washington to Major General William Heath*, Headquarters at Keith's 14 December 1776.
119. Ibid.
120. See note 117.
121. See note 118
122. See note 109.
123. See note 117.
124. University of Virginia, *George Washington to his brother, John Augustine,* Camp near the Falls of Trenton, 18 December 1776, *WW,* 6, pg n.g (http://etext.virginia.edu).
125. Lesser, 43.
126. NARA, No. 36. 1 December 1776, *Return of the Army under General Washington at Trenton: Colonel Weedon's Regiment*, M 246 MR 137 *Returns of the Army*.
127. Lesser, 43,
128. Fischer, 207.
129. University of Virginia, *George Washington to Colonel John Cadwallader*, 6 p.m., 25 December 1776, *WW*, 6, pg n.g (http://etext.virginia.edu).
130. Ibid., *George Washington to Major General Israel Putnam*, Camp above the Falls of Trenton, 25 December 1776.
131. Ibid., See note 86 in letter for specifics. "Stryker, in his *Battles of Trenton and Princeton* (p. 113) states that early on Christmas morning, Washington issued [these] orders for the march to Trenton. He does not state his source." See also Fischer, 221–226.
132. Fischer, 228–229.
133. See note 131. Scanned image on this page of the men on the march to Trenton was taken from John Grafton, *The American Revolution, A Picture Sourcebook* (New York: Dover Publications, 1975), 64.
134. Fischer, 231.
135. William M. Dwyer, *The Day is Ours: An Inside View of the Battles of Trenton and Princeton, November 1776 to January 1777* (New Brunswick: Rutgers University Press, 1998), 247.
136. Ibid., 255.
137. Ibid.
138. Ibid., 255–256.
139. Fischer, 231–232.
140. There are three academic historians whose books are still in print who have written about Trenton. David Hackett Fischer's *Washington's Crossing*, Richard Ketchum's *The Winter Soldiers,* and William Dwyer's *The Day is Ours* have been used extensively here. In addition, Arthur Lefkowitz's The *Long Retreat* contains an account of the action at both Trenton and Princeton. Samuel Stelle Smith's *The Battle of Trenton* presents yet another account of this action.
141. Richard Ketchum, *The Winter Soldiers: The Battles for Trenton and Princeton* (NY: Owl Books, 1999), 260, 355.
142. Fischer, 247.
143. Ibid., 234–235.
144. Bull Run Library, "Washington's Description of Battle at Trenton," *Virginia Gazette* (Dixon), 10 January 1777, 3, col. 2; 4, col. 1, RELIC M 071.055 Vir MR 6, *Virginia Gazette, 1776–1777.*
145. University of Virginia, *George Washington to the President of Congress*, from headquarters at Newtown, 27 December 1776, *WW*, 6, pg. n.g (http://etext.virginia.edu).
146. Ibid.
147. Boatner, 742.
148. *Letters* 5: 675–676.
149. Haller, 19.
150. NARA, *Edward Abbey's Pension File* S 34621, M 804 MR 1.
151. Ibid., *Spencer Anderson's Pension File* S 37672, M 804 MR 58.
152. Ibid., *David Baker's Pension File* W 1822, M 804 MR 115.

153. Ibid., *Isaac Barr's Pension File* S 41419, M 804 MR 155.
154. Ibid.
155. Christmas fell on a Wednesday. See Smith, 17.
156. Bull Run Library, "Colonel Weedon's Arrival in Philadelphia with Hessian Prisoners," *Virginia Gazette*, 24 January 1777, 2, col. 2, RELIC M 071.55 Vir, MR 6 *Virginia Gazette, 1776–1777*.
157. *JCC:* 1042–1045. See also University of Virginia, *George Washington to the President of Congress*, Trenton, 1 January 1777, *WW*, 6, pg n.g (http://etext.virginia.edu).
158. Fischer, 270–271.
159. Ibid., 271–272.
160. Ibid., 272–273.
161. Ibid., 273.
162. University of Virginia, *George Washington to Commanding Officer at Morristown*, 30 December 1776, *WW*, 6. pg. n.g (http://etext.virginia.edu).
163. Fischer, 274.
164. Fischer, 277–278.
165. Rhodehamel, *The American Revolution: Writings*, 256–257.
166. *Letters*, 6: 58–62.
167. *Letters* 6: 26–27.
168. Ibid.
169. Colonial Williamsburg Foundation, "Battle of Princeton described", *Virginia Gazette* (Purdie), 24 January 1777, 1, col.2; 2, col. 1 & 2 (http://research.history.org).
170. Ibid.
171. *Letters* 6: 26–27.
172. Ibid.
173. Benson Lossing, *Pictorial Field Book of the Revolution* CD 3261(Westminster: Heritage Press, 2004) II, 28–29.
174. "Diary of John Chilton" *Tyler's Quarterly* XII: 283–289.
175. Colonial Williamsburg Foundation, "Capture of General Mercer," *Virginia Gazette* (Purdie) 27 January 1777, 1, col. 2 and 2, col. 1 & 2 (http://research.history.org).
176. Lossing II., 29–30.
177. Colonial Williamsburg Foundation, "Body of General Mercer brought to Philadelphia," *Virginia Gazette* (Dixon), 31 January 1777, 6, col. 2 (http://research.history.org).
178. Ibid.
179. Ibid. See individual service records for these men and their death dates in the compiled service records of the 3rd Virginia.
180. Ibid.
181. Ibid. See individual service records for these men and their death dates in the compiled service records of the 3rd Virginia.
182. Ibid.
183. Bull Run Library, *PWCOB* 1778–1784, July 1778 Court, 9.
184. NARA, *George Peart's service records*, 3rd Virginia.
185. Ibid. See compiled service records in the 3rd Virginia for men enrolled in the companies of these captains.
186. VHS, *Letter from John Chilton to his brother Charles Chilton*, Morristown, 11 February 1777, Mss K 2695a1–11, *Keith Family Papers*. See also Cecere, 90–93.
187. Joan W. Peters, *Military Records, Certificates of Service, Discharges, Heirs, Pension Declarations & Schedules from the Fauquier County Virginia Court Minute Books* 1784–1840 (Westminster: Willow Bend Books, 1999), 55. Hereafter Peters, *Military Records 1780–1840*.
188. NARA, *John Deane's compiled service records*, 3rd Virginia.
189. Peters, *Military Records 1780–1840*, 55.
190. See note 186; Cecere, 92–93.
191. While a search in the *Virginia Gazette* for small pox turned up quite a few entries, there was nothing in this newspaper regarding the disease as a major cause of death in the Virginia regiments.
192. John W. Rae, *Morristown: A Military Headquarters of the American Revolution* (Charleston: Arcadia Publishing, 2002), 21, 23.
193. See note 186.
194. Ibid.
195. "Diary of John Chilton," *Tyler's Quarterly* XII: 283–289.

196. VHS, *Letter from John Chilton to Major Martin Pickett & others,* from Hanover Township, 11 March 1777, Mss K2694a1–11, *Keith Family Papers*.
197. Ibid.
198. Ibid.
199. Colonial Williamsburg Foundation, "Small pox in Virginia regiments cured," *Virginia Gazette* (Purdie Supplement) 11 April 1777, 1, col. 2 (http://research.history.org).
200. Rhodehamel, *The American Revolution: Writing,* 295–300; 824.
201. University of Virginia, *General Orders,* Headquarters Morristown, 13 January 1777, *WW,* 7, pg. n.g (http://etext.virginia.edu).
202. See note 193.
203. Sanchez-Saavedra, 38.
204. NARA, *George Gregory's compiled service records,* 3rd Virginia.
205. Ibid., *Henry Harrison's compiled service records.*
206. Ibid., *Alex Burk's compiled service records.*

CHAPTER 5

SKIRMISHES & BATTLES: 2
APRIL 1777 TO OCTOBER 1777

Spring 1777: Promotions and resignations in the 3rd Virginia's Field & Staff officers, captains, and subalterns alter the regiment's appearance.

The first four months of 1777 saw significant changes in the regiment's field and staff organization. Their commanding officer, Colonel George Weedon had been promoted out of the regiment to become acting adjutant-general of the army on 13 January 1777.[1] On 21 February 1777, Weedon became a Brigadier-General, and received his own brigade.[2] As a result of this promotion, the regiment's lieutenant colonel, Thomas Marshall, became the colonel of the 3rd Virginia.[3] William Heth, a Major in the 11th Virginia, was promoted from the 11th Virginia to the Lieutenant-Colonelcy of the 3rd Virginia on 1 April 1777.[4] William McWilliams, an early captain of the 3rd Virginia, had been promoted to Brigade Major in October 1776 and in March 1777 was appointed an aide-de-camp to Lord Stirling.[5]

The changes in the command structure of the regiment were echoed in the promotion of two captains in the regiment. Captain William Washington, who had been wounded at Trenton, was promoted out of the regiment in late January 1777.[6]

> William Washington, in less than four months of active campaigning with the Continental Army, had proven himself on several occasions—to the point of being wounded while leading his men. He had become an officer who could be trusted with independent command and a battlefield leader capable of initiative and personal bravery at decisive moments.
>
> His grueling service in the New Jersey campaigns of 1776 gave him valuable exposure to the hit-and-run tactics necessary for the small American forces to eventually wear down the powerful British army...[7]

Captain Washington's company remained together until August 1777 when twenty of his men, including the officers and sergeants, were transferred into Captain Gustavus Brown Wallace's company.[8]

In March 1777, Captain John Thornton, who had distinguished himself in the New Jersey campaign in the preceding year in the attempt to capture the notorious Major Robert Rogers, received a promotion to a newly raised Virginia battalion.

On 20 March 1777, General Washington wrote to Captain Thornton of his "desire to appoint you the Major" of a new battalion to be raised under the command of Charles Mynn Thurston:

> I have not forgot, that it was in contemplation for you to fill the office of Lieut. Colonel, of Colo. Henley's battalion; but, besides the improbability, from his own account, that success will attend this attempt in New England, I discover that there are several Captains in the Virginia Line, with older commissions than yours, who will complain of so rapid a promotion;
>
> For theses reasons I think it more for the public good to offer you this majority. Angus McDonald Esqr of Frederick is designed for the Lieutt Colonel. This [is] at present doubtful whether he will come into service. Should he refuse, perhaps circumstances may justify you supplying the vacancy. Be pleased to communicate your determination to me immediately...[9]

John Thornton's company of riflemen languished without a captain for two months. Then, in June 1777 ten of his men were selected for Daniel Morgan's independent rifle regiment. The remaining men filled out Captain John Ashby's rifle company whose ranks had been somewhat depleted by Colonel Morgan's selection process for his rifle command.[10]

Two cadets in the 3rd Virginia received promotions out of the regiment. Robert Randolph was promoted to a cornet in the 3rd Continental Dragoons in February 1777.[11] Alexander Keith was promoted to a 1st Lieutenant in the 10th Virginia on 20 March 1777.[12] Another cadet, William Robertson, resigned in April 1777.[13] There was also a resignation of a Lieutenant in March 1777—that of Lieutenant Matthew Whiting.[14]

The final adjustment to the 3rd Virginia took place on a brigade level. On 10 May 1777 the 3rd Virginia was transferred out of Lord Stirling's Brigade and joined the 7th, 11th, and 15th Virginia as part of Brigadier General William Woodford's new Virginia Brigade. In a letter to General William Woodford, from Headquarters at Morristown on that date, Washington declared

> The duties [of the brigade] you are immediately to enter upon, and to make yourself master of the true state of those regiments, as early as possible.
>
> The necessity of occupying so many posts, as we at present do, will prevent your drawing the Brigade into compact order, till further orders; but the regiments should be kept as much together, as the nature of the service will admit.
>
> You will in a particular manner inquire, what officers are absent form those regiments of your Brigade now here, a d have alls such, as have gone off without leave, exceeded their furloughs, or are on any frivolous business, recalled and kept close to their duty.
>
> You will likewise enquire into the state and condition of the non-commissioned officers and privates, know where the absentees are, and endeavour to get them to their respective regiments, as soon as possible.
>
> The completing these regiments to their Establishment, is to become an object of your greatest attention, discreet and active officers should be employed in this service, and no others; as we must, if possible, put an end to idleness and dissipation, not only in camp, *but upon all duties detached from it.*
>
> Whenever your brigade can be drawn together, you should make them practice, as much as possible...[15]

General Orders, issued at Morristown on 11 May 1777 made this transfer official.

> The 3rd, 7th, 11th, and 15th Virginia Regts are to compose a brigade, under the command of Brigadier General Woodford; And the 4th, 8th, 12th, and 16th Virginia Regts, are to compose another under the command of Brigadier Genl. Scott.
>
> Benjamin Day Esqr., is appointed Brigade Major to Genl Woodford...to be respected and obeyed as such.[16]

General Orders issued on 22 May 1777 were even more explicit relating to the Virginia line. The 1st, 5th, 9th, and 13th Virginia, along with Hazen's regiment was to comprise the 1st Virginia Brigade, to be under the command of Brigadier General Muhlenberg. The 2nd, 6th, 10th, and 14th Virginia was designated as the 2nd Virginia Brigade, under the command of Brigadier General George Weedon. These two brigades were placed in Major General Nathanael Greene's division.

The 3rd, 7th, 11th, and 15th Virginia was to be part of the 3rd Virginia Brigade, under the command of Brigadier General William Woodford. The 4th Virginia Brigade was to be made up of the 4th, 8th, and 12th Virginia, and along with William Grayson's[17] and John Patton's[18] additional Continental Regiments, were to form another division to be commanded by Major General Stephen.[19]

April to June 1777: A pause in the action

All during the spring, newly enlisted troops trickled into New Jersey. While his army was slowing recuperating, Washington wanted an immediate return of his officers many of whom were on leave to escape the associated illnesses of winter camp life. In General Orders, issued from headquarters at Morristown, on 7 April 1777, Washington gave orders

> In the most pointed terms, that all the Officers of the 1, 3, 4, 5, 6, and 9th Virginia Regiments, who are absent without leave in writing from himself or Major General Stephen, or are not upon any special command, or not on the recruiting service (the two last cases by proper authority) do immediately join their respective corps, without the smallest hesitation or delay[20]

Meanwhile, recruiting officers were out in force through out the newly formed states. No regiment needed a successful recruiting effort more than the 3rd Virginia. The regiment's numbers were depressingly low.

In a General Return of Continental Forces in New Jersey, filed, on 28 May 1777, the 3rd Virginia regiment reported a colonel, a lieutenant colonel, five captains, eight lieutenants, one ensign, a chaplain and surgeon, an adjutant, and a quartermaster among its staff. There were nineteen sergeants, two drummers, three fifes, a quartermaster sergeant, and a sergeant major among the non-commissioned officers in the regiment. Only 123 of the rank and file were fit for duty, not counting the thirteen who were sick and present and fourteen who were sick and absent. The regiment totaled only 169 men and officers on that date.[21]

In spite of these trifling numbers, Washington "put on the boldest, most aggressive face for the benefit of the British army in New Jersey. Sentries in their camp around New Brunswick were constantly sniped at, and foraging parties were met by skirmishers who harassed them with volleys from woods and fences, killing and wounding dozens of officers and men."[22]

Some of the 3rd Virginia troops may have been part of these troops. Captain William Washington's payrolls for April to May 1777 showed four men as British prisoners, all privates: George Adams, William Aigin, Thomas Hunt, and John Knight.[23]

John Chilton recorded the events of April in summary form in his diary. The regiment marched to Newark "with an intent to cross over to Bergen where we hear 4 or 500 Tories were assembled, but being disappointed in boats, did not cross; [we] staid at Newark [for] 2 or 3 day[s], then marched to the Matuchin [Metuchen] lines where we staid til 4th May when we were ordered to join the Grand Army at Middlebrook."[24]

While the 3rd Virginia totals were low according in the 22 May 1777 return, as May brought warmer weather, the Continental army slowly swelled to more than 10,000 men and officers on Continental duty in New Jersey.[25]

Washington badly needed a respite to allow new troops to arrive and supplies from France to be delivered to the army. The military supply depot at Danbury, Connecticut had been raided successfully by the British during the last part of April. The enemy had destroyed nineteen dwellings in the town and twenty-two barns and storehouses filled with provisions, clothing and nearly 1700 tents.[26]

Richard Henry Lee wrote Patrick Henry on 13 May 1777 that

> We have no late intelligence from France, tho we have reason every day to expect it, Capt Weeks in the Continental Ship Reprisal of 16 guns & 1000 & odd men has taken & sent into Port :'Orient a Lisbon packet of equal force to himself, with three ships that were under her convoy, and the provisions we have taken at sea, more than compensate for the Danbury loss, since the latter was only 1700 barrels of meat with some flour & grain and we have brought in 5000 barrels of meat bound to N. York.[27]

While supplies remained a constant worry, Washington shared several concerns about the state of his small army with the President of Congress, in a letter written from his headquarters at Morristown on 12 May 1777.

The pay of regular soldiers was foremost on his list " The conduct of too many officers," he said, "in withholding the pay of their soldiers, I am persuaded, is reprehensible, and has been the cause of uneasiness and of many desertions." He suggested a reform of the system with auditors to settle the accounts. "They would be a check on the Pay Masters, and, I am persuaded, will be the means of the accounts being fairly and justly liquidated. If a settlement can be once obtained, I trust the confusion will never take place again, as the pay masters will receive and pay all money due to the regiments and account for it..."[28]

The General then turned to the issue of the condition of his army. "Our army is weak and by no means equal to that of the enemy", he stated "and till their designs are known, and we are more reinforced with regular troops, we should be prepared in the best manner we can." He reluctantly advised calling out the militia from Delaware and Pennsylvania, "tho' it gives me pain," he went on, "that we should be under the necessity of recurring to such a measure, yet I should suppose it to be advisable."[29]

Piscataway

While there was frequent skirmishing with the British in the form of harassing their forage parties, the skirmish at Piscataway in the second week of May was an attempt to surprise the vaunted Scottish Black Watch regiment stationed there.

Washington reported the skirmish in a letter to the President of Congress written from Morristown on 12 May 1777.

> On Saturday a smart skirmish happened with a detachment of our troops, who attacked a number of the enemy near Piscataway, in which our men behaved well and obliged the enemy to give way twice, as reported to me, with loss; the enemy receiving a strong reinforcement, our people retreated to their posts. I cannot give the particulars, as they have not been sufficiently ascertained.[30]

At least one 3rd Virginia veteran remembered being at Piscataway, according to his pension declaration, filed in Green County, Tennessee in January 1829. This was Edmond Bolling, a private in Captain William Washington's company.[31] Two other soldiers—William Leitch and Butler Silvey—in this company may have been in this skirmish as well, as they were listed as prisoners in the May 1777 payrolls for Captain Washington's company.[32]

June to August 1777 – Armies on the move

On 30 May 1777, Washington gave orders that "the whole Army be ready to move by 4 o'clock tomorrow morning; their tents struck; their baggage loaded, and men under arms—it is expected that everything in the Quarter Master General and Commissary General's departments will be ready to move at the same time. Brigadiers commanding brigades, and commanding officers of regiments, and corps, are to pay strict attention to see their officers, and men, in camp this evening, and well supplied with ammunition."[33]

A false alarm. Washington wanted to see "whether a proper distribution of baggage waggons had been made, to the several regiments, and with what degree of alertness and expedition, the army could be ready to march, on a sudden emergency." While the general was happy with most of the results, he wished that "a greater punctuality to the time had been more generally observed...It will be expected in [the] future, that a precise conformity to the moment pointed out will mark the conduct of every corps."[34]

Washington wrote to his brother John Augustine from Middlebrook on 1 June 1777.

> I am now assembling the troops of this state, and those southward of it, at this place [Middlebrook] which lays about seven miles from the enemys principal post at Brunswick and convenient for following them either to Philadelphia or to the eastward. There has been no considerable movement among them of late; from every appearance Philadelphia is their object, and to facilitate their passage across the Delaware a number of flat bottom'd boats are provided and now ready upon carriages to form a bridge with.
>
> I cannot learn that the enemy have, as yet, received more than a few recruits as a reinforcement, but I fancy they hourly expect transports with their foreign mercernarys. I can no[t] otherwise acct for Genl. Howes inactivity, as his numbers all along have greatly exceeded mine and at times double and tripled them.[35]

While Washington thought the enemy was concentrated on taking Philadelphia, General Howe had other plans. His intent was to flush out the American army, "holed up in the well-fortified hills around Boundbrook" and destroy it. He planned a feint on Philadelphia which, he thought, would bring Washington and his army down from the hills. Then somewhere around Princeton, the British could force a battle in the open, where they had a decided advantage.[36]

On 13 June, the British set this plan into motion. Two equal divisions, totally 11,000 men, moved out of Brunswick, under the command of Major General Charles Cornwallis and Lieutenant General Charles Heister. Howe accompanied the Hessian general.

The British ran into difficulties right from the start. Cornwallis's troops were brought to a halt when the Americans destroyed the bridge over the Millstone River near Hillsborough. Then they ran into well-aimed rifle fire from rebel troops as they repaired the bridge. Heister and Howe's troops were bogged down with broken-down wagons and narrow passes.[37]

Washington had no intention of challenging the British so directly. He had different plans. He planned to deploy troops from his main army at Boundbrook to harass the British right and rear flank. General Benedict Arnold, meanwhile, was to collect Continentals and militia at Philadelphia and set up a line of defense behind the Delaware River. Then the British would be caught between two armies, the main army commanded by Washington and the army around Philadelphia commanded by General Arnold.

When Washington heard that the British were at the Millstone River, he sent Colonel Daniel Morgan and his newly-formed independent rifle regiment to accost them.[38] Among his riflemen were twenty-three men from Captains Ashby and Thorntons' rifle companies.[39]

Morgan and his riflemen took a position near the intersection of the New Brunswick-Delaware road and in a direction heading north towards the Millstone River and the American camp. That way the British could be stopped either way they approached. Morgan was to attack the enemy's flanks.

> Washington advised him to 'dress a company or two of true woods men in the right Indian style and let them make the attack accompanied with screaming and yelling as the Indians do, it would have very good consequences.'[40]

Colonel Morgan came to a halt on the Millstone Road before sunrise on 14 June. He dispatched scouts who quickly came back with the news that Howe was headed in their direction. The colonel then positioned his men throughout the woods to await the British. When they came into view, the riflemen opened fire, so devastatingly, that the enemy was brought to a temporary standstill. When the British were reinforced with more troops, Morgan sounded his turkey call from the instrument he used to assemble his men and retreated to higher ground. There, they set up camp and dispatched news of this encounter to Washington.[41]

The British, unsuccessful in their attempt to draw the wily General out, returned to Brunswick. On 21 June, Howe retreated across the Raritan River towards Amboy, thinking this ploy might lure the Americans out from his encampment at Middlebrook.

Instead, Washington sent Major Generals Greene and Waynes' divisions, along with Morgan's rifle men to Brunswick, to attack the British rear guard.

> After flushing a Hessian picket near the outskirts, Morgan joined Greene and Wayne inside the town, and the three American commanders drove the rear guard across the river bridge into redoubts on the east bank...The Americans [attacked and] dislodged the British and harassed them as they withdrew, sometimes advancing within thirty yards. At Piscataway the Americans gave up the chase, whole the British continued to Amboy.[42]

Captain John Chilton described this action a little differently in a 29 June 1777 letter from Steele's Gap to his brother Charles. On the 26 June, Chilton told his brother, the 3rd Virginia was at Piscataway which the enemy had abandoned just a few days earlier.

> Col^o Morgan with the Rifle Regt was on the Mattuchin Lines at [the] same time and our main Army had come down into the plains. The enemy unexpectedly stole a march in the night of the 25th and had nearly surrounded Morgan before he was aware of it. He, with difficulty, saved his men and baggage and after a retreat, rallied his men and sustained a heavy charge until reinforced by Maj^r Genl Stirling, who gave them so warm a reception that they were obliged to retreat so precipitately that it had like to have become a rout.
>
> But being strongly reinforced, he was obliged to retreat with the loss of 2 pieces of Artillery & Brigadier Genl Maxwell was on the left and had a severe engagement but was also obliged to retreat. The enemy pursued their advantage as far as the Scotch Plains, which place they left that

night and suddenly returned unto Perth Amboy...There were but few Virginians except Morgans in this battle ... [43]

Chilton went on to report that "two thirds of our army were not in action." Chilton, himself "was in 4 miles of this engagement and heard it all." Then,

> just as the battle ended, Colo. Marshall received orders to leave Piscataway and march up by way of Bound Brooke. A party of the enemy had advanced within 2 miles of us, about 2000, and had set down to refresh themselves. We marched off with colours flying and drums beating, which they hearing and expect^g we were coming to attack them, made the best of their way to P. Amboy, since when they seem peaceably disposed and keep closed...
>
> Tell the children I have some hopes of seeing them this fall as there is some talk of our Reg^t being sent home in order to recruit and enlist the old soldiers again, tis thought by this piece of indulgence they will enter the service again (but keep this secret.)...Let the fathers of my boys know that their sons are all well... Tell Mr Tomlin not to cry any more about Billy, he's a fine soldier.[44]

On the night of 25 June, General Washington sat down and wrote to the President of Congress about this encounter. "He included praise for the 'conduct and bravery of Genl. Wayne and Colo. Morgan and of their Officers and Men...as they constantly advanced upon an enemy far superior to them in numbers.' He further stated his intention to follow Howe and to observe his next move."[45]

The next day, while the 3rd Virginia was at Piscataway, Washington came down from the hills, to New Market. The enemy, however were already on the move. During the early hours of the 26 June, the British were headed towards Westfield, "intent on getting between the Americans and the passes leading back to Middlebrook. But near Woodbridge, a patriot reconnaissance party sighted the enemy and warned Washington in time to escape. Morgan, sent to delay the British thrust, found that Howe had wind of Washington's flight and had headed for Amboy, where he transferred his entire army to New York."[46]

The general was aware of this transfer almost as soon as it happened. In a letter to his brother John Augustine, written from camp at Middlebrook on 29 June 1777,

> I expect from appearances and my Intelligence, [the British] will be imbarked in a few hours for Staten Island, or New York; for what other expedition time, [I cannot] discover. By means of their shipping and the easy transportation that that shipping affords, they have it much in their power to lead us a very disagreeable dance ...[47]

In early July, Howe, unable to flush out the Americans from their base in New Jersey, decided it was time to turn his attention to Philadelphia. Instead of attacking by land, he decided to attack by sea. His troops began embarking from Staten Island for an amphibious assault on the capital.[48]

The American army meanwhile was held in a constant state of readiness. In the General orders issued on 2 July, "the whole army [was] to get ready to march tomorrow morn at 7 o'clock, with the tents and baggage, all property put up in the waggons."[48]

Two days later, the general orders were even more specific.

> As it is impossible to tell with certainty how soon, or how suddenly the army may be called upon to march (as it is an event dependent upon the enemy's movements) The General orders that no officer, or soldier shall be absent from camp, but that ever thing be held in the most perfect readiness, except striking of tents.
>
> As no opportunity can be more favorable than the present, to get rid of all heavy baggage; the General once more strongly urges the officers to store what they can possibly spare, at Morristown. If after this second notice they continue to fill and 'cumber waggons with old tables, chests, chairs &c, they are not to be surprised if they are left in the field; This must be the inevitable consequence of a scarcity or failure of teams ...

From the after orders, issued on the same date,

> When the order is given to march, and the men are paraded for that purpose, the rolls are to be called; and the commanding officer of each corps is to see that his men are all present, or know with certainty where and why they are absent.
> When they are told into sub-divisions, in platoons, and officers assigned to each, such officers are to abide constantly with them; and upon a march see that no man is suffered to quit his rank, upon any occasion, without a non-commissioned officer with him, who is to bring him to his place again.
> Whenever a halt is made, and the ranks are suffered to be broken, in order for the men to sit, or refresh themselves, the officers commanding each division, as above, is, so soon as they are ordered *to Arms* again, to see that they have every man of their division in his place...
> When a march is to begin, after a halt, the drummers are to beat the first division of the foot march, to be taken from front to rear; and upon the last *flam* of the first division being struck, the whole are to move ...[49]

On 8 July 1777, Captain Chilton wrote a letter sharing his discontent with the army life to Captain William Pickett.

> ...Here I am 300 miles from home, under the mortifying circumstance of being known to the whole Army by the name of old Chilton, and seeing boys, which I would not have made Serg^{ts} of, every day put over my head and for no earthly reason but that they wear a finer coat, [and] gambol and play the fool more kittenishly than I can.[50]

Perhaps this disgruntlement came from the regiment having been on the march almost continuously since the 3rd July. On that date, Washington and his army marched from Middlebrook to Morristown by way of White's Tavern. They remained just eighteen miles out of Middlebrook until 12 July when they marched and encamped at the western end of Pumpton plains.[51]

It appeared that the regiment was kept on the march through out July. On 13 July, a Sunday, Chilton recorded that it was raining and he had lost his journal from 15 April to this day. On 26 July, Captain Chilton recorded the unpleasant encounter he had when he was refused his post in the battalion.[52]

The situation did not improve when, on Sunday, the 27 July, they were not able to get an early start due to the rain.

> The regiment marched so late into the night before that nothing could be cooked. No wagons [were] allowed to carry our cooking utensils. The soldiers were obliged carry their kettles, pans &c in their hands, clothes and provisions on their backs as our marched was a forced on & the season extremely warm; the victuals became putrid by sweat & heat—the men badly off for shoes, many being entirely barefoot and in our regi^t a too minute inspection was made into things relative t6o necessaries that the men could not do without, which they were obliged to throw away.[53]

The regiment reached Pittstown at noon on Monday, 28 July where they stayed until four in the afternoon, "to refresh and draw provisions." They then moved to Quakerstown and encamped there for the night. By 30 July, the regiment had finally arrived at Howell's Ferry on the Delaware River.

On Thursday, 31 July, misfortune struck Captain Chilton and the 3rd Virginia once again. In fording the river, his wagon overturned. "This scheme of fording," Chilton stated in his diary, "had like to have proved fatal to several soldiers, two were drowned a day or two before."[54] Luckily for the Captain, his bed clothes had been wrapped up in Lieutenant Mountjoy's tent and their bulk kept the water from soaking through the clothing so that these garments at least were saved. However, the regiment was forced to sleep in the woods, two miles from the river—tentless—since these accommodations had been lost in the river.[55] Not a good month for Captain Chilton or the 3rd Virginia.

August to September 1777, The 3rd Virginia's arrival in Pennsylvania, the British landing in Pennsylvania, and preliminary skirmishing fill out the month as the Americans plan to defend Philadelphia.

The 3rd Virginia arrived at Germantown on Saturday 2 August and remained in that general vicinity until 23 August. The next day, they marched through Philadelphia, crossed the Schuylkill and camped at Darby.

On 14 August, Chilton wrote his brother Charles from the camp in Pennsylvania. He was still very much dissatisfied with his position in the regiment.

> ...I confess your prognostication of my ill success of rising in the Army was well founded and has turned out according to your suspicion. It was confessed that my fortune was hard and that they wished it in their powers to give me a post my services and hardships entitled me, but by so doing they should break the great rule of rising by seniority of commissions. This I was told was said, had I been by I should have told them that if due consideration had been observed, the appointing the Officers and disposing of posts in the Army, a remonstrance from one would have never happened.

He did, however, he related, continued to be in favor with the generals although he had an unfortunate run-in with General Stevens.

> I was with ... three officers one evening at the Sutlers. I had just went up to drink, our getting grog, the retreat beat, I told the Adjutant to step down while I paid the check which I was doing when a Serg^t and a file of men came and informed [me] we must go to the Genl.
> I went down very angry, making the poor Serg^t and his men keep their distance. 'When', says the Genl 'Capt Chilton, is it possible that you should be out of your duty?' I told him it was possible but could not submit that I then was. That the strictest disciplinarian allowed 5 minutes but that I had not required two. That I knew my duty and had done it, and admitting I had made a slip, thought it too trifling to be sent for in that manner. He then said he did not know we were Officers, asked our pardons, asked us to drink grog which we refused and went, very angry away. The next day he called to me ... across a platoon to know how I did, and seemed sorry for what he had done. So I even thought it was best to be on good terms again.[56]

Then, he added, somewhat disconsolately his feelings about Colonel Marshall's second in command, Lieutenant Colonel William Heth,

> But we have a gentleman in our Reg^t, one Col^o Wm Heth, who takes great things upon himself, he intirely rules Col^o Marshall and will cause him to be as much despised as himself. Heth does not want sense but is imperious to the last degree. I was never tired of the service till he joined our Reg^t. I have a small notion of entering into the sea service if I could have the command of some clever little snug vessel for I have no notion of Colonels. They are too over bearing to inferior Officers and as remarkably mean and cringing to their superiors.
> Heth has greatly the ascendancy over Marshall which I could not have believed. Anything clever that is done in the Reg^t Heth takes the credit of and what is not well done is thrown on Marshall, which will sink his credit as Heths rises ... I am sorry for it but cant help it. If Capt Wm Blackwell was not out I should be almost tempted to quit the service, his tent and mine almost join so that we are always together when off duty.
> I pity yours, Keiths & Picketts case ... Have this consolation, however. Ill gotten, power is seldom lasting.[57]

Captain Chilton's assessment of William Heth may have been one that Colonel Marshall came to share. In October 1777, Washington wrote to Governor Patrick Henry that

> Colo. Thomas Marshall of the 3d Virginia Regt informs [me] that the State are about raising a new Regiment of Artillery. He seems desirous of exchanging the Foot Service for that of the Artillery, as he thinks he could render his Country more service in that line. His mathematical abilities are sufficiently known in Virginia, and he possesses in addition to those necessary

> qualifications for an Artillery officer, that of indubitable bravery, of which he has given proofs upon every occasion. Col. Marshall has solicited the command of this regiment and requested me to mention, that if the State should please to honor him, that his leaving the foot service would not be disagreeable to me, it being his choice.[58]

It took awhile. However, he was able to resign in early December 1777 to take up a post with the Virginia State Regiment of Artillery.[59] The loss of his men at Brandywine and Germantown, along with Regimental politics, may have occasioned this move.

To return to the events of August, on Monday, 25 August 1777, Chilton reported in his diary that the army marched to Chester, "a smart, little, but irregular built town." They camped outside Wilmington.

> The road runs within sight of the Delaware whose course is nearly west & sometimes a few pints to the southward. The land here is not so rich as the other side [of the] Delaware, but well cultivated, fine meadows and better cattle. The inhabitants too, have not that griping importunate countenance as they have up to the N. Westward.
> Rain this even^g, as indeed there has been, particularly thro' this month, this whole summer.[60]

"The enemy," Chilton noted in his journal, "it is said, have landed and about 3000 last night took possession of Iron Hill, which is about 12 miles near the place of their landing and about 12 M^s from us. His Excellency the Genl has gone down to observe their position." More rain, last night and part of this morning—now the 27th August.[61]

The enemy had indeed landed. On 27 August, Washington wrote the President of Congress from Wilmington,

> I this morning returned from the Head of Elk, which I left last night. In respect to the enemy, I have nothing new to communicate, they remain where they debarked first. I could not find out from inquiry what number is landed, nor form an estimate of it, from the distant view I had of their encampment. But few tents were to be seen from Iron Hill and Grey's Hill, which are the only eminences about Elk.
> I am happy to inform you that all the Public Stores are removed from thence, except about seven thousand bushels of corn. This I urged the Commissary there to get off, as soon as possible, and hope it will e effected in the course of the few days if the enemy should not prevent, which their situation gives them but too easy an opportunity of doing; The scarcity of teams, in proportion to the demand, will render the removal rather tedious, though I have directed the Quarter Master to send some from hence, to expedite the measure.
> A part of the Delaware Militia are stationed there and about nine hundred more from Pennsylvania are now on the March ... I also intended to move part of the Army that way today, am under the necessity of deferring it, till their arms are put in order and they are furnished with ammunition, both having been greatly injured by the heavy rain that fell yesterday and last night...[62]

ACTION AT WHITE CLAY CREEK

In the General Orders, issued from headquarters at Wilmington on 27 August 1777, Washington ordered "Genl. Greene's division...to march tomorrow morning, and take post, on a piece of ground, which will be marked out for him, on White Clay Creek ... General Stephen's division is to march [in the] morning, immediately after General Green's."[63]

On Thursday 28 August, Generals Green and Stephen's division, of which the 3rd Virginia was a part, returned to Brandywine; Chilton described the town in some detail in his diary. It was

> a small town chiefly consisting of mills and taverns, 8 or 10 mills being within 100 yards of each other; a navigable creek runs up to the Mills [and] the water is brought in canals from Brandywine Creek. There appears to be a smart fall of waters just above the Mills about ½ mile farther; on the south side of a gradual hill is Wilmington. The fron or Road Street is regular enough, paved within the rails; the town is built irregularly towards the west—they have a Markett house; a Navigable Creek makes to the Southw^d of the Town (called Christeen). 4 M^s farther [is] an inconsiderable town, Newport.[64]

Captain Chilton spent 28 August as captain of the rear guard. Colonel Hollingsworth[65] went past the guard around noon, going to be treated for wounds in the cheek or neck. The commissary's wagons returned around two in the afternoon along with some men who "heard that the Ministerials were advancing within a few miles of us (scary creatures), [and] said there were 16,000, which our soldiers as much believed as they believe George III and his corrupt ministry have a right to tax America ..." The rear guard was relieved at sunset and rejoined the regiment.[66]

Washington wrote the President of Congress from his headquarters at Wilmington on 29 August to report that

> ... The enemy advanced a part of their Army yesterday to Greys Hill, about two miles on this side of Elk, whether with intent to take post there, or to cover, while they remove what stores they found in the town, I cannot yet determine. ...Our light parties yesterday took between thirty and forty prisoners, twelve deserters from the navy and eight from the army have already come in, but they are able to give us very little intelligence.[67]

Chilton noted in his diary that "within these three days, 50 prisoners have been brought in. The enemy seems to be bold but very imprudent. Should they continue to act as they have done, a few months will give them into our hands without fighting. We have better than 1000 men near them who will, I expect, give a good account of those bloodsuckers, who shall be guilty of the temerity of leaving their camp for the atrocious crime of robbery, rapine & murder ..."[68]

September 1777
Prelude to Brandywine.

The Skirmish at Iron Hill

On the 1 and 2 September, Colonel Heth of the 3rd Virginia was ordered out with an advanced detachment to reconnoiter the enemy's position. While rain kept him in camp, when he left on Tuesday, 2 September, Captain Chilton noted in his diary, Captain Ashby, Lieutenant White and Lieutenant Peyton, all of the 3rd Virginia, accompanied him.

> The enemy advanced as high as the Red Lion; they were met by our advanced party under Colo. Crawford—the engagement got pretty hot. Several on each side were wounded and some slain. Strong reinforcements were sent which obliged our men to give ground. The enemy returned. Our division (Genl Stephen's) went to our alarm posts, staid a few hours and returned to camp. [We] pitched our tents and slept heartily.[69]

General Washington wrote a description of this skirmish to the President of Congress, from Wilmington, at 8 p.m. on 3 September 1777.

> This morning the enemy came out with considerable force and three pieces of Artillery, against our Light advanced Corps, and after some pretty smart skirmishing obliged them to retreat, being far inferior to them in number and without cannon. The loss on either side is not yet ascertain'd. Ours, tho' not exactly known is not very considerable. Their's, we have reason to believe, was much greater, as some of our parties composed of expert marksmen, had opportunities of giving them several close, well directed fires, more particularly in one instance, when a body of riflemen formed a kind of ambuscade. They advance about two miles this side of Iron Hill, and then withdrew to that place, leaving a picket at Couch's Mill about a mile in front. Our parties now lie at White Clay Creek, except the advanced pickets, which are at Christiana Bridge.[70]

In the same letter, Washington described the action Captain Chilton took note of in his diary.

> On Monday a large detachment of the enemy landed at Cecil Court House and this morning I had advice of their having advanced on the New Castle Road, as far as Carson's Tavern. Parties of horse were sent out to reconnoitre them, which went three miles beyond the Red Lion, but could neither see nor hear of them. Whence I conjecture, they filed off by a road to their left and fell in with their main body. The design of the movement this morning, seems to have been to disperse our Light Troops, which have been troublesome to them and to gain possession of Iron Hill, to establish a post most probably for covering their retreat in case of accidents.[71]

Preparations along Red Clay Creek and the move to Newport.

On Thursday, 4 September, Captain Chilton was on guard, with two subalterns, two Sergeants, two corporals and forty privates, at a bridge over Red Clay Creek and spent a "peaceable" guard, that night.

> Lieut Davis of the Pennsylvania Troops and Ensn. Westfall,[72] both of Scotts Brigade were with me; early this morning, came down about 600 men ... 200 first with the Qr. Masters, bearing entrenching tools. Colo. Febigar[73] with 200 & Colo. Willis[74] with 200; they were followed by waggons loaded with axes with which they felled trees, plashing them to form a line. About 2 in [the] afternoon, Majr. Genl. Sullivans Division came down & took possession of the lines we had been plashing. [Sullivan's division] consist[ed] of between 2 & 3000 effective men.[75]

Washington's general orders, issued on 4 September reflected Chilton's observations.

> The tents of Genl Sullivan's, Lord Stirling's and Wayne's division, and Nash's brigade, are to be struck and packed by five o'clock tomorrow morning (if the weather permit) these corps, together with Genl Potter's brigade, are to hold themselves in readiness to march at a moment's warning afterwards upon receiving orders.
> For which purpose, each brigade should be paraded, their arms grounded, and the men ready to take them up at the first call.
> The Quarter Master General will shew the ground they are to encamp upon, in the following order: Genl Sullivan's on the right, Lord Stirling's on the left; Genl Nash's on the left of Genl Sullivans; and Genl Potter's on the right of Lord Stirling's...Genl Stephen's division and Genl Irvine's brigade, when it leaves this place are to form a second line; Stephen's on the right. The division commanded by Genl Wayne is to form a third line; Genl Greene's division [is to] remain where it is.[76]

On 5 September, Washington wrote to the President of Congress from his headquarters at Wilmington, observing that "the enemy have remained intirely quiet" since his last correspondence.[77]

On Saturday, the 6 September, General Stephen's division marched "by the sun" for about a mile and camped near Newport. The division stayed at Newport as they "expected the enemy would be in motion early in the morning of Sunday."[78]

In general orders issued from his headquarters at Newport, on 7 September 1777, Washington

> received confirmation ... that the enemy have disencumbered themselves of all their baggage, even to their tents, reserving only their blankets, and such part of their cloathing as is absolutely necessary. This indicates a speedy and rapid movement, and points out the necessity of following the example, and ridding ourselves for a few days of every thing we can possible dispense with." The tents of the whole army are to be struck and packed up in the waggons, tomorrow morning, an hour before day; and the horses tackled. All the Corps of horse are to be saddled at the same time; and the whole Army drawn up in their respective lines.[79]

On Sunday, 7 September, Chilton recorded in his diary that "every necessary order was given to be in readiness—the deserters from the enemy inform that on Saturday morn^g, they drew 5 days provisions which were to serve them to Philadel^a or Wilmington at least."[80] On Monday morning, Chilton reported, "the enemy approached as near as Newark. We all lay at our alarm posts."

On 9 September, the British army was on the move, "with a seeming intention of attacking us at our post near Newport."

> We waited for them the whole day, but in the evening they halted at a place called Mill Town about two miles from us. Upon reconnoitering their situation, it appeared probable, that they only meant to amuse us in front, while their real intent was to march by our right and by suddenly passing the Brandywine and gaining the heights on the north side of that River, get between us and Philadelphia and cut us off from that city.
> To prevent this it was judged expedient to change our position immediately, the Army accordingly marched at two O'Clock this morning and will take post this evening on the high grounds near Chad's Ford...[81]

Captain Chilton echoed these orders in his diary, when he observed in his 9 September 1777 entry that "at 2 in the morning we had orders to march; took the road from Newport to Wilmington 2 miles, then turned to almost north, about 2 m[ile]s more; we then marched west course 10 miles S.W. & crossed Brandywine Creek and encamped on the heights of the Creek."[82]

Believing that a battle was eminent, General Washington issued orders from his headquarters at Birmingham on 10 September 1777.

> Two hundred and fifty men of Genl Greene's, and two hundred of each other division, and one hundred of Genl Nash's brigade, of Continental troops, and four hundred of Genl Armstrong's division of militia, are to be drawn out daily, as picquets, and to assemble, those of Genl Greene's, Genl Wayne's, Lord Stirling's and General Stephen's divisions, and Genl Nash's brigade, on the most convenient ground near the Artillery park. Genl Sullivan's at the centre of his division.
> From these picquets, all the necessary outguards are to be furnished; and the residue to remain at their respective places of assembling, ready to reinforce the out guards, or other duty, until relieved by new picquets ...[83]

Washington's preparations.

On 10 September, Washington positioned his troops along the east side of Brandywine Creek. The forces straddled the main road north to Chester and Philadelphia. The army began to build earthen batteries for the artillery just north of Chad's Ford, to cover the ford and provide support for the center of Washington's line.

His left flank was held by nearly 2000 Pennsylvania militia, under the command of General John Armstrong. They were situated on the hills several hundred yards south of the main road and covered Gibson's and Pyle's Fords.

Chad's Ferry was guarded by General Nathanael Greene's division, consisting of nearly 1800 Virginia Continentals. The ford itself was defended by General Anthony Wayne's Pennsylvanians, all part of the Pennsylvania line. These troops made up the center of Washington's arrangement

Brinton's Ford, a mile to the north of Chad's ford, was defended by General John Smallwood and his twelve hundred man continental contingent from Maryland. Jones' Ford, a mile away, was to be defended by some eighty soldier of the Delaware Regiment, while another two hundred troops of the 1st Battalion of Hazen's regiment covered Wistar's Ford. Hazen's 2nd Battalion was responsible for holding Buffington's Ford, just below the forks of Brandywine.

The residue of the army, some 4300, remained behind with Greene and Wayne, to provide a defense for the center of the American line, including General Stephen's division. Some 800 men, from General Maxwell's Light Infantry and Continental Light Dragoons, along with elements of the Chester County, Pennsylvania militia, were to cross Brandywine Creek at Chad's Ford, acting as an advance guard.[84]

BRANDYWINE
11 SEPTEMBER 1777

Since the Colonel Thomas Marshall's 3rd Virginia did not become involved in this battle until late afternoon, it is necessary to recount the events up to that time in order to understand their part in the battle. There were three distinct phases to this encounter. The 3rd Virginia's role did occur until the commencement of the third phase.

Phase 1: 5 a.m. to 11 a.m. – Action at Welsh's Tavern/ Kennett Meeting House.

The British were on their way well before dawn, divided into two columns, one under the command of Lieutenant General Knyphausen, the other, by Lieutenant General Lord Cornwallis. Kynphausen's column consisted of four Hessian regiments, two brigades under General Grant, the 71st Highland Regiment, a squadron of mounted Hessian dragoons, and 350 loyalists known as the Queen's Rangers, under Captain James Wemyss as well as English riflemen, directed by Captain Patrick Ferguson. The Hessian General's entire force totaled about 5,000 men.[85] Their march was aided by an early morning fog which served to hide the British forward movement.

On their way to Welsh's Tavern, the British were unexpectedly met by members of General Maxwell's light infantry. The Americans took up their first line of defense behind a stone wall of the Kennett graveyard, with Captain Charles Porterfield, of the 11th Virginia,[86] in charge. His orders were to fire on the British and then fall back to the second defensive position held by General William Maxwell and his New Jersey Continentals.[87]

Porterfield and his men fired their volley as the Queen's Rangers and Ferguson's rifles approached the meeting house. He retreated as ordered, with the British riflemen in pursuit. Maxwell then abandoned the meeting house's stone wall and used another stone house nearby to set up his defensive line. At the same time, Maxwell's men discharged volley upon volley into the oncoming British. The Americans put up a stubborn defense and slowed down the British advance which was their objective.[88]

The British plan, too, seemed to be working well. Howe had decided to outflank his opponent. Kynphausen's forces were to oppose the Americans at Chad's Ford, "with instructions to 'amuse' the Americans: fire artillery, make as many troop movements as possible, and give Washington the impression that the main attack would be there."[89]

Cornwallis's forces, in the meantime, were to move north through the hilly countryside west of Brandywine Creek, and cross the Creek above the American right flank. If possible, then Cornwallis was to attack the Americans from their right flank and their rear.[90]

That was the plan. Unfortunately for the British, not everything went quite as planned. The Queen's Rangers thought that the Americans were surrendering and advanced only to be suddenly cut down at close range. Ferguson's riflemen lost nearly two-thirds of its numbers by the end of the battle, including their captain who was severely wounded.

By mid-morning, Maxwell's light troops had fallen back across the Brandywine and an artillery barrage erupted on both sides.

> The valley between the two armies shook and reverberated with the thunder of cannons from both sides, and the humid air quickly filled with clouds of thick, white smoke. Knyphausen was following his instructions to 'amuse' the Americans and patiently waited to hear gunfire from the north, which would indicate that Cornwallis had gained Washington's right flank.[91]

Phase 2: 11 a.m. to 4 p.m. British tactics proceeded according to plan – Knyphausen attacked across the Brandywine while Cornwallis fell on the American's right flank.

Cornwallis and Howe reached Trimble's Ford, defended by Pennsylvania riflemen, an hour or so before noon. A "sharp skirmish" ensued there resulting in the withdrawal of the American forces. Their commanding officer, Lieutenant Colonel James Ross of the 1st Pennsylvania[92] sent an urgent dispatch to Washington saying "a large body of the enemy from every account 5000, with 16 or 18 field pieces, marched along this road just now." Ross described the strategic importance of the roads the British now occupied.

> This road leads to Taylor's and Jefferies ferries on the Brandywine and to the Great Valley at the Sign of the Ship on the Lancaster Road to Philadelphia. There is also a road from Brandywine to Chester by Dilworth's Tavern.

> We are close to their rear with 70 men. Capt (Michael) Simpson lay in ambush with 20 men, and gave them three rounds within a small distance, in which two of his men were wounded, one mortally. I believe Genl Howe is with this party, as Joseph Galloway is here known by the inhabitants with many of whom he spoke, and told them that Genl Howe is with him ...[93]

Washington received this message around noon. It just confirmed what he already believed: that the British were definitely going to make a flanking movement on his forces. In response, the General decided to launch an attack on Kynphausen's forces across the Brandywine. He ordered Major General Sullivan to cross the Creek at Brinton's Ford and directed General Maxwell to move his Light Infantry back across Chad's Ford. Maxwell did as ordered and overran a British artillery battery. Sullivan skirmished with the British 4th Regiment.

Then, an erroneous report relaying information from Sullivan that Cornwallis's forces were "nowhere to be seen" west of the Brandywine or near the forks, caused Washington to rethink his strategy. So he sent these orders to Sullivan: "Unresolved conflict of intelligence—rash to assume the offensive. Enemy might be waiting. Orders revoked."[94] Thus he recalled Sullivan from across the Creek and sent him instead to the vicinity of the Quaker Birmingham Meeting House. At the same time, he sent out scouts to gather better intelligence regarding the positions of the British columns under Cornwallis.

He realized also, with growing irritation, that he had not heard from Colonel Theodorick Bland who was responsible for reconnoitering the roads above Jones' Ford. For several hours, there was no news from the right flank of the American army.[94]

The British under Cornwallis, in the meantime, had crossed the east branch of the Brandywine and were headed up the road to the Birmingham Meeting House. The advanced party of Cornwallis's column was led by the Hessians Jaegers, accompanied by some of the British Light Infantry and a company of Highlanders. Moving cautiously through a steep gorge to Sconnelsville, they were astounded to find some of the American forces two miles away, positioned near Birmingham Meeting House.

As the British forces approached Osbourne Hill, still undetected, they were now in a position to launch an attack on the American's right flank. At this point, however, Colonel Theodorick Bland's scouting party *finally* spotted the British. He scrawled a hurried message to Washington:

> '1/4 past one o'clock. Sir, I have discovered a party of the enemy on the heights just on the right of the Widow Davis's who live close together on the road call'd Forks road, about half a mile to the right of the Meeting House. There is a higher hill on their front.'[96]

At the same time Bland dispatched another message to Sullivan, notifying him "that the enemy are in the rear of my right, about two miles, doming down as he says, about two Brigades Chasseurs [Jagers]. He also says he saw dust rise back in the country for about an hours... 2 o'clock p.m."[97]

Now that Washington had some definitive intelligence about Cornwallis' movements, he quickly conveyed orders to two of his reserve divisions—Stirling's and Stephen's, totaling around 3500 men from Virginia, Pennsylvania and New Jersey—to move with all dispatch to Birmingham Meeting House.

Events moved quickly. At 2:30 in the afternoon, Washington ordered Sullivan to march to Birmingham with his division—1300 Marylanders—to "take command of all the forces on the Continental right flank."[98]

At 3 p.m. Stirling's and Stephen's troops reached the area around the Meeting House. They took up positions on a hill just south of the building. Sullivan's troops came into the vicinity soon after from the west and occupied a site on a hill half a mile to the left, in front of Stirling's troops.[99]

Phase 3: 4 p.m. to 8 p.m. – British launch an attack on Birmingham Hill.

Sullivan, when he arrived at the American lines, was not happy with the position of his troops, and he rode up to Birmingham Hill to consult with Stirling, Stephen, Brigadier General William Woodford and other officers. He ordered Stirling and Stephen to shift to the right while his own men were to close the half mile gap between the two divisions. He then ordered General Woodford, in Stephen's division, to shift his men behind the hill to the American right.

Unfortunately, his order came too late to adjust the position of Colonel Marshall and the 170 men of his 3rd Virginia Regiment. The regiment had been placed in the woods to the right of the American line, near the Birmingham Meeting House, in order to protect the flank and several artillery pieces. When Sullivan shifted the line to get rid of the gap, he unwittingly left Marshall and the 3rd Virginia in front of the American main line.

At 4 o'clock the British struck the right flank,[100] just as Sullivan's division were trying to close the gap between Stirling and Stephens. The British suddenly appeared, with fixed bayonets, and began crossing the divide between the two armies. The Maryland and Delaware brigades, to the rear, broke and ran.[101] Stirling's brigade, in the center, were slowly driven back by the ferocity of the British attack.[102]

While this fighting was going on, the 3rd Virginia was contesting the British advance, from their own position in an orchard behind the Meeting House. They were opposed by the British Light Infantry and Hessian troops.[103]

The British began their march across wheat and corn fields, their advance hampered because they had to tear down or climb over fences belonging to local farmers. The Americans began firing their artillery when the enemy was halfway between the Osbourne and Birmingham Hills. It did not appear to deter the British and Hessian advance, even after the Americans replaced solid shot with canisters filled with "deadly small missiles." Howe's aide-de-camp, Captain von Muenchhausen, entered this account in his diary:

> 'When we got close to the rebels, they fired their cannon; they did not fire their small arms till we were within 40 paces of them, at which time they fire whole volleys and sustained a very heavy fire. The English, and especially the English grenadiers, advanced fearlessly and very quickly; fired a volley, and then ran furiously at the rebels with fixed bayonets.'[104]

General Sullivan said, in his account, "five times did the Enemy drive our troops from the Hill & as often was it regained ... The general fire of the Line lasted an hour & forty minutes, fifty one minutes of which the Hill was disputed almost muzzle to muzzle in such a manner that General Conway who has seen much service says he never so close & sever a fire."[105]

Stirling and Stephen, outflanked on the right, began to retreat. This brought about a collapse of the American center. Lord Stirling was able to beat back the British attack on the center until the brigades on the American right broke and ran. Now threatened on both flanks, and to avoid being taken prisoner, Stirling successfully moved his men into the cover of nearby woods. Most of the remaining troops made it to the second line of defense southeast of Birmingham Hill. In their flight, they abandoned nine of their cannons. Sullivan attempted to rally the American right flank but failed. Only Hazen's forces in his division, placed on the left, were able to hold off a charge of the Hessians.

While this was going on, Colonel Marshall and this 3rd Virginia regiment continued to harass the enemy who were assaulting the area around the Meeting House.

> The 1st battalion of British light infantry advanced on Marshall's position and thus avoided artillery fire by Stephen's gun. The light infantry was joined by other British troops near the meeting house and they advanced on Marshall with the 17th light infantry on the right and 42nd Foot on the left. Marshall's unit fired and retreated to the Birmingham Meeting House where they took positions behind a stone wall and continued to fire upon members of the light infantry.[106]

Intense pressure from the British from both flanks caused a collapse. Only Woodford's brigade remained on Birmingham Hill.[107]

> On the American right, German and British light infantry worked their way around Stephen's flank and assaulted Marshall's isolated Third Virginia from two sides. After hand-to-hand fighting, the Virginians fell back from their forty-five minute stand, losing heavily in the process.[108]

Losing heavily, doesn't begin to describe it. The regiment was badly mauled. They managed to reach Woodford's position by circling around behind the hill. Colonel Marshall was on foot, his horse shot from under him. Captain John Chilton had been killed. Captain Phillip Lee was badly wounded and eventually died of his wounds in January 1778. Two lieutenants lost their lives in this battle: William White and Apollos Cooper. Ensign Robert Peyton was killed. Lieutenants John Francis Mercer, John Blackwell, and

John Peyton were wounded. Thirteen non-commissioned officers and sixty privates out of 150 men were dead in this unsuccessful defense of Birmingham Hill.[109]

Once the 3rd Virginia had reached their brigade, Woodford decided to stay where they were to give Sullivan's troops time to regroup. He changed his mind when British artillery began firing at them. His captain of Artillery and three of his lieutenants were wounded. More than half of his men were killed in the cannonading. Horses were shot down which necessitated the abandonment of his division's field pieces. Then Woodford was wounded in the hand by cannon fire and he left to have his hand dressed. When the cannonade stopped, the British charged. They were within sight of the battered American unit, when the brigade retreated, making for the woods behind the hill.[110]

While the battle continued for several more hours, and the British earned a hard-won victory, Colonel Marshall and his regiment played no further part in the action.

The *Virginia Gazette*, in its 3 October 1777 edition carried an account of the regiment's role and casualties suffered at Brandywine. Dated 22 September 1777, from a camp near Schuylkill, a General Officer wrote

> I have only time to inform your Excellency, that on the 11th last, we had very nigh given the enemy a sever drubbing. The action commended about 8 o'clock in the morning, and with several intermissions, continued till night. About 5 o'clock it resembled an earth quake, far exceeding the loudest thunder.
>
> Lieut. Col. Neaville, of the 12th [Virginia], began the attack at Birmingham meeting house, and his regiment was the last that left the field; they behaved well. Col. Marshall, of the 3d regiment, attacked the enemy's left column with his single regiment, and at first repulsed them; but, overpowered by numbers, was obliged to retire, which he did in good order. In this contest, which continued violent for near three quarters of an hour, this brave regiment lost four officers on the spot, amongst them a brave young Gentleman, Lieutenant Peyton, and Captain Chilton, who, brave as Wolfe, imitated his manner in death, inquiring about the success of the day as he expired...[111]

Late on the evening of 11 September 1777, General Washington wrote John Hancock about the events at Brandywine Creek.

> I am sorry to inform you, that in this day's engagement, we have been obliged to leave the enemy masters of the field. Unfortunately the intelligence received of the enemy's advancing up the Brandywine, and crossing at a ford about six miles above us, was uncertain and contradictory, notwithstanding all my pains to get the best. This prevented my making a disposition, adequate to the force with which the enemy attacked us on the right; in consequence of which the troops first engaged, were obliged to retire before they could be reinforced.
>
> In the midst of the attack on the right, that body of the enemy which remained on the others side of Chad's Ford, crossed it, and attacked the division under the command of General Wayne and the light troops under General Maxwell who, after a severe conflict, also retired.
>
> The militia under the command of Major Genl Armstrong, being posted at a ford, about two miles below Chad's, had no opportunity of engaging. But though we fought under many disadvantages, and were from the causes, above mentioned obliged to retire, yet our loss of men is not, I am persuaded, very considerable, I believe much less than the enemy's.
>
> We have also lost about seven or eight pieces of cannon, according to the best information I can at present obtain. The baggage having been previously moved off, is all secure, saving the men's blankets, which being at their backs, many of them doubtless are lost.
>
> I have directed all the troops to assemble behind Chester, where they are now arranging for this night. Notwithstanding the misfortune of the day, I am happy to find the troops in good spirits; and I hope another time we shall compensate for the losses now sustained. The Marquis La Fayette was wounded in the leg and Genl Woodford in the hand. Divers other officers were wounded and some slain, but the number of either cannot now be ascertained.[112]

Although the British had won the battle on Brandywine Creek, the American forces were still between the redcoats and Philadelphia.[113] Washington issued General Orders from his Headquarters at Chester, the next day for brigade officers to send officers to pick up stragglers "on the roads leading to the places of action yesterday, and on any other roads where [they] may be found; particularly to Wilmington, where 'tis said, many have retired … In the mean time," he continued, "the troops are to march on in good order thro' Derby to the bridge over Schuylkill, cross it, and proceed up to their former ground near the falls of Schuylkill and Germantown and there pitch their tents."[114]

Washington issued this statement in his General Orders on 13 September. He gave

> …thanks those gallant officers and soldiers, who, on the 11th instant, bravely fought in their country and its cause…Altho' the event of that day, from some unfortunate circumstances, as not so favorable as could be wished, the General has the satisfaction of assuring the troops, that from every account he has been able to obtain, the enemy's loss greatly exceeded our; and he has full confidence that in another Appeal to Heaven (with the blessing of providence, which it becomes every officer and soldier humbly to supplicate), we shall prove successful.[115]

In the aftermath of Brandywine: Casualties in the 3rd Virginia.

Dr. David Griffith, the 3rd Virginia's surgeon described the part the regiment played at Brandywine, in a letter to his wife Hannah on 14 September.

> Fame will [have] inform you by this time that we have had a battle.—The unfortunate, it will by no means, be so ruinous as report & the tongues of tories will make it. We were repulsed & lost the ground but our enemy purchased it dearly. Their loss is very considerable by all accts. Our no so great as might be expected…
>
> Our regt suffered more than any in the line & acquired greater glory. We lost upwards of 40 men killed & wounded. Three officers are killed & 4 wounded, one, I fear mortally. The officers of ours killed are Captn. Chilton, Lieut Appollos Cooper, Bob Peyton, Lieut. White, shot thro the belly. Capt. Briscoe, Lieut. Mercer & Capt[n] Lee are slightly wounded.
>
> The loss of this action is not so bad in its consequences as might be expected… The spirits of the army is not [broken]—they rallied the same night & retired the next day in good order & in as good spirits as they were before the action, & are now as desirous of fighting as ever.[116]

Captains John Ashby, David Arell, John Chilton, Phill Lee, John Peyton, Robert Powell, Gustavus Brown Wallace, and Captain Charles West/ Reuben Briscoe all returned men wounded at Brandywine in their September 1777 muster rolls. Table 6 below illustrates the losses to the regiment after Brandywine.

Table 6: Casualties in the 3rd Virginia at Brandywine from Compiled Service Records, 3rd Virginia[117]
Abbreviations: n.g. = not given; yrs = years; all dates abbreviated; PR = Company Payroll; exp = expired.

Name	Rank	Enlistment/Discharge	On Wm. Mountjoy's List of Absentees	Muster Roll
Captain Arell's Company:				
Thomas Daley	Private	n.g.	Dead. (date n.g.)	9/77 to 10/77: Wounded.
William Sanford	Private	Enlisted for 2 yrs.	Dead. (date n.g.)	9/77 to 10/77: Absent, Wounded at Brandywine.
Captain Ashby's Company:				
Christopher Burn	Private	n.g.		9/77 Absent, wounded at Hospital. 10/77 Wounded.
Matthew Carney	Private	Enlisted 2/12/76 for 2 yrs.		**9/77 Killed 9/11/77.**
John Cullins	Corporal	Enlisted until 3/18/78. Discharged 2/18/78.		9/77 Absent, wounded & sent to hospital.
Edward Riley	Private	Enlisted 1/77 for 3 yrs.		9/77 Absent, wounded & sent to hospital. 10/77 Wounded.
Armistead White	Sergeant	Enlisted 2/12/76 for 2 yrs.		9/77 Absent, wounded & sent to hospital.

Table 6: Casualties in the 3rd Virginia at Brandywine from Compiled Service Records, 3rd Virginia[117]

Name	Rank	Enlistment/Discharge	On Wm. Mountjoy's List of Absentees	Muster Roll
Captain John Chilton's Company:				
Henry Bradford	Sergeant	Enlisted until 4/10/78. Discharged 12/23/77.		9/77 Wounded.
Robert Coffee	Rank n.g.	Enlisted 4/10/76 for 2 yrs.		9/77 **Killed 9/11/77.**
John Chilton	Captain	Commissioned 4/29/76.		9/77 **Killed 9/11/77.**
John Brown (2)	Private	Enlisted until 4/10/78.		9/77 to 11/77 Absent, wounded. **11/15/77 Dead.**
Michael Hynd	Drummer	Enlisted until 4/10/78.		9/77 Absent, missing since Brandywine.
Joshua Jenkins	Sergeant	Enlisted until 4/10/78.		9/77 **Killed 9/11/77.** PR 9/77 for 11 days.
Peter Moore	Private	Enlisted until 4/10/78. Discharged 2/14/78.		9/77 to 10/77 Absent, wounded.
John Murphy	Private	Enlisted until 4/10/78. Discharged 12/23/77.		9/77 Absent, wounded.
Captain Phill Lee's Company:				
Phill Lee	Captain	Commissioned 3/19/76.		9/77 Wounded **1/29/78 Dead.**
Robert Peyton	Lieutenant	Commissioned 8/15/77.		9/77 **Killed 9/11/77.**
William Norman	Private	Enlisted 2/1/76 Discharged Yorktown.		9/77 to 1/78: Absent, wounded.
John Young	Private	Enlisted for 3 yrs. Deserted 7/77; returned 8/77. Discharged Yorktown.		9/77 to 11/77: Wounded. 12/77 to 1/78 Absent, wounded.
Captain John Peyton's Company:				
Micajah Farrow	Corporal		Killed. (date n.g.)	9/77 Wounded, 9/11/77.
Charles Lenox	Private	Enlisted 2/5/76 for 2 yrs.		9/77 to 10/77 Wounded. 11/77 to 1/78 Absent, wounded.
John Matthews	Private	Enlisted until 2/5/78.	Discharged. (date n.g.)	9/77 Wounded.
Jonathan Williams	Private	Enlisted until 2/5/78. Time exp: 1/78		9/77 to 10/77 Wounded. 11/77 to 12/77 Absent, wounded.

Table 6: Casualties in the 3rd Virginia at Brandywine from Compiled Service Records, 3rd Virginia[117]

Captain Robert Powell's Company:

Name	Rank	Enlistment/Discharge	On Wm. Mountjoy's List Of Absentees	Muster Roll
Thomas Cosby	Private	n.g. Reenlisted 12/23/77 in Light Horse.		9/77 Absent, with wounded at Bethlehem.
Forrest Green	Private	Enlisted for 2 yrs. Discharged 2/4/78.		9/77 Absent, wounded at Bethlehem.
Samuel Hill	Private	Enlisted 76 for 2 yrs. Discharged 2/13/78.		9/77 Absent, with wounded at Bethlehem.
Stephen Terry	Private	n,g, Discharged 11/8/77.		9/77 Absent, with wounded at Bethlehem.
Daniel Turner	Private	Enlisted for 2 yrs. Discharged 2/10/78.		9/77 Absent, with wounded at Bethlehem.
John Whitlock	Private	Enlisted for 2 yrs.		9/77 to 10/77 Absent, wounded at Bethlehem.

Captain Gustavus Brown Wallace's Company

James Arrowsmith	Private	Enlisted 2/23/76 for 2 yrs. Discharged Yorktown. (date n.g.)		9/77 Wounded, at Reading; 10/77 Wounded.
Jeremiah Kendall	Private	Enlisted 2/12/76 for 2 yrs. Discharged 2/1/78. (as Sergeant.)		9/77 to 10/77 Wounded.
Valentine King	Private	Enlisted 2/23/76 for 2 yrs. Discharged, 2/78 Yorktown.		9/77 to 10/77 Wounded. 11/77 Wounded, at Reading.
John Francis Mercer	Lieutenant.	Promoted to Captain 1/27/78.		9/77 to 10/77. Wounded.

Captain West/Briscoe's Company

Hugh Henderson	Private	Enlisted for war.	9/77 "Left on the field 9/11/77." PR 1/78 for 5 mo. "Being wounded & taken prisoner at Brandywine, since came up, though not mustered."	
Apollo Cooper	Lieutenant	Commissioned 2/9/76.		9/77 **Killed 9/11/77.**

Note: The compiled service records for officers of 3rd Virginia Regiment identified these officers as having died either at Brandywine or of wounds suffered at Brandywine: Cadet Robert Peyton, dead 9/11/77;[118] Lieutenant Apollo Cooper, dead 9/11/77;[119] and Lieutenant William White, died 9/16/77 of wounds from Brandywine.[120]

Two twentieth-century historians gave this stirring description of Captain John Chilton's demise.

> The first column of British infantry had just reached the edge of the wood as Captain John Chilton fell with a gaping wound ion his side. Fully conscious, he realized that the musket ball that had torn through his vitals had done damage beyond the power of any physician to repair. Around him the battle surged. There were so few against so many, too few to spare to take him from the field. Here he would stay, under a tree, and watch their valiant efforts. Perhaps his presence might give them greater courage. He had nothing more to give.

As pain dimmed his vision he asked how they had fared. The position could not be held. The retreat had been sounded, they told him. They carried him to an old Meeting House that was being used as a field hospital. Tradition says that it was Birmingham, but Weedon identified it as Concord Meeting House on the Chester Road near Marshall's Wood. Captain Chilton's work was not finished, but his time had run out. Others would have to finish the course.[121]

In the wake of Captain Chilton's death at Brandywine, his brother-in-law, 1st Lieutenant John Eustace Blackwell, was promoted to the captaincy of his company just three days later on 14 September 1777.[122] John's brother Lieutenant Joseph Blackwell had also survived the battle although his smallpox-weakened eyes still bothered him. Sergeant William Moore had been promoted to Ensign and could help "carry some of the load." Only Sergeants Chichester Matthews and William Tomlin were able to return to duty. Jonathan Crooke, a private in Chilton's company, was assigned hospital duty and took care of the company's wounded.[123]

Private Robert English, one of the original members in Chilton's company, had been sick and absent in Virginia since June 1777. He had just returned to the regiment in September when his company was battered at Brandywine. He deserted. Company Muster rolls for October showed him as "absent, confined for desertion." Since the penalty for desertion was hanging, he must have been very persuasive as he was found on Company muster rolls from November 1777 until his discharge on 14 February 1778.[124]

Captain Phill Lee, although wounded, remained the commanding officer of his company—at least on paper.[125]

With Woodford, temporarily incapacitated, the reins of the brigade fell to Colonel Thomas Marshall.[126] Captain John Ashby, though wounded, remained with his company. His lieutenant, Valentine Peyton, had also come through the battle unharmed.[127]

While the 3rd Virginia as a regiment had survived the British attack on the hill of the Birmingham Meeting house, the regiment anxiously awaited the arrival of new recruits which would help fill out their companies. Six of these men had had been left in Leesburg to be inoculated for small pox, including William Bradford and Stephen Tomlin, whose brothers were already in the regiment.[128]

Overall consequences of Brandywine.

After the battle, the American army was in total disarray. While most of the American officers and men headed towards Chester during the night of 11 September, others kept going, to Philadelphia and beyond. "Hundreds exited the war this way, making it difficult to ascertain exact American casualties at Brandywine."[129] The Americans losses—wounded, killed, or taken prisoners were thought to be double those of the British and included 315 deserters. The British losses were 543 killed, wounded or missing.[130]

By 14 September, the Washington's exhausted army had reached Germantown. In order to delay Howe and Cornwallis from another assault on the American position, and to give his army time to refit and regroup, Washington reverted to the strategy he employed so successfully the previous spring. He ordered Generals Smallwood and Gist and their Maryland militia to harrass the British supply lines.

Washington was "happy to find the troops in good spirits; and ... hoped another time we shall compensate for the losses now sustained."[131]

In a letter form Eliphalet Dyer to Joseph Trumbull, written from Philadelphia on the day after Brandywine, he reported "our Army are much fatigued but not at all discouraged, but on the contrary, are said to be very alert & in high spirits. We hope for [a] rest [for] two or 3 days when we expect 3 or 4000 Jersey Militia."[132]

Cornelius Hammet, in a letter to William Wilkerson, written from Philadelphia on 13 September 1777, echoed this sentiment. "Our Army," he said, "are in high spirits & very desirous of having another brush with the enemy who, by the last accounts, still remain on the field."[133]

Another delegate, William Williams, wrote Jonathan Trumbull Jr from Philadelphia on 13 September "As our army was much dispersed, having man by posts & passes to defend, not near all were ever engaged [in the battle] & few or none of the militia. Tis said by every one that they behaved with great bravery, but were under many disadvantages of ground &c, & also that they are yet in good spirits & not dismayed."[134]

It appeared, then, that while the Americans had lost this battle, they had not lost the war. The realization that they held their own against the best the British could throw at them, no doubt accounted for these "high spirits" reported by both General Washington and several delegates to Congress. The 3rd Virginia certainly found they could match their men favorably against the British, despite the severe pounding they took.

On the March.

Washington issued orders on 14 September for the army to be ready to move.

> The troops are to march to Swedes' Ford in the following order, be subdivisions from the right, viz: First, two-thirds of the Light Dragoons, from which their commanding officer will detach small parties in front, to reconnoitre on the flanks to a considerable distance.
> Second, a Captain's command from General Smallwood's Brigade, 800 years in their rear. Third, one regiment from [the] same brigade, 200 yards in *their* rear.
> Fourth, the main body of the army 500 yards in their rear, in the following order, viz: 1st. General Sullivan's Division, 2d. Lot, Stirling's 3d. General Wayne's, 4th Park of Artillery, 5th General Nash's Brigade, 6th General Stevens' Division, 7th. General Greene's.
> Fifth, the wagons with stores, hospital stores, and commissaries' stores. Sixth, a rear guard of two regiments from Weedon's Brigade. Seventh, a Captain's command from these two regiments, at the distance of 200 yards. Eight, the remaining third of the Light Dragoons, 500 yards from the foot. Ninth, a subaltern's command from these Dragoons, at the distance of 500 yards.
> The guards in front and rear, and each brigade, to send out small flanking parties on their left. The rear guard of foot, and the Light Dragoons, to pick up all stragglers.[135]

By 15 September, the army had reached the area around Warren Tavern. Washington ordered

> In [the] future, whenever the men are formed for action, the Serjeants are to be placed in the ranks, on the flanks of subdivisions, that the benefit of their fire may not be lost. The Brigadiers and Officers commanding regiments are also to post some good officers in the rear, to keep the men in order; and if in time of action, any man, who is not wounded, whether he has arms or not, turns his back upon the enemy, an d attempts to run away, or to retreat before orders are given for it, those officers are instantly to put him to death. The man does not deserve to live, who basely flies, breaks his solemn engagements, and betrays his country.[136]

On the same day Washington reported to the President of Congress that the British lay near Dilworth Town, not far from Brandywine. "We," he continued, "are moving up this road to get in between the enemy and the Swedes Fort and to prevent them from turning our right flank, which they seem to have a violent inclination to effect, by all their movements."[137]

BATTLE OF THE CLOUDS
16 SEPTEMBER 1777

Washington and his army arrived in the vicinity between the Warren and White Horse Taverns on 16 September 1777. The army was, he reported to the President of Congress, "so far advanced, as to be in a position to meet the enemy on the route to Swedes Ford." The general ordered his troops to be "refreshed" this morning since they were late in setting up camp the night before. He communicated his worry about the lack of ammunition for some of his troops, knowing it would be needed if there was an engagement.[138]

The British indeed were on the move. General Howe was still of the opinion that if he could lure Washington and his army into one large engagement, he could finish off the rebel army, force Washington to surrender and end the rebellion.

As day dawned on 16 September, in a heavy rain, Howe sent a battalion of Light Infantry in advance of the two British columns, one headed by Knyphausen, the other by Cornwallis. Skirmishing took place as the British advanced, met by American rifle fire, whereupon the American lines withdrew. Then, just as the two sides began to fire in earnest, a "northeaster that had been brewing struck."

The Americans had positioned themselves in a heavily wooded area. The Hessian Jagers, under the command of Captain Ewald, were ordered to attack and moved forward in a very heavy downpour. American rifle fire met the column although the rain began to stifle its effect as weapons and powder became soaked. The Hessian rifles also began to misfire due to the downpour, and "Ewald ordered his men to draw their short hunting swords. 'I reached the wood at top speed', he said, "and came to close quarters with the enemy, who during the furious attack forgot he had bayonets and quit the field.'"[139]

It did not appear that the 3rd Virginia took any part in this battle, so-called because it seemed that the clouds opened up and the resulting heavy downpour effectively stopped any further engagement between the two armies. None of the accounts of the action mentioned the 3rd Virginia.

Washington described the action and the effect the lack of ammunition had on the American forces in a letter to the President of Congress on 19 September.

> When I left Germantown with the Army, I hoped I should have had an opportunity of attacking them, either in front or on their flank, with a prospect of success; But unhappily a variety of causes concurred to prevent it.
>
> Our march, in the first place, was greatly impeded thro' want of provisions, which delayed us so long that the enemy were apprized of our motions and gained the grounds near the White Horse Tavern, with a part of their army turning our right flank, whilst another part, composing the main body, were more advanced towards our left.
>
> We should have disappointed them in their design by getting on their left; but the heavy rain which fell that [on Tuesday] evening and in the course of the night, totally unfitted our guns for service and nearly the whole of the ammunition with which the Army had been completed a day or two before, amounting to forty rounds per man.
>
> At first I expected that the loss was by no means so considerable, and intended [only] to file off with the troops a few miles to replace it and clean their arms and then to proceed on my original plans; but upon examination, found it as I have mentioned, and that we had not a sufficient supply with us to furnish the men with the necessary complement.
>
> In this situation it was judged necessary, that we should proceed as far as Reading Furnace for the security of the army. Owing to these accidents, particularly the latter, matter have not been conducted as I intended and wished, and the enemy have had an opportunity of making their advances without being attacked.
>
> I yet hope, from the present state of the River, that I shall be down in time to give them a meeting and if unfortunately they should gain Philadelphia that it will not be without loss ...[140]

He said later, that "upon examining the state of our ammunition I find it so generally hurt by the rain that we are not in a condition to make a stand."[141] The American army crossed the Schuylkill, undetected, "over roads that had become quagmires, a grueling thirty-six mile march." This put the Americans on the left bank of the river.

PAOLI

Washington had left General Anthony Wayne behind, with orders to follow and harrass the British rear. He gave the same orders to General Maxwell and his Light Infantry.

Unfortunately, the British knew of the American plans and the exact whereabouts of Wayne's forces, thanks to their intelligence. Howe decided to make a surprise night attack on the American's forces camped at Paoli Tavern.[142] A British officer described the attack.

> On approaching the right of the Camp we perceived the line of fires, and the Light Infantry being ordered to form to the front, rushed along the line putting to bayonet all they came up with, an overtaking the main herd of fugitives, stabbed great numbers.[142]

The British light infantry then hit the Americans from the rear and the flank. Lieutenant Martin Hunter, a British officer, recalled later in his life that the bayoneting "with the cries of the wounded formed altogether the most dreadful scene I ever beheld. Every man that fired was immediately put to death."[143]

The British Light Dragoons followed up with an attack on the camp from the woods along, and with other British troops with fixed bayonets they charged into the midst of the American camp. Amongst the last forces to attack was the Black Watch who fired the American huts.

Throughout all the confusion, Wayne managed to get many of his officers and rank and file away. The British, frustrated in their unsuccessful attempt to capture the American Brigadier, turned their attack on General Smallwood's Maryland militia. The militia, unused to such brutality, "flung down their guns & run off & have not been heard of since, whilst the Artillery men & waggoner cutting their horses loose and running off with them." [144]

This action came to be known as the Paoli Massacre although most of Wayne's troops managed to elude the British. Unfortunately, for the Americans, Howe's rear was now secure and General Wayne's brigade was no where near ready for another battle. Since the action involved Pennsylvania troops, the 3rd Virginia was not involved here either.

Washington's chief problems: collecting stragglers and winter clothing for the troops.

Meanwhile Washington was doing his best to address several other issues that *were* to affect the regiment: picking up stragglers who retreated from Brandywine and finding the necessary winter clothing for the troops. Foremost on his mind was the necessity to round up the stragglers who had not yet returned to the army after Brandywine.[145] Equally important, with the expected advent of cold weather, was the lamentable want of clothing, shoes and blankets. One of his first steps was to recommend to the President of Congress the appointment of a committee to obtain blankets for his soldiers.

> Many are now without, and the season becoming cold, they will be injured in their health and unfitted for service, unless they are immediately provided with them. Our supplies in this instance, as well as in every article of cloathing, can not be too great as there are frequent losses, not easily to be avoided.
>
> I would also observe, that I think, in point of prudence and sound policy, every species of provisions, should be removed from the city [Philadelphia], except such as will be necessary to supply the present demands of this army.[146]

On 22 September, Washington ordered his Clothier-General to "distribute all the cloathes and shoes in his possession."[147] On 23 September, in a letter to the President of Congress from his camp near Potts Grove, he requested that Lancaster and its vicinity to be scoured for shoes and blankets for the army including "large parcels of shoes, in particular."[148]

On the same day, realizing that the shortage of clothes, shoes and blankets was quickly becoming critical, Washington ordered Lieutenant Colonel Alexander Hamilton to go to Philadelphia and "there procure from the inhabitants, contributions of blankets and clothing and materials to answer the purposes of both, in proportion to the ability of each." Washington told Hamilton that

> The distressed situation of the army for want of blankets and many necessary articles of clothing, is truly deplorable; and must inevitably be destructive to it, unless a speedy remedy be applied. Without a better supply than they at present have, it will be impossible for the men to support the fatigues of the campaign in the further progress of the approaching inclement season. .... No supply can be drawn from the public magazines. We have therefore no resource but from the private stock of individuals. I feel, and I lament, the absolute necessity of requiring the inhabitants to contribute to those wants which we have no other means of satisfying, and which, if unremoved, would involve the ruin of the army, and perhaps the ruin of America.[149]

By the end of September, Washington and his army were on the Shippack Road, five miles from Pennybacker's Mill. Here, he informed his troops of Burgoyne's surrender at Saratoga.[150] His own army had been swelled by the arrival of additional Continental forces and militia: Brigadier General McDougal's Continental troops from Peekskill, consisting of around 900 men; General Smallwood's 1100 man contingent of Maryland militia; and Brigadier General Forman's Jersey militia of some 600 men. A group of Virginia militia had arrived at Lancaster, although they were reported to be badly armed.

In a Council of War, called on 28 September at the American headquarters at Pennybacker's Mill, it was decided that the "Army should move to some grounds proper for an encampment within about 12 miles of the enemy, and there wait for a further reinforcement, or be in readiness to take advantage of any favourable opportunity that may offer for making an attack.[151]

THE ROAD TO GERMANTOWN

On 1 October, Washington ordered

> the whole army ... to strike their tents tomorrow morning at 8 o'clock, and get ready to march. At *nine* the march is to begin, Genl Sullivan's division leading, followed by Lincoln's McDougall's Greenes'; these form the first line; then the park of artillery, then the second line in this order, Stirling's division, Nash's, Stephen's.
> Genl Sullivan's division to beat a march as a signal for marching, the beat to be continued by the others successively. The whole are to encamp on the new ground in the same order...the waggons to go in the rear of the army, in the order of the brigades to which they belong; all the tent waggons first.[152]
> At *nine* the march is to begin, Genl Sullivan's division leading, followed by Lincoln's McDougall's, Greene's; these form the first line; then the park of artillery, then the second line in this order, Stirling's division, Nash's, Stephen's ... The whole [army] are to encamp on the new ground in the same order.[152]

The next day the American army moved to within fifteen miles of the British encampment at Germantown. Washington and his senior officers had decided to attack the British at Germantown. These forces were General Howe's minus British and Hessian Grenadiers, and two squadrons of Light Dragoons taken by Cornwallis to Philadelphia. Howe's forces were further weakened when two other regiments of foot had been dispatched to assault the American forts on the Delaware.[153]

GERMANTOWN
4 October 1777

The American Plan.

The American preparation for the attack against the British at Germantown was spelled out in Washington's General Orders, issued 3 October 1777. Troops were furnished with two days worth of cooked provisions and issued forty rounds of ammunition. The sick were all sent to Bethlehem around noon. At six in the evening the whole army was on the move. Packs and blankets were left behind.
Washington was to accompany the two divisions, under Sullivan and Wayne, which were to form the right wing. They were to march down the Shippack Road to Germantown Pike and attack the British left flank. General Conway's troops were to take out the pickets on the left flank. General John Armstrong, positioned to the right of Sullivan, was to take his Pennsylvania militia down the Manatawny Road along the Schuylkill. His troops, once they dealt with the British pickets, were to attack the left flank and rear of the enemy. Washington assigned General Maxwell's Light Infantry and Brigadier General Francis Nash's brigade of North Carolinians to act as the reserve for the right wing.
The American left wing, was under the overall command of Major General Nathanael Greene.[154] Greene's division was the stronger force in numbers—with three divisions, his, Stephen's on his right and McDougall's on his left. It was two-thirds of Washington's forces—including the entire Virginia line. Greene's left was protected by General Smallwood's Marylanders and General Forman's Additional Continental Regiment. These troops were to move down the old York Road, sweeping around the British right, to attack from the rear.[155]
The columns were to do their best to arrive by two in the morning on 4 October, so they were within two miles of the enemy's pickets. They were to halt there and wait until five in the morning when the attack was to begin. Each column was to make their own dispositions in such a way that their advanced forces would be able to attack the enemy's pickets "precisely at five oClock with charged bayonets

without firing and the columns to move on to the attack as soon as possible." Washington wanted "every officer and soldier to have a piece of white paper in their hatt."[156]

That, at least, was the plan. However, the ground over which the army was to march was rugged and broken. The roads were quagmires since it had been raining for days. The distances to be covered by all of the advancing columns were different for each. Communication between the American divisions was difficult.

The British position at Germantown.

Howe's force at Germantown numbered between seven and eight thousand. His main line of defense lay on the southern edge of the village. General Kynphausen's left wing would face Sullivan's right wing. Beyond Howe's main defense line, on the outside edge of Germantown, was the 40th Foot, commanded by Lieutenant Colonel Thomas Musgrave. They were camped near a large stone house—the Chew mansion, also known as Cliveden. The British 2nd Light Infantry, the unit who attacked Anthony Wayne's forces at Paoli, was posted on the Germantown Road at Mount Pleasant. Their pickets were just to the north, at Mount Airy.

The British right wing was commanded by General Grant and extended northeastward beyond Lime Kiln Road where Greene's division would be coming. The 1st Light Infantry Battalion, with pickets, was situated on Lime Kiln Road, just north of General Grant.[157]

Phase 1: 5:30 a.m. to 6:15 a.m. – Preliminaries at Mount Airy along the British Left Wing.

The 6th Pennsylvania was the lead regiment in General Conway's brigade and was the first infantry unit in action on the morning of 4 October, sometime between five and five thirty in the morning. They moved with fixed bayonets noiselessly in a line down the southern end of Chestnut Hill along the Germantown Road.

With a troop of dragoons accompanying them, the Pennsylvania regiment proceeded up the rise of Mount Airy, having been ordered to silence the British pickets with their bayonets and sabers to keep them from raising the alarm. Unfortunately for the Americans, the British pickets, alerted, fired at the column with musket fire and cannons. The British sentries, shouting a warning as they retreated, were forced back to the camp of the 2nd Light Infantry at Mount Pleasant.

The sun came up as the Americans attacked the British pickets at their outposts. The ground, already damp from the incessant rain, was soon covered with a dense, patchy, nearly impenetrable fog. These conditions, combined with the smoke from the guns, reduced visibility to almost nothing.

The Americans moved to attack the 2nd Light Infantry at Mount Pleasant and, after heavy fighting, forced the British line back, Then followed a see-saw battle, with the Americans forced back, regrouping, pushing the British light infantry back who regrouped and again attacked the American forces under Conway.

Behind Conway's forces was the rest of the American right wing. Sullivan's Maryland troops formed up west of the Germantown Road while Wayne's Brigade formed up on the east. Both brigades set out to reinforce Conway.

When these fresh troops arrived, they found that they had outflanked the British on both sides, with Conway forces along the road and in the fields. Wayne's troops attacked the Light Infantry with a vengeance. Because of the part this British infantry unit played at Paoli, the Americans took no prisoners. They bayoneted every Light Infantryman they found. The remaining force fell back from Mount Pleasant.[158]

In the meantime, Greene's division became lost when he took a wrong turn. It was an hour before he was able to find his way back. The roads, a moonless night and heavy fog had slowed his columns down.

Colonel Thomas Marshall, the acting commander of Woodford's Brigade, began to lose contact with the main column when he veered off to his right. As dawn broke, heavy gunfire was heard from the right. Marshall halted his men. He had no idea where he was since the firing now seemed to be coming from his rear. The fog made it impossible to see and distorted the sound of the gunfire.[159]

Phase 2: 6:15 to 7:30 a.m. – The action around the Cliveden.

General Howe, hearing sounds of battle, took his staff and rushed up the Germantown Road to see what was happening. He was stunned to find his Light Infantry in full retreat. So, he quickly ordered Musgrave's 40th Regiment to cover the Light Infantry's retreat.

> The British situation changed by the minute. The 2nd Battalion of Light Infantry put up a fight at every fence, ditch and hedge. The American advance was fluid. The Continentals near the road slowly moved forward against opposition, while the right of Sullivan's line and the left of Wayne's brigade encountered little or no opposition.[160]

By the time the battle had reached the Chew Mansion, the "retreat had become a rout." The British abandoned their two pieces of artillery but not before slashing the dragropes and killing the horses to prevent the Americans from using them.

Musgrove, upon learning that an American force, part of Wayne's brigade, was already at his camp behind Cliveden, split his force, ordering part to stay and cover the Light Infantry's retreat while the rest of the regiment went into the mansion. He deployed his men through out the mansion, manning positions at doors and windows. Musgrove ordered his men to bayonet anyone who tried to enter the mansion.[161]

As the American forces came up to the mansion, the British fired on them. Conway's men disengaged and marched off to the right but not before the Pennsylvanians fired a few volleys back at the British. They were behind Sullivan's men and formed the extreme right flank of his forces. Sullivan's men also passed the house. Major John Eager Howard, in command of the Maryland regiment due to an injury to Colonel Josias Hall, also passed by unaffected by the enemy fire from the mansion.

Meanwhile, Washington was getting worried. He and his staff had accompanied Wayne and Sullivan's troops and had witnessed the fighting between the British Light Infantry and the Americans. However, he could hear nothing of any battle along Limekiln Pike which meant that General Greene's forces had not yet arrived on the scene.

Greene had gotten lost and by the time Colonel Marshall emerged with the brigade from the blinding fog to see a massive stone mansion ahead of him, it seemed every window and door in the house was belching gun fire at the brigade. The brigade halted and the four artillery pieces accompanying them, were unlimbered and opened fire on the rear of the house. Cannon shot tore off the back door of the mansion.[162]

FIGURE 2. The action at Cliveden

At the same time, Lord Stirling's men appeared, with Washington, from the opposite side. Washington did not like the idea of a British force holed up on his rear, so he sent Lieutenant William Smith of the 15th Virginia (part of Woodford's Brigade) under a flag of truce to negotiate its surrender. The British responded with musket fire, shattering the lieutenant's leg. Henry Knox, enraged by such a breach in the rules of war, moved up his artillery and also shelled the Mansion—to no effect.

Finally Washington realized he could wait no longer and moved on, posting a force to lay siege to the mansion.[163]

Phase 3: 7:30 to 8 a.m. – Stephen v. Wayne: The dangers of friendly fire.

When General Wayne's forces heard the sound of gunfire from their rear, they became concerned that the British might be making a concerted counterattack. Since the dense fog and smoke from the gunfire immobilized their visibility, it became impossible to see what was happening. Thus, Wayne's right flank lost contact with Sullivan's men, who were busy engaging the British, several hundred yards away to the right

Some of Wayne's troops began to march back towards the action at Cliveden and came up on the mansion from the south. Maxwell and Nash's forces were already hitting the house from the north and west. Woodford's Brigade was engaging from the east. Wayne's approach would then completely encircle the British at the mansion.

> As General Adam Stephen's troops moved southwest between Limekiln Pike and Abington Road, they lost contact with Woodford's brigade on their right. While the remainder of Greene's division drove the 1st Battalion of British Light Infantry from their camp, Stephen headed toward the main British camp.
> Suddenly, in the smoke and fog, Stephen's troops encountered a battle line advancing in their direction. They halted, dressed the line, presented their muskets and fired a volley—right into Wayne's Pennsylvania troops who were countermarching toward the fight at Cliveden where they assumed a British counterattack was underway.[164]

Wayne's division broke. So did Sullivan's.

Phase 4: 8 a.m. – Retreat and Counterattack.

Greene's division, meanwhile, was encountering difficulties of its own. The division had lost support from both the left and right. Only a part of Stephen's troops remained on the right while McDougall's forces, left to cover Greene's left flank, had moved off to the north.

Greene took what was left of his division and attacked the British right wing with bayonets. He "penetrated the enemy line [for] more than a half mile." Fearing he would be surrounded Greene ordered a withdrawal when he realized that both his flanks were exposed to the enemy. Most of his Virginia troops managed to withdraw—except for the 9th Virginia which were captured by the British.

Washington was still near Cliveden when the American withdrawal began. It soon became a rout and American attempts to stop the retreat went for naught. When the army realized the British were too disorganized to attempt a counter attack, "the panic subsided, and Washington was able to lead his beaten army back to Pennypacker's Mill in fairly good order."[165]

In the aftermath of Germantown: Casualties in the 3rd Virginia.

There appeared to be only one private who died in the 3rd Virginia in this battle, although Captain John Ashby was still suffering from being wounded at Brandywine. He was further hindered by rheumatism from the rainy and cold fall weather.[166] He was forced to resign his commission on 30 October and was replaced by his lieutenant, Valentine Peyton.[167]

The compiled service records for the 3rd Virginia show only two men in the regiment's muster rolls as having been wounded. Robert Doyle was a private in Captain Ashby's company. He was wounded at Germantown. He had enlisted in March 1776 and was had an early discharge—in November 1777,[168] probably because of his wounds. David Wickliffe, a private in Captain John Peyton's company, was also wounded in this battle. Captain Peyton's muster rolls show him as wounded in October and November 1777. John Anderson, a private in Captain Peyton's company was killed.[169]

Contemporary accounts of the Battle at Germantown.

There was a plethora of accounts of the battle from eyewitnesses or participants. The *Virginia Gazette* had at least seven different accounts of the battle. Three of the accounts spoke of the action at the Chew Mansion where Colonel Marshall and the 3rd Virginia found themselves, as they came out of the fog and smoke, early on the morning of 4 October.

Two of these accounts were in the 24 October 1777 edition of the *Gazette*. The first was an extract of a letter from camp, by an unidentified writer, dated 5 October 1777. The writer was with the right wing of the army, under Washington, Sullivan, and Wayne.

> ... The fogginess of the morning was very much against us. I believe in my soul, had it not been for that, we would have totally routed their army. Our men were afraid to follow up their advantages after driving them, as they could not see any distance who were before them. General Green did not come up for some time, but when he did advance he also drove them.
>
> We completely surprised the foe, and did not make an attack in a single place without routing them. I was attached to General Washington, and had an opportunity of seeing the behaviour of the centre; we drove them near three hours.
>
> Another unfavourable circumstance was our engaging them in Germantown. They took possession of the houses, from which they annoyed us exceedingly; one party from Mr. Chew's house was very troublesome. I was apprehensive for the General. They fired on us from the windows. The General ordered some field pieces to be drawn up against it, which raked it pretty well. We then sent a flag, to summon them to surrender; they fired on the flag, shatter the gentleman's leg who carried it, and kept us in play from this house till they had a reinforcement, I believe their grenadiers from Philadelphia, and then pushed down a column on us, which we are not able to withstand...[170]

The second account was posted on 10 October from Yorktown, in Pennsylvania.

> On Saturday morning, about day-break, our troops attacked the enemy in Biggar's town and Germantown, two miles below it, nearly at the same time. We continued to drive them from every post we assaulted for three hours; they at last took shelter in the stone houses, and churches, from whence they annoyed us much.
>
> While our men were endeavouring to dislodge them from Mr. Chew's house, they had time to bring up reinforcements of fresh troops. In the mean while two of our divisions, falling in from different quarters, mistook each other for reinforcement of the enemy; a mistake occasioned by the thick fog., which prevented our seeing the distance of thirty yards. This accident threw our troops in some confusion, and contributed to bring on a retreat; however, the enemy did not dare to pursue.[171]

Still another account appeared in the 19 December 1777 edition of the *Virginia Gazette*, an extract of a letter from Captain William Pierce[172] to Patrick Henry, dated 5 November 1777.

> At present I am more enabled to give you an accurate account of the battle at Germantown than I was the day on which it was fought. Immediately after the hurry of an action it is not easy to ascertain the particulars of it; the various accounts from different quarters confuse, and render the whole imperfect.
>
> When our men first made the attack we had the most pleasing prospect before us. The plan was evidently good, and the complete surprise given the enemy promised a glorious victory. They were routed, pursued, and charged with fury; but after flying before our arms in the utmost confusion, for some distance into Germantown, the fortune of the day was turned agains us, and we were compelled to yield the laurels we had won.
>
> The circumstance of this misfortune was owing to the enemy taking to a large stone house; and our men, attempting to surround it, were put to the rout, by the prospect of being outflanked. What part of the army gave way it is impossible to say...
>
> As to the Virginia line, I cannot, in justice to the officers and men, point out any particular honour to one that was not due to another.[173]

Then there were the letters written by the delegates to Congress. There were at least eight letters written by delegates to Congress about Germantown to various correspondents in the weeks following that battle.[174]

One of the most representative accounts of the battle at Germantown was given in a letter from Richard Henry Lee of Virginia to Governor Patrick Henry.

> ...we have had another general engagement with the enemy at and near German Town. With ours, we attacked their army. The plan was well concerted, and the execution was so bravely conducted, that a most brilliant victory was on the moment of being obtained, when accident alone removed it from us.
>
> The morning was so foggy, which with the state of the air keeping down the smoke of the cannon &c effectually prevented our people from knowing their success, occasioned delay, and gave the enemy time to rally and return to the charge which they did five several times.
>
> But this was not the worse. Our right & left columns mistook each other for enemies and apprehending a fresh reinforcement gave way too soon to a last effort of the enemy, and quitted a glorious victory absolutely in their power. However, they retired in order and had so severely handled the enemy that they dared not pursue, and our wound and every thing valuable was brought off. Our Army is now upon the ground they left before the battle, in the high spirits, and satisfied they can beat the enemy ...[175]

All the correspondents blamed the weather and foggy conditions for the British recovery. For example, Eliphalet Dyer wrote Joseph Trumbull on 8 October 1777 about the attack on the British at Germantown.

> ... It happened to be a very foggy morning & no wind. The Enemies picket was attacked a little before sun rise drove at once on upon the first part of their main army which was their light infantry, who soon gave way & indeed their whole army & were successfully drove about tow miles & for the space of more than 2 hours tho we were greatly embarrassed by the fog & thickness of the weather which with the smoke of the cannon so darkned the air that the enemy could not be distinguished n or our different persons see the operations of each other & sometimes taking friends for foes which was most unhappily the case in Genll Greens Division who fired on each other & threw each other into the great confusion avoiding each other which confusion catched from column to column.
>
> A confused retreat took place & to rally them was impossible tho our troops before had behaved with the greatest spirit & bravery, and a most Compleat Victory seemed full in prospect. Till this unfortunate mistake occasioned by the fog snatched it out of hands the prospect was full, of our Army in a very few hours again entering Philadelphia but once more disappointed.[176]

John Hancock, the President of the Continental Congress, was another member of that august body who commented on the action at Germantown. He wrote his wife Dolly on 8 October.[177] James Duane also described the engagement, in a letter to George Clinton, saying "...a heavy fog which totally obstructed all communication among our different divisions; and indeed destroyd all distinction between friends and foes; seemingly in the midst of conquest, put an end to all those sanguine expectations by a sudden retreat of our troops.[178]

Finally, the delegate from South Carolina, Henry Laurens,[179] in a letter to the Marquis de Lafayette written on 12 October 1777, weighed in with his opinion. "The action of the 4th at German Town," he said, "is a subject for a condolence & congratulation, tis very evident we ran away from complete victory which had invited us to proceed & embrace her. " Laurens continued "... several & distinct accounts of four General Officers of the Enemy ... are attended by such circumstantial proofs as put them little below the line of certainty."[180]

It should be noted here not only was the delegate from South Carolina *not* at Germantown; he did not mention the fire fight at Cliveden in this correspondence nor did he appear to be aware of the weather on that fateful morning. He drew his conclusions based on observations of *British* generals.

General Washington, himself, had written Mr. Laurens on 5 and 7 October, with a detailed account of the battle, including his plan of attack. On the 5th, Washington wrote

> ... We marched about seven o'clock the preceding evening and Genl Sullivan's advanced party, drawn from Conways Brigade, attacked their picket at Mount Airy or Mr. Allen's House, about sun rise the next morning, which presently gave way, and his main body, consisting of the right wing, following, soon engaged the Light Infantry and other troops, encamped near the picket, which they forced from the ground, leaving their baggage.
> They retreated a considerable distance, having previously thrown a party into Mr. Chew's House, who were in a situation not to be easily forced, and had it in their power, from the windows, to give us no small annoyance, and in a great measure to obstruct our advance.
> ... The morning was extremely foggy, which prevented our improving the advantages we gained, so well as we should otherwise have done. This circumstance, by concealing from us the true situation of the enemy, obliged us to act with more caution and less expedition than we could have wished, and gave the enemy time to recover from the effects of our first impression; and what was still more unfortunate, it served to keep our different parties in ignorance of each others movements and hindering their acting in concert.
> It also occasioned them to mistake one another for the enemy, which, I believe, more than any thing else, contributed to the misfortune which ensued. In the midst of the most promising appearances, when every thing gave the most flattering hopes of victory, the troops began suddenly to retreat, and intirely left the field, in spite of every effort that could be made to rally them.[181]

Washington indeed thought "upon the whole, it may be said the day was rather unfortunate than injurious. We sustained no material loss of men and brought off all our artillery, except one piece which was dismounted ... our troops, who are not in the least dispirited by it, have gained what all young troops gain by being in Actions ..."[182]

On the 7th of October, Washington again wrote the erstwhile southern delegate with a return of American losses at Germantown. He went on to say

> ... that the enemy had been severely handled. It is with much chagrin and mortification, I add, that every account confirms the opinion I first entertained, that our troops retreated t an instant when victory was declaring herself in our favor. The Tumult, disorder and even despair, which it seems had taken place in the British Army, were scarcely to be paralleled; and it is said, so strongly did the ideas of a retreat prevail, that Chester was fixed on as their rendezvous. I can discover no other cause, for not improving this happy opportunity, than the extreme haziness of the weather.[183]

Overall consequences of the Battle of Germantown.

5 October 1777: General Orders thanking officers and men involved in the attack on Germantown.

Perhaps more than anyone else, General Washington appreciated what his officers and men accomplished in the attack on the British at Germantown. Had it not been for an unfortunate combination of weather and terrain conspiring to form a dense fog, Germantown might well have been another Princeton. As it was, the army retired in fairly good order, some twenty miles from the scene of the action.[183]

On the following day, General Washington published, in his general orders at his headquarters at Perkiomy "his thanks, to the Generals and other officers and men concerned in yesterday's attack, on the enemy's left wing, for the spirit and bravery they manifested in driving the enemy from field to field." He went on to say that

> ... altho' an unfortunate fog, joined with the smoke, prevented the different brigades seeing and supporting each other, or sometimes even distinguishing their fire from the enemy's and form some other causes, which as yet cannot be well accounted for, they finally retreated, they nevertheless see that the enemy are not proof against a vigorous attack, and my be put to flight when boldly pushed.
> This they will remember and assure themselves that on the next occasion, by a proper exertion of the powers which God has given them, and inspired by the cause of freedom in which they are engaged, they will be victorious.

> The Commander in Chief not seeing the engagement with the enemy's right wing, desires the General officers who commanded there, to thank those officers and men who behaved with becoming bravery...[184]

On 11 October 1777, Washington's General Orders expressed the following:

> The Commander in Chief has the pleasure to inform the army, that Congress have, in a unanimous resolve, expressed their thanks to the officers and men concerned in the attack, on the enemy near Germantown on the 4th instant, for their brave exertions on that occasion; and hopes the approbation of that honorable body, will stimulate them to still nobler efforts on every future occasion.[185]

Overall Casualties at Germantown: American & British.

In the letter to his brother, John Augustine, written 18 October 1777, Washington detailed his losses: around 1000 were killed, wounded and missing. "Of the missing," he reported, "many, I dare say took advantage of the times, and deserted." General Nash of North Carolina died of his wounds. "Many valuable offices of our was also wounded and some killed. The enemys loss is variously reported; none make it less than 1500 (killed and wounded) ... Genl. Agnew of theirs was certainly killed, many officers wounded... In a word, it was a bloody day."[186]

Richard Henry Lee, in his 8 October letter to Governor Patrick Henry, was a little more specific.

> Our loss is pretty well fixed to 700 killed, wounded, and missing. That of the enemy not certainly known, but surely very great, as you may judged by the following intelligence brot this evening by Gen. Greens Aid and which he says may be relied on—Gen. Agnew, Colonels Woolcot, Abercrombie & Tho. Byrd (form Virga) with General De Heitsers son killed, Gen. Kniphausen wounded in the hand, and between 20 and 300 waggons loaded with wounded sent into Philadelphia.
> That Gen. Howe had sent about 2000 Hessians over Schuylkill (denoting a retreat) and that he refused to let any of the inhabitants of Philadelphia to go to see the field of battle.[187]

Overall Consequences of Germantown: Court of Inquiry and General Court Martial of Major General Adam Stephen.

Perhaps the most significant victim after Germantown was Major General Adam Stephen. He "was drunk" on the march to Germantown and when Marshall and Febinger asked for directions, they were "given orders so nonsensical that Febiger, who was closer to the main column, ignored them and followed closely on Greene's right" during the march to Germantown. Because of the confusion in his division leader's instructions, Colonel Marshall lost contact with Greene's column and eventually ended up at the Chew Mansion.[188]

Generals Weedon and Muhlenburg had decided to stay with Greene after they realized that Stephen's orders were unintelligible. However, Brigadier General Charles Scott had the most cause for bitterness. It was his men who fired into Wayne's Brigade, bringing about the misconception that the British were counterattacking.

With acrimonious accusations running back and forth between the two generals—Scott placed the blame for his brigade firing into the rear of General Wayne's men squarely on Stephen's drunken, incoherent orders and Stephens accused Scott of cowardice—Washington called for a court of inquiry into Stephen's conduct between 11 September and 4 October. The Court of enquiry, under the leadership of General Greene, would take place, according to his After Orders, on 26 October at nine in the morning at the president's quarters, to

> enquire into the conduct of Major General Stephen, on the march from the Clove to the Schuylkill falls, in the action of the 11th September last on the Brandywine, and more especially in the action oth the 4th instant at and about Germantown, on which occasions he is charged with 'Acting unlike

an officer.' Also into the charge against him for 'Drunkenness, or drinking so much, as to act frequently in a manner, unworthy the character of an officer.'[189]

The General Court Martial was put off until nine in the morning of 3 November. This was brought about by the "delay that may arise from the appointment of new members, and the impracticability of changing the General Officers, without introducing those who have already been on the court of enquiry, relative to the same charges, renders it necessary that this trial should be before the same court."[190]

The Court Martial took place on 3 November. Major General Stephen was charged with three counts—two of behavior unbecoming to an officer on the march from the Clove and again at both Brandywine and Germantown and one count of drunkenness.

The Court rendered the following opinion and sentence:

> The Court having considered the charges against Major General Stephen, are of opinion, that he is guilty of unofficerlike behaviour, in the retreat from Germantown, owing to inattention, or want of judgement; and that he has been frequently intoxicated since in the service, to the prejudice of good order and military discipline; contrary to the 5th article of the 18th Section of the articles of war. Therefore [we] sentence him to be dismissed [from] the service. The Court find him not guilty of any other crimes he was charged with, and therefore acquit him, as to all others, except the two before mention.' The Commander in Chief approves the sentence.[191]

Two weeks after this sentence was published in the General Orders of 20 November 1777, Congress appointed Marie Joseph Paul Yves Roch Gilbert du Motier, Marquis de Lafayette, an inexperienced twenty year old, as the new commander of Woodford's and Scott's brigades.

> The young 'Markwiss', as the Virginians like to call him, had many qualities going for him besides age and experience. He was hard-working, willing to learn, naturally brave and completely loyal. He sought good advice and took it. He mastered English quickly and thereafter rarely spoke French, to the annoyance of his compatriots. In addition, he was utterly unassuming.[192]

Overall Consequences of Germantown: Court of Enquiry and General Court Martial of Brigadier General Maxwell.

Another Court of inquiry was held on the same day with General Greene presiding. This enquiry involved a complaint by Lieutenant Colonel William Heth of the 3rd Virginia against Brigadier General Maxwell while Maxwell was commanding the light infantry. Lieutenant Colonel Heth brought charges against Maxwell, while commanding the Light Infantry, for having been "disguised with liquor" to the point of not being able to do his duty. The Court had fully inquired into the complaints by Lieutenant Colonel Heth and were

> clearly of opinion, that [the complaints] are without foundation; saving that it appears, he was once during said time disguised with liquor in such a manner, as to disqualify him in some measure, but not fully, from doing his duty; and that once or twice besides his spirits were a little elevated by spirituous liquor...

The Court left it to Washington and his "better judgment" as to whether the charges were serious enough to bring to trial by a Court Martial.[193]

Washington felt the charges should be looked into and directed that a General Court Martial be set up, under the direction of General Sullivan, to proceed to the trial of Brigadier General Maxwell, upon the complaints filed in the report. This General Court Martial was held on the 30th October through the 1 November 1777, under the direction of General Sullivan. The Court considered the charges and the evidence and was "unanimously of opinion that Brigadier General Maxwell, while he commanded the light troops, was not at any time disguised with liquor, so as to disqualify him in any measure from doing his duty. They do therefore acquit him of the charge against him."[194] In orders issued on 8 November, Washington approved the sentence.[195]

The impact on the 3rd Virginia of Colonel Marshall's request to resign his colonelcy of the regiment.

General Washington had communicated Colonel Marshall's request to resign as the commanding officer of the 3rd Virginia to become the colonel in the Virginia State Artillery regiment to Governor Patrick Henry on 3 October, the day before the Battle at Germantown.[196]

Since the artillery regiment had only been in existence since August 1777 and no field officers had yet been appointed, Colonel Marshall remained with the 3rd Virginia through December. Although he was commissioned as the colonel of the Virginia State Artillery Regiment on 15 November 1777,[197] he did not actually resign his continental commission until 4 December 1777.[198]

This resignation meant that Lieutenant Colonel William Heth became the acting colonel of the 3rd Virginia.[199] As early as July 1777, William Heth was given the title of colonel even though he was commissioned on 1 April 1777 as a *Lieutenant Colonel*.[200] In a 5 July 1777 Return of Virginia officers absent on command on Furlough, "— Heth," *Colonel* of the 3rd Virginia was listed as being "on furlough."[201] Wm. Heth was listed as *Colonel Wm. Heth* in a Regimental Account of Captain John Francis Mercer, dated 10 December 1777.[202] He was promoted to a full colonel in April 1778.[203]

Lieutenant Colonel Christian Febiger of the 11th Virginia had been promoted out of that unit to be the colonel of the 2nd Virginia in late September 1777. Then, on 9 October, Colonel Febiger was assigned to the 3rd Virginia, no doubt to help with the transition caused by Colonel Marshall's eventual transfer out of the regiment. Febiger and Heth had served together as officers in Daniel Morgan's 11th Virginia.[204]

END NOTES
CHAPTER 5
BATTLES & SKIRMISHES, 2
APRIL TO OCTOBER 1777

1. University of Virginia, *General Orders*, Morristown, 13 January 1777, *WW*, 7, pg. n.g (http://etext.virginia.edu).

2. Boatner, 1179. See also NARA, *George Weedon's compiled service records*, "Schedule of Promotions in General Weedon & Woodford's Brigade, Virginia Line," Officers, 3rd Virginia. This undated schedule shows Weedon's promotion as 21 February 1777.

3. NARA, *Thomas Marshall's compiled service records*, "Schedule of Promotions in General Weedon & Woodford's Brigade, Virginia Line," Officers, 3rd Virginia. See also University of Virginia, *General Orders*, Headquarters 22 March 1777, *WW*, 7, pg. n.g (http://etext.virginia.edu).

4. Heitman, 287.

5. University of Virginia, *General Orders*, Headquarters at Morristown, 19 March 1777, *WW*, 7, pg. n.g (http://etext.virginia.edu). See also Heitman, 376.

6. Heitman, 574, See also Haller, 27.

7. Haller, 20.

8. See 3rd Virginia compiled records and Chapter 2, note 167

9. University of Virginia, *George Washington to Major John Thornton*, Headquarters at Morristown, 20 March 1777, *WW*, 7, pg. n.g (http://etext.virginia.edu).

10. See the compiled service records for the 3rd Virginia for records of men in Captain John Thornton's company.

11. NARA, *Robert Randolph's compiled service records*, Officers, 3rd Virginia. See also Heitman, 458.

12. Heitman, 328.

13. NARA, *William Robertson' compiled service records*, Officers, 3rd Virginia.

14. Ibid., *Matthew Whiting's compiled service records*.

15. University of Virginia, *George Washington to Brigadier-General William Woodford*, Headquarters at Morristown, 10 May 1777, *WW*, 7, pg. n.g (http://etext.virginia.edu).

16. Ibid., *General Orders*, Morristown, 11 May 1777.

17. Sanchez-Saavedra, 73.

18. Heitman, 430. John Patton had been a Major, 2nd Battalion of Miles Pennsylvania Rifle Regiment in March 1776. He had been promoted to Major, 9th Pennsylvania, in October. On 11 January 1777 he became a colonel of one of the sixteen additional Continental Regiments.

19. University of Virginia, *General Orders*, Headquarters at Morristown, 22 May 1777, *WW*, 8, pg. n.g (http://etext.virginia.edu).
20. Ibid., *General Orders*, Headquarters at Morristown, 7 April 1777.
21. NARA, no. 46. 28 May 1777, *General Return of Continental Forces in New Jersey*, M 246 MR 137, *Returns of the Army*.
22. Thomas Fleming, *Liberty, The American Revolution* (New York, Viking Press, 1997), 235.
23. See NARA, Service Records for George Adams, William Aigin, Thomas Hunt, and John Knight, in the 3rd Virginia's compiled service records.
24. "Diary of John Chilton" *Tyler's Quarterly*, XII: 283–289.
25. Lesser, 47.
26. Boatner, 315.
27. Library of Congress, "Richard Henry Lee to Patrick Henry," *Letters*, 7: 76 (http://memory.loc.gov).
28. University of Virginia, *George Washington to the President of Congress*, Headquarters at Morristown, 12 May 1777, *WW*, 8, pg. n.g (http://etext.virginia.edu).
29. Ibid.
30. Ibid. See also Boatner, 872.
31. NARA, *Edmond Bolling's Pension* S39206, M 804 MR 282.
32. NARA, *Compiled service records for William Leitch and Butler Silvey*, M 881 MR 954 and 956.
33. University of Virginia, *General Orders, After Orders*, Headquarters at Middlebrook, 30 May 1777, *WW*, 8, pg. n.g (http://etext.virginia.edu).
34. Ibid., *General Orders*, Headquarters at Middlebrook, 31 May 1777.
35. Ibid., *George Washington to John Augustine Washington*, Middlebrook, 1 June 1777.
36. Taafe, 36.
37. Ibid., 37.
38. Ibid., 38.
39. See Chapter 7 for the names of these 3rd Virginia riflemen.
40. Higginbotham, 58.
41. Ibid.
42. Ibid., 59.
43. VHS, *Captain John Chilton to his brother Charles Chilton*, MssK2694a1–11, *Keith Family Papers*, VHS, Richmond.
44. Ibid.
45. Higginbotham, 59. The only letter to the President of Congress in this time period (20–29 June 1777) in the University of Virginia's online website for *Washington's Writings* was written on 28 June 1777. It did not specifically mention either the conduct of Colonel Morgan or General Wayne's troops. Washington did report the loss of three field pieces.
He also recounted that "as soon as we had gained the passes, I detached a body of Light Troops under Brigadier General Scott, to hang on their flank and watch their motions and ordered Morgan's corps of Riflemen to join him since." That was the only mention of Morgan in this letter. See University of Virginia, *George Washington to the President of Congress*, Camp at Middlebrook, 28 June 1777, *WW*, 8, pg. n.g (http://etext.virginia.edu). His 29 June 1777 letter to the President of Congress did not mentioned Morgan at all. See University of Virginia, *George Washington to the President of Congress*, Middlebrook, 29 June 1777.
46. Higginbotham, 59–60.
47. University of Virginia, *George Washington to John Augustine Washington*, from his camp at Middlebrook, 29 June 1777, *WW*, 8, pg. n.g (http://etext.virginia.edu).
48. Taafe, 44.
49. University of Virginia, *General Orders & After Orders* issued at headquarters, 4 July 1777, *WW*, 8, pg. n.g (http://etext.virginia.edu).
50. VHS, *John Chilton to Captain William Pickett*, MssK2694a1–11, *Keith Family Papers*, VHS, Richmond.
51. "Diary of John Chilton," *Tyler's Quarterly*, XII: 283–289.
52. Ibid.
53. Ibid.
54. Ibid.
55. Ibid.
56. VHS, *John Chilton to his Brother Charles Chilton in Fauquier*, Mss K2694a1–11, *Keith Family Papers*, VHS, Richmond.

57. Ibid.
58. University of Virginia, *George Washington to Governor Patrick Henry*, Headquarters, 20 miles from Philadelphia, 3 October 1777, *WW*, 8, pg. n.g (http://etext.virginia.edu).
59. "Diary of John Chilton," *Tyler's Quarterly*, XII: 283–289.
60. Ibid.
61. Ibid.
62. University of Virginia, *George Washington to the President of Congress*, Wilmington, 27 August 1777, *WW*, 8, pg. n.g (http://etext.virginia.edu).
63. Ibid, *General Orders*, Headquarters, Wilmington, 27 August 1777, *WW*, 8, pg. n.g (http://etext.virginia.edu).
64. "Diary of John Chilton," *Tyler's Quarterly*, XII: 283–289.
65. Colonel Hollingsworth was Henry Hollingsworth, colonel of the Maryland Militia 1776–1781. See Heitman, 297.
66. "Diary of John Chilton," *Tyler's Quarterly*, XII: 283–289.
67. University of Virginia, *George Washington to the President of Congress*, Headquarters at Wilmington, 29 August 1777, *WW*, 8, pg. n.g (http://etext.virginia.edu).
68. "Diary of John Chilton," *Tyler's Quarterly*, XII: 283–289.
69. Ibid.
70. University of Virginia, *George Washington to the President of Congress*, from Wilmington, 8 p.m., 3 September 1777, *WW*, 9, pg. n.g (http://etext.virginia.edu).
71. Ibid.
72. Ensign Westfall was Cornelius Westfall, of the 8th Virginia. See Heitman, 583; Colonel John Patton was the colonel of one of the sixteen Additional Continental Regiments. See Heitman, 430; Patton's Regiment was assigned to Brigadier General Charles Scott's Brigade. See Lesser, 54; see also John B. B. Trussell, *The Pennsylvania Line, Regimental Organization and Operations, 1775–1783* (Harrisburg: Pennsylvania Historical & Museum Commission, 1993), 150.
73. Colonel Febiger was Christian Febiger, Lieutenant Colonel of the 11th Virginia. He was assigned to the 3rd Virginia Regiment on 9 October 1777. See Heitman, 223.
74. Colonel Willis may have been Lieutenant Colonel Lewis Willis of the 10th Virginia which was part of General George Weedon's Brigade. . See Sanchez-Saavedra, 72. See also Lesser, 54.
75. "Diary of John Chilton," *Tyler's Quarterly*, XII: 283–289.
76. University of Virginia, *General Orders*, Headquarters at Wilmington, 4 September 1777, *WW*, 9, pg. n.g (http://etext.virginia.edu)
77. Ibid, *George Washington to the President of Congress*, Headquarters at Wilmington, 5 September 1777.
78. "Diary of John Chilton," *Tyler's Quarterly*, XII: 283–289.
79. University of Virginia, *General Orders*, Headquarters at Newport, 7 September 1777, *WW*, 9, pg. n.g (http;//etext.virginia.edu)
80. "Diary of John Chilton," *Tyler's Quarterly*, XII: 283–289.
81. University of Virginia, *George Washington to the President of Congress*, 6 miles from Wilmington, 9 September 1777, *WW*, 9, pg. n.g (http;//etext.virginia.edu)
82. "Diary of John Chilton," *Tyler's Quarterly*, XII: 283–289.
83. University of Virginia, *General Orders*, Headquarters at Birmingham, 10 September 1777, *WW*, 9, pg. n.g (http://etext.virginia.edu).
84. Thomas J. McGuire, *Brandywine Battlefield Park, Pennsylvania Trail of History Guide* (Mechanicsburg: Stackpole Books, 2001), 19–20. See also map on page 24. Hereafter, McGuire, *Brandywine Battlefield Park*.
85. Ibid.
86. Heitman, 448.
87. Bruce E. Mowday, *September 11, 1777, Washington's Defeat at Brandywine Dooms Philadelphia* (Shippensburg: White Mane Books, 2002), 85.
88. McGuire, *Brandywine Battlefield Park*, 23.
89. Ibid.
90. Ibid.
91. Ibid.
92. Heitman, 474.
93. Mowday, 104.
94. Ibid., 107.
95. McGuire, *Brandywine Battlefield Park*, 25–26.
96. Ibid., 31–32.

97. Ibid., 32.
98. Ibid.
99. Ibid.
100. Mowday, 118–119.
101. Taafe, 72.
102. McGuire, *Brandywine Battlefield Park*, 33.
103. Mowday, 120.
104. Ibid., 121.
105. Ibid.
106. Ibid. See also Taafe, 73.
107. Ibid., 125.
108. Taafe, 74.
109. Mowday, 125–126.
110. Ibid.
111. Colonial Williamsburg Foundation, "The 3rd Virginia at the Battle of Brandywine," *Virginia Gazette* (Dixon) 22 September 1777, 3, col. 1 (http://research.history.org). A full description of the battle with a map may be found in the Library of Virginia's *George Weedon Papers*. See LVA, *George Weedon to John Page*, 2 October 1777, Accession 22965a, *George Weedon Papers*, LVA, Richmond. See also Gott and Russell, 204–205.
112. Rhodehamel, *Washington: Writings*, 274.
113. John B. Frantz & William Pencak, eds., *Beyond Philadelphia, The American Revolution in the Pennsylvania Hinterland* (University Park: Pennsylvania State University Press), 15.
114. University of Virginia, *General Orders*, Headquarters at Chester, 12 September 1777.
115. Ibid., *General Orders*, Headquarters near Germantown, 13 September 1777.
116. VHS, *David Griffith to his wife Hannah*, Mss 2 G8755b, *Letters &c of David Griffith*, VHS, Richmond.
117. See the compiled service records in the 3rd Virginia
118. Ibid., *Robert Peyton's compiled service records*, Officers,, 3rd Virginia.
119. Ibid., *Apollo Cooper's compiled service records*.
120. Ibid., *William White's compiled service records*.
121. Gott and Russell, 206.
122. Heitman, 105.
123. Gott and Russell, 213–214.
124. NARA, *Robert English's compiled service records*, 3rd Virginia. See also Gott and Russell, 214.
125. See NARA, 3rd Virginia regiment's compiled service records for John Alvey, John Brown and other rank & file in Captain Phill Lee's company. The muster rolls filed between September 1777 and January 1778 for officers, non-comms, and rank and file for Captain Philip Richard Francis Lee's company are all under his command. In February 1778, his company muster roll is listed as the "late" Philip Richard Francis Lee's company.
126. Gott and Russell, 212.
127. Ibid., 214.
128. Ibid.
129. Taafe, 76.
130. Gregory T. Edgar, *The Philadelphia Campaign, 1777–1778* (Bowie: Heritage Books, 1998), 39.
131. Rhodehamel, *Washington: Writings*, 274. This sentiment was expressed in a letter to John Hancock, written at midnight on 11 September 1777 from Chester.
132. *Letters*, 7: 649–651.
133. Ibid., 7: 655–656.
134. Ibid., 7: 657–660.
135. University of Virginia, *General Orders*, Headquarters, 14 September 1777, *WW*, 9, pg. n.g (http://etext.virginia.edu).
136. Ibid., *General Orders*, Headquarters, near Warren Tavern, 15 September 1777.
137. Ibid., *George Washington to the President of Congress*, 15 September 1777, *WW*, 9, pg. n.g (http://etext.virginia.edu).
138. Ibid., *Washington to the President of Congress*, at Camp between Warren & White Horse Taverns, 16 September 1777, *WW*, 9, pg. n.g (http://etext.virginia.edu).
139. John Buchanan, *The Road to Valley Forge, How Washington Built the Army That Won The Revolution*. (New York: John Wiley and Sons, 2004), 254.
140. University of Virginia, *George Washington to the President of Congress*, 19 September 1777, *WW*, 9, pg. n.g (http://etext.virginia.edu).

141. Buchanan, 255.
142. Ibid., 260. See also Thomas J. McGuire, *Battle of Paoli* (Mechanicsburg, Stackpole Books, 2000), 95–102.
143. Buchanan, 260.
144. Ibid., 261.
145. See University of Virginia, *General Orders,* Headquarters at Yellow Springs, 17 September 1777 and *General Orders,* Headquarters, 20 September 1777, *WW,* 9, pg. n.g (http://etext.virginia.edu).
146. University of Virginia, *George Washington to the President of Congress,* 19 September 1777, *WW,* 9, pg. n.g (http://etext.virginia.edu).
147. Ibid., *General Orders,* Headquarters, 27 September 1777.
148. Ibid., *George Washington to the President of Congress,* Camp near Potts Grove, 23 September 1777.
149. Ibid., *George Washington's Instructions to Lieutenant Colonel Alexander Hamilton,* 22 September 1777; *George Washington's Instructions to Colonel Clement Biddle* 26 September 1777, to impress all blankets shoes, stockings for the use of the Army, from Bucks, Philadelphia, and Northampton Counties, Pennsylvania.
150. Ibid., *General Orders,* Headquarters at Pennypacker's Mill, 28 September 1777.
151. Ibid., *Council of War,* Headquarters at Pennypacker's Mill, 28 September 1777.
152. Ibid., *After Orders,* Headquarters, Shippack, 1 October 1777.
153. Buchanan, 270.
154. Ibid., 271–272. See also University of Virginia, *General Orders,* 3 October 1777, *WW,* 9, pg. n.g (http://etext.virginia.edu).
155. Gott and Russell, 216–217. See also Buchanan, 271–272.
156. University of Virginia, *General Orders,* 3 October 1777.
157. Buchanan, 273–274.
158. Thomas M. McGuire, *The Surprise at Germantown* (Germantown, Cliveden for the National Trust for Historic Preservation & Thomas Publications, 1994), 41–46. Hereafter, McGuire, *Germantown.*
159. Gott and Russell, 217–218.
160. McGuire, *Germantown,* 47–49.
161. Ibid.
162. Ibid. The scanned image of the action at Cliveden was taken from Grafton, 66.
163. Gott and Russell, 218.
164. McGuire, *Germantown,* 79–81.
165. Gott and Russell, 219.
166. Ibid.
167. NARA, *John Ashby's compiled service records,* Officers, 3rd Virginia.
168. Ibid., *Robert Doyle's compiled service records,* 3rd Virginia.
169. Ibid., *David Wickliffe's compiled service records,* 3rd Virginia; See also NARA. *John Anderson's compiled service records,,* 3rd Virginia.
170. Colonial Williamsburg Foundation, "Description of Battle at Germantown," *Virginia Gazette* (Dixon) 24 October 1777, 2, col. 1 (http://research.history.org).
171. Ibid.
172. William Pierce was a captain in the 1st Continental Artillery and served as an Aide-de-Camp to Generals Sullivan and Greene. See Heitman, 441.
173. Colonial Williamsburg Foundation, "Battle of Germantown Described," *Virginia Gazette* (Purdie) 19 December 1777, 2, col. 1 (http://research.history.org).
174. These letters have been taken from Paul Smith's *Letters of Delegates to Congress,* extracted in June 2006 from the Samford University Library in Homewood, Alabama, and their online counterparts at the Library of Congress's American Memories website.
175. *Letters,* 8: 82–83.
176. Library of Congress, *Eliphalet Dyer to Joseph Trumbull,* 8 October 1777, *Letters,* 8: 76, (http://memory.loc.gov).
177. *Letters,* 8: 77–78.
178. Ibid., 75.
179. Henry Laurens was a delegate from South Carolina. He was elected President of the Continental Congress on 1 November 1777. See Boatner, 599–601.
180. Library of Congress, *Henry Laurens to the Marquis de Lafayette,* 12 October 1777, *Letters,* 8: 116–117 (http://memory.loc.gov).
181. University of Virginia, *George Washington to the President of Congress,* at Camp near Pennypacker's Mill, 5 October 1777, *WW,* 9, pg. n.g (http://etext.virginia.edu).
182. Ibid.

183. Washington wrote his brother John Augustine from Philadelphia County on 18 October 1777 that "after the engagement [at Germantown] we removed to a place about 20 miles from the enemy, to collect our force together, to take care of our wounded, get furnished with necessaries again and be in a better posture either for offensive or defensive operations." See Rhodehamel, *Washington: Writings*, 277–278.

184. University of Virginia, *Washington to President of Congress*, 7 October 1777, *WW*, 9, pg. n.g (http://etext.virginia.edu)

185. Ibid., *General Orders* at Headquarters, Towsamensing, 11 October 1777.

186. Rhodehamel, *Washington: Writings*, 277–278.

187. *Letters*, 8: 82–83.

188. Gott & Russell, 217–218.

189. University of Virginia, *After Orders, as part of General Orders*, Headquarters, Whitpain Township, 25 October 1777, *WW*, 9, pg. n.g (http://etext.virginia.edu).

190. Ibid., *General Orders*, Headquarters, White Marsh, 2 November 1777.

191. Ibid., *General Orders*, Headquarters, White Marsh, 20 November 1777.

192. Gott & Russell, 244.

193. University of Virginia, *General Orders*, Headquarters, White Plains, 26 October 1777, *WW*, 9, pg. n.g, (http://etext.virginia.edu).

194. Ibid., *General Orders*, Headquarters, White Marsh, 4 November 1777.

195. Ibid., *General Orders*, Headquarters, 8 November 1777.

196. See note 58.

197. Sanchez-Saavedra, 124.

198. Heitman, 389.

199. Sanchez-Saavedra, 38. The author shows William Heth as a Lieutenant Colonel of the 3rd Virginia, commissioned 1 April 1777; At the time, Thomas Marshall was the colonel of the 3rd Virginia, so upon his resignation, Heth would have been raised to the acting colonel. Christian Febiger, the newly promoted colonel in the 2nd Virginia, and a former officer with Heth in Daniel Morgan's 11th Virginia, was assigned to the 3rd Virginia in October 1777. See Heitman, 223. John Chilton, in his letter to his brother Charles Chilton, written a little more than three weeks before his death at Brandywine, shared his dislike for Heth with his brother. See page 126 and note 57.

200. Sanchez-Saavedra, 38. See also NARA, *William Heth's compiled service records*, 3rd Virginia.

201. Ibid., *Return of Virginia Officers absent on furlough*.

202. Ibid.

203. Sanchez-Saavedra, 38. See also Heitman, 287.

204. See note 199.

Chapter 6

Skirmishes & Battles, 3
October 1777 to June 1778

Recap of Events

The 3rd Virginia did not emerge from Germantown entirely unscathed. While they did not suffer significant losses via casualties, their command structure was appreciably altered between October and December.

Major General Adam Stephen, their divisional commander, was dismissed from the service in November 1777 and replaced by Marquis de Lafayette in December. General Woodford, who was forced to turn the reins of the brigade over to Colonel Marshall when he was wounded at Brandywine, returned to duty.

Colonel Marshall, meanwhile, was set to depart from the regiment to take up command of a Virginia State Artillery Regiment. Lieutenant Colonel William Heth was poised to take over the 3rd Virginia and eventually became the colonel of the 1st Battalion of Woodford's Brigade.[1] Colonel Christian Febiger, of the 2nd Virginia, was assigned to the 3rd Virginia, probably to make the transition from Marshall to Heth easier.

A return for Woodford's Brigade dated 3 November 1777, noted a total of 1558 men and officers in the 3rd, 7th, 11th, and 15th Virginia making up the unit. These figures did not include the 406 who were sick, absent, the twenty-six on furlough or the 234 on command. The return listed a colonel, four lieutenant colonels, two majors, eighteen captain, thirty-seven lieutenants and twenty-two ensigns in the command structure. The brigade contained two chaplains, five adjutants, five quarter masters, three pay masters four surgeons and one surgeon's mate. The corps had ninety-five sergeants and thirty-two drum and fife. The Fauquier County, Virginia, militia had also arrived, swelling the brigade's numbers with ninety-nine privates fit for duty.[2]

A week later, Woodford's Brigade showed a shocking modification in their numbers. There was still a colonel in the brigade, Colonel Marshall, according to the return; the rest of the staff decreased— one Lieutenant Colonel, one major and five captains, eleven lieutenants and five ensigns were reported in this return. Likewise, the totals for the brigade declined—now there were only 330 men and officers. There were 188 rank and file present and fit for duty. One man had deserted. Twenty-two more privates had joined the brigade.

The comments for the brigade in this return were very revealing, "In the 3rd Virginia Regiment, 24 men [were] wanting cloths, [and] unfit for duty;" in the 11th Virginia, four sergeants and thirty-four men needed clothes and were unfit for duty; in the 12th Virginia, two sergeants, two Drum and Fife, and thirty privates lacked clothes and blankets and were thus unfit ford duty, although they had been returned among those present and fit for duty.[3]

The 3rd Virginia, a little more than a month after Germantown, was suffering from a lack of clothes needed to survive the coming winter. The rest of the brigade was little better off. The lack of supplies did not bode well for the Brigade and the army especially if the weather turned cold early.

Interlude
October to December 1777

Between Germantown and the skirmish at White Marsh in early December, other than periodic harassment of the redcoats, Washington's army was not actively engaged with the enemy. It was a time for the officers and men to regroup, care for their wounded and recover from the rigors of the fall campaign. There were already problems surfacing that caused the commander-in-chief a good deal of anxiety. A deplorable lack of shoes, blankets, clothes, tents and arms for his army distressed him greatly.

September to October 1777, Washington's growing concerns about supplies and provisions for the Army.

As early as 26 September, a lack of shoes for his troops had prevented Washington from keeping pace with the British, fearing a move on Reading where quantities of Continental military stores were being kept.

> Messrs Carrol, Chase and Penn, who were some days with the Army, can inform Congress, in how deplorable a situation the troops are for want of that necessary article, at least one thousand men are bare footed and have performed the late marches in that condition. I was told of a great number of shoes in the hands of private people in Philadelphia and sent down to secure them, but I doubt the approach of the enemy will prevent it ...
>
> If there are any shoes and blankets to be had in Lancaster or that part of the Country I earnestly entreat you to have them taken up for the use of the Army. I have been informed, that there are large parcels of shoes, in particular there. Finding that the inclosed came from Colo Gibson, I took the liberty of opening it, as I wanted much to know what Route he was taking.[4]

Those men in the Virginia militia who were well armed, he ordered to join the army; the rest were to remain in Frederick, Maryland, to see if arms could be procured for them.[5]

On the same day, to forestall possible shortages in needed supplies, Washington ordered Colonel Clement Biddle[6] to "impress all the blankets, shoes, stocking and other articles of cloathing for the use of the army that can be spared by the inhabitants in the counties of Bucks, Philadelphia, and Northampton, paying for the same at reasonable rates or give certificates."[7]

Two days after Germantown, on 6 October 1777, Washington authorized Brigadier General William Woodford, to take shoes, stockings and blankets for the use of the army that could be spared by the residents of Bethlehem. Those appointed to take these goods were to give Certificates of payment at a reasonable price, noting the quantity and quality of the items collected, which could be turned over to the Clothier General for payment.[8]

On 10 October, writing to the President of Congress, from his camp twenty-six miles from Philadelphia, Washington was still concerned about arms for the militia and shoes and stockings for his men. These concerns were joined by a new one, pay for the men.

The militia, he reported, was in camp and totaled about 1100 men, although "their arms are indifferent, and almost the whole are destitute of pouches and other necessary accoutrements." The "military chest" he complained "is nearly exhausted, not having more than ten thousand dollars in it." That money was to go to pay the army for August.

Washington protested again about the lack of shoes and stockings.

> Our distress for want of shoes and stockings is amazingly great, particularly for want of the former. On this account we have a great many men, who cannot do duty and several detained at the hospitals for no other cause. I must request Congress to continue their exertions to relieve us, and to direct every supply of these and other necessaries to be forwarded as soon as they possibly can after they are collected. It will be proper to send them on, as fast as they can be procured, without waiting to make up a considerable quantity to be brought at one time.[9]

Three days later, on 13 October 1777, he sent another urgent missive to the President of Congress. He shared his unease on five distinct issues with Hancock. After reporting that there was no material news to convey vis-à-vis his army and the army under General Howe, and relating some other war news regarding the cannonading of Fort Mifflin and the capture of Fort Montgomery by the British and evacuation of Peekskill, Washington turned once again to the need for basic supplies for his army.

> It gives me pain to repeat so often, the wants of the Army and nothing would induce me to it, but the most urgent necessity. Every mode hitherto adopted for supplying them, has proved inadequate, notwithstanding my best endeavours to make the most of the means which have been in my power ... What new expedient Congress can devise for more effectually answering these demands I know not, persuaded as I am, that their closest attention has not been wanting to a matter of so great importance.[10]

In this same letter, Washington had enclosed a return which showed the Army's "deficiency in the most essential articles."[11] This return was for the troops present in camp, "besides which there are numbers in the several hospitals totally destitute of the necessaries they require to fit them for the field, and on this account alone are prevented from joining their corps. The recruits coming in are also in the same melancholy predicament." Washington could not tell how much clothing was actually in the hands of James Mease, the Clothier-General,[12] but he did know "he is intirely bare of some of the most capital articles we want."[13]

The army stores appeared to be completely out of military supplies, like cartouche boxes,[14] "without which it is impossible to act ... several of the continental troops are deficient in this instance, and what adds to our distress, there are but very few of the southern militia that are provided." The general went on to recommend to take great care in selecting the leather—only the best and thickest would serve the purpose. Each box should have an inner flap to better protect cartridges in rainy weather. The present flap, he said, was too small and did not project sufficiently over the ends or sides of the boxes to protect the contents.[15]

Finally, Washington conveyed his disquiet regarding the "general defective state of the regiments which compose our army" which, in "his opinion, has a claim to their most serious attention."

> Congress will find, from a view of the returns transmitted from time to time, that they do not amount to near half of their just complement. What can be done to remedy this I know not.. But it is certain every idea of voluntary inlistments seems to be at an end; and it is equally certain, that the mode of drafting had been carried on, with such want of energy in some states and so much disregarded in others, that but a small accession of force has been derived from it.
>
> These facts are sufficiently interesting of themselves, but there are others to be added. I am told that Virginia, in her regulations for drafting extended her plan only to nine regiments that were first raised. In what policy this was founded, I cannot determine but the other six, are to receive no reinforcements from that source.
>
> Nor to matters stop here. The engagements of the first nine regiments, I am informed were temporary, and according to the officers accounts, the longest period to which any of the men are bound to serve is next April; many are not obliged so long, and there are some, who claim a discharge at this time.[16]

On 18 October, Washington wrote his brother John Augustine, from Philadelphia County. After telling him about Germantown, he expressed his anguish about "our distress on acct of cloathing". It was "great, and in a little time must be very sensibly felt, unless some expedient can be hit upon to obtain them."[17]

On the 21 October, Washington took a break from his continuing anxiety about the state of his army and informed the President of Congress, instead, of the General Howe's evacuation of Germantown and the British withdrawal within lines near Philadelphia. He also conveyed the news of the continuing siege of Fort Mifflin, without any material damage being done to the fortification.[18]

In a 24 October 1777 letter to the President of Congress, Washington had some good news and some bad news to convey. The good news was the repulse of the Hessian troops under Count von Donop at Fort Mercer.[19] The bad news concerned the continuing now near desperate need for shoes and stockings for continental troops.

> It gives me great concern, to inform Congress, that after all my exertions we are still in a distressed situation for want of Blankets and shoes. At this time, no inconsiderable part of our force are incapable of acting thro' the deficiency of the latter, and I fear, without we can be relieved, it will be the case with two thirds of the Army in the course of a few days.[20]

In a letter written to the same respondent on 1 November, Washington addresses the reasons for his inactivity vis-à-vis the British. There were four principal causes: Chief among them was the lack of ammunition, followed by "the distress of the soldiers for want of shoes", the superior numbers and discipline of the enemy in respect to their troops, and the need for reinforcements, preferably from Gates's northern army.[21]

In addition to these concerns, Washington was apprehensive about the state of the enlistments of the original nine Virginia regiments. "We should suffer greatly by the loss of so large a part of our force, which have been long inured to service," he believed. He thought it advisable, he said "to consult the officers commanding them upon the mode which should appear to them best calculated to reinlist them."

Washington enclosed their recommendations, and requested Congress's "earliest attention" and their opinion on "whether the indulgence and allowance they have proposed may be granted, and if any additional bounty may be given." Washington thought this was necessary, given the amount now paid for substitutes and drafts, even for the militia. He did not think that soldiers would reenlist for the war or for three years, given what was currently being paid.[22]

November 1777: Protest of subaltern officers of Virginia Line regarding the reduction of ten companies to eight in the Virginia line.

The General also sent along to Congress a protest by the subaltern officers in the Virginia line. He explained that he had reduced the number of companies in each regiment from ten to eight in order to equal the companies in other line regiments. Washington did this to "prevent a considerable, unnecessary expence." In order to bring about this reform, Washington ordered a freeze on promotions, either to vacancies "at the time of the regulation, or to any future ones that may happen" for subalterns in the 9th and 10th companies in the various regiments of the Virginia line.

"The subalterns were to remain," he said, "in their rank and command till they can be promoted in the other eight companies and their men incorporated." This, in essence, was the complaint of these junior officers. Washington sent the remonstrance on to Congress with a request that they determine the question.[23] Evidently, Congress viewed this reduction from ten companies to eight in the regiments of the Virginia line as necessary as Washington did.

In the 3rd Virginia, the gradual merging of the companies of Captains Phill Lee, who died in January 1777, and David Arell, who resigned in February 1778, into other existing companies in the regiment confirmed this.

Muster rolls for the men and officers in Captain Lee's company for February through May were listed as "late Captain Lee's." In June 1778, Captain John Peyton absorbed Captain Lee's late company into his own.[24]

Captain David Arell resigned his commission in February 1778. His muster rolls were listed as "Late Captain Arell's Company" from March through May 1778. In June 1778, Captain Reuben Briscoe merged the men of Captain Arell's old company with his own.[25]

November to December 1777: Washington's ongoing consternation over the lack of money and clothes for his army.

Washington communicated his growing apprehension over the state of pay for his army in a letter to the President of Congress from his headquarters at White Marsh on 8 November 1777. He informed Mr. Laurens that "the military chest is again empty and the Army... unpaid for the months of September and October..." He directed him to "be pleased to direct that a supply of cash be sent on as expeditiously as possible."[26] It wasn't until 26 November, that Washington notified his troops through his General Orders that "the money for the payment of the army for September and October is expected every moment."[27]

Would that the issue of clothing for his troops could have been solved so easily. Washington addressed this critical need in no less than six letters to various respondents.[28] He viewed this with such alarm that he issued powers to his officers to collect clothing in November 1777.

> By virtue of the powers vested in me by the Honorable Congress I hereby authorize to collect all such blankets, shoes, stocking and other clothing suitable to the use of the Army, within the counties of the State of Pennsylvania ... You are to give certificates to the inhabitants of the quantity and value of each species you receive from them, directed to James Mease Esqr. Clothier General at Lancaster of which you are to keep an exact entry; And at the end of this service you are to make an exact return of each certificate to the Clothier Genera and another to me. Whatever blankets and clothing you may collect, is to be sent, with an account of it, to the commanding officer of the Brigade you belong to.[29]

On 13 November, Washington addressed the pressing need for clothing for his troops.

> There is another matter of as much importance and no less difficult than the raising of the soldier, and that is the cloathing of him. Our importations from abroad are so uncertain from the number of the enemy's cruisers that infest our coats that we can scarcely count upon any supplies thro' that channel, and the stock of goods that are upon hand are so nearly consumed that I look with the greatest concern, upon the sufferings of the soldiers for the reminder of this year; and as for the next I view them as naked, except some measures can be fallen upon to collect from the inhabitants of the different states part of their stock of cloathing, which I fear is but scanty.
>
> In this state very great collections have been and are now making, and I have sent officers to Jersey, Delaware and Maryland, with the most pressing letters to the respective Governors, to give what assistance they can in procuring necessaries for their troops. Blankets, shoes and stocking are most immediately wanted, but cloathing of any kind would be acceptable at this inclement season, and more especially as we have the greatest prospect of a winter campaign.[30]

David Griffith, the regimental surgeon and chaplain, was worried about provisions. He informed his wife about the scarcity and prices of foodstuffs in his 13 November 1777 letter from camp at White Marsh to her.

> I saw ... Doc^r Hutchinson yesterday, who came out of the city the day before & he told me that all kinds of provisions were extremely scarce & dear—That the little flour to be sold went at 2 half-Joes a hundred—that very bad beef sold from 2/ to 3/9 per pound, hard money & that no other kind of meat & no vegetables were brought to market. The Doc^r, who is a Quaker & a very reputable man, says that our prisoners in town are almost starved & kept from perishing only by the bounty of some well disposed inhabitants.[31]

By 17 November 1777, the clothing situation had grown desperate.

> I am informed that it is matter of amazement, and that reflections have been thrown out against this Army, for not being more active and enterprising, than, in the opinion of some, they ought to have been., If the charge is just, the best way to account for it will be to refer you to the returns of our strength and those which I can produce of the enemy, and to the inclosed abstract of the cloathing now actually wanting for the Army, and then I think the wonder will be, how they keep the field at all, in Tents, at this season of the year. ...There are besides, most of those in the hospitals more bare than those in the field. Many remain there, for want of clothes only.[32]

The circumstances had become so critical that several General Officers employed agents to purchase what could be found in different parts of the country. Since these agents needed to be paid, Washington did not know whether the application should be made to the Treasurer or to the Clothier General. If Congress thought the Clothier General should handle the payment for clothes then Washington would go ahead and order it to be done.[33]

On 1 December 1777, the general wrote the President of Congress from his headquarters at White Marsh, that "the officers, or at least a large proportion of them, as well as the men, are in a most disagreeable condition as to cloathing, and without any certain prospect of relief; And what is still more painful, if perchance they have an opportunity of purchasing, which is seldom the case, they have the mortification to find themselves totally incompetent to it, from the depreciation of our money and the exorbitant p0rice demanded for all articles in this way."[34]

On 3 December, 1777 General Woodford filed a brigade return that reflected his commander-in-chief's dismay over the lack of clothes for his army. The brigade strength totaled 1397 officers and men. Out of the 1397, a little over half, some 726, were present and fit for duty. There were 329 men who were sick and absent while eighty-four were reported as sick and present. The brigade had 229 men on command. Twenty-nine of his men were on furlough. In his comments, Woodford reported "among those returned fit for duty are included several hundred really unfit from the want of shoes and clothing and some returned sick, present are only unfit for duty as waning clothing and shoes ..."[35]

Shipments of clothing began to arrive from Virginia by 10 December, "which," Washington told Governor Patrick Henry "tho' not very great will be very acceptable, as far as it will go." [36] He elaborated further:

> I beg that whatever you can spare may be immediately sent forward to the head quarters of the Army, where ever that may be, and I have no doubt but we can get the cloaths more readily made up by the tailors of the army, than you can in the country.
> I observe that there is a small supply of cloth, suitable for the officers. I should be extremely glad if that could be sent up for the use of those who remain in the field and not delivered out to those, who under various pretences will find means to winter at home. I hope the Gentlemen, who are appointed in your state to make a collection of clothing for your troops will exert themselves; for altho' large quantities are order from Europe, the arrival is so precarious, that we ought by no means to put a dependence upon a supply thro' that channel.[37]

While shipments of clothing, shoes, and stocking began to arrive for Washington's army, Woodford's brigade return, filed 22 December 1777, when the army was in winter quarters at Valley Forge, still showed 180 of his men "unfit for want of clothes." This brigade return showed, out of a total of 1308 men and officers, from the 3rd, 7th, 11th, and 15th Virginia, only 319 who were present and fit for duty. There was no colonel recorded in the staff numbers, so Colonel Thomas Marshall had already departed for his state artillery command by this date. The brigade return showed 333 sick and absent, eighty-five sick and present; 212 men were on furlough while 179 were on command.[38] This return demonstrated the plight of this Virginia brigade with regards to their general health and the need for warm winter clothes, shoes and stockings.

By 31 December 1777, the Brigade return showed a further deterioration. The brigade's strength totaled only 286 men and officers. A lieutenant colonel, a major, four captains, two lieutenants, and three ensigns made up the officers and subalterns. Fifty-nine were sick and absent; sixteen were sick but present with the brigade. In this return, seventy men were listed for "want of shoes & cloathes." One man had died, one had been discharged, and one had deserted. Fifty-three were on furlough while forty others were on command. Timothy Pickering, Adjutant General noted that 'Some brigades have distinguished the men unfit for duty from the want of cloathes, from the sick, present, other include them, with the sick, present and some have retd [returned] all those fit for duty who were well, although barefooted ..."[39]

In comparing this return with the 22 December one, taken a week earlier, there were five less captains, eighteen less lieutenants, and one less ensign reported in this return. While there were now seventy rather than 180 men unfit for want of shoes and cloths in the New Year's Eve return, the brigade had lost three men—one had died, one had been discharged, and one had deserted.[40]

It was apparent that the men of the 3rd Virginia was hanging on until their terms of enlistment was over which would occur between January and March 1778.

Concerns about the expiration of terms of enlistment of the Virginia Line.

The commander-in-chief had already grappled with the anticipated discharges for the first nine Virginia regiments[41] scheduled to occur in the first three months of the New Year and come up with a proposal from the officers in the Virginia line to submit to Congress.

> The Virginia officers believed that, if the men were allowed to spend Christmas at home, they might be induced to re-enlist in the spring. They also proposed an increase in the Continental bounty for re-enlistment, as state militia units were offering amazing sums.[42]

David Griffith had written his wife in mid-November to tell her that he hoped "our Regt will get leave to return to Virginia before Christmas to remain there till April. It is thought this method will be adopted in order to encourage the men to reinlist for the war as the time of most of them will be expire in the beginning of the spring. This is the case with 6 other regiments, and the affair is now under the consideration of Congress."[43]

During the last of November, Washington addressed this concern to the President of Congress.

> I must take the liberty to request the decision of Congress on the case of the nine first raised Virginia regiments as early as circumstances will permit. If the plan proposed for reinlisting them Is judged expedient, one capital inducement to that end suggested by the Officers, will cease, if it is longer delayed. It is a matter of considerable importance, and of which I wish to be satisfied as soon as possible.[44]

Unfortunately, by 4 January 1778, only forty Virginians had decided to re-enlist for another tour of duty,[45] so Washington was still faced with losing his most experienced Virginia troops and officers. Other than a mass early discharge, this was a problem that had no readily perceived solution.

END OF THE INTERLUDE
18 NOVEMBER TO 4 DECEMBER 1777

Return of Colonel Daniel Morgan's Independent Rifle Command.

Meanwhile, Colonel Morgan and his men had been released by General Gates, after their triumph at Saratoga, on 2 November 1777. The *Virginia Gazette* reported that "Morgan's excellent corps of light infantry is by this time near Germantown" in their 14 November 1777 edition.[46] His "excellent corps of light infantry" had evidently reached Washington's army on 18 November 1777.[47]

Loss of the Delaware River Forts

The last two weeks in November were not good ones for the American army in Pennsylvania. Three days before Morgan's arrival in the American camp, Washington ordered Woodford, now in temporary command of Stephen's division, to get ready to move with baggage and provisions by seven in the morning.[48] David Griffith, in a letter to his wife written two days later, reported that "our division (Stephens) is under orders to march over [the] Schuylkill—the weather prevented it yesterday and wether we shall go at all is uncertain at this time."[49]

It may be that Washington had in mind a relief force of Woodford's men to attempt to break the siege of Fort Mercer on the Delaware. However, Fort Mifflin had already been lost when Woodford received the orders to march on 15 November and Fort Mercer was evacuated successfully and fell to the British five days later.[50]

There did not appear to be any of the 3rd Virginia engaged in these two actions. Certainly, the brigade returns for November indicate that this unit was well under strength and had at least two dozen men needing clothes along with several dozen who were sick and absent from the unit. Woodford's return, dated 10 November, 1777, five days before the British began their assaults on the river forts, showed only 330 officers and men fit for duty.[51]

In a report of the loss of the Delaware River forts made to the President of Congress on 23 November 1777, Washington explained the situation as best he could. The garrison at Fort Mercer had to be evacuated when Lord Cornwallis with 2000 men landed to assault the fort.

When he received information about Cornwallis's movements, he detached General Huntington's Brigade to join General Varnum in his defense of these forts. He ordered General Greene's division, to march through New Jersey and join up with Glover's Brigade which was already there. Together they were to attack Cornwallis in an effort to stop his assault on the Delaware fortifications. Unfortunately, the British were too quick for the Americans and the forts fell.

Thus on the 23 November, Greene and Glover were still in New Jersey while some 170 men from Morgan's rifle command had been sent to reinforce Greene. Washington was hopeful that once the Greene and Glover's troops had joined forces, with Morgan's rifle men, a concerted attack could then be made on Cornwallis.[52]

Skirmish at White Marsh
5–8 December 1777

On 4 December General Howe and some 10,000 British troops moved to the vicinity around Chestnut Hill, just two or three miles from the American army. The British sent out parties to reconnoiter to see if Washington's forces could be drawn out again in a general engagement.[53]

This time, Washington was ready. He had already issued an "Order of Battle" to his army. Morgan's riflemen had an important part in this skirmish[54] which was envisioned by Washington as an attempt to "harrass the enemy as much as possible, taking especial care to gain their flanks and rear, if possible."[55] Indeed, the riflemen were to give the British army more than they bargained for.[56]

On 6 and 7 December, Howe took a large segment of his army from Philadelphia to Germantown and then to Jenkintown, coming within two and a half miles of the American left wing. After probing the American outposts and taking a position along the high ground around Edge Hill,[57] the presence of Morgan's riflemen persuaded the British general that the American defenses were too strong to attempt a general attack. The redcoats withdrew to Philadelphia.[58] In the skirmishing, General James Irvine and seventeen of his Pennsylvania militia men were taken prisoners by the British.[59]

David Griffith gave a synopsis of the events of December in a letter to his wife, written at White Marsh on 11 December 1777.

> I flattered myself, some time ago, that the inclemency of winter would have inclined both the contending parties to go into winter quarters & that I should be able to return about Christmas. I see not great prospect of this as yet. Both armies are yet in the field and this day they were so nigh as to cannonade each other across the River Schuylkill at Mallisons Ford.[60]

Dr. Griffith then described the skirmish in some detail:

> Genl Howe came out of the city with his whole army (within 3 miles of us) to look at our right flank. After staying there two days, he crossed over to Jenkin Town to view our left & came within a mile of us. His view was either to draw us from our strong situation or to attack us in it if there was any probability of succeeding.
>
> After keeping us under arms 4 days & as many nights, he returned in the dead of night to Philadelphia after plundering the country in the most shocking manner & stripping the people, without distinction of all their provisions, stock, furniture and cloths.
>
> Our riflemen and some militia had frequent skirmishes with them, and from the best intelligence we can collect, they killed and wounded three or four hundred of them. Our loss is not yet exactly known, but is not great. Brigadier Genl Irwin of the Pens^a Militia was slightly wounded and his horse falling with him and bruising his head much, he became their prisoner.[61]

Griffith informed his wife that the "whole army marched this morning & intended to cross the Schuylkill, it was expected by many that we were going into quarters on Chester C° & that the army were to build hutts & cabins for themselves in the woods. The enemy were apprised of our designs and marched up the other side of the river to the place they had thrown a bridge over & got there time enough to prevent us from doing what was intended."[62]

The American army was forced to back up for a few miles and Griffith heard that "the enemy are likewise gone back."[63] Successful as this skirmish may have been for the Americans, Washington was forced to give up any thought of a winter campaign. His generals in the Virginia line agreed. "Half of their men were already in the hospitals, many of the rest were half-naked, hungry and shoeless."[64]

FIGURE 3. Marching to Valley Forge

WINTER QUARTERS, VALLEY FORGE
19 DECEMBER 1777 THROUGH MAY 1778

The condition of Woodford's Brigade on its arrival at Valley Forge.

FIGURE 4. Winter Quarters, Valley Forge

Washington broke camp on 11 December and arrived at his winter quarters at Valley Forge on 19 December 1777. The 3rd Virginia, along with the rest of Woodford's brigade, was in an appalling situation. Woodford's Brigade consisted of the 3rd, 7th, 11th, and 15th Virginia regiments, and for a time—a very brief time—ninety-nine privates from the Fauquier County militia.

The 22 December 1777 brigade return amply demonstrated the plight of the brigade. Out of the 1308 men and officers on paper, the brigade had 180 men unfit for duty due to a lack of clothes, 333 who were absent and sick in area hospitals—probably due to a deficiency of clothing and the ill-health which resulted.

There were additional eighty-five men who were sick but present with the brigade. Less than one-quarter of the men—only 319—were fit for duty. There were 212 men on furlough and 179 more on command.

The brigade had two lieutenant colonels so two of the four regiments had commanding officers. Nine captains were present, spread out among the four regiments. If the regiments were up to full strength, with eight companies apiece, there should have been thirty-two captains. Twenty lieutenants and two ensigns were found through out the four regiments.

Only two regiments had adjutants while there was one quarter master and one pay master for the brigade. Each regiment had its own surgeon while there was only one surgeon's mate for the brigade. One of those regimental surgeons was David Griffith who also served a double duty as one of the two chaplains who served the brigade.

Among the non-comms, there were sixty-eight sergeants, a drop of ten from the 3 December return, and twenty-one drum and fife, which also showed a decrease from the early December return, when thirty-four musicians were listed in the brigade.[65] A field return for the brigade, filed on the 23rd, revealed 257 men unfit for want of clothes. There were a further 261 on guard or on detachment, further reducing the effectiveness of this unit.[66]

The situation had not improved much by New Year's Eve, either. The Brigade return then, recorded one Lieutenant Colonel, probably William Heth, a major and only four captains, two lieutenants, and three ensigns for the entire brigade. David Griffith was evidently still with the brigade as a chaplain and a surgeon were found within the unit along with a surgeon's mate. The really shocking figure was the low amount of men fit for duty—forty-seven! The brigade reported one man dead[67] which may have been Private George Strong in Captain Blackwell's company who died on New Years Eve.[68]

In December 1777, there were actually two other deaths in the 3rd Virginia which occurred between 12 December and the end of the year which did not show up in the earlier December brigade returns.[69]

Both of these men had enlisted in September 1777 in Captain Gus Wallace's company. Peter Williams was a private who died on 12 December 1777.[70] Henry Martrim died two days later, on 14 December 1777.[71]

December 1777: Discharges and resignations deplete the rosters of the 3rd Virginia.

Although the exact plight of the 3rd Virginia cannot be ascertained with any certainty through the brigade returns, the compiled service records for the regiments do contain hints as to their situation. Four captains in the regiment suffered some losses in men and officers via the resignation or discharge route.

In Captain David Arell's company, his lieutenant, Robert Slaughter, was the first to resign on 10 December 1777. Two of his corporals, Philip Langford and Francis Hagan, were discharged 23 December 1777.[72]

Captain John Blackwell, who had been promoted to take over John Chilton's old company, lost eight experienced veterans, when they were discharged on 23 December 1777. Sergeants Henry Bradford and Wm. Tomlin, Drummer John Auber, privates Thomas Bates, John Hopper, Thomas Kelly, John Murphy, and John Strong all received discharges on that date.[73]

Captain Valentine Peyton, who had absorbed some of John Thornton's and John Ashby's old rifle companies, was fortunate that only four men left the company in December. One was his lieutenant, Joseph Baynham, who resigned on New Years Eve. Private James Harris was discharged on 23 December. The remaining two men had served with Colonel Morgan at Saratoga. Privates Benjamin Powell, who was discharged on 3 December, and Martine Wingate who was discharged on 1 December 1777, were still being carried on Captain Peyton's muster rolls and pay rolls.[74]

Captain Gustavus Brown Wallace's company, now commanded by John Mercer, had just two men who left in December. One was Lieutenant Allan Mountjoy who resigned 10 December 1777, after the skirmish at White Marsh. Private John Garner was discharged 23 December 1777.

November 1777 to January 1778: The number of sick soldiers further reduces the strength of the regiment.

In order to see whether it was possible to discover if the regiment suffered from ill-health or were in the hospital for want of clothes, it was necessary to assemble this information from the compiled service records for the 3rd Virginia regiment. These records were, in turn, compilations of muster rolls, pay rolls and a variety of lists which related to the regiment.[75] The information was recorded on cards, arranged by the soldier or officers' name, and then by muster roll or pay roll on a month by month basis. The rolls provided the reports of those who were sick, absent; sick, present; or sick at a specific location, like the hospital or a place.

Thus, there was no way to know how many were suffering specifically from a lack of winter clothing. Table 7 on the next page presents the information on the sick in the regiment between November 1777 and March 1778.

FIGURE 5. Conditions of the troops at Valley Forge

Table 7. Those men and officers who were recorded as "sick" in the 3rd Virginia as extracted from the Compiled Service Records for the 3rd Virginia, November 1777 to April 1778.[76]
Abbreviations: all dates abbreviated; MR = Muster Roll; PR = Pay Roll; Va.= Virginia.

Captain Arell's Company			
Name	Rank	Enlistment/Discharge	Date of entry
David Arell	Captain	Resigned 2/14/ 78	MR 12/ 77 to 1/ 78 Sick, absent.
William Berry	Private	2/8/ 76 for 2 yrs Time expired: 1/ 78.	MR 11/ 77 to 12/ 77 Sick, absent.
James Deekins	Private	1/14/ 77 for 3 yrs DEAD 3/15/ 78.	MR 11/ 77 to 2/ 78 Sick, absent. PR 3/ 78 for 15 days. DEAD.
John Elliott	Sergeant	Enlisted 2/8/ 76 for 2 yrs.	MR 9/ 77 to 1/ 78 Sick, absent.
Robert Godfrey	Private	Enlisted 9/15/ 77 for war.	MR 11/ 77 Sick, absent.
Thomas Jenkins	Private	Enlisted for war. DEAD 1/15/ 78.	MR 10/ 77 to 12/ 77 Sick, absent. PR 1/ 78 for 15 days. DEAD.
James Wilkes	Private	Enlisted 9/5/ 77 for 3 yrs. DEAD 4/15/ 78.	MR 11/ 77 to 3/ 78 Sick, absent. PR 4/ 78 for 15 days. DEAD.
Daniel Wright	Private	Enlisted 3/2/ 77 for 3 yrs.	MR 10/ 77 Sick, absent. MR 11/ 77 to 3/ 78 On furlough. MR 3/ 78 Deserted 3/15/ 78
Captain Briscoe's Company			
George May	Private	Enlisted for 2 yrs.	MR 11/ 77 Sick, Bethlehem. MR 12/ 77 Sick, hospital.
Captain Phill Lee's Company			
Captain Phill Lee		Commissioned 3/19/ 76 DEAD 29 January 78	MR 9/ 77 to 12/ 77 wounded. MR 1/ 78 DEAD.
Thomas Mason	Private	Enlisted 2/2/ 76.	PR 8/ 77 to 11/ 77 Sick, Va. MR 8/ 77 to 1/ 78 Sick, Va.
Henry Westall	Private	Enlisted 3/8/ 77 for 2 yrs.	MR 6/ 77 to 10/ 77 Sick in Va. MR 11/ 77 Sick in Alexandria, Va.
Obadiah Philbert	Private	Enlisted for 2 yrs.	MR 9/ 77 Sick at Flying hospital. MR 10/ 77 to 1/ 78 Sick, Reading.

Table 7. (Continued) Those men and officers who were recorded as "sick" in the 3rd Virginia as extracted from the Compiled Service Records for the 3rd Virginia, November 1777 to April 1778.

Captain John Mercer's Company			
Name	Rank	Enlistment/Discharge	Date of entry
James Arrowsmith	Private	Enlisted 2/23/ 76 for 2 yrs.	MR 12/ 77 to 1/ 78 Sick, absent.
George Boyle	Private	Enlisted 2/23/ 76 for 2 yrs.	MR 11/ 77 to 12/ 77 Sick, absent.
John Ethrington Jr.	Private	Enlisted 10/7/ 77 for 3 yrs.	MR 11/ 77 to 12/ 77 Sick, absent.
John King	Private	Enlisted 2/23/ 76 for 2 yrs.	MR 11/ 77 to 1/ 78 Sick, absent.
William McCullough	Private	Enlisted for 2 yrs.	MR 12/ 77 Sick, present.
Colbert McDonald	Private	Enlisted 2/23/ 76 for 2 yrs.	MR 11/ 77 Sick at Black River. MR 12/ 77 Sick, absent.
David Price	Private	Enlisted 2/23/ 76 for 2 yrs.	MR 11/ 77 to 1/ 78 Sick, absent.
George Smith	Private	Enlisted 2/3/ 78 for 3 yrs. DEAD 4/ 78.	MR 11/ 77 to 4/ 78 Sick, absent. PR 4/ 78. DEAD.
Elijah Taylor	Private	Enlisted 2/23/ 76 for 2 yrs.	MR 11/ 77 Sick at Lancaster. MR 12/ 77 Sick, absent.
John Vigor	Private	Enlisted 2/23/ 76 for 2 yrs.	MR 11/ 77 Sick in Va. MR 12/ 77 to 1/ 78 Sick, absent.
Captain John Peyton's Company			
William Fitzpatrick	Private	Enlisted until 2/5/ 78.	MR 11/ 77 to 1/ 78 Sick, absent.
Edward Phelps	Private	Enlisted 2/5/ 76 for 2 yrs.	MR 9/ 77 Sick at Reading. MR 10/ 77 Sick at hospital. MR 11/ 77 to 1/ 78 Sick, absent.
John Towers	Private	Enlisted until 2/5/ 78. Discharged 1/31/ 78.	MR 10/ 77 to 12/ 77 Sick, absent.
Captain Robert Powell's Company			
John Harrod	Private	Enlisted 3/12/ [yr. n.g.] DEAD 3/ 78.	MR 11/ 77 Sick, absent. MR 1/ 78 to 2/ 78 Sick, absent. PR 3/ 78 DEAD.

In the list of Captains in Table 7, it should be noted that these company's original captains had been replaced. Only Captain Lee was an original Captain and he was to die in January 1778 of wounds suffered at Brandywine. David Arell had replaced Captain John Fitzgerald in November 1776; Reuben Briscoe had taken over Captain Charles West's company upon his promotion to Major in the 3rd Virginia in July 1777; and John Mercer had become the Captain of Gustavus Brown Wallace' old company when he was promoted out of the regiment after Germantown in October 1777;[77] John Peyton had received a Captain's commission in the 3rd Virginia in June 1776 while Robert Powell Sr. became a captain in the regiment in October 1776.[78]

While it was not possible to discern a cause for the men who were recorded as "sick," several useful observations may still be made from the data recorded here. It appeared that Captains Mercer and Arells' companies were the hardest hit with some kind of sickness.

Mercer's men were sick in November and December, with one death, to George Smith, occurring in April 1778. Captain Arell's men, on the other hand, had three privates sick in September and October as well as the six who became sick in November or December. Three of his privates died—James Deekins, sick form November 1777 until his death on 15 March; Thomas Jenkins, sick from October 1777 until he died on 15 January 1778; and James Wilkes, who was sick from November 1777 until his death on 15 April 1778.

Captain Robert Powell's company suffered a death as well from a soldier being sick and that was Private John Harrod, who became sick in September 1777 and was sick and absent from his company from September 1777 until February 1778. He died in March 1778.

Eight of the soldiers in this table were sick well before November 1777 and continued so into the New Year. John Elliott, a sergeant in Captain Arell's company became sick in September 1777 and remained so through January 1778. Thomas Jenkins, as has been noted, died in January 1778 after having been sick for some three and a half months.

Daniel Wright, a private in Captain Arell's company, became sick in October and never returned. The muster rolls listed him as "on furlough" from November 1777 through 15 March 1778. The March showed him as "deserted" on 15 March 1778.

Thomas Mason, a private in Captain Phill Lee's company, was listed as sick in July 1777, although one of the muster rolls noted that he had been sick in Virginia since 26 August 1776. He apparently never made it out of Virginia although he was carried on the muster rolls and pay rolls as "sick, in Virginia" until January 1778.

Henry Westall was another private in Captain Lee's company listed as sick in Virginia, beginning in September 1777. He had enlisted in March 1776 and apparently become sick in June 1777 while in Virginia. He, too, never returned to his company. The January 1778 muster roll entry stated "sick in Va. Entire entry cancelled by time."[79]

Obadiah Philbert, also a private in Captain Lee's company, was listed in September 1777 as "sick at Flying hospital" and then, from October 1777 to January 1778, as "sick at Reading." The three men in Captain Lee's company had all enlisted in the early months of 1776 and were due to be discharged between January and March 1778.

Edward Phelps, a private in Captain John Peyton's company, was "sick at Reading" in September 1777. In October he was sick at the hospital and apparently spent November through January 1778 sick there as he was listed as "sick, absent" in those months' muster rolls. Phelps had enlisted in February 1776 and was also scheduled for a discharge in February 1778.

John Towers was sick and absent from Captain John Peyton's company from October to December 1777. He was discharged on 31 January 1778, five days before his term of enlistment was over.

Only one officer's death was recorded during this period. This was Captain Philip Richard Francis Lee. who was wounded at Brandywine and died of these wounds on 29 January 1778.

January to April 1778: Deaths and Desertion in the 3rd Virginia.

The early winter months of 1778 were not especially kind to the regiment. Twenty-one men died, their numbers spread through five companies. Captains David Arell, Phill Lee, John Peyton, and Robert Powell saw their rank and file diminish at the demise of these men. In addition, there were three desertions, one in December 1777 and two in March and April 1778.

Table 8 shows the men and officers who died or deserted while in winter quarters at Valley Forge.

Table 8. Deaths and Desertions in the 3rd Virginia December 1777 to April 1778[80]
Abbreviations: All dates abbreviated; VF = Valley Forge; n.g. = not given; yrs = years; retd = returned

Name	Rank	Enlisted	Date of Death	Deserted?/ Date
Captain Arell's Company				
Thomas Clack	Sergeant	9/1/ 77 for war.	4/15/ 78	No
George Gordon	Sergeant	1/13/ 77 for 3 yrs.	2/28/ 78	No
James Deekins	Fifer	For 3 yrs.	3/15/ 78	No
William Bryant	Private	9/8/ 77 for war.	3/15/ 78 VF	No
Thomas Jenkins	Private	9/8/ 77 for war.	1/15/ 78	No
Richard Shepherd	Private	For war.	1/15/ 78	No
James Wilkes	Private	n.g.	4/15/ 78	No
William Williamson	Private	For 3 yrs.	2/20/ 78 VF	8/ 77; retd 9/12/ 77
John Lawler (2)	Private	2/8/ 76 for 2 yrs. Reenlisted 12/ 77 for war.		4/15/ 78 Never retd from furlough.
William Russell	Private	8/30/ 77.		3/8/ 78
William Williams	Private	For war.	3/8/ 78.	
Daniel Wright	Private	3/2/ 77 for 3 yrs.	3/15/ 78	
Captain John Blackwell's Company				
John Walton	Private	4/10/ 76 for 2 yrs.		4/10/ 78 Never retd from furlough.
Captain Phill Lee's Company				
Philip Richard Francis Lee	Captain		1/29/ 78	No
George Armstrong	Private	3/1/ 76. Reenlisted 12/1/ 77 for 3 yrs in Captain Mercer's Company.	4/24/ 78	No
Captain John Peyton's Company				
Thomas Steele	Private	Reenlisted 9/11/ 77 for 3 yrs.	1/ 78	No
Captain John Mercer's Company				
John Wells	Private	2/23/ 76 for 2 yrs. Reenlisted 11/ 77 for 3 yrs.	5/31/ 78	No
William Bland	Soldier	9/ 77 for war	3/15/ 78	No
George Collop	Private	9/ 77 for 3 yrs.	3/15/ 78	No
Captain Robert Powell's Company				
John Harrod	Private	12/ 77 for 3 yrs.	3/ 78	No
Thomas Rice	Private	9/ 77 for war.		3/21/ 78
John Wilburn	Private	8/ 77 for war.		12/ 77

This data in this table indicates that the men who died in 1778 had enlisted or re-enlisted in the waning months of 1777 for a term of three years or for the war. This information also points out the commencement of a successful recruitment effort in the late summer and early fall of 1777, not only in attracting new enlistees but in persuading some of the original members of the regiment to reenlist.

January to March 1778 Discharges completely alter the structure and organization of the 3rd Virginia.

General Washington realized that the enlistment terms for the first nine regiments of the Virginia line were about to expire in the first three months of 1778. When his attempts to induce these veterans to reenlist failed, in January he "released all soldiers whose terms of service had expired or would expire in the next two months."[81]

The compiled service records for the 3rd Virginia indicated that a large majority of those men who enlisted in February and March of 1776 went home.[82] Only a few reenlisted.

Corporal Burr Harris [83] and Private George Armstrong,[84] in Captain Phill Lee's company, reenlisted on 1 December 1777 in Captain John Mercer's company. George Armstrong died in April 1778.[85] Another private in the same company, Spencer Anderson, was said to have re-enlisted in the Light Horse,[86] along with Private Francis Turner,[87] in December 1777.

Three men in Captain John Peyton's company reenlisted in the Light Horse on 23 December 1777. They were Sergeant Moses Dalton,[88] and Privates James Kehoe,[89] and John Randolph.[90] Sergeant John Wells, in Captain Gus Wallace's company re-enlisted in Captain Mercer's company in November 1777 and went on furlough until March 1778. When he returned to Captain Mercer's company in April, the muster roll listed him as "present, sick at the Church Hospital." He died 31 May 1778.[91]

Privates Charles Colley, Thomas Cosby, and James Harris, in Captain Robert Powell's company all reenlisted in the Light Horse in December 1777.[92] Sergeant Thomas Kane in Captain Powell's company, also reenlisted—with Powell, in December 1777. He deserted in May 1778 and returned in July 1778. He was reduced to the ranks that month.[93]

The men, who re-enlisted as shown above and in Table 7, were all found in the compiled service records of the 3rd Virginia regiment.[94]

Discharges to original men and officers of 3rd Virginia forced a transition to a regiment composed of men recruited in 1777 and 1778.

Most of the men in the regiment returned home in small groups through March 1778. Some of the officers were already home, busily trying to recruit new men to fill out their companies. Captain Valentine Peyton had arrived in Fauquier in December, hoping to find a 1st Lieutenant. Nathaniel Ashby, who had resigned his commission in the 3rd Virginia in November, was already home—preparing to marry Peggy Mauzy.[95] Unfortunately Captain Peyton could not persuade the young man to come back to the regiment.

Captain John Blackwell and his brother Lieutenant Joseph Blackwell arrived home in Fauquier in January. So had the men wounded at Brandywine in September, in Captain Chilton's old company; they had all been discharged, including Sergeant Henry Bradford, and Privates John Brown, John Murphy, and Thomas Kelly. Colonel Marshall also discharged some of the men whose terms had expired, among them John Dulin and Samuel Cox.[96]

Since most of the men who enlisted in Captain Chilton's company in February and March 1776 did not return to the army after their discharge, Captain Blackwell was badly in need of new recruits. Both he and Val Peyton had little success in recruiting Fauquier men probably due to competition from other Virginia line regiments, Colonel Marshall and Captain Elias Edmond's organization of the State Artillery, and George Rogers Clark's endeavours to raise men in the county for seven companies to set out for Fort Pitt, ostensibly for the defense of Kentucky. Since there were Fauquier county residents with ties to Kentucky, these men were not interested in service in what had already proved to be dangerous duty in a Virginia line regiment.[97]

Captain Blackwell was able to persuade only a few of the regiment's veterans to return with him. Sergeant Moses Allen, and newly promoted Sergeant William Bawcut, Jonathan Crooke, Benjamin Hamrick, John Walton, Daniel Pennington, William Bailey, and John Russell[98] all returned to Valley Forge.[99]

Captain Valentine Peyton fared little better. When he was not able to persuade Nathaniel Ashby to return, he was forced to carry Isham Keith on his rolls as his 1st Lieutenant. It was a short assignment as Keith resigned his commission in April 1778.[100] Peyton's company consisted of just thirty-four men in March and gained just six more as he returned to winter quarters.[101]

Similar troubles accosted the other Captains of the regiment in their endeavors to fill their companies with fresh recruits.[102] It probably did not help recruiting efforts, when the army returns for February through June 1778 for Woodford's Brigade showed the effects of a continual shortage of clothes and an increasing rate of desertion and an equally alarming rise in the death toll throughout regiments in the brigade. The numbers of men being discharged in the January through March 1778 period in the regiments within the brigade merely emphasized the impact as more and more men left, not to return.[103]

It would be an extremely difficult task to replace the sheer numbers of experienced, battle-hardened veterans who returned home. Thus it was left to those men who had enlisted in 1777 and early 1778 to carry the regiment.[104]

A brigade return in early May amply showed what a massive task it was to fill the ranks of the four regiments Woodford commanded. By the second week in May, his brigade still needed 48 sergeants, thirty-one drum and fife, and 1555 rank and file to complete its regimental ranks. Just one sergeant had joined along with four new recruits. The brigade showed 995 men and officers fit for duty on paper, although this did not take into account the 357 men who were sick and present and the ninety-two who were sick and absent. Nor did it count the eighty-five men who were still out on furlough.[105]

The Politics of Promotion: Woodford versus Muhlenberg, Weedon, and Scott.

In mid-March, after much successful maneuvering by Woodford, a General Board of Officers met to decide the fate of the commissions of the Virginia generals—William Woodford, Peter Muhlenburg, and George Weedon. Woodford had been "implacable in his demand for precedence over the other three Virginia Brigadiers and was constantly intriguing to bring it about."[106]

The Board of General Officers rendered a decision in his favor. Accordingly, on 19 March, Congress passed a resolution for Washington to call in and cancel the commissions of the three Virginia Brigadiers. Instead, he was to issue new ones that were to rank in a different configuration. Woodford was to be the senior general, followed by Muhlenberg, then Scott, and finally, Weedon.

This created a firestorm. Weedon resigned and went home to Virginia. Muhlenberg was incensed and considered resignation. He decided to stay only after Congress gave assurances that the change in the seniority was not due to any perceived stain on his character or service. Charles Scott did not complain of the new ranking since Woodford had already outranked him in the previous arrangement in seniority.[107]

The Brigade's furor over the Oath of Allegiance.

The promotion of William Woodford to be the ranking brigadier in the Virginia line did have some unintended consequences. Congress had passed a resolution in February 1778 requiring all officers, holding a continental commission, to take and subscribe to the following oath of allegiance.

> I do acknowledge the United States of America to be free, independent and sovereign states and declared that the people thereof owe no allegiance or obedience to George the Third, King of Great Britain and I renounce refuse and abjure any allegiance or obedience to him, and I do swear (or affirm) that I will to the utmost of my power support, maintain, and defend the said United States against the said King George the third, his heirs and successors and his and their abettors, assistants and adherents and will serve the said United States in the office of which I now hold with fidelity according to the best of my skill and understanding.[108]

The officers in both Woodford's and Weedon's brigade, when asked to take and sign the oath, point-blank refused to do so. They were the only brigades in the army who declined. Washington was baffled.

In a memorial signed by twenty-six officers of the two brigades, they stated four objections to taking and signing the oath. First, they considered the tenor of the oath an indignity; it presupposes that some have acting against their sentiments. It may even be unnecessary, since they have "ventured their lives and fortunes in support of American Independence."

Secondly, many of the officers "at present are injured in their rank" so they consider this an impropriety to sear to continue in their present posts as "the rank of the juror is to be taken when the oath is administered."

Third, the officers wondered whether the oath would debar an officer from being able to resign. Finally, the majority of the officers thought that this oath would lay considerable restraints on any attempts on their part that would bring about a change "that would put them on an honorable and advantageous footing."[109]

Washington wrote the Woodford's brigade's divisional leader, Marquis de Lafayette on 17 May expressing his dismay.

> I received yesterday your favor of the 15th Inst., inclosing a paper, subscribed by sundry officers of General Woodford's brigade, setting forth their reasons for not taking the Oath of Abjuration, Allegiance and Office, and thank you much for the cautious delicacy, used in communicating the matter to me.
> As every Oath should be a free act of the mind, founded on the conviction of the party, of its propriety, I would not wish, in any instance, that there should be the least degree of compulsion exercised; or to interpose my opinion in order to induce any to make it, of whom it is required. The Gentlemen therefore who signed the paper, will use their own discretion in the matter, and swear or not swear, as their conscience and feelings dictate.
> At the same time, I cannot but consider it, as circumstance of sing singularity, that the scruples against the Oath should be peculiar to the Officers of one Brigade, and so very extensive.
> The oath in itself is not new. It is substantially the same with that required of all governments, and therefore, does not imply any indignity; and it is perfectly consistent with the professions, actions, and implied engagements of every officer.
> The objection, founded on the supposed unsettled rank of the officers, is of no validity (rank being only mentioned as a further designation of the party swearing); Nor can it be seriously thought, that the oath is either intended, or can prevent their being promoted, or their resignations.
> The fourth objection stated by the Gentlemen, serves as a key to their scruples, and I would willingly persuade myself, that their own reflexions will point out to them the impropriety of the whole proceeding, and not suffer them to be betrayed in future into a similar conduct. I regard them all, and cannot but regret that they were ever engaged in the measure. I am certain they will regret it themselves. Sure I am they ought.[110]

Lafayette pointed out to the General that the objection to the oath lay in the words "in the office I now hold."

> In a nutshell, they did not trust Woodford. They thought of resignation as a last resort if serving under his command should become unbearable. Would not this oath be a weapon he could use against them if they decided to resign, or more important, seek a more agreeable post under another commander.[111]

Washington was able to reassure the officers of Woodford and Weedons' brigade that the oath would not prohibit them from resigning to leave the army or from seeking a more amenable position in another command. With that guarantee the officers in both brigades took and signed the oath without further protest.[112]

SKIRMISH AT BARREN HILLS
18–20 MAY 1778

8 May 1778 Council of War

Washington met with Major Generals Gates, Greene, Stirling, Mifflin, Lafayette, DeKalb, Armstrong, and Steuben and Brigadier Generals Knox, and Duportail in early May to determine a course of action for the ensuing spring and summer campaign against the British. He explained the current deployment of both army and their relative strengths.

The British forces, he said were split into three separate entities—one at Philadelphia, one at New York and the last in Rhode Island. The force in Philadelphia "consisting of the flower of their army," totaled somewhere around 10,000 rank and file and was fortified by a string of forts from the Schuylkill to the Delaware River along with a small detached fortification at Billingsport.

The New York and Long Island forces amounted to around 4000, consisting of both British and German troops and new levies. New York would be difficult to take, secured as it was by British shipping on their front and both flanks and by the Harlem River in the rear. Forts Independence and Washington also guarded any American access.

The Rhode Island contingent was the smallest, held by 2000 or so German troops. Their security was occasioned by the insularity of their location and by protection from their ships.

The American army, on the other hand, was concentrated in Pennsylvania and Delaware and on the Hudson. It totaled in al around 15,000 rank and file for the field, not counting horses and the artillery. The main Army was at Valley Forge and added up to around 11,800 rank and file, fit for service, not counting the sick, present and the men currently on command. A much smaller force of 1400 men were at Wilmington, Delaware. The force on the Hudson, he thought, probably amounted to around 1800 rank and file fit for duty.

Once this explanation was made, Washington requested "after a full and candid discussion of the matter in council, each member would furnish him with his sentiments in writing on some general plan, which, considering all circumstances, ought to be adopted for the operations of the next campaign."[113]

His officers unanimously decided to remain on the defensive unless the enemy "should afford a fairer opportunity than at present exists." There would difficulties in any attempt to wrest Philadelphia from the British—the officers did not believe it could be taken by assault nor could it be blockaded successfully with the numbers the American currently had in their main army. The same consensus was reached regarding an assault on New York.[114]

A Need for Reconnaissance.

As early as April 1778, rumors had been flying around the American camp at Valley Forge that General Howe was about to be replaced by Sir Henry Clinton. In May, another equally tantalizing report circulated—the British were about to evacuate Philadelphia.

In order to discover whether this intelligence had any reality attached to it or was simply wishful thinking, Washington decided to dispatch a large enough force from the American base to determine an anticipated time period of withdrawal, if true. The force dispatched would also have an additional advantage—they were to annoy British communication lines and foraging parties that would have to be sent out for a change of headquarters. He hoped this would attain two objectives, bring in accurate intelligence as to the British plans and harass the British supply lines which had worked so well for the army in the past.

To accomplish this, he assigned this responsibility to Marquis de Lafayette whose division included 2,200 men, five guns, and the entire Virginia line. Lafayette left camp with Enoch Poor's Massachusetts brigade, and the two Virginia brigades under Muhlenberg and Scott. In addition to Muhenberg's own brigade, he also had the command responsibility for Woodford's and Weedon' brigades.[115]

While this was a larger force than ordinary for a reconnaissance and hit and run mission, Washington did not want a repeat of the action that had occurred on 5 May. On that day, young Lieutenant John Hill Carter, of Colonel Baylor's Regiment of Light Dragoons, through a misunderstanding of Captain MacLane's orders, left roads unguarded from Barren Hill Church to Philadelphia. Because of this, the British were able to march to the church undetected and captured a subaltern officer and his party who had returned to the church "for refreshment."[116]

On 18 May, Washington gave Lafayette and his men their marching orders.

> The detachment under your command with which you will immediately march towards the enemy's line is designed to answer the following purposes: to be a security to this camp and a cover to the country between the Delaware and Schuylkill, to interrupt the communication with Philadelphia, obstruct the incursions of the enemy's parties, and to obtain intelligence of their motions and designs.
>
> This last is a matter of very interesting moment, and ought to claim your particular attention. You will endeavour to procure trusty and intelligent spies, who will advise your faithfully of whatever may be passing in the city; and you will without delay communicate to me every piece of material information you obtain.
>
> A variety of concurring accounts make it probable the enemy are preparing to evacuate Philadelphia. This is a point, which it is of the utmost importance to ascertain; and if possible the place of their future destination.
>
> Should you be able to gain certain intelligence of the time of intended embarkation; so that you may be able to take advantage of it, and fall upon the rear of the enenmy in the act of

withdrawing, it will be a very desirable event. But this will be a matter of no small difficulty, and will require the greatest caution and prudence in the execution. Any deception or precipitation may be attended with the most disastrous consequences.

You will remember that your detachment is a very valuable one, and that any accident happening to it would be a severe blow to this army. You will therefore use every possible precaution for its security, and to guard against a surprise. No attempt should be made nor anything risked without the greatest prospect of success, and with every reasonable advantage on your side.

I shall not point out any precise position to you; but shall leave it to your discretion to take such posts occasionally as shall appear to you best adapted to the purposes of your detachment. In general I would observe that a stationary post is unadvisable, as it gives the enemy an opportunity of knowing your situation and concerting plans successfully against you. In case of any offensive movements against this army, you will keep yourself in such a state as to have an easy communication with it and at the same time harrass the enemy's advance.[117]

On the night of 18 May, Lafayette and his detachment settled into positions near Matson's Ford, on the Schuylkill, at Barren Hill, situated midway between the two armies. Meanwhile on the same night, the British began celebrating in grand manner the preparations to welcome Sir Henry Clinton, their new commander and to gather to for the imminent departure of General Sir William Howe.

The next morning, spies brought news of Lafayette's position and the British, in an excess of zeal and as part of a farewell gesture to Howe, decided to attack Lafayette's force with some 5000 men under General Grant, 15 pieces of artillery and 2000 grenadiers under General Grey. Grey would lead the forward detachment and Howe and Clinton would attack the center. They set up the ambush carefully, until on the 20 May, they were ready to move. If the British were successful, the Americans were going to be outnumbered and out maneuvered. Just exactly what Washington wanted the young Major General and his detachment to avoid.

Fortunately for the American forces, Captain Allan McLane of Patton's Continental Regiment,[118] with a detachment of Oneida Indians, was able to take two British grenadiers prisoners at Three Mile Run who told him all about the British plan. He deployed some riflemen to delay the British and hurried to Lafayette to warn him. McLane knew the vicinity well, having grown up in the area and knew of a little known escape route on a sunken road to Matson's Ford.

Thanks to the intensive drilling and discipline instilled in the forces at Valley Forge by Baron von Steuben,

> Lafayette formed his men into a compact platoon columns and after setting up a small rear guard to simulate a defense, coolly slipped away with only minor casualties. On the morning of the 20th Clinton moved from the south on Barren Hill, only to meet the scouts of Grey's column moving cautiously down from the north. The birds had flown.[119]

The Virginia Gazette carried an account of this skirmish in an "extract of a letter from a gentleman who was in camp when the Marquis de la Fayette lately returned with his detachment."

> I have inquired very particularly into the Marquis's enterprise, and have learned from a gentleman, on whose veracity and accuracy I can depend, the following articles. The objects of the detachment are well known to every body.
> On the 19th instant, that detachment, consisting of about 2000 rank and file and an irregular body of 45 Indians, marched from camp, and halted within 11 miles of Philadelphia, between Barren Hill church and Schuylkill. The following night a chain of guards and sentinels were stationed, for commanding the avenues into and out of the city.
> In the meantime some infamous Tory must have betrayed the design; for, notwithstanding the vigilance of the sentinels, the enemy, in force of full 7000, came out near midnight, and by a round-about hard march penetrated the country so far as to reach the spot where the Marquis had occupied the preceding night, and the first intelligence of their progress reached the Marquis no sooner than break of day the 21st.
> From the account of their number, and the direction of their march, there was nothing left for the detachment but to decamp with all haste, consistent with good order.

> The column of the enemy, as it approached the detachment divided and took different roads, the most effectually to surround it; at the same time another column marched out of Philadelphia, advancing towards the Marquis's front. The retreat was conducted in excellent order, in presence of the enemy's advance parties of horse. Sir Henry Clinton, who is said to have been commander of the enemy's party, or whoever he was, must have been deceived by the regularity and good order of the retreat, and apprehensive of being drawn into an ambuscade, otherwise nothing but want of courage can excuse him for letting the Marquis get off with so trifling a loss as three men killed and four prisoners.
>
> The enemy had two horsemen killed, and many wounded. When the Indians had fired off their pieces at the light horse, they set up the war whoop, and scampered about according to their custom. The light horse, terrified at the unusual sound, scampered off too, as fast as their horses would carry them. The Indians collected some of their cloaks, which were dropped in the flight, and soon converted them into leggings.[120]

The Americans managed to dodge a major bullet and Lafayette's division was lucky to have escaped with their lives. Washington must have breathed a massive sigh of relief when Lafayette and his men returned safely to camp.

May to June 1778: The British preparations and evacuation of Philadelphia.

By the last week in May 1778, Washington had come to believe that the British were indeed about to leave Philadelphia, he thought, thought to go to New York. He shared this sentiment with Landon Carter, in a letter written at Valley Forge on 30 May.

> The enemy seems to be upon the point of evacuating Philadelphia, and I am persuaded are going to New York, whether as a place of rendezvous of their whole force, for a general imbarkation, or to operate up the North River, or to act from circumstances is not quite so clear.
>
> My own opinion is, that they must either give up the Continent or the Islands; which they will do, is not clear; and yet, I think, they will endeavour to retain New York, if they can by any means spare troops enough to garrison it.[121]

Washington could only "lament that the number of our sick (under inoculation, &c.), the situation of our stores, and other matters, will no allow me to make a large detachment from this army till the enemy have actually crossed the Delaware ... then it will be too late."[122]

Regimental Surgeon and Chaplain David Griffith concurred. On 3 June 1778, he penned a quick note to his wife Hannah from the camp at Valley Forge.

> My Dearest Hannah,
> I have the satisfaction to acquaint you that I arrived here in good health. After a tedious journey, in which, I believe the shortness of the sages was a means of preventing a complaint I so much dreaded: I have, at times a little remains of the pains in my back—I am, I thank God, otherwise, very well.
>
> We are in Daily expectation of going into Philadelphia. Every account received from that place for three weeks past confirms the opinion that they are about to leave it. I have seen several reputable People from that City within a few days & they all agree that their cannon & baggage is mostly on board, that the Tories are all embarked with their effects, that many of their ships are moved Downwards. In short, the Circumstances are so many & so probable that no body here doubts of this being their design.
>
> The British Officers in Philad[a] make no secret of their being about to go, & they likewise say that their troops are about to evacuate Rhode Island. If accounts from New York are to be credited, they are likewise preparing to evacuate that place. Remember what I told you before our parting— If God spares me, I expect to see New York before next Christmas. Upon the enemys quitting Philad[a] we shall immediately march through Jersey towards New York as it is expected they are [to] be at that Place till their Whole Army is collected.
>
> Every appearance, in short, is favourable to the American Cause. All the news you have heard from France is abundantly confirmed & in the most authentic manner. The last papers from Boston mention the arrival of 5 large ships at that place from France with goods, one of them a Kings frigate.

Our army is tolerably healthy at present. They had a bilious fever among them which has Destroyed some, but they are now much healthier. They are all well clothed at present & well furnished with necessarys.[123]

With the likelihood of a British evacuation of the city, Washington realized he needed a more exact idea of the strength of his army. To that end, on 22 May 1778, he sent urgent dispatches to the commanding officers of the Virginia Brigades "to order the commanding officers of the different regiments in your brigade to make you, as soon as possible, an exact return of the men in their respective corps who came out as draughts or substitutes, distinguishing those of the old from the new. If" he ordered, "you can obtain a return of those who either died or deserted after they joined their regiments, I should be glad to have it... He added a P.S: "Let the county be mentioned from whence the draughts came."[124]

The May 1778 returns reflected the strength of Woodford's brigade, which included the return, ordered by Washington on 22 May, and are presented in Table 9 below.

Table 9. Woodford's Brigade Returns 2 May to 23 May, Returns No. 66–70. *General Returns of the Army at Valley Forge.* Abbreviations: Lt. Cols = Lieutenant Colonels; Lts = Lieutenants; QM = Quarter Master; PM = Pay master; Sgt = Sergeant; D&F = Drum & Fife; R&F = Rank & File.

No. 66. 2 May 1778. *Monthly Return, Valley Forge: Woodford's Brigade.*
0 Colonels   2 Lt. Cols   1 Major 10 Captains   7 1st Lts   11 2nd Lts   11 Ensigns
3 Adjutants   3 QM   1 PM   1 Chaplain   1 Surgeon   1 Mate
2 Sgt Majors 4 QM Sgts   0 Drum Majors   1 Fife Major 29 D&F   60 Sgts.
321 present, fit for duty   370 sick, present   93 sick, absent   94 on furlough   132 on command
Since last return: 23 Dead   2 discharged   7 deserted   4 promoted
Total: 1010
    Wanting to complete: 42 Sgts   33 D&F   1550 R&F
    Joined: 3 Sgts.   4 D&F   211 R&F

No. 67. 9 May 1778. *Weekly Return at Valley Forge:. Woodford's Brigade*
0 Colonels   1 Lt. Col   1 Major 11 Captains   7 1st Lts   12 2nd Lts.   12 Ensigns
3 Adjutants   3 QM   2 PM   1 Chaplain   2 Surgeons   1 Mate
2 Sgt. Majors 4 QM Sgts   3 Drum Majors   1 Fife Major 30 D&F   48 Sgts
330 present, fit for duty   357 sick, present   92 sick, absent   85 on furlough   131 [?] on Command
Since last return: 5 Dead   3 Discharged   9 Deserted
Total: 995.
    Wanting to complete: 48 Sgts   31 D&F   1555 R&F
    Joined: 1 Sgt   0 D&F   4 R&F

No. 68. 16 May 1778. *General Return at Valley Forge: Woodford's Brigade*
0 Colonels   2 Lt. Cols   1 Major   11 Captains   9 1st Lts   15 2nd Lts.   12 Ensigns
4 Adjutants   4 QM   3 PM   1 Chaplain   3 Surgeons   1 Mate
3 Sgt Majors 4 QM Sgts   1 Drum Major   1 Fife Major   34 D&F   54 Sgts
390 present, fit for duty   331 sick, present   79 sick, absent   26 on furlough   178 on Command
Since last return: 11 Dead   2 Discharged   1 Deserted   1 Promoted
Total: 1004.
    Wanting to Complete: 50 Sgts   30 D&F   1556 R&F
    Joined: 2 Sgts   3 D&F   24 R&F

No. 69. 23 May 1778. *General Return, Valley Forge: Woodford's Brigade.*
0 Colonels   2 Lt. Cols.   1 Major   11 Captains 7 1st Lts   13 2nd Lts   7 Ensigns
4 Adjutants   3 QM   2 PM   1 Chaplain   3 Surgeons   1 Mate
4 Sgt Major   4 QM Sgts   1 Drum Major   1 Fife Major 37 D&F   61 Sgts
356 present, fit for duty   329 sick, present   76 sick, absent   26 on furlough   240 on Command
Since last return: 8 Dead   1 Discharged   2 Deserted
Total: 1027.
    Wanting to Complete: 46 Sgts   26 D&F   1533 R&F
    Joined: 1 Sgt.   0 D&F   23 R&F

Table 9. Woodford's Brigade Returns 2 May to 23 May, Returns No. 66--70. (Continued)
General Returns of the Army at Valley Forge.

No. 70. May 30, 1778. *Monthly Return at Valley Forge : Woodford's Brigade*

0 Colonels	2 Lt. Cols./	1 Major	13 Captains	10 1st Lts.	15 2nd Lts.	9 Ensigns
4 Adjutants	3 QM	2 PM	2 Chaplains	3 Surgeons	1 Mate	
3 Sgts Majors	4 QM Sgts	2 Drum Majors	1 Fife Major	32 D&F	58 Sgts	

489 present, fit for duty   267 sick, present   109 sick, absent   25 on furlough   158 on Command
Since last return: 28 Dead   12 discharged   9 deserted   3 promoted
Total: 1048.
  Wanting to complete: 41 Sgts   27 D&F   1512 R&F
  Joined: 2 Sgts   5 D&F   72 R&F
Comments: **Since last return 23 R&F killed and missing**
  1263 R&F unfit for duty for want of arms, clothing and Accoutrements.

Source: NARA, No. 66–70, 2 May to 30 May 1778 *Returns at Valley Forge*, M 246 MR 137, *Returns of the Army.*

An examination of Woodford's Brigade returns for this month reveals a very seriously undermanned unit. Winter had come and gone. Warmer weather had arrived. Yet new enlistees had not. The brigade was still experiencing considerable difficulties equipping and clothing the men and officers of the four regiments within the unit.

These returns also amply illustrated the frustration at the lack of success of recruiting officers in filling up their companies in the four regiments. It was not just the captains of the 3rd Virginia who were having difficulties, it was a widespread problem throughout the brigade.

Eight days later, on 30 May 1778, brigade returns for the Virginia brigades revealed a serious problem in the areas of men and officers fit for duty. In a brigade return for Charles Scott's unit, on 30 May 1778 composed of the 4th, 8th, and 12th Virginia along with two additional Continental regiments under the command of William Grayson and John Patton of Pennsylvania, the numbers were even more troubling when compared with Woodford's return of the same date. The entire 4th regiment numbered only seventy-two men; the 8th Virginia, ninety-eight; the 12th Virginia had the most men—275. Grayson's regiment contained 105 men, while the Patton's regiment was down to eighty-three men.[125]

Weedon's Brigade, composed of the 2nd, 6th, 10th, 13th Pennsylvania, and 14th Virginia presented these figures on 30 May, 1778: 150 men and officers in the 2nd Virginia; sixty-three men and officers in the 6th Virginia; 252 men and officers in the 10th Virginia; 237 men and officers in the 13th Virginia; and 218 in the 14th Virginia. Clearly this Brigade was in much better shape—at least as far as the totals in each regiment.[126]

Peter Muhenberg's Brigade, on 30 May 1778, comprised the 1st Virginia, the 5th and 9th Virginia, the 13th Virginia, the 1st Virginia State Regiment, and the German Battalion. His brigade was by far in the best shape as far as the numbers were concerned. With the exception of the 1st Virginia, the regiments in his brigade all contained more than 100 men.[127]

By the last of May, Washington wanted *all* of his Virginia officers, unless on furlough, to return without delay to Valley Forge. On 29 May, Washington issued the following orders, as published in *the Virginia Gazette* on 12 June 1778.

> The Commander in Chief positively requires all officers absent from the camp, belonging to the troops of the state of Virginia, except those who are detained on publick service by His Excellency the Governour of that state, or any general officer of the same, or those who have furloughs not yet expired, immediately to join their respective corps.[128]

Perhaps the continuing absence of officers and the overall strength of his army, especially if the other May brigade returns mirrored those of the Virginia ones, were the "other matters" Washington was referring to in his 30 May 1778 letter to Landon Carter, when he lamented his inability to put together a large enough force to harrass the British until they were across the Delaware.[129]

On 10 June, the General was *still* awaiting word that the British had departed. He wrote his brother John Augustine, from camp near Valley Forge. He was "at a loss", he said, since the British had embarked their baggage and stores on board transports and proceeded below the Cheveaux de Frieze. Then a Peace Commission made up of British diplomats appeared in Philadelphia which may have further held up the evacuation. Washington was skeptical of any success of this latest move by the British to end the war. The negotiators, while willing to accede to any terms, conditioned them upon a "return to our dependence on Great Britain."[130]

Washington was also discouraged about the latest recruiting efforts to bring fresh Virginia troops into camp. How was he to engage the British without sufficient reinforcements from new recruits?

> Out of your first and sec. draught by which we ought to have had upwards of 3500 men for the regiments of that state we have received only 1242 in all. I need only mention this fact in proof of what other states do; of our prospects also; and, as a criterion by which you may form some estimate of our real numbers when hear them, as I doubt, not you often do, spoke of in magnified terms. From report, however, I should do injustice to the states of Maryland and New Jersey, were I not to add, that they are likely to get their regiments nearly completed.[131]

He told his brother the "extreme fatigue and hardship which the soldiers underwent in the course of the winter, added to the want of cloath, an, I may add, provisions, have rendered them very sickly, especially in the [North Carolina Brigade]; many deaths have happened in consequence, and yet the army is in exceeding good spirits.[132]

When the British finally did evacuate Philadelphia, on 18 June 1778,[133] it must have been a relief and, at the same time, anticlimactic what with all the rumors and visual evidence of the impending departure, swirling about the city and its environs.

EVENTS LEADING
TO BATTLE OF MONMOUTH
JUNE 1778

17 June 1778: The American Plan.

On 17 June, Washington held a Council of War with his general staff. Lafayette was there; so were Woodford and Muhlenberg. Washington had four matters to bring up for discussion.

First on his agenda was the anticipated evacuation of Philadelphia by the British. He thought they were headed for New York, either by marching through New Jersey or going by water. However, he could not discount this to be a feint, meant to "draw us out of this strong position, throw us off our guard and attack us to advantage." The redcoats could, he opined, even "intend a southern expedition." The enemy numbered around 10000 rank and file, fit for duty.

Second, he considered the strength of his army at Valley Forge. This had to be taken into consideration in any overall plan for an attack against the British. He thought, counting those who were sick, but not too sick and still capable of acting in an emergency, he might field a force of a little over 12000 rank and file. There were a still a little over 2000 men who were sick or lacked clothing and arms, "unable to march." Most of these men, however, could travel at a moderate pace to somewhere safer, if the rest of the army had to move. On the other hand, the plight of the seriously sick and wounded, now ten to twelve miles away from camp, would have to be carried out by wagons so as not to impede the Army's main force.

It was of paramount importance that the Council consider and plan for the disposition of the large number of military stores and magazines in camp or its vicinity, as well as Quarter Master's general stores at Reading and the depositories at Lebanon and Carlisle, if the army were to march.

Third, the 800 man force in New Jersey comprised of a Continental brigade and New Jersey Militia had "been notified of the probability of the enemy's marching through it" had been ordered to harrass the British with "all the annoyance and disturbance in their power" should the British decide on that route to their interim or final destination.

Fourth, the commander in chief reminded the Council that the British already have between 14,000 and 15,000 troops in New York. The American army, on the other hand, once united with reinforcements from the North River, will have "near 14,000 Continental troops, fit for service."

Having informed the Councils of these four items on his agenda, he requested, after a personal discussion of these points takes place, a written opinion for a course of action for the army to follow. He was especially desirous for the Council to deliver a judgment on five major points:

1) Should any enterprise now be taken against Philadelphia?
2) Should the army remain here until *all* the British have departed the City or should the army move immediately to the Delaware River?
3) If the army stays her until the British leave the city and if the British go through the Jersies towards Amboy, is it practicable, for this force to join the American forces in the Jersies to continue to harass the redcoat army further? Should the Army, instead, march to the North River to secure communication lines between the eastern and southern states?
4) In the event that the army here is able to overtake the enemy on their march, will it be prudent, with aid from the New Jersey militia, to make an attack on the British—should this be a partial or general attack?
5) In case of the "immediate removal of this army," what should be done to safeguard the sick and the military stores?

Only two generals were in "unequivocally" in favor of attacking the British if they moved through New Jersey to New York. Four of the generals, including Lafayette, were in favor of harassing the British as much as they could *without* annoying them to a point of bringing on a general engagement. General Muhlenberg favored an attack only if the British departed from Philadelphia to go somewhere other that did not entail a New Jersey route. Everyone was opposed to moving from Valley Forge before the British actions could be correctly deciphered. Most of the Council were opposed to sending a detachment to the Jersies in anticipation of a British move there.[134]

Armies on the move.

The next day, the British left the city. Washington took action immediately to secure the city with American troops.[135] At the same time, he wrote Major General Lee, with orders to stop "on the first strong ground after passing the Delaware at Coryells ferry" until further orders. He was to proceed only he received "authentic" intelligence of the enemy taking a direct route across New Jersey to South Amboy or lower. If that occurred, than Lee and his force were to continue their march to the North River.[136]

The General established the order of march from Valley Forge, on 18 June, after Generals Lee and Mifflins' division had marched. The Light Horse was to march in front of the army and right flank during the day and encamp at the rear of the army at night. The second division was Lafayette's division, with Woodford and Scott's Virginia brigades, followed by the North Carolina brigades; they were to lead the march from Valley Forge. Following Lafayette's division was Baron De Kalb and the brigades of John Glover, Samuel Patterson, and Ebenezer Learned. The artillery units were to be the last to leave with the stores of spare ammunition.[137]

On 20 June, in a letter to the President of Congress, the general explained the disposition of his army; they had reached the vicinity around Coryell's Ferry, north of Trenton; he halted there for the night due to heavy rain and was waiting for the expected arrival of General Lee with six brigades. At last account, the British forces were in New Jersey, around three miles from Mount Holley, where they were repairing a bridge destroyed by the Americans. The forces in New Jersey, under the command of General Maxwell, had followed orders to harrass the British while avoiding a general engagement.[138]

Washington had 12200 Continental and militia troops when they crossed the Delaware at Coryell's Ferry. Major General Charles Lee commanded the right wing composed of the Virginia brigades of Woodford and Scott, North Carolina, Pennsylvania, and Massachusetts troops.

The left wing was Lord Stirling's, made up of New Englanders and Pennsylvania troops. The second line—to be under the command of Major General Lafayette—was composed of Maryland line troops, Muhlenberg and Weedon's Virginia Brigades, Maxwell's New Jersey troops, who were then harassing the enemy, were to join Lafayette's division.[139]

On 23 June, Washington brought his army to a halt at Hopewell, New Jersey. He was still waiting for intelligence regarding the expected route the British planned to take to New York. He took the opportunity the intense heat and rain afforded to rest his men and call another Council of War.[140]

The general quickly brought the Council up to date. The British, he said appeared to be found in two columns, one on the Allentown road and the other on the Bordentown road. He thought their army numbered somewhere between 9,000 and 10,000 rank and file.

The American Army, according to field returns made on 21 June,[141] had 10,684 rank and file, along with and additional 1200 men in General Maxwell's brigade. General Dickinson had 1200 more militia who had been "collected in the neighbourhood of the enemy, [and] who in conjunction with General Maxwell are hovering on their flanks and rear and obstructing their march."[142]

While a week had passed since the British left Philadelphia, still they had traveled less than forty miles. Neither Washington nor Dickinson thought that the obstructions—destroying bridges and knocking down trees to cover roads—were sufficient to cause such a delay. "Under the circumstances," he asked his Council, was it advisable to "hazard a general action?" Is so, should such an attack be a major one on the British or be one that "obliges them to attack us?"

If, on the other hand, this should not prove to be advisable, what measures can be taken "to annoy the enemy in their march, should it be their intention to proceed through the Jerseys?"

The Council of War, which included Major General Lafayette and Brigadier General Woodford, decided against pursing a general action against the British. Instead, they approved a detachment of 1500 men "to annoy the left flank and rear of the British."[143] The generals, in reaching this decision, were divided. Some wanted to act more aggressively against the British. General Lee, however, argued persuasively against this idea. He did not believe the Americans could stand up to such an attack on the British.

While several of "Washington's officers already doubted Lee's abilities and judgment... no one was willing to speak out against him.[144]

> Talking among themselves, many of Washington's generals regretted their timid and halfhearted recommendations. Greene, Wayne, and Lafayette each wrote to Washington to urge more aggressive action. Greene lamented that they were missing an opportunity to strike the vulnerable British column because of unfounded and exaggerated fears of failure, adding that he was confident that the army could win any big battle that might ensue.
>
> Lafayette said that he, Greene, Steuben, Duportail, Wayne, and Paterson all wanted to send more troops after the British.[145]

Apparently, Washington was of like mind. He first offered the command of the advanced troops to General Lee, who turned it down. Lee did not agree with the mission.[146] So, on 25 June, he issued a orders to Lafayette instead to proceed immediately with General Poor's detachment and join up with Charles Scott's Virginia brigade to "use the most effectual means for gaining the enemy's left flank and rear" and give them "every degree of annoyance." Lafayette was take command of all the continental forces on the lines and, with General Dickinson, "take such measures... as will cause the enemy most impediment and loss in their march." Washington added a precaution: "You will naturally take such precautions as will secure you against surprise and maintain your communications with this army."[147]

Washington's aide-de-camp, Alexander Hamilton wrote Lafayette the same day to tell him that the enemy had filed off the Allentown Road and onto the Monmouth road.

> Their rear is said to be a mile westward of Laurence Taylor's Tavern, six miles from Allen Town. General Maxwell is at Hyde's Town, abt. Three miles from this place, General Dickinson is said to be on the enemy's right flank, but where cannot be told. We can hear nothing certain of General Scott but from circumstances he is probably at Allen Town.
>
> We shall agreeable to your request consider and appoint some proper place to rendezvous, for the union of our force, which we shall communicate to General Maxwell and Scott and to your self. In the meantime, I would recommend to you to move towards this place as soon as the convenience of your men will permit. I am told Col. Morgan is on the enemy's right flank...[148]

Lafayette's advanced corps—now composed of the brigades of Maxwell, Morgan, Scott and Wayne—moved onto Hightstown and took up a position there. Washington moved his army from Kingston to Cranbury. At this point, General Lee had a change of mind, finding that the advance corps was composed of nearly 5,000 men or half the American forces.

> ... his pride and ego overcame his principles, and he asked Washington for the job. Washington, who did not want to offend Lee or Lafayette, crafted another peculiar compromise. He put Lee in charge of the advanced corps and reinforced it with two additional brigades, but he ordered him to refrain from interfering if he discovered that Lafayette had already decided to commit his troops into action. As it was, Lafayette had already determined against any such attack for now, and he cheerfully agreed to serve under Lee. On 27 June, Lee took control of the tip of the American army's spear at Englishtown.[149]

While Lee was in overall command of the advanced forces at Englishtown on the evening of the 26 June, Washington brought up the rest of his forces to Manalapan, some three miles behind. The British and American forces were now just five miles apart.[150]

On 27 June, Washington met with Generals Lee, Wayne, Maxwell, Scott, and Lafayette to decide on a plan for the upcoming engagement. Lee was to attack the enemy's rear guard the next day if at all possible.

> Lee, however, saw things differently. As far as he was concerned, the Americans should avoid any major engagement with the superior British army, and he believed that recent conferences at Valley Forge and Hopewell confirmed this policy. He was unwilling or unable to see that Washington had gradually changed his mind over the past week. Lee was ready to attack the British column, but only if he could do so without provoking a full-fledged battle, whereas Washington was now prepared to run that risk.[151]

When Lee met with his the officers in his division, did not have orders for them "because he claimed that the current military situation was too fluid to make any concrete plans." In his opinion, it was far more likely that the British would attack the Americans, than vice versa. Washington, however, was more worried about whether the British would escape, thus avoiding a general engagement. With this in mind, the general instructed Lee to deploy troops to delay a British march long enough for the rebel army to overtake them before they reached Middletown. He further directed Lee to attack the enemy if he had the chance to do so.[152]

At 11:30 on 28 June, Washington sat down to write the President of Congress. He was at Englishtown, around sixteen miles from Monmouth Court House.

> I am now here with the main body of the Army and pressing hard to come up with the enemy. They encamped yesterday at Monmouth Court House, having almost the whole of their front, particularly their left wing, secured by a marsh and thick wood and their rear by a difficult defile, from whence they moved very early this morning.
>
> Our advance, from the rainy weather and intense heat, when it was fair (tho' these may have been equally disadvantageous to them) has been greatly delayed. Several of our men have fallen sick from these causes, and a few unfortunately have fainted and died in a little time after. We have a select and strong detachment more forward under the general command of Major Genl. Lee, with orders to attack their rear, if possible. Whether the detachment will be able to come up with it, is a matter of question, especially before they get into strong grounds.
>
> Besides this, Morgan with his corps and some bodies of militia are on their flanks. I cannot determine yet, at what place they intend to embark. Some think they will push for Sandy Hook, whilst other[s] suppose they mean to go to Shoal Harbour. The latter opinion seems to be founded in the greatest probability, as, from intelligence, several vessels and craft are lying off that place.
>
> We have made a few prisoners, and they have lost a good many men by desertion. I cannot ascertain their number, as they came in to our advanced parties and pushed immediately into the country. I think five or six hundred is the least number that have come in, in the whole. They are chiefly foreigners.[153]

Monmouth Court House
28 June 1778

The most accurate account of this engagement came from Washington himself, in a letter to the President of Congress, published in the *Virginia Gazette* in July 1778. While some of this account of the Army's preparation and deployment before 28 June has already been alluded to, Washington's descriptions of the weather and condition of his troops makes a fuller narrative desirable.

The American deployment.

... The slow advance of the enemy had greatly the air of design, and led me, with others, to suspect that General Clinton, desirous of a general action, was endeavouring to draw us down into the lower country, in order, by a rapid movement to gain our right, and take possession of the storng grounds above us. This consideration, and to give troops time to repose and refresh themselves from the fatigues they had experienced from rainy and excessive hot weather, determined me to halt at Hopewell township, about five miles from Princetown, where we remained till the morning of the 25th.

On the preceding day I made a second detachment of 1500 chosen troops under Brigadier Genl Scott, to reinforce those already in the vicinity of the enemy, the more effectually to annoy and delay the march. The next day the Army moved to Kingston, and having received intelligence that the enemy was prosecuting their rout toward Monmouth Court House, I dispatched a third detachment of a thousand select men under Brigadier General Wayne and sent the Marquis de la Fayette to take the command of the whole advance corps, including Maxwells Brigade and Morgans light infantry; with orders to take the fair opportunity of attacking the enemy's rear.

In the evening of the same day, the whole Army marched from Kingston where our baggage was left, with intention to preserve a proper distance for supporting the advanced corps, and arrived at Cranberry early the next morning. The intense heat of the weather, and a heavy storm unluckily coming on made it impossible to resume our march that day without great inconvenience and injury to the troops.

Our advanced corps, being differently circumstanced, moved from the position it had held the night before, and took post in the evening on the Monmouth Road, about five miles from the enemy's rear; in expectation of attacking them the next morning on their march. The main body having remained at Cranberry, the advanced corps was found to be too remote, and too far upo0n the right to be supported either in case of an attack upon, or from the enemy, which induced me to send orders to the Marquis to file off by his left towards English town, which he accordingly executed early in the morning of the 27th.

The enemy in marching from Allentown had changed their disposition, and placed their best troops in the rear, consisting of all the grenadiers, light infantry, and chauffeurs of the line. This alteration made it necessary to increase the number of our advanced corps; in consequence of which I detached Major General Lee with two brigades to join the Marquis at Englishtown, on whom, of course, the command of the whole devolved, amounting to about five thousand men. The main body marched the same day, and encamped within three miles of that place. Morgan's corps was left hovering on the enemy's right flank, and the Jersey militia, amounting at this time to about seven or eight hundred mend, under General Dickinson, on their left.

The enemy's position.

The enemy were now encamped in a strong position, with their right extending about a mile and a half beyond the Court House, in the parting of the roads leading to Shrewsbury and Middletown, and their left along the road from Allen Town to Monmouth, about three miles on this side the Court House.

Their right flank lay on a skirt of a small-wood, while their left was secured by a very thick one, and a morass running towards their rear, and their whole front covered by a wood, and for a considerable extent towards the left with a morass. In this situation they halted till the morning of the 28th.

Washington's Plan: Attack the British rear guard with the advanced corps.

>Matters being thus situated, and having had the best information, that if the enemy were once arrived at the Heights of Middletown, ten or twelve miles from where they were, it would be impossible to attempt anything against them with a prospect of success. I determined to attack their rear the moment they should get in motion from their present ground. I communicated my intention to General Lee, and ordered him to make his disposition for the attack, and to keep his troops constantly lying upon their arms, to be in readiness at the shortest notice. This was done with respect to the troops under my immediate command.

The British front lines begin to move.

>About five in the morning General Dickinson sent an express, informing that the front of the enemy had began their march, I instantly put the Army in motion, and sent orders by one of my Aids to General Lee to move on and attack them, unless there should be very powerful reasons to the contrary; acquainting him at the same time, that I was marching to support him and for doing it with the greater expedition and convenience, should make the men disencumber themselves of their packs and blankets.

General Lee orders a retreat of advanced guard without encountering opposition.

>After marching about five miles, to my great surprise and mortification, I met the whole advance corps retreating, and, as I was told, by General Lee's orders, without having made any opposition, except one fire given by a party under the command of Colo. Butler, on their being charged by the enemy's cavalry, who were repulsed.

Washington and other officers halt the advance of the enemy on the advanced corps.

>I proceeded immediately to the rear of the corps, which I found closely pressed by the enemy, and gave directions for forming part of the retreating troops, who by the brave and spirited conduct of the officers, and aided by some pieces of well served Artillery, checked the enemy's advance, and gave time to make a disposition of the left wing and second line of the Army upon an eminence, and in a wood a little in the rear covered by a morass in front. On this were placed some batteries of cannon by Lord Stirling who commanded the left wing, which played upon the enemy with great effect, and seconded by parties of infantry detached to oppose them, effectually put a stop to their advance.

General Greene moves the right wing up to join Washington on the right.

>General Lee being detached with the advance corps, the command of the right wing, for the occasion, was given to General Greene. For the expedition of the march, and to counteract any attempt to turn our right, I had ordered him to file off by the new church two miles from English Town, and fall into the Monmouth road, a small distance in the rear of the Court House, while the rest of the column moved directly on towards the Court House. On intelligence of the retreat, he marched up and took a very advantageous position on the right.

General Poor received orders to move around the right flank, General Woodford, around the left flank of the enemy.

>In this situation, the enemy had both their flanks secured by thick woods and morasses, while their front could only be approached thro a narrow pass. I resolved nevertheless to attack them, and for that purpose ordered General Poor with his own and the Carolina Brigade, to move round upon their right, and General Woodford upon their left, and the Artillery to gall them in front. The Troops advanced with great spirit to execute their orders. But the impediments in their way prevented their getting within reach before it was dark.
>They remained upon the ground, they had been directed to occupy, during the night, with intention to begin the attack early the next morning, and the army continued lying upon their arms in the field of action, to be in readiness to support them.

The British retreat, undetected.

In the meantime, the enemy was employed in removing their wounded, and about 12 Oclock at night marched away in such silence, that tho' General Poor lay extremely near them, they effected their retreat without his knowledge. They carried off all their wounded except four officers and about fifty privates whose wounds were to dangerous to permit their removal.

Washington decides not to pursue, due to fatigue and weather.

The extreme heat of the weather, the fatigue of the men from their march thro' a deep, sandy country almost entirely destitute of water, and the distance the enemy had gained by marching in the night, made a pursuit impracticable and fruitless. It would have answered no valuable purpose, and would have been fatal to numbers of our men, several of whom died the preceeding day with heat.

FIGURE 6. The scene at Monmouth[154]

Praise for the officers and troops.

Were I to conclude my account of this day's transactions without expressing my obligations to the officers of the army in general, I should do injustice to their merit, and violence to my own feelings. They seemed to vie with each other in manifesting their zeal and bravery. The catalogue of those who distinguished themselves is too long to admit of particularizing individuals; I cannot however forbear mentioning Brigadier General Wayne whose good conduct and bravery thro' the whole action deserves particular commendation.

The behaviour of the troops in general, after they recovered from the first surprised occasioned by the retreat of the advanced corps, was such as could not be surpassed.

All the Artillery both officers and men that were engaged, distinguished themselves in a remarkable manner.

Return of losses for Americans and British troops.

Inclosed Congress will be pleased to receive a return of the killed, wounded and missing. Among the first were Lieut. Colo. Bunner of Penna and Major Dickinson of Virginia, both officers of distinguished merit and much to be regretted. The enemys slain left on the filed and buried by us, according to the return of the persons assigned to that duty were four officers and two hundred and forty five privates. In the former number was the Honble Colo Monckton. Exclusive of these they buried some themselves, as there were several new graves on and near the field of battle. How many men they may have had wounded cannot be determined; but from the usual proportion to the slain, the number must have been considerable. There were a few prisoners taken…

Washington places Lee under arrest, to await a Court Martial into his conduct.

The peculiar situation of General Lee at this time requires that I should say nothing of his conduct. He is now in arrest. The charges against him, with such sentence as the Court Martial may decree in his case, shall be transmitted for the approbation or disapprobation of Congress as soon as it shall have passed.

FIGURE 7. Washington relieving General Lee of command.[155]

Washington decides to harass the British withdrawal with a detachment of a New Jersey brigade, Morgan's corps and other light parties.

> Being fully convinced by the gentlemen of this country that the enemy cannot be hurt or injured in their embarkation at Sandy Hook the place to which they are going, and being unwilling to get too far removed from the North River, I put the troops in motion early this morning and shall proceed that way, leaving the Jersey Brigade, Morgan's corps and other light parties (the militia being all dismissed) to hover about them, countenance desertion and to prevent their depredations, as far as possible. After they embark the former will take post in the neighbourhood of Elizabeth Town. The latter rejoin the corps from which they were detached.[156]

THE ROLE OF THE VIRGINIA BRIGADES AT MONMOUTH.

While Washington's account provided an over-all description of this battle, it did not precisely define the part the various brigades played in the action, especially those Virginia brigades associated with Lafayette and Woodford.

When Lee went to take over the overall command of the advanced corps, Washington sent further reinforcements of Virginia and Massachusetts regulars under the immediate command of Colonel William Grayson of Virginia. When Grayson's command arrived at Englishtown very early in the morning of 28 June, Lee ordered him to Tennant Meeting house, two miles from Monmouth Court House. He followed, arriving around five in the morning with Lafayette's, Wayne's and Scott's detachments.

By this time, Clinton was already on the move, having left Cornwallis to guard the rear with nearly 2000 grenadiers and dragoons. When Lee learned of this, he ordered Grayson's troops to attack. As Grayson prepared to carry out these orders, his men came upon General Dickinson's New Jersey militia fleeing from the scene. The militiamen had mistakenly thought that Cornwallis's men were the entire enemy force. Grayson and Dickinson were discussing this when Lee arrived. With this information, Lee thought that Clinton's portion of the British army had left Monmouth, so he sent his advanced corps across a causeway, flanked on either side by swamp, to rout the enemy's covering party on the other side.

Sir Henry Clinton, realizing that his force was in danger of being surrounded and outflanked, sent dragoons and a brigade of foot to reinforce Cornwallis. Cornwallis now was able to put increasing pressure upon the American advance corps which was forced to give way. This placed the Pennsylvania and Virginia brigades of Anthony Wayne and Charles Scott in peril. When the advanced force was forced to retreat, Wayne and Scott and their men were abandoned. Grayson's troop was decimated.

When Washington arrived, he was mortified to learn that the entire advance corps was retreating, he was told, by the orders of General Lee.[157]

> Coming abreast of Lee still floundering in a morass of conflicting orders, [Washington] demanded an explanation. Lee muttered something about false intelligence and an attack against his better judgement. Washington peremptorily ordered him to the rear and took over his command.[158]

Now that the rear guard had held under Cornwallis against the advanced American forces, Sir Henry Clinton, the British commander-in-chief, decided to use that opportunity to bring about a general engagement with the American forces. Thanks to the training and discipline instilled in the rebel forces by Baron von Steuben over the long winter at Valley Forge, Colonel Henry Livingston's New York regiments halted the enemy's advance. This allowed the artillery to shift into action. Greene's artillery and the 1st Continental artillery, assisted by covering fire from Brigadier General William Woodford's brigade, swept the length of the British left wing and center with cannon fire.

The Americans were able to bring their lines together on ground behind the west morass. Greene's division was in firm possession of the right wing. Wayne's Pennsylvania troops were deployed along a hedge row just forward of the American center. Stirling held the left wing.

When Clinton attacked the left wing, Stirling's troops held. As the British attack wavered, two New Hampshire regiments and the 1st Virginia rushed in from the extreme right flank, forcing the redcoats back. When this maneuver failed, Clinton ordered Cornwallis's elite troops to attack the right wing under Greene. General Peter Muhlenberg with his and Weedon's brigades saw action in this confrontation. The attack failed.

And what of the 3rd Virginia and Woodford's brigade? The brigade fought under for a time under Lafayette in Lee's division and then under Greene. Those in Woodford and Scott's brigade under Lafayette fought in the thick of the action, as part of the advanced corps. Part of the brigade apparently were detached to go with Greene as they added covering fire to the enfilade of cannon fire alluded to above.

A twentieth century historian has summed up involvement of the 3rd Virginia regiment at Monmouth as follows: "the Fauquier men in the 3rd Virginia Regiment under Heth, and John Cropper's 11th Regiment bore the palm" of the battle.[159] They were, then, in the very heart of the action.

3rd Virginia veterans remember Monmouth.

Long after the battle, veterans who applied for pensions remembered Monmouth. Although they gave no details of what happened, veterans in Captains Arell, Ashby, Chilton, Washington, and Briscoe all stated they had been at Monmouth.

Table 10. Some Virginia veterans who mention Monmouth in pension applications.

Name	Captain	Comments
James Alverson[160]	Val Peyton	
John Atkinson[161]	David Arell	
Moses Allen[162]	John Chilton	
	John Blackwell	
Charles Baker[163]	John Ashby	
Isaac Barr[164]	John Ashby	
John Bridges[165]	William Washington	
Philip Conner[166]	Charles West	
Samuel Cox	John Ashby	"severely wounded at Monmouth"[167]
John Cockerill[168]	John Ashby	

Charles Bettisworth, who had enlisted in February 1778 in Captain Reuben Briscoe's company as a substitute, said he was not at the battle, "being a raw recruit with his gun out of repair." He and others, he stated, were placed as a "guard over the baggage wagons, stationed about 1 ½ miles from the action."[169]

Factors in the success at Monmouth: Baron von Steuben's training.

Beyond a doubt, one of the paramount grounds for the success at both Barren Hills and Monmouth was the training and discipline instilled into the American troops by an irascible Prussian Lieutenant General, Friedrich Wilhelm Augustus von Steuben. In February 1778, he appeared to offer his services to Washington and his army. Together with Nathanael Greene and Alexander Hamilton, he developed a training program for the troops.

He stood before the shivering, half-starved provincials in a magnificent uniform and put on a show worthy of paid admission. According to tradition, when he could no longer curse his awkward recruits in German and French he would call on his French-speaking American aide, Capt. Benjamin Walker to swear for him in English: '*Viens*, Walker, *mon ami*...Goddam de *gaucheries of* dese *badauts* ... '[170]

FIGURE 8. Von Steuben training the troops.[171]

Roughly translated, he said, "Come, Walker, my friend, Goddamn the awkwardness of these idlers." It worked. Baron von Steuben transformed these troops into a disciplined fighting force. Heretofore, soldiers were prone to question orders from superiors, especially if they did not understand their necessity. They also were reluctant to march about aimlessly barefoot and without sufficient winter clothing to keep out the bitter cold. Baron von Steuben managed to put iron into their backs and resolve into their character. The hard work paid off.[170]

Lafayette was the first recipient to enjoy this new training—at Barren Hills when he was able to turn his men and escape the British ambush. At Monmouth, the discipline showed itself once more when Livingston's New Yorkers stiffened and halted the British, giving time for the artillery and Woodford's men to deploy. He was with Washington and helped steady the men during the last attack by the British before they retreated.[172]

Epilogue

The Philadelphia campaign which had begun as a defense for Philadelphia finally ended in June 1778. The previous fall had seen defeats at Brandywine and Germantown which opened the city to the British. After the skirmish at White Marsh, the Americans had gone into winter quarters at Valley Forge. The army that left Valley Forge in May was a different one that entered those winter quarters. It emerged stronger and more discipline, in good spirits and renewed resolve. In June 1778, troops entered Philadelphia again, claiming it again for Congress. The Battle at Monmouth Courthouse resulted in a British retreat. The summer campaign *was* this battle. Clinton retired, to nurse his wounds in New York. Washington soon followed, setting up his headquarters at White Plains.

Meanwhile, the composition of the 3rd Virginia had been altered almost beyond recognition from the regiment of 1776. The regiment was left with a few veterans and those men who were recruited between January and December 1777 and January and May 1778. Those who enlisted in 1777 may have fought at Brandywine although some had been sequestered either in Virginia or Philadelphia to be inoculated for small pox. They arrived too late for Brandywine; instead they saw action at Germantown. Recruitment still proved difficult. These efforts were not improved when Captain Phill Lee had died in January 1778 and Captain David Arell resigned in February 1778.

The last battle for the men of the 3rd Virginia was Monmouth Court house. The regiment was already in transition—with the conversion of these new recruits—transformed by von Steuben—into an efficient fighting force.

September 1778, White Plains: Reorganization of the Virginia Line.

In September 1778 at White Plains, Washington reorganized the Virginia line, which was still lacking more than 2000 recruits. The 1st and 9th Virginia was combined under Colonel Richard Parker. The 2nd and 6th Virginia was merged together under the command of Colonel Christian Febiger. The 3rd and 5th Virginia was combined under Colonel Wm. Heth. The 4th and 8th Virginia was consolidated under Colonel John Neville. Then the 7th Virginia became the new 5th Virginia under Colonel Wm. Russell. The 10th through the 15th Virginia regiments were renumbered as the 6th through the 10th Virginia.

Officers in eliminated regiments became supernumeraries "unless a vacancy of equal rank existed in the regiment with which theirs was combined." Thus, John Tebbs of the old 3rd Virginia became a supernumerary Captain. He was forced into this status in the new combined 3rd & 5th Virginia when no Captaincy was available for him in the newly consolidated 3rd Virginia.

September 1776 to September 1778: Full circle for the 3rd Virginia.

The need for defense in December 1776 was responsible for the creation of the original six Virginia Regiments, one of which was the 3rd Virginia. Once the regiment had been created, staffing it was next on the agenda. With officers appointed with continental commissions, recruitment went smoothly. Men signed on between February and April 1777 for a tour of two years. By June, the field officers had been taken care of and the regiment started north to join Washington's army in New York.

In September 1776, the 3rd Virginia received its baptism as a continental line regiment at Harlem Heights. The regiment went on to participate in the skirmishes and battles fought in New York, New Jersey, and Pennsylvania over the next two years. They spent a horrifying winter in Morristown in 1777, watching helplessly as comrades died by the dozens between January and March 1777. They spent a terrible winter at Valley Forge, bereft of basic necessities—clothes, shoes, stockings, blankets, arms.

Many went home in January, February, and March their enlistments over. Now the regiment had to depend on its 1777 and 1778 recruits—those who enlisted for a three year tour or for the war—along with the few veterans who remained. The officer corps, by and large, remained intact, losing only Phill Lee and David Arell. Thanks to von Steuben, the regiment was learning to become a well-ordered, disciplined unit.

After Monmouth, the 3rd Virginia, now a well-ordered, disciplined unit, returned to New York, where their continental line experience had begun. They had come full circle.

FIGURE 9. Soldiers, Continental Line.[173]

END NOTES
CHAPTER 6 BATTLES, 3
OCTOBER 1777 TO JUNE 1778

1. NARA, *William Heth's compiled service records*, 3rd Virginia.
2. NARA, no. 51. 3 November 1777, *Weekly Return of the Continental Army in Pennsylvania, Woodford's Brigade*, M 246 MR 137, Returns of the Army.
3. Ibid., no. 47. 10 November 1777, *General Return of the Continental Army at White Marsh.*
4. University of Virginia, *George Washington to the President of Congress*, Camp near Potts Grove, 23 September 1777, *WW*, 9, pg. n.g (http://etext.virginia.edu).
5. Ibid.
6. Clement Biddle was the Commissary-General of Forage from 1 July 1777 to June 1780. See Heitman, 102.
7. University of Virginia, *George Washington to Colonel Clement Biddle*, Camp near Potts Grove, 26 September 1777, *WW*, 9, pg. n.g (http://etext.virginia.edu).
8. Ibid., *George Washington to Brigadier General William Woodford*, given at Headquarters, 6 October 1777.
9. Ibid., *George Washington to the President of Congress*, at Camp, 26 miles from Philadelphia, 10 October 1777.
10. Ibid., *George Washington to the President of Congress*, Headquarters, 13 October 1777.
11. This return was no. 51, filed in November 1777. See note 2 above. See also Lesser, 50–51.
12. Heitman, 387.
13. See note 10 above.
14. Cartouche boxes were usually a small, thin paper box meant to carry ball and powder needed to load one round in a firearm. Here it appears that Washington is actually referring to cartridge boxes, which are usually made of cloth or leather. Cartridge boxes "usually hung from the waist by a belt-loop." See Drake, 36.
15. See note 10 above.
16. Ibid.
17. Rhodehamel, *Washington, Writings*, 274.
18. University of Virginia, *George Washington to the President of Congress*, Headquarters, 24 October 1777, *WW*, 9, pg. n.g (http://etext.virginia.edu).
19. Ibid. See also Boatner, 382–383, for the particulars of the repulse of Hessian troops at Fort Mercer and the shelling of the enemy troops from American river vessels below.
20. See note 18 above.
21. University of Virginia, *George Washington to the President of Congress*, Headquarters at White Marsh, 1 November 1777, *WW*, 9, pg. n.g (http://etext.virginia.edu).
22. Ibid.
23. Ibid.
24. See NARA, 3rd Virginia compiled service records for Thomas Terry, Hugh Ferguson, and James McGlothlin, for just three of the soldiers in Captain Lee's company whose muster rolls for March through May listed the company as "Late Captain Lee's company."
25. Ibid., *George Jeffrey's and William Kent's compiled service records*, 3rd Virginia. These were two soldiers whose service records indicated that Captain David Arell's company, after February 1778 was "Late Captain Arell's.
26. University of Virginia, *George Washington to the President of Congress*, Headquarters, White Marsh, 8 November 1777, *WW*, 10. pg. n.g (http://etext.virginia.edu).
27. Ibid., *General Orders*, Headquarters, White Marsh, 26 November 1777.
28. Ibid., *Powers to Officers to Collect Clothing*, Headquarters, November 1777; *George Washington to Governor Patrick Henry*, Headquarters, White Marsh, 13 November 1777; *George Washington to the President of Congress*, Headquarters at White Marsh, 17 November 1777; *George Washington to the President of Congress*, Headquarters at White Marsh, 1 December 1777; *George Washington to Governor Patrick Henry*, Headquarters at White Marsh, 10 December 1777; and *George Washington to Governor Patrick Henry*, from Camp 14 miles from Philadelphia, 19 December 1777.
29. Ibid., *Powers to Officers to Collect Clothing &c* Headquarters, November 1777.
30. Ibid., *George Washington to Governor Patrick Henry*, Headquarters at White Marsh, 13 November 1777.
31. VHS, *David Griffith to his wife Hannah*, at White Marsh, 13 November 1777, Mss 2 G 8755a1, *Letters &c of David Griffith*, VHS, Richmond.

32. University of Virginia, *George Washington to the President of Congress,* Headquarters at White Marsh, 17 November 1777, *WW,* 10, pg n.g (http://etext.virginia.edu).
33. Ibid.
34. Ibid., *George Washington to the President of Congress,* Headquarters, 1 December 1777.
35. NARA, no. 48, 3 December 1777, *General Return of the Continental Army at White Marsh, Pennsylvania, General Woodford's Brigade,* M 247 MR 137 *Returns of the Army.*
36. University of Virginia, *George Washington to Governor Patrick Henry,* Headquarters at White Marsh, 10 December 1777, *WW,* 10, pg n.g (http://etext.virginia.edu).
37. Ibid.
38. NARA, no. 49. 22 December 1777, *General Return at Valley Forge, Woodford's Brigade.*
39. Ibid., no. 50. 31 December 1777, *General Returns at Valley Forge, Woodford's Brigade.*
40. See totals in the two returns posted at Valley Forge as referenced in notes 38 and 39 above.
41. See page 160.
42. Gott and Russell, 243.
43. VHS, *David Griffith to his wife Hannah,* from Camp at White Marsh, 13 November 1777, Mss 2G 8755b, *Letters &c of David Griffith,* VHS, Richmond.
44. University of Virginia, *George Washington to the President of Congress,* Headquarters 26–27 November 1777, *WW,* 10, pg n.g (http://etext.virginia.edu).
45. Gott and Russell, 243
46. Colonial Williamsburg Foundation, "Colonel Morgan near Germantown" *Virginia Gazette* (Dixon), 14 November 1777, 2, col. 1 (http://research.history.org).
47. Ibid., "Morgan joins Washington's Army," *Virginia Gazette* (Dixon), 28 November 1777, 2, col. 1.
48. University of Virginia, *George Washington to Brigadier General William Woodford,* Headquarters, 15 November 1777, *WW,* 10, pg n.g (http://etext.virginia.edu).
49. VHS, *David Griffith to his wife Hannah,* Mss 2G 8755b, *Letters &c of David Griffith,* Richmond.
50. For details of siege and evacuation of Fort Mercer, see Boatner, 382–383; for loss of Fort Mifflin, Boatner, 383–384.
51. NARA, no. 47. 10 November 1777, *Return of Continental Army at White Marsh, Pennsylvania, Woodford's Brigade.*
52. Ibid.
53. Gott and Russell, 237–238.
54. See Chapter 7 for full details of the part Morgan's riflemen played in this skirmish.
55. University of Virginia, *Order of Battle, 4–5 December 1777, WW,* 10, pg n.g (http://etext.virginia.edu).
56. Library of Virginia, *George Weedon to John Page,* Accession 22954a, *George Weedon Papers,* LVA, Richmond.
57. Boatner, 1199–1200.
58. See note 56.
59. Boatner, 1199.
60. VHS, *David Griffith to his wife Hannah,* Mss 2G 8755b *Letters &c of David Griffith,* VHS, Richmond.
61. Ibid.
62. Ibid.
63. Ibid.
64. Gott and Russell, 238.
65. NARA, no. 49. 22 December 1777, *General Return at Valley Forge, Woodford's Brigade.*
66. Ibid., no. 52. 23 December 1777, *Field Return.*
67. Ibid., no. 50. 31 December 1777, *General Return at Valley Forge, Woodford's Brigade.*
68. NARA, *George Strong's Compiled Service Record,* 3rd Virginia.
69. See NARA, no. 49. 22 September 1777, *Return for Woodford's Brigade.*
70. NARA, *Peter Williams's compiled service records,* 3rd Virginia.
71. Ibid., *Henry Martrim's compiled service records.*
72. Ibid., *Robert Slaughter's, Francis Hagen's and Philip Langford's compiled service records.*
73. Ibid., The compiled service cards for these eight men contain the date of their discharge, found in the compiled service records of the 3rd Virginia.
74. Ibid.

75. The muster rolls and pay rolls for the 3rd Virginia are found on NARA, *Revolutionary War Rolls*, M 246 MR 97–98. Unfortunately many of these rolls are extremely difficult to decipher due to their age and condition. These facts make the carded information extracted from the rolls all the more valuable to researchers.

76. See the compiled service records for the 3rd Virginia in M 881 MR 951–956. These records were extracted from the muster rolls and payrolls, which contained the data on the sick personnel in the regiment.

77. See Chapter 2 for the changes in the 3rd Virginia on a company level.

78. Sanchez-Saavedra, 40.

79. NARA, *Henry Westall's compiled service records*, 3rd Virginia.

80. Ibid., See the compiled service records for the 3rd Virginia, listed in this table, on M 881, MR 951–956, *CSR, 3rd Virginia*.

81. Gott & Russell, 243.

82. For example, the men receiving early discharges or discharges in February 1778 included eighteen men in Captain Arell's company, twenty-one men in Captain Ashby's Company, and nearly all of Captain Blackwell's men, among the companies of the regiment. See the compiled service records for the 3rd Virginia for dates of discharge of men who enlisted in 1776 for two years in the 3rd Virginia on NARA, *compiled service records* 3rd Virginia.

83. NARA, *Burr Harris's compiled service records*, 3rd Virginia.

84. Ibid., *George Armstrong's compiled service records*.

85. Ibid.

86. Ibid., *Spencer Anderson's compiled service records*.

87. Ibid., *Francis Turner's compiled service records* .

88. Ibid., *Moses Dalton's compiled service records*.

89. Ibid., *James Kehoe's compiled service records*.

90. Ibid., *John Randolph's compiled service records*.

91. Ibid., *John Well's compiled service records*.

92. Ibid., *Charles Colley's, Thomas Cosby's and James Harris's compiled service records*, 3rd Virginia.

93. Ibid., *Thomas Kane's compiled service records*.

94. Ibid., See the 3rd Virginia compiled service records for these men.

95. Gott & Russell, 246.

96. Ibid., 247.

97. Ibid., 250–256.

98. Service records for William Bawcutt, Jonathan Crooke, Benjamin Hamrick, and Daniel Pennington may be found on NARA, *Compiled service records for 3rd & 4th Virginia*, M 881 MR 957–970. John Walton's compiled service record is found in the compiled service records for the 3rd Virginia. Richard Basye's compiled service record for the 3rd Virginia ends with his discharge on 14 February 1778. He was not found in the compiled service records for the 3rd & 4th Virginia. See NARA, *Richard Basye's compiled service records*, 3rd Virginia.

99. Gott and Russell, 266.

100. Heitman, 328.

101. Gott and Russell, 266.

102. See NARA for the compiled service records for the 3rd & 4th Virginia, on M 881 MR 957–970 for men who enlisted in the 3rd Virginia companies in 1777 and 1778.

103. See Chapter 2, Table 1, page 44; and Chapter 3, pages 65–67 for details regarding the condition of Woodford's Brigade between January and June 1778.

104. See note 102 above.

105. NARA, No. 67. 9 May 1778, *Weekly Returns at Valley Forge, Woodford's Brigade*, M 246 MR 137 *Returns of the Army*.

106. Gott and Russell, 261–262.

107. Ibid., 263.

108. University of Virginia, *General Orders*, Headquarters, Valley Forge, 7 May 1778, *WW*, 11, pg. n.g (http://etext.virginia.edu).

109. Ibid., *George Washington to Marquis de Lafayette*. The memorial was extracted from the end note attached to this letter.

110. Ibid., *George Washington to Marquis de Lafayette*, the text of the letter itself as referenced in note 109.

111. Gott & Russell, 273.

112. Ibid, 112.

113. University of Virginia, *Council of War*, Headquarters, Valley Forge, 8 May 1778, *WW*, 11, pg. n.g (http://etext.virginia.edu).

114. Ibid., See foot note accompanying the above Council of War.
115. Gott and Russell, 273.
116. Lieutenant John Hill Carter was court-martialed for neglect of duty for this although the Court thought Carter had misunderstood Captain McLane's orders which "considerably alleviated his neglect of duty." Washington approved a reprimand, discharged the Lieutenant from arrest so he could return to his regiment. Washington "hopes that he will in the future, he said, "pay very strict attention to the orders of his commanding officer, as he must plain perceive the ill effects that have arisen from misapprehension." See University of Virginia, *General Orders,* Headquarters, Valley Forge, 14 May 1778, *WW,* 11, pg. n.g (http://etext.virginia.edu).
117. Ibid., *George Washington to Marquis de Lafayette*, Headquarters 18 May 1778.
118. Heitman, 373.
119. Gott & Russell, 274. See also Wayne Bodle, *Valley Forge Winter* (University Park, Pennsylvania, Pennsylvania State University Press, 2002), 235–238.
120. Colonial Williamsburg Foundation, "Skirmish at Barren Hill," *Virginia Gazette,* (Purdie) 12 June 1778, 2, col. 1 (http://research.history.org). See also Boatner, 59–60.
121. Rhodehamel, *George Washington, Writings,* 312.
122. Ibid.
123. VHS, *David Griffith to his wife Hannah,* Mss 2G 8766b, *Letters &c of David Griffith,* VHS, Richmond.
124. University of Virginia, *George Washington to Brigadier General Charles Scott, WW,* 11, pg. n.g (http://etext.virginia.edu).
125. Lesser, 68. The only return for May 1778 is the return dated 30 May 1778.
126. Ibid.
127. Ibid.
128. Colonial Williamsburg Foundation, "Orders from General Washington, Headquarters, Valley Forge, 29 May 1778" *Virginia Gazette* (Purdie), 12 June 1778, 2, col. 2 (http://research.history.org).
129. See page 176 and end notes 121 and 122.
130. University of Virginia, *George Washington to John Augustine Washington,* Camp near Valley Forge, 10 June 1778, *WW,* 12, pg. n.g (http://etext.virginia.edu).
131. Ibid.
132. Ibid.
133. Boatner, 856.
134. University of Virginia, *Council of War,* Headquarters, Valley Forge, 17 June 1778, *WW,* 12, pg. n.g (http://etext.virginia.edu).
135. Taafe, 208.
136. University of Virginia, *George Washington to Major General Charles Lee,* 18 June 1778, *WW,* 12, pg. n.g (http://etext.virginia.edu).
137. Ibid., *Order of March from Valley Forge,* 17 June 1778 & *Order of March from Valley Forge,* 18 June 78.
138. Ibid., *George Washington to the President of Congress,* 20 June 1778.
139. Ibid., *General Orders,* Headquarters, Coryell's Ferry, and 22 June 1778.
140. Gott & Russell, 277.
141. There were no returns filed for 22 June 1778 in the *Returns of the Army,* M 246, MR 137.
142. University of Virginia, *Council of War,* Hopewell New Jersey, 24 June 1778, *WW,* 12, pg. n.g (http://etext.virginia.edu).
143. Ibid. See also Taafe, 209 and Gott and Russell, 277–278.
144. Taafe, 209.
145. Ibid.
146. Ibid., 210.
147. University of Virginia, *George Washington to Marquis de Lafayette,* Kingston, 25 June 1778, *WW,* 12, pg. n.g (http://etext.virginia.edu).
148. Ibid., See also note 22.
149. Taafe, 210.
150. Ibid.
151. Ibid., 211.
152. Ibid.
153. University of Virginia, *George Washington to the President of Congress,* Englishtown, 28 June 1778, *WW,* 12, pg. n.g (http://etext.virginia.edu).

154. Grafton, 85
155. Ibid., 83.
156. Colonial Williamsburg Foundation, "General Washington's Account of the Battle at Monmouth Court House, *Virginia Gazette* (Dixon), 1, col. 2; 2, col. 2 & 3 (http://research.history.org).
157. Gott and Russell, 278–279.
158. Ibid., 279. See also Taafe, 218–219.
159. Gott & Russell, 280.
160. NARA, *James Alverson's Pension File* W 8236, M 804 MR 42.
161. Ibid., *John Atkinson's Pension File* S 37683, M 804 MR 807.
162. Ibid., *Moses Allen's Pension File* S 2487, M 804 MR 40.
163. Ibid., *Charles Baker's Pension File* S 45231, M 804 MR 141.
163. Ibid., *Isaac Barr's Pension File* S 41419, M 804 MR 115.
165. Ibid.. *John Bridges's Pension File* W 4904, M 804 MR 333.
166. Ibid., *Philip Conner's Pension File* S 42134, M 804 MR 630.
167. Ibid., *Samuel Cox's Pension File* S 39343, M 804 MR 672.
168. Ibid., *John Cockerell's Pension File* S 353854, M 804 MR 592.
169. Ibid., *Charles Bettisworth's Pension File* S 32117, M 804 MR 230.
170. Boatner, 1055–1057.
170. The translation and comments in this paragraph are my own.
171. Grafton, 79.
172. Boatner, 1057.
173. *American Historical Illustrations & Emblems, CD & Book*, 9.

Chapter 7

The 3ʳᴰ Virginia
& Colonel Daniel Morgan's Light Infantry

June to July 1777: Formation of an independent rifle regiment under the command of Colonel Daniel Morgan.

Early in June 1777, George Washington gave Colonel Daniel Morgan his own independent command, a rifle corps operating as a light infantry corps. This corps consisted of some 500 specially selected Continentals from the western counties of Pennsylvania, Maryland, and Virginia.[1] Twenty-three men from the rifle companies of John Thornton and John Ashby of the 3ʳᵈ Virginia were selected for this independent light infantry command in June 1777 and served through the Saratoga campaign until their discharge, either in December 1777 or February 1778.[2]

In a letter to Colonel Morgan from General Washington, written at headquarters at Middlebrook 13 June 1777, the general called his men a "corps of Rangers newly formed." Washington told Morgan his corps was to be considered as a body of light infantry. For that reason they were exempted from the common duties of the line.

Washington ordered Morgan and his newly formed regiment to the Van Veghten Bridge to watch the enemy's left flank and the roads from Brunswick to Millstone and Princeton. He wanted this done with "very small scouting parties" to avoid fatiguing his men. If the enemy were to move at all, Morgan and his men were to immediately fall upon their flanks. He cautioned the colonel to take care that he was not surrounded or have his retreat to the main army cut off.

Washington had already ordered spears for the regiment as a defence against enemy Light Horse units which he expected to receive and deliver to the men shortly. He again cautioned Morgan to take care not to be caught in any situation which would give the British an advantage. Washington's final bit of advice in this letter dealt with fighting the enemy "Indian style":

> It occurs to me that if you were to dress a company or two of true woods Men in the right Indian style and let them make the attack accompanied with screaming and yelling as the Indians do, it would have very good consequences especially if as little as possible was said, or known of the matter beforehand.[3]

Morgan and his men saw action the next day on the Millstone Road where they temporarily checked the British advance. A few weeks later, Anthony Wayne's brigade, along with Morgan's men, successfully harassed the British as far as Piscataway, leaving the redcoats to retreat to Amboy. The same day, Washington wrote Congress about the encounter and praised the "conduct and bravery of Genl. Wayne and Colo. Morgan and of their officers and men... as they constantly advanced upon an enemy far superior to them in numbers."[4]

Meanwhile Washington was attempting to ascertain the enemy's destination. For a time, it was thought that Howe was going north to meet up with Burgoyne. As a result, Morgan's rifle corps was kept busy marching, waiting and marching again. The last week in July, Washington wrote from the Clove to Morgan:

> While you are lying at Hackinsack you may be subject to a surprise by a party of the enemy from fort Washington; [Expect] you to keep your Guard advanced to Hackinsack Ferry and the Bridge above. Patrolling Parties may safely lay be day at Fort Lee, from whence they may observe what is doing at Fort Washington, or down the River toward New York. When you move it will probably be at a very short warning, you are therefore to hold your Corps in readiness to march in an Hour after you receive Notice either by Night or day ...[5]

When this did not prove to be the case, Washington ordered Morgan, if he had not passed the Delaware River, to halt at Trenton "unless you should receive such information, as you deem authentic of the arrival of the Enemy's Fleet within the Capes of Delaware."

If Morgan had already crossed the river, then he was to proceed to Bristol, unless he obtained satisfactory intelligence of the Enemy's arrival in the Delaware Capes. In that case he was to march to Philadelphia "with the utmost expedition ..."[6]

August 1777: Morgan's Rifle command ordered to proceed to Peekskill, New York.

In August, Washington received disturbing news from upper New York. The Americans there had lost Fort Ticonderoga and Fort Miller to the British under Burgoyne who was now less than forty miles from Albany. Burgoyne's plan, once he reached Albany, was to meet up with General Howe and thus, control the Hudson in order to isolate New England from the rest of the colonies.

Washington moved quickly. First, he persuaded Congress to transfer Benedict Arnold to the Northern Army. He was also under pressure from Congress and New Yorkers, who promoted the idea of assigning Morgan's rifle corps to the same theatre. "Oh for some Virginia rifle-men!" cried an Albany gentleman. "Colonel Morgan's regiment would be of great use this way."[7]

On 16 August 1777, Colonel Morgan received orders from Washington to march with his riflemen and baggage, "as soon as possible" to Peekskill. There the rifle corps was to place themselves under the command of General Putnam, who will have vessels to take them to Albany.

> I know of no other Corps so likely to check their [the British] progress in proportion to their number, as the one you Command. I have great dependence on you, your Officers and Men, and am firmly persuaded, you will do honor to yourselves and essential Service to your Country ...[8]

Horatio Gates, the commander of the Northern Army, found most of his command, including Morgan's men awaiting him on his arrival at the Northern Army headquarters in August 1777.

Washington was able to part with the rifle corps, albeit reluctantly, because General Howe had decided to move his army to Philadelphia by sea. So Washington decided he could spare reinforcements for Gates and chose two of the Continental regiments then at Peekskill along with Morgan's riflemen. Congress was also pressuring the commander-in-chief to do something about the continuing Indian attacks that were terrorizing the northern department, civilians and soldiers alike. It was hoped that the rifle corps would check the Indian and prevent Burgoyne from acquiring intelligence while boosting the morale of the army by ridding them of Indians.

Morgan arrived with so many men on the sick list that he could count on only 374 men who were healthy enough to fight.[9] Added to this pressure was Gates' dependence on the riflemen to scout out an area that was as yet unfamiliar to them. His men were hampered by forests that were impenetrable in places and filled with dense early morning fog.[10] On 13 September, Morgan's men skirmished with the British about two miles away from their Bemis Heights camp.[11]

FIRST BATTLE OF SARATOGA
(A.K.A. FREEMAN'S FARM)
19 SEPTEMBER 1777

Early morning 19 September: As a dense fog lifts, American pickets spot the British on the march.

Gates placed Morgan's riflemen, along with Henry Dearborn's light infantrymen, in the left wing under the command of Benedict Arnold.[12] On Friday, 19 September, both British and American camps were blanketed with a dense fog. When it lifted, American pickets patrolling on the east bank of the Hudson and sentries in the trees spotted what could only be British preparations to attack.

The British artillery and 1200 Germans were forming up to march down the river road. At the same time, the British regiments under Brigadier General Simon Fraser, part of Burgoyne's right wing, were beginning to move ahead with 2200 redcoats, Tories and Indians. Gates, through Arnold, gave Morgan orders to move out, supported by Dearborn, to investigate British movements and if necessary blunt any attack towards the left wing of Arnold's division.[13]

Arnold dispatches Morgan to watch the enemy's left flank.

Accordingly, Arnold dispatched Morgan and Dearborn with instructions to watch the army's left flank and harass any enemy troops that came into sight. Arnold, in a compromised reached with Gates, decided to engage the enemy in a heavily wooded area north of the American camp. If a battle was fought in the forest, Burgoyne could not effectively use his artillery and bayonet charges.

Midday, 19 September: Morgan's riflemen take their position, using the terrain to their advantage.

Around one o'clock, on a warm September afternoon, approximately three hundred riflemen and light infantry advanced through the trees and reached the southern edge of Isaac Freeman's farm. Some moved through the field and took possession of a log hut; others hid behind a rail fence. Still others stationed themselves behind trees or hovered in the branches above. This was a forest of large trees—maples, oak and white pine—which provided shade and relief from the sun and cover from the enemy.

Morgan's riflemen fire on the British and, at British retreat, unwittingly charge into the enemy's massed lines.

Before long, the Americans saw the enemy skirmishers emerging from the tree line, unaware of the waiting Americans.[14]

> Almost invisible in the woods and in back of the rail fence, the riflemen took careful aim, especially at the officers, and along with the Americans waiting inside the log cabin fired with devastating effect, routing [the] astonished redcoats. Running forward for the kill, Morgan's men burst into the open and dashed after the fleeing British, not realizing until too late that they were headed straight for the massed British line.[15]

That charge was very nearly fatal, as the British light infantry commanded by Captain Fraser, brought up cannon and shots hit the unsuspecting Americans squarely on their left flank. Morgan, hearing the shooting, rushed forward to find out what had happened. He found a near disaster. Major Jacob Morris of the Maryland troops in his rifle corps, after forcing the British into a precipitate retreat, had dashed ahead, straight into Burgoyne's center. In their eagerness to escape, the Marylanders scrambled in all directions.

"I am ruined, by God ..."

Morgan was sure that Morris's haste had led to part of his rifle corps' destruction. According to his aide, James Wilkinson, he broke into angry tears. "I am ruined, by God... my men are scattered God knows where."[16] Fortunately Morgan had his ever present turkey call with him and the sharp whistle enabled the riflemen to gather around him so they could retreat into the woods. Captain Van Swearingin of the Pennsylvania light infantry was wounded, and with twelve others, was captured by the British.[17]

Morgan regrouped his rifle corps and moved within sight of Freeman's farm, which was now occupied by Burgoyne's column. The farmhouse was in a clearing about three hundred fifty yards long. At the north end of the clearing, the British artillery and three regiments waited. As Morgan positioned his men just inside the woods, Arnold dispatched two regiments of the New Hampshire line in his command who took up their stations to the Morgan's left.

A full-scale battle ensues ...

A full engagement erupted between Morgan's corps and the Continentals and Burgoyne's regiments. Sheltered by the fall foliage, the Americans opened up and kept up a brisk fire until the British retreated into a pine grove to the north. Quickly reforming, Burgoyne's men executed a bayonet charge, hurling the Americans back across the opening. The riflemen kept behind cover with some climbing trees to get a better view of the action and their targets. The British pointed their artillery at the woods and the resulting cannon shot caused branches to plunge from shattered trees. The noise was deafening.

Through the day, Morgan's men kept their positions and aimed with care at the enemy artillery men. The result? Nearly all the British gunners had been killed or wounded.[18]

By midafternoon, Arnold had thrown his entire division into the battle. As the American battle line moved further and further to the left, Burgoyne became fearful that his right wing might be outflanked so he ordered the 21st Regiment which held the right wing, to turn to the right. This caused the 62nd Regiment in the center to shift slightly to its right, thus exposing both its flanks.

Morgan quickly took advantage of this by ordering his men to concentrate their fire on the 62nd Regiment in the center. Neither side was able to gain a decided advantage in the farmyard. Dearborn and Morgan and their men "rolled the enemy back, only to give way themselves in the face of vicious counterattacks."[19] Burgoyne lost many of his officers from sharpshooter's fire. The same fate held true for tories in the British ranks as the riflemen picked them off as well.

As the afternoon wore on, Burgoyne's situation became critical. His artillery was gone. Many of his companies lacked officers. The 62nd Regiment was nearly annihilated. Sometime after four in the afternoon, Burgoyne got word to the Germans on the river road to reinforce the British center. The Germans responded, appearing on the British left and pushed the Americans from the clearing. As the daylight ended, so did the battle. Morgan and Arnold's Continentals moved back to the American breastworks, leaving the enemy to throw up fortifications on the battlefield.

American and British casualties in the First battle of Saratoga

The American loss was 320 men to the Burgoyne's nearly 600. Though Morgan's corps was the first to engage the enemy and among the last to leave the field, his riflemen suffered very few casualties: four killed, eight wounded, and three missing. Dearborn's losses were more severe: nineteen dead, twenty—two wounded, and three missing.[20]

> Accounts by British participants show that Morgan's corps was the most successful unit engaged that day. The riflemen were primarily responsible for reducing the 62nd Regiment to fewer than 60 effectives, and they also accounted for many of the casualties among Burgoyne's officers and gunners.[21]

Less than a week later, on 24 September 1777 General Washington wrote to General Gates to request that he release Morgan and his men so they could return to the main Army. In a letter written at Camp near Potts Grove, the General admitted to Gates that

> This Army has not been able to oppose Genl. Howe's with the success that was wished and needs a reinforcement. I therefore request, if you have been so fortunate, as to oblige Genl. Burgoyne to retreat to Ticonderoga, or if you have not, and circumstances will admit, that you will order Colo. Morgan to join me again with his Corps. I sent him up, when I thought you materially wanted him, and if his services can be dispensed with now, you will direct his immediate return.
>
> You will perceive, I do not mention this by way of command, but leave you to determine upon it according to your situation. If they come, they should proceed by water from Albany, as low down as Peeks Kill, in such case you will give Colo. Morgan, the necessary orders to join me with dispatch ...[22]

General Gates replied to Washington on October 5, 1777 with a letter of his own:

> Since the Action of the 19th Instant, [ultimo] the enemy have kept the ground they occupied the morning of that day; and fortified their camp. The advanced centrys [sentries] of my picquets, [pickets] are posted within Shot, And opposite the enemy's; neither side have given ground an inch. In this situation, Your Excellency would not wish me to part with the corps the army of General Burgoyne are most afraid of.[23]

Second Battle of Saratoga
(A.K.A. Battle of Bemis Heights)[24]
7 October 1777

September to October: A hiatus in the fighting.

During the next two and a half weeks the Americans put intense pressure on Burgoyne's men; every night there was skirmishing and the rebels forced the British into sleeping in their clothes with their weapons nearby. The British also faced dangerous shortages of food. The enemy began to complain about the chilly October weather as their uniforms became torn and tattered from fighting and by marching through the impenetrable wilderness.

Burgoyne became convinced that he must either retreat for fight his way out to get to Albany. He decided to fight his way out and set out on 7 October to do that very thing. He moved his men across a wheat field. There appeared to be nothing but trees on their front and sides.

Morgan's proposal.

Gates quickly took the initiative and ordered Morgan to "begin the game." Morgan then suggested his own proposal—he and his men would sneak through the woods on the American left to a hill near the British right flank and strike immediately. At the same time another American force could attack Burgoyne's left flank. Gates accepted the idea[25] and ordered Brigadier General Enoch Poor's division, made up of the veterans of the 1st, 2nd, and 3rd New Hampshire Continental line, to attack from the American right flank.

Morgan's riflemen put the British to flight.

Poor's Continentals put the British to flight, captured cannon and turned it on the enemy. Morgan and his men, supported by Dearborn's light infantry, were also on the move. His riflemen had taken longer to reach the field because of their wide swing around the enemy's right flank. Following his plan, he reached the wooded hill 150 yards behind the British right flank. From this vantage point, the men could see Poor's men in action. The firing was intense. The British were positioned behind a rail fence.[26]

As Poor was forcing the British back, Morgan's riflemen poured down the hill and opened fire. As the British changed their front to meet this threat, Dearborn's troops took this opportunity to push forward and attacked the British rear, halting sixty yards from the British positions behind the rail fence. There they discharged their muskets and, jumping the fence, shouting and hollering at the top of their voices, charged with fixed bayonets. Balcarre's light infantry broke and ran, pursued by the Americans for about three-quarters of a mile. Balcarres was able to rally his disoriented troops and formed another line behind a fence, utilizing the 24th Regiment and what remained of his light infantry.

Arnold and Learned attack the Germans.

While all this was going on Arnold, who had been relieved of his command in a power struggle with Gates, decided to take command of Learned's brigade which had been held in reserve. They attacked the Germans with artillery. The whole line of battle, on both sides, erupted into flame and smoke. The Americans were not able to displace the Germans and finally began to withdraw in the face of intense fire. Just as this occurred, Morgan and Dearborn drove Balcarre's forces back, exposing the German flank. The Germans finally began to pull back, seeing that they were now almost completely surrounded.

Morgan's rifles take out Captain Simon Fisher of the 24th Infantry.

Meanwhile, Captain Simon Fraser, mounted on a gray horse, was riding back and forth calmly along his lines, reassuring the light infantry and his own 24th regiment and attempting to form a second line of attack. Morgan, seeing this, called on one of his riflemen, Tim Murphy, "whose skill with his double-barreled rifle was legendary" and told him to "get rid of the man on the gray horse."

Murphy climbed a tree. "His first shot cut the horse's crupper, the strap looped under its tail; his second went through the main, just behind the horse's ears, and an aide pleaded with Fraser, to draw out of range. No, the brigadier said, his duty was here. Murphy's third shot hit him squarely in the stomach, wounding him badly" as he doubled up and fell forward on his horse's neck. The wound was to prove fatal.[27]

Arnold and Morgan combine forces to attack the von Breymann Redoubt.

Arnold, with two brigades, attacked the British center while Morgan made for Burgoyne's redoubt on the right, commanded by Lt. Colonel Heinrich von Breymann's Germans. Arnold's drive was repulsed initially until he cut to his left and led Learned's troops in attacking and taking several cabins held by the Canadians and Indians. Once he was successful there, he joined Morgan's forces, who were besieging the Germans at the Breymann redoubt.

While Morgan was attacking the front of the Breymann redoubt, Arnold came around from behind and assaulted the German's unprotected rear. His charge took the Germans completely by surprise. Unfortunately Arnold was wounded when he rode around the back of the redoubt. He was shot in the leg, his borrowed horse was killed and his leg was broken when the horse fell on top of him. The German commander was dead, killed by his own men, and the redoubt defenders were over whelmed by the American forces. This battle was over.[28]

Burgoyne's casualties were extensive: 184 killed, 264 wounded, 183 captured—631 men, of whom thirty-one were officers. The Germans alone had ninety-four dead, sixty-seven wounded, and 102 captured—more than half his force had been lost.

The American assault on Balcarre's redoubt continues.

Meanwhile, the American assault on the Balcarre's redoubt continued unabated. As night fell, Burgoyne ordered his worn out troops to strike their tents and move in total silence to the heights overlooking the river.[29]

Riflemen continually harrass the British retreat.

The next day was a day of short marches and repeated delays for the British and Germans. At ten in the morning, the heavens opened up and the dispirited British were pummeled by a cold, driving rain. Their rear was continually harassed by American riflemen. At nine that night, the exhausted British troops forded the Fishkill Creek, in water up to their waists and moved on to the heights. They were only eight miles from the battlefield.

Burgoyne gave orders for his men to dig in to the previously arranged fortifications on the heights. The Germans on the right flank found this impossible to dig out foxholes much more than a foot and a half deep, due to the composition of the soil. Out on the perimeter, not far from where Saratoga Lake empties into the Fishkill, the British had thrown up a small redoubt of logs, to serve as an observation point. Three companies crowded into the post, with orders not to start a fight with the Americans.

Morgan's men had other ideas. They had been positioned nearby and every morning at daybreak, climbed into the tall trees nearby where they could fire into the observation post. Several soldiers, who looked over the wall to see what was happening, paid for it with their lives. The grenadiers came up with another less dangerous idea. To see if the riflemen were still about, a grenadier would raise his cap on a pole just high enough to look as if a man was peering over the logs. Almost every time this was done, a bullet would pierce the cap; one time, three bullets smacked into a cap.[30]

Burgoyne seemed to have lost his grasp of the situation. He became indecisive, discipline was deteriorating, and the army's infrastructure was collapsing. Troops were starving because the commissary had neglected to distribute food. Water was scarce. Not one dared to go to the river for water for fear of being picked off by rebel riflemen. Further more, the American artillery barrages were increasing, the British boats were under constant attack and every day, there were more and more skirmishes.

17 October 1777: Burgoyne surrenders.

On 11 October, the rank and file of a German picket guard left their post and deserted to the Americans. By 13 October, the rebel forces had taken 120 prisoners and received 160 deserters. Four days later, Burgoyne surrendered.[31]

The 3rd Virginia Regiment's involvement at Saratoga.

It is not possible to distinguish the part the men from the 3rd Virginia played in the events surrounding the battles fought in September and October at Saratoga. They were, after all, but twenty-three men among five hundred. While they were, on paper at least, part of 3rd Virginia companies, it is not known under which of the captains in Morgan's corps these men actually served.

Only two 3rd Virginia men in Morgan's rifle command died during the Saratoga campaign. According to 3rd Virginia company muster rolls, Thomas Cragin was listed as sick in November 1777 while James Williams were reported as sick in September 1777; both were reported dead in December 1777. Weather conditions being what they were, with rain and a cold October, Privates Cragin and Williams could have caught cold or worse. None of the rest of the men from the 3rd Virginia in Morgan's command were otherwise wounded or killed in these engagements with the British. The names of the men known to have been 3rd Virginia soldiers on command with Colonel Morgan are found in Table 11 on pages 205–206.

November 1777: The return of Morgan's men to Washington's army.

Washington had wanted Morgan and his riflemen back in late September but Gates demurred. "Your Excellency," he said, "would not wish me to part with the corps the army of General Burgoyne are most afraid of."[32] It was not until after the surrender of Burgoyne on 17 October, that Gates sent Morgan and his men back to Washington.

> Tramping southward over roads crowded with homeward-bound militia, the rifle corps reached Fishkill, New York, by October 31. There Morgan attended a council of war convened by General Putnam to assign regiments to garrison duty along the Hudson.
> On the morning of November 2, just beyond New Windsor, New York, Morgan met Hamilton and was exhilarated to learn that his corps was so valuable to the Commander in Chief; of all the officers he ever served under, Morgan respected Washington most. [He] accelerated his pace, even though each day several of his men complained of having to throw away their worn-out shoes.[33]

The *Virginia Gazette* reported that "Morgan's excellent corps of light infantry is by this time near Germantown" in their 14 November 1777 edition.[34] This "excellent corps of light infantry" reached Washington's army, stationed at White Marsh, on 18 November 1777.[35]

Washington kept Morgan's men busy upon his return, giving him the responsibility of reconnoitering the British position up and down the Delaware.[36]

SKIRMISH AT WHITE MARSH
5–8 DECEMBER 1777

When General Howe heard that Washington was moving his troops from Whitemarsh, he and the 10,000 troops under his command moved to the vicinity around Chestnut Hill. He sent out reconnoitering parties to probe the American position to see if the could draw the rebel forces out and into a general engagement. The two armies were within several miles of one another; only a small valley lay between them.[37]

Morgan, sent to keep an eye on the British bombarding American forts on the Delaware, was with Greene when he received orders to return to the American camp. He and his men made good speed since he knew that Howe, now rejoined by Cornwallis, was approaching White Marsh. His rifle command arrived in camp on 7 December.

He and his corps, assisted by Colonel Christopher Gist's Maryland militia, occupied a wooded elevation overlooking the Limekiln Road, a mile or so in front of the American center. Presently a British column under Major General Charles Grey came into view.

At Morgan's command, the Americans opened and sustained a blistering fire as the British hurried toward the protection of the woods. The patriots fought heroically I the furious contest that ensued, despite an overwhelming disadvantage in men.

After a time the Hessian jaegers... and Major John Simcoe's Tory Queen's Rangers gained their opponents' flanks. Morgan, galloping back and forth in an effort to keep a battle line, had his horse shot from under him. At length, he and Gist retired in good order while part of the riflemen, slithering from tree to tree, covered the movement with their deadly marksmanship.[38]

The British commander had enough. So had Howe. The British withdrew to Philadelphia.

George Weedon, in a letter to John Page on 17 December described the skirmish at White Marsh. Wryly, he observed that "Genl Howe is a very troublesome man and will not at all times afford license to write or indeed to sleep ..."

[Howe], by a sudden and rapid march on the night of the 4th instant, possessed a post on this side Chestnut hill within one mile and quarter of our Army. In the morning of the 5th, the two armies lay like Saul & the Philistines with only a small vally between, and a general action every moment expected.

He came out in full force, about 12,000 effectives and declared his intention of routing us. His excellency had previous intelligence of his move & designs, and made the proper disposition for his reception, he spent the 5th and 6th in reconnoitering us, the pickets of the two armies skirmishing alternately. [On] the 7th he maneuvered towards our left wing where Mr Morgan's core [sic] engaged a column and kept up a brisk fire till 3 oClock. At four, it was resumed & continued till dark without being able to bring on anything decisive and that night these mighty men retreated back to their strong lines with precipitation, leaving us masters of the ground, and without attempting the army which was their object.

In the different skirmishes we had about 30 kill'd & wounded; their loss in kill'd, wounded, prisoners & deserters was upwards of 300.

Among our wounded is a Major Morris of [the] Marquis core [sic], a brave and good officer, he is like to recover. Brig[r] Genl Irvin of the Pensylvania [sic] Militia, was in the first skirmish wounded in the hand, was thrown from his horse and made prisoner.

We have now moved the army on this side [of the] Schuylkill where we shall hutt the troops during winter.[39]

Once ensconced in winter quarters at Valley Forge, Morgan and his riflemen had the responsibility "of patrolling the area between Gulph Mills and Radnor Meeting House on the west side of the Schuylkill River." His men were to report the appearance of British foraging parties. He was also given the task of establishing checkpoints on the roads in the area in order to prevent tories from supplying the British with provisions.[40]

Meanwhile, the men in the 3rd Virginia in his command were nearing the end of their enlistments. Martin Wingate, Benjamin Powell, and Mitchell Burk all received early discharges in December 1777.[41] The rest of the 3rd Virginia men in the rifle corps served out their enlistments until their discharge in the early months of 1778.

3rd Virginia riflemen selected by Colonel Morgan for his independent rifle command, June 1776.

Table 11 on the next two pages contains a list of the twenty-three men from the 3rd Virginia who served in Colonel Daniel Morgan's Light Infantry. This table provides the soldier's name and rank, his 3rd Virginia Captain, his service with the Light Infantry, and his enlistment date and discharge, if known. This information was extracted from three sources: NARA, *Revolutionary War Rolls*, M 246 MR 97, *3rd Virginia Regiment*, NARA, Compiled *Service Records*, M 881 MR 951-956, *CSR, 3rd Virginia* and M 881 MR 958 and 960, *CSR, 3rd & 4th Virginia*. While the riflemen served under Morgan after June 1777, they were carried on paper as members of John Ashby's rifle company or of his successor Val Peyton.

Table 11. Men selected by Colonel Daniel Morgan from the 3rd Virginia to serve in his Independent Rifle corps, June, 1776. Abbreviations: All dates abbreviated; Prvt = Private; Corp = Corporal

Name	Rank	Captain	Service with Colonel Morgan
Reuben Bryant	Prvt/Corp	John Ashby	6/ 77to 10/ 77
		Valentine Peyton	11/ 77 to 12/ 77.
			Enlisted March 18, 77 for 2 yrs.
Peter Bryant	Prvt	Valentine Peyton	12/ 77
William Breedlove	Prvt	John Ashby	8/ 77 to 12/ 77
Mitchell Burk	Soldier	John Thornton	6/ 77 to 8/ 77
	Soldier	John Ashby	8/ 77 to 10/ 77
	Soldier	Valentine Peyton	11/ 77
			Discharged 12/1/ 77.
Shadrach Butler	Prvt	John Thornton	6/ 77 to 8/ 77
	Prvt	John Ashby	9/ 77 to 11/ 77
	Prvt	Valentine Peyton	11/ 77 to 12/ 77
			Enlisted 2/12/ 76 for 2 yrs.
Listra Baughan	Prvt	John Ashby	10/ 77
As Listra Vaughan	Prvt	John Thornton	7/ 77 to 9/ 77
	Prvt	Valentine Peyton	11/ 77
John Bazzill	Prvt	John Ashby	10/ 77
Thomas Cragin	Corp	John Ashby	6/ 77 to 11/ 77
			Enlisted 3/18/ 76 for 2 yrs.
			DEAD 12/22/ 77.
Joseph Cromwell	Prvt/Corp	John Ashby	6/ 77 to 2/ 78
			Enlisted 3/18/ 76 for 2 yrs..
Dennis Crow	Soldier	John Thornton	6/ 77 to 1/ 78
John Crow	Prvt	John Thornton	6/ 77 to 7/ 77
	Prvt	John Ashby	8/ 77 to 10/ 77
	Prvt	Valentine Peyton	11/ 77
			Enlisted 2/12/ 76 for 2 yrs.
Reuben Earthern	Prvt	John Ashby	8/ 77 to 10/ 77
		Val Peyton	11/ 77
		Robert Powell	12/ 77
Thomas Gambell	Prvt	John Thornton	6/ 77 to 7/ 77
	Prvt	John Ashby	8/ 77 to 10/ 77
	Prvt	Valentine Peyton	11/ 77 to 1/ 78
			Enlisted 2/12/ 76 for 2 yrs.
William Hinson	Prvt	John Thornton	7/ 77
		John Ashby	8/ 77 to 10/ 77
			Enlisted 2/12/ 76 for 2 yrs.
Baylor Jennings	Prvt	John Ashby	7/ 77; 8/ 77 to 10/ 77.
	Prvt	Valentine Peyton	11/ 77 to 1/ 78
			Enlisted 3/18/ 76 for 2 yrs.

Table 11. (Continued) Men selected by Colonel Daniel Morgan from the 3rd Virginia to serve in his Independent Rifle corps, June 1776.

Name	Rank	Captain	Service with Colonel Morgan
Martin Johnson	Prvt	John Thornton	6/ 77 to 7/ 77
	Prvt	John Ashby	8/ 77 to 10/ 77
	Prvt	Valentine Peyton	11/ 77 to 1/ 78
			Enlisted 2/12/ 76 for 2 yrs.
Abram Milhousan	Prvt	John Ashby	6/ 77 to 10/ 77
	Prvt	Valentine Peyton	11/ 77 to 1/ 78
			Enlisted 3/18/ 76 for 2 yrs.
Benjamin Powell	Prvt	John Thornton	6/ 77 to 7/ 77
	Prvt	John Ashby	8/ 77 to 9/ 77
	Prvt	Valentine Peyton	10/ 77 to 11/ 77
			Enlisted 2/12/ 76 for 2 yrs.
			Discharged 12/3/ 77.
John Slaughter	Corp	John Thornton	6/ 77 to 7/ 77 Size: 5 ft. 7 in.
	Corp	John Ashby	8/ 77 to 9/ 77
	Prvt	John Ashby	10/ 77
	Prvt	Valentine Peyton	11/ 77 to 1/ 78
			Enlisted 2/12/ 76 for 2 yrs.
David Tharp	Prvt	John Thornton	6/ 77 to 7/ 77
	Prvt	John Ashby	8/ 77 to 10/ 77
	Prvt	Valentine Peyton	11/ 77 to 1/ 78
James Williams	Prvt	John Thornton	6/ 77 to 7/ 77
	Prvt	John Ashby	8/ 77 to 9/ 77
		Valentine Peyton	9/ 77 – **Sick**; 11/ 77
			Enlisted 2/12/ 76 for 2 yrs.
			DEAD by 12/22/ 77.
Pearson Williams	Prvt	John Ashby	6/ 77 to 10/ 77
	Prvt	Valentine Peyton	11/ 77
			Enlisted 3/18/ 76 for 2 yrs.
Martin Wingate	Prvt	John Ashby	6/ 77 to 10/ 77
	Prvt	Valentine Peyton	11/ 77
			Enlisted 3/18/ 76 for 2 yrs.
			Discharged 12/1/ 77.

SOURCE for all men except Listra Vaughan: NARA, Compiled Service Records, M 881 MR 951–956, *CSR, 3rd Virginia*. For Listra Vaughan, see NARA, Compiled Service Records, M 881 MR 970, *CSR, 3rd & 4th Virginia*.

The Final Days: June to December 1778

Morgan's rifle regiment, now minus the 3rd Virginia men, served through the spring of 1778 on routine patrol, harassing the British foraging parties and checking on known tories to make sure they were not providing supplies to the British. He and his riflemen were involved only peripherally at Monmouth, having been given the responsibility to shadow the enemy's right flank. He *did* capture fifteen grenadiers but because he received no other orders from General Lee, he and his men did not take part in the main engagement.[42]

In September 1778, he reluctantly relinquished his rifle command to a junior officer when he took over permanent command of the 7th Virginia. There was no longer sufficient manpower to sustain a separate command as Washington had diluted its strength when he sent rifle companies to guard the Northern frontier against Indian attacks. By the end of the year, Morgan's elite unit would be disbanded.[43]

END NOTES
CHAPTER 7
THE 3RD VIRGINIA & COLONEL DANIEL MORGAN'S
LIGHT INFANTRY

1. Don Higginbotham, *Daniel Morgan: Revolutionary Rifleman* (Chapel Hill: UNC Press, 1961), 57.
2. NARA, 3rd Virginia compiled service records for Peter Bryant, Mitchell Burk, Shadrach Butler, Thomas Craigin, Joseph Cromwell, Dennis Crow, John Crow, Thomas Gambell, William Henson, Baylor Jennings, Martin Johnston, Abraham Milhousen, Benjamin Powell, John Slaughter David Tharp, James Williams, Pearson Williams and Martin Wingate.. See also NARA, compiled service records for William Breedlove, Listra Baughan, and Reuben Earthern, 3rd & 4th Virginia.
3. University of Virginia, *George Washington to Colonel Daniel Morgan,* 13 June 1777, *WW,* 8, pg. n.g (http://etext.virginia.edu).
4. Higginbotham, 59.
5. University of Virginia, *George Washington to Colonel Daniel Morgan,* Headquarters at the Clove, 23 July 1777, *WW,* 8, pg. n.g (http://etext.virginia.edu).
6. Ibid., *George Washington to Colonel Daniel Morgan,* 8 miles east of Morristown, 26 July 1777.
7. Higginbotham, 61.
8. University of Virginia, *George Washington to Daniel Morgan,* 16 August 1777, *WW,* 8, pg. n.g (http://etext.virginia.edu).
9. Richard M. Ketchum, *Saratoga: Turning Point of America's Revolutionary War* (New York: Henry Holt & Company, 1997), 345–346.
10. Ibid., 347.
11. Ibid., 349.
12. Higginbotham, 65.
13. Ibid.
14. Ketchum, 356 and Higginbotham, 65.
15. Ketchum, 360.
16. Higginbotham, 67.
17. Ibid.
18. Ketchum, 362.
19. Higginbotham, 67–68.
20. Ibid.
21. Ibid., 69.
22. University of Virginia, *George Washington to Major General Horatio Gates, WW,* 8, pg. n.g (http://etext.virginia.edu).
23. Ibid., *Gates to Washington* 5 October 1777, found in footnote in text.
24. W. J. Wood, *Battles of the Revolutionary War, 1775–1781* (New York: DeCapo Press, 1995), 132. See also Boatner, 971. Both of these references refer to the 19 September 1777 battle as the Battle of Freeman's Farm or the First Battle of Saratoga. Likewise, for the October 1777 engagement, it is known alternatively as the Battle of Bemis Height or the Second Battle of Saratoga.
25. Higginbotham, 72.
26. Ketchum, 395.
27. Ketchum 399–400. A similar account may be found in Higginbotham, 73–74.
28. Ketchum, 402–403.

29. Ibid., 403. See also Higginbotham, 75.
30. Ketchum, 403.
31. Ibid., 414–415.
32. University of Virginia, *George Washington to Major General Horatio Gates,* Camp near Potts Grove, 21 September 1777, *WW,* 8, pg. n.g (http://etext.virginia.edu).
33. Higginbotham, 79.
34. Colonial Williamsburg Foundation, "Colonel Morgan near Germantown," *Virginia Gazette* (Dixon), 14 November 1777, 2, col. 1 (http://research.history.org)
35. Ibid, "Morgan joins Washington's Army," *Virginia Gazette* (Dixon), 28 November 1777, 2, col. 2.
36. Higginbotham, 80.
37. Boatner, 1199; Gott and Russell, 237–238.
38. Higginbotham, 81. See also footnote 5 in Higginbotham, on page 81, for sources regarding the part Morgan's rifle corps played at the skirmish at White Marsh.
39. Library of Virginia, *George Weedon to John Page,* Accession 22954a, *George Weedon Papers,* LVA, Richmond.
40. Higginbotham, 81.
41. NARA, See the 3rd Virginia compiled service records for these three men.
42. Higginbotham, 88–91.
43. Ibid., 92.

Index, Volume 1

This index is an every name index for Volume 1 of the History of the Third Virginia: With Flags Flying and Drums Beating. Some place names appear and any of the revolutionary war battles in which the regiment participated are also found here.

The index is in a two column format in order to place more entries onto the page. Officer and soldiers' ranks may appear as abbreviations due to space constraints with this format. Likewise, states may also appear as their abbreviated versions.

INDEX, VOLUME 1

NAME	REMARKS	PAGE
ABBEY, Edward	Soldier, 3rd Virginia	52, 82, 103
ABBERCROMBIE, Colonel	Death at Germantown	151
ADAMS, George	Soldier, 3rd Virginia British Prisoner	123
AGNEW, General	Death at Germantown	151
AIGIN, William	Private, 3rd Virginia British Prisoner	123
ALEXANDER, Morgan	Captain, 2nd Virginia, 8th Virginia	15
ALEXANDER, William (Lord Stirling)	Major General, Brigadier General, Continental Army	43–44, 84, 86–95, 134
ALLEN, John	Captain, Massachusetts Artillery	101
ALLEN, Moses	Corporal/Sergeant, 3rd Virginia	20, 173, 189
ALVERSON, James	Private, 3rd Virginia	189
American Army	Crosses Delaware into Pennsylvania, December, 1776	186
American Artillery	Ordered to attack British at Monmouth	183
American Field Returns	Filed June 1778 before Monmouth	183
ANDERSON, Enoch	Captain, Hazlet's Delaware Brigade	75
ANDERSON, John	Captain, 5th Virginia, transferred into 3rd Virginia, September 1778	45
ANDERSON, John	Private, 3rd Virginia, Killed at Germantown, October 1777	147
ANDERSON, Spencer	Private, 3rd Virginia	17, 19, 54, 82, 103, 172
ARELL, David	Captain, 3rd Virginia	18, 29–30, 33, 41, 45, 103, 162, 169, 171, 190
ARMSTRONG, John	Brigadier General, Continental Army	175

Name	Remarks	Page
ARMSTRONG, George (1)	Private, 3rd Virginia Died 24 April 1778	173 172
ARNOLD, Benedict	Major General, Continental Army	198, 202
ARROWSMITH, James	Private, 3rd Virginia	139, 170
ASHBY, John	Captain, 3rd Virginia	17, 19, 20, 29, 30–31, 35–37, 42, 52–53, 55, 77–78, 82–83, 103, 108, 130, 140, 197
ASHBY, Nathaniel	Ensign, 3rd Virginia	17, 52, 173
ASHBY, Stephen	Captain, 12th Virginia	63
ATKINSON, John	Private, 3rd Virginia	189
AUBER, John	Drummer, 3rd Virginia	168

B

Name	Remarks	Page
BAILEY, William	Private, 3rd Virginia	172
BAKER, Charles	Soldier, 3rd Virginia	189
BAKER, David	Private, 3rd Virginia	54, 83, 103
BAKER, Richard	Killed at Trenton, December 1776	56, 103
BALCARRE's	British Light Infantry	201
Baltimore, Maryland	Continental Congress removes to	94
BARR, Isaac	Private, 3rd Virginia	103, 189
Barren Hill, Pennsylvania	Skirmish at, 25 May 1778	67, 175–178
BASYE, Benjamin	Private, 3rd Virginia Death reported 26 February 1777 Heirs-at-Law	110 112
BASYE, Jesse	Private, 3rd Virginia Death during war, at Philadelphia Heirs-at-Law	112 112
BASYE, Jeremiah	Heir-at-Law to Benjamin and Jesse Basye	112

NAME	REMARKS	PAGE
BATES, Thomas	Private, 3rd Virginia Discharged 23 December 1777	168
Battle of the Clouds	Description, 16 September 1777	141–142
BATTUT, John	British Lieutenant, 14th Regiment	11, 13–14, 16
BAUGHAN, Listra	Private, 3rd Virginia, in Morgan's Rifle Corps. SEE ALSO VAUGHAN, Listra	205
BAWCUTT, William	Sergeant, 3rd Virginia	173
BAYNHAM, Joseph	Lieutenant, 3rd, Resigned January 1778	168
BAZZILL, John	Private, in Morgan's Rifle Corps	205
BEALE, Robert	Captain, 5th Virginia, transferred into 3rd Virginia, September 1778	45
BEALE, Robert	Lieutenant, 3rd Virginia	19
Beall's Brigade	Ordered to evacuate Fort Lee	87
BEALL, Reazin	Brigadier General, at White Plains	83
BEARMORE, William	Private, 3rd Virginia Died 22 February 1777	110
BELT, —	Sergeant, Maryland troops, killed at White Plains, October 1776	83
Bemis Heights aka 2nd Battle of Saratoga	Description of Battle, 7 October 1777	201–202
BENTLEY, William	Captain, 5th Virginia, transferred into 3rd Virginia, September 1778	45
Bergen, New Jersey		57
BERRY, William	Private, 3rd Virginia	83
BETTISWORTH, Charles	Private, 3rd Virginia	189
BIDDLE, Clement	American Colonel	160
BLACKWELL, John	Lieutenant/ Captain, 3rd Virginia	2, 5, 17–20, 29, 31–32, 45, 52, 135, 140, 173
BLACKWELL, Joseph	Lieutenant, 3rd Virginia	17–18, 32, 57, 112–113, 173

Name	Remarks	Page
BLACKWELL, William	Captain, Fauquier Minute Men as part of Culpeper Minute Battalion	5, 9
BLAND, Theodorick	Colonel, 1st Continental Dragoons	134
BLAND, William	Private, 3rd Virginia Died 15 March 1778	172
BOLLING, Edmond/Edward	Private, 3rd Virginia	124
Bordentown, New Jersey		93
Boundbrook, New Jersey		59
BOYLE, George	Private, 3rd Virginia	170
BRACCO, Bennett	Captain, Beall's Independent Maryland company, killed at White Plains, October 1776	83
BRADFORD, Henry	Sergeant, 3rd Virginia, wounded at Brandywine, 11 September 1777 Discharged 23 December 1777	138 168, 173
BRADFORD, William	Private, 3rd Virginia	140
Brandywine	Description of Battle	51, 63, 64, 132–141
BREEDLOVE, William	Private, 3rd Virginia, in Morgan's Rifle Corps	205
BRENT, Willoughby	Sergeant, 3rd Virginia Died February 1777	110
BRIDGES, John	Private, 3rd Virginia	189
BRISCOE, Reuben	Lieutenant/ Captain, 3rd Virginia	4, 19, 29, 141, 171
British movements in New Jersey December 1776		89
BROWN, John (2)	Soldier, 3rd Virginia, wounded at Brandywine 11 September 1777 Died 15 November 1777	138
BRUIN, William	Died by 1 March 1777	110
Brunswick, New Jersey		56, 70
BRYANT, Reuben	Private/ Corporal, 3rd Virginia, in Morgan's Rifle Corps	205

Name	Remarks	Page
BRYANT, William	Private, 3rd Virginia Died 15 March 1778 at Valley Forge	172
BUFORD, Abraham	Captain, Culpeper Minute Battalion	7–9
BUNNER, Rudolph	Lieutenant Colonel, 3rd Pennsylvania Killed at Monmouth, June 1778	187
BURGOYNE, John	British General at Saratoga	201–203
BURK, Alex	Private, 3rd Virginia	114
BURK, Mitchell	Private, 3rd Virginia, in Morgan's Rifle Corps; early discharge December 1777	206
BURN, Christopher	Private, 3rd Virginia, wounded at Brandywine, September 1777	137
BURN, Peter	Soldier, 3rd Virginia, Died 15 January 1777	110
BUTLER, Richard	Colonel, 9th Pennsylvania Role at Monmouth	186
BUTLER, Shadrach	Private, 3rd Virginia in Morgan's Rifle Corps	205
BYRD, Thomas	Colonel, Virginia, Killed at Germantown, October, 1777	151

C

Name	Remarks	Page
CADWALLADER, John	Colonel, Pennsylvania Militia	91, 89
CAGE, Joshua	Soldier, 3rd Virginia Died 15 January 1777	108–110
CALVERT, George	Private, 3rd Virginia Died 15 January 1777	108–110
CALVERT, Reuben	Sergeant, 3rd Virginia Died 15 January 1777	110
CAMPBELL, —	Captain, Fincastle Militia	15
CARNEY, Matthew	Private, 3rd Virginia, killed at Brandywine, September 1777	137
Carolina Brigade	At Monmouth	186

Name	Remarks	Page
CARROLL, Isaac	Soldier, 3rd Virginia Died 15 January 1777	110
CARTER, Landon	Received letter from General Washington May 1778	181
CARTER, Moses	Soldier, 3rd Virginia Died 14 February 1777	108–110 111
CARTER, Robert	Received letter from Francis Lightfoot Lee, December 1775	9
CHASE, Samuel	Maryland Delegate to Congress, Letter To Horatio Gates, 21 September 1776	80
Chatham, New Jersey		57
CHESTER, John	Colonels, Connecticut State Regiment	43
Chesterfield, Virginia Minute Men		9
Chew Mansion	aka Cliveden or Battle at Germantown	146
CHILTON, Charles	Letter from brother Captain John Chilton, 30 November 1776	88
	Letter from Captain John Chilton, February 1777	32
	Letter from Captain John Chilton, August 1777	128
	Letter from Captain John Chilton, June 1777	125–126
	Letter from Captain John Chilton, August 1777	128
CHILTON, John	Captain, 3rd Virginia,	2, 17–20, 29, 31–32, 42, 52–54, 58–59, 101, 108
	Arrest for being late at Roll Call	61
	Captain, Fauquier County company in Culpeper Minute Battalion	5, 9, 15
	Deaths in his company	108
	Killed at Brandywine, September 1777	135, 138 139–140
	Diary Entries, January to March 1777 Death of General Mercer	53–54, 58–59 59
	Diary Entries, March to April 1777 Small pox in 3rd Virginia	60
	Diary Entries, April to July 1777	61–62, 123, 125, 127
	Diary Entries, August to September 1777	60–66, 108, 129–132

Name	Remarks	Page
CHILTON, John	Captain 3rd Virginia	
	Guarded Pass at Steel's Gap	60
	Inoculated for small pox	57, 112–113
	Late for roll call, denied post, Sword ordered returned	60–61
	Letters	
	Describing Battle at Harlem Heights	77
	To Friends in Fauquier reporting death of Major Andrew Leitch	81
	To brother Charles Chilton	60
	To brother Charles Chilton, November 1776	81
	To brother Charles Chilton, February 1777	112–113
	To brother Charles Chilton, June 1777	125–126
	To brother Charles Chilton, August 1777	128
	To Joseph Blackwell, September 1776	31
	To Captain William Pickett, July 1777	127
	Loss of Baggage in Delaware River	127
	Officer of the Day, August 1777	63
CHILTON, Letitia	Wife of Captain John Chilton, Died 9 December 1775	15
CHILTON, Stephen	Brother of Captain John Chilton, death reported in 1774	17
CHILTON, William	Brother of Captain John Chilton, death reported	17
CHINN, Rawleigh	Sergeant, 3rd Virginia Died 15 January 1777	110
CLACK, Thomas	Sergeant, 3rd Virginia Died 15 April 1778	172
CLARK, James	Soldier, 3rd Virginia Died 15 January 1777	110
CLARK, Sarah	Cared for Brigadier General Hugh Mercer	108
CLAYTON, Philip	Colonel's home in Culpeper where Culpeper Minute Battalion rendezvoused	5
CLENDENNY	Soldier, 3rd Virginia Died 1 February 1777	110
CLINTON, George	General, Continental Army Letter to New York Convention, September 1776	79
Cliveden	aka Chew Mansion/ Battle at Germantown	146

Name	Remarks	Page
COCKRELL, John [aka COCKERILL]	Private, 3rd Virginia	189
COFFEE, Robert	Soldier, 3rd Virginia Killed at Brandywine, September 1777	138
COLLEY, Charles	Private, 3rd Virginia	173
COLLOP, George	Private Deserted 15 March 1778	172
Connecticut Militia	Flight at Harlem Heights described	76
Continental Congress	Letter from Executive Committee to John Hancock, January 1777	106
CONNER, Douglas	Corporal, 3rd Virginia Died 15 January 1777	110
CONNER, Philip	Private, 3rd Virginia,	189
CONWAY, Thomas	Brigadier General, Continental Army	62
COOK, —	Governor of Connecticut Received letter from General Washington	76
COOKE, Eppa	Soldier, 3rd Virginia Died 11 January 1777	110
COOPER, Apollos	Lieutenant, 3rd Virginia Killed, Brandywine, September 1777	135
COPPAGE, John	Private, 3rd Virginia	83, 86
CORNWALLIS, Charles	British Major/ Lieutenant General	124–125, 133
Coryell's Ferry		67
COSBY, Thomas	Private, 3rd Virginia	139, 173
Council of War by Americans		175–176, 183
COX, Samuel	Private, 3rd Virginia	82, 173, 189
CRAIGIN, Thomas	Corporal, 3rd Virginia, in Morgan's Rifle Corp; died 22 December 1777	203, 205
CRAWFORD, William	Colonel, 7th Virginia	63
CROCKETT, Joseph	Captain, 7th Virginia	19, 36

Name	Remarks	Page
CROMWELL, Joseph	Private/ Corporal, 3rd Virginia, in Morgan's Rifle Corps	205
CROOK, Jonathan	Private, 3rd Virginia	140, 173
CROOK, Zachary	Corporal, 3rd Virginia Died 15 January 1777	110
CROW, Dennis	Soldier, 3rd Virginia, in Morgan's Rifle Corps	205
CROW, John	Soldier, 3rd Virginia, in Morgan's Rifle Corps	205
CULLINS, John	Soldier, 3rd Virginia Wounded at Brandywine, September 1777	137
Culpeper Minute Men		2–3, 5, 9
CUNNINGHAM, Henry	Colonel, 1st Pennsylvania Battalion	84

D

Name	Remarks	Page
DADE, Robert	Lieutenant, 3rd Virginia Died in August 1776	53
DALEY, Thomas [aka DAILEY]	Private, 3rd Virginia Wounded, Brandywine, September 1777 and died of wounds	137
DALTON, Moses	Sergeant, 3rd Virginia	173
DANSEY, John	Private, 3rd Virginia May have died 15 February 1777	111
DAVIS, John (1)	Private, 3rd Virginia Died before 1 April 1777	110
DAVIS, Presley	Sergeant, 3rd Virginia Died 1 February 1777	110
DAY, Benjamin	Brigade Major, Woodford's Brigade	122
DEAN, John [aka DEANE]	Soldier, 3rd Virginia Affidavit for Benjamin Basye's Heirs	112
DEANE, Silas	Letter to Robert Morris	105, 107
DEARBORN, Henry	Lieutenant Colonel, Light Infantry	198–201

NAME	REMARKS	PAGE
DEBUTY, John	Private, 3rd Virginia May have died 1 February 1777	111
DEEKINS, James	Fifer, 3rd Virginia Died 15 February 1778	169, 171–172
DeKALB, John, Baron	Major General, Continental Army	175
Delaware Blues	aka John Hazlet's 1st Delaware	88
Delaware River		92, 94
Delaware River Forts		165
DICKINSON, Edmond	Major, 1st Virginia Killed at Monmouth, June 1778	187
DOYLE, Robert	Private, 3rd Virginia Wounded at Germantown, October 1777	147
DUNMORE, Lord		6-12, 14, 16–17, 19
DUPORTAIL, Louis Lebique	Brigadier General, Engineers	175
DURHAM, Edward	Soldier, 3rd Virginia Died by 1 March 1777	110
DYER, Eliphalet	Letter to Joseph Trumbull re Brandywine, 12 September 1777	140

E

NAME	REMARKS	PAGE
EARTHERN, Reuben	Private, 3rd Virginia, in Morgan's Rifle Corps	205
EDWARDS, Leroy	Lieutenant/ Captain, 5th Virginia; transferred into 3rd Virginia, September 1778	45
Elizabethtown, New Jersey		55
ELLIOTT, John	Sergeant, 3rd Virginia	169, 171
ENGLISH, Robert	Private, 3rd Virginia	140
ETHRINGTON, John Jr	Private, 3rd Virginia	170
EWING, James	Brigadier General, Pennsylvania Militia Mentioned as Ewing's Brigade	87
Executive Committee, Continental Congress	Letter to John Hancock, January 1777	106

Name	Remarks	Page
F		
FARROW, Micajah	Private, 3rd Virginia Wounded at Brandywine, September 1777, and died of wounds	138
Fauquier County Virginia Militia		65
FEBINGER, Christian	Lieutenant Colonel/ Colonel, 2nd Virginia	153
FERGUSON, Patrick	British Captain, Rifle Regiment	133
FERMOY De, Matthias Alexis	Brigadier General, Continental Army	94, 99
FEWELL, Henry	Private, 3rd Virginia Died 1 February 1777	110
FITZGERALD, John	Lieutenant, Fairfax Independent company	4
	Captain, Prince William County Minute Battalion	5
	Captain, 3rd Virginia	18, 29, 33, 52–54, 83, 103
FITZGERALD, John H.	Lieutenant, 5th Virginia, transferred into 3rd Virginia, September 1778	45
FITZPATRICK, William	Private, 3rd Virginia	170
FLEMING, Charles	Lieutenant-Colonel, 3rd Virginia, transferred to 8th Virginia, September 1778	27
FLEMING, Thomas	Colonel, 9th Virginia	40
FONTAINE, Bechet de Roche	Captain Engineers	9
FORD, Elijah	Soldier, 3rd Virginia May have died 15 February 1777	111
FORDYCE, Charles	British Captain, 14th Regiment, at Great Bridge	11–14
FORMAN, David	Brigadier General, New Jersey Militia	144
Fort Lee, New Jersey		86
Fort Washington		54, 70, 85
FOWLER, William	Captain, 5th Virginia, transferred into 3rd Virginia, September 1778	45

Name	Remarks	Page
FRASER, Simon	British Brigadier General	198
FRASER, Simon	British Captain, 24th Regiment, At Saratoga	201
	Killed by Tim Murphy, rifleman, Morgan's Rifle Corps	202
FRAZER, Persifor		52
Freeman's Farm	aka 1st Battle of Saratoga	198–200

G

Name	Remarks	Page
GALLOWAY, Joseph	American Tory	133
GAMBELL, Thomas	Private, 3rd Virginia, in Morgan's Rifle Corps	205
GAMBRELL, Richard	Soldier, 3rd Virginia Died 15 January 1777	110
GARNER, Jeremiah	Soldier, 3rd Virginia Died 1 February 1777	110
GARNER, John	Private, 3rd Virginia	168
GASKINS, Thomas	Colonel, 5th Virginia, transferred into 3rd Virginia, September 1778	27
GATES, Horatio	Major-General, Continental Army, Commander-in-Chief, Northern Department	198
	Letter from Samuel Chase, September 1776	80
	Letter from General Washington, December 1776	97
	Letter from General Washington, September 1777	200
	Letter to General Washington, October 1777	200
	Member of Council of War	175
General Orders		122, 137, 144, 150
Germantown	Description of Battle, 4 October 1777	64, 144–152
GIST, —	Maryland Militia at White Marsh	204
GLOVER, John	Brigadier General, Continental Army His brigade mentioned	182
GODFREY, Robert	Private, 3rd Virginia	169

Name	Remarks	Page
GOLDSMITH, Thomas	Lieutenant, Smallwood's Maryland Regiment	83
GORDON, George	Sergeant, 3rd Virginia Died 26 February 1778	172
GRANT, —	British General, in command of right wing at Germantown	145
GRAY, —	British Major General, at White Marsh	204
GRAYSON, William	Colonel, Prince William Minute Battalion	3, 15
Great Bridge, Virginia	Skirmish described	9–15
GREEN, —	Militia Captain at Great Bridge	16
GREEN, John	Major, 1st Virginia In charge of Virginia troops detached to capture Major Robert Roger's Tory troops Wounded at New Rochelle	82 37, 82
GREENE, Nathaniel	Brigadier and Major General, Continental Army	63, 85, 98, 122, 124, 129, 144–145, 175, 183, 186
GREGORY, George	Private, 3rd Virginia	114
GRIFFITH, —	American Colonel	79
GRIFFITH, David	Chaplain/ Surgeon, 3rd Virginia	42, 52, 56, 64, 101
	Letter to Richard Henderson, about he death of Major Andrew Leitch,	80
	Letter to wife Hannah re Brandywine	137
	Letter to wife Hannah, November 1777	163–164
	Letter to wife Hannah re evacuation of Philadelphia	178–179
	Prior military experience	19
	Surgeon Prince William County Minute Battalion	5
	Surgeon, treating wounded in Philadelphia, December 1776	93
	Surgeon, ordered to send health men back to Continental Army	93
GRIFFITH, Hannah	Wife of David Griffith Letters from husband David	52, 56 64, 137, 163–164, 178–179

Name	Remarks	Page

H

Name	Remarks	Page
Hackensack, New Jersey		55, 87
HAGAN, Francis	Corporal, 3rd Virginia	168
HALLER, Henry	Colonel, Pennsylvania Battalion of the Flying Camp	84
HAMMET, Cornelius	Letter to William Wilkerson, re Brandywine, September 1777	140
Hampton, Virginia	British attack on	7
HAMRICK, Benjamin	Private, 3rd Virginia	173
HAMRICK, Uriah	Private, 3rd Virginia Died 21 January 1777	110
HANCOCK, Dolly	Letter from husband John re Germantown, October 1777	149
HANCOCK, John	Letter to wife Dolly re Germantown, October 1777	149
	Letter from Executive Committee of Continental Congress	106
	Letters from General Washington, December 1776	89, 91
	Letter from General Washington, re Brandywine, September 1777	136
Hanover, New Jersey	Inoculation of 3rd Virginia Companies	58
Harlem Heights, New York	Description of Battle	53, 75, 77–81
HARRIS, Burr	Private, 3rd Virginia	173
HARRIS, James	Private, 3rd Virginia	168, 173
HARRISON, Henry	Soldier, 3rd Virginia	172
HAWKINS, John	Adjutant, 3rd Virginia	45
HAYS, John	Captain, 9th Virginia	27
HAZLETT, John [aka HASLET]	Colonel, 1st Delaware	28, 42, 55, 83–84, 88
HEARD, Nathaniel	Brigadier General, New Jersey Militia Brigade mentioned	87
HEATH, William	Major General, Continental Army	89, 91

Name	Remarks	Page
HEISTER, Charles	Hessian Lieutenant General	124–125
HENDERSON, Hugh	Soldier, 3rd Virginia	139
HENDERSON, Richard	Letter from Surgeon David Griffith re death of Major Andrew Leitch, October 1776	80
HENLEY, David	Colonel, Massachusetts	121
HENRY, Patrick	Letter from General Washington re Colonel Thomas Marshall	128–129
	Letter from General Washington, December 1777	
	Letter from Richard Henry Lee May 1777	123
	Letter from Richard Henry Lee re Germantown, October 1777	151
Hessian Hunting	At Fort Washington, in Virginia Gazette November 1776	85
Hessian Prisoners	Captured at Trenton, escorted to Philadelphia by 3rd Virginia	56, 103
HETH, William	Major, 11th Virginia	121
	Lieutenant Colonel/ Colonel, 3rd Virginia	27, 128, 130, 152, 153
	Complaint against Brigadier General William Maxwell for conduct at Germantown	152
HILL, Samuel	Private, 3rd Virginia	139
HINSON, William	Private, 3rd Virginia, in Morgan's Rifle Corps	205
HITCHCOCK, Daniel	Colonel, 11th Continental Infantry and 2nd Rhode Island	98, 112
HOLIFIELD, Daniel	Private, 3rd Virginia May have died 15 February 1777	112
HOPPER, John	Private, 3rd Virginia	168
HOWE, Robert	Lieutenant Colonel/ Colonel, Carolina Forces	10, 15–16
HOWE, William	British General	55, 58, 82, 83, 90, 145, 203
HUNGERFORD, Thomas	Lieutenant, 3rd Virginia	41

Name	Remarks	Page
HUNT, Thomas	Private, 3rd Virginia Prisoner of British, April to May 1777	123
HYND, Michael	Drummer, 3rd Virginia Missing in Action after Brandywine, September 1777	138

I

Name	Remarks	Page
Innes, James		6
Iron Hill	Description of Skirmish	130–131
IRVIN, James	Brigadier General, Pennsylvania Militia Wounded in hand at White Marsh Captured by British, December 1777	204 204 204

J

Name	Remarks	Page
JACKSON, Henry	Colonel, one of Massachusetts's Additional Continental Regiments	68
JAMESON, John	Captain, Culpeper Minute Battalion	5, 9
JEFFERSON, Thomas		53
JEFFREY, George		41
JENKINS, Joshua	Sergeant, 3rd Virginia Killed at Brandywine	138
JENKINS, Thomas	Private, 3rd Virginia Died 15 January 1778	169, 172
JENNINGS, Baylor	Private 3rd Virginia, in Morgan's Rifle Corps	205
JOHNSON, John	Private, 3rd Virginia Died 1 January 1777	110
JOHNSON, Martin	Private, 3rd Virginia, in Morgan's Rifle Corps	205
JOHNSON, Thomas [aka JOHNSTON]	Captain, 3rd Virginia Company Returns Resignation, November 1776	18, 29, 36, 52, 53 33–34 34
JONES, Charles	Soldier, 3rd Virginia Died 1 February 1777	17, 19 110
JONES, John	Soldier, 3rd Virginia May have died 9 February 1777	17 111

NAME	REMARKS	PAGE

K

KANE, Thomas	Sergeant, 3rd Virginia	173
KEHOE, James	Private, 3rd Virginia	173
KEITH, Alexander	Cadet, 3rd Virginia	121
KEITH, Isham	Lieutenant, 3rd Virginia	15, 52
KELLY, Thomas	Private, 3rd Virginia	168, 173
KENDALL, Jeremiah	Private, 3rd Virginia	139
KING, John	Private, 3rd Virginia	171
KING, Valentine	Private, 3rd Virginia Wounded, September to November 1777	139, 170
King's Bridge, New York		53
KNIGHT, John	Private, 3rd Virginia Prisoner of War, April to May 1777	123
KNOWLTON, Thomas	Lieutenant Colonel/ Colonel 20th Continental Infantry	76, 78
	Killed at Harlem Heights	76, 79
KNOX, Henry	Brigadier General/ Chief of Artillery, Continental Army	100-101 175
KNYPHAUSEN —	Hessian Lieutenant General, at Germantown October 1777	133, 134 151

L

LaFAYETTE, Marquis de	Major General, Continental Army	68, 152, 176–177, 182, 183, 185
	Letter from Henry Laurens, October 1777	149
	Letter from General Washington re Refusal of Officers in Woodford and Weedons' Brigade to take Oath of Allegiance	175
LANGFORD, Philip	Corporal, 3rd Virginia	168
LANKFORD, John	Private, 3rd Virginia Died 15 January 1777	110
LAURENS, Henry	Letter to Marquis de LaFayette, October 1777	149

NAME	REMARKS	PAGE
LAWLER, John (2)	Private, 3rd Virginia Deserted 15 April 1778	172
LAWS, William	Private, 3rd Virginia Died 15 January 1777	110
LEARNED, Ebenezer	Brigadier General, Continental Army His Brigade mentioned	182
LEARNEY, John	Soldier, 3rd Virginia May have died 31 December 1776	110
LEE, —	Captain	45
LEE, Charles	Major General, Continental Army	38, 87–89, 91, 95, 183
	Command of right wing at Monmouth	182
	Court Martial for conduct at Monmouth	187
	Letter from General Washington, December 1775	95–96
	Letter from General Washington, Re Evacuation of Fort Washington, November 1776	87
	Letter from General Washington, Re need for his troops to defend Philadelphia, December 1776	90
	Letter from General Washington requesting he and his troops to join American Army, December 1776	93
	Placed under Arrest after Monmouth	187
LEE, Francis Lightfoot	Letter to Robert W. Carter, December 1775	9
LEE Philip Richard Francis	Captain, 3rd Virginia	3, 18–19, 29, 31, 35, 52, 53–54, 103, 138, 140
	At White Plains, October 1776	82
	Company Returns	34
	Wounded at Brandywine	29, 135
	Died 29 January 1778 from wounds suffered at Brandywine	169, 171–172, 190
LEE, Richard Francis	Letter to Governor Patrick Henry, Re Germantown	149
	Letter to Catherine Macauley, Re Dunmore's Proclamation freeing slaves November 1775	9
LEITCH, Andrew	Captain, Prince William Minute Battalion	5
	Captain, 3rd Virginia	18, 52. 114
	Promoted to Major, 1st Virginia	34, 53, 114
	Role at Harlem Heights	78

Name	Remarks	Page
LEITCH, Andrew (Continued)	Wounded at Harlem Heights	34, 76, 79, 80
	Circumstances surrounding his death	35, 81
	Letters describing his death from lockjaw	80
81LEITCH, William	Private, 3rd Virginia	124
	Prisoner of War, May 1777	
LENOX, Charles	Private, 3rd Virginia	138
	Wounded at Brandywine, September 1777	
LESLIE, Samuel	British Captain, 14th Regiment, at Great Bridge	11–12, 14
LEWIS, George	Reports death of General Hugh Mercer	108
LINCOLN, Benjamin	Major General, Continental Army	59
LINTON, Hilvy	Soldier, 3rd Virginia	110
	Died 16 February 1777	
LIVINGSTON, William	Letter from General Washington Re Evacuation of Fort Lee	87
Long Island	Battle of	53
LUCAS, James	Major, transferred into 3rd Virginia, September 1778	27
LYNCH, James	Soldier, 3rd Virginia	110
	May have died in March 1777	
LYNN, —	Captain of Minute company, at Hampton	7

M

Name	Remarks	Page
MACAULEY, Catherine	Letter from Richard Francis Lee, November 1775	9
MARKHAM, —	Militia captain at Norfolk	16
MARLOE, John	Private, 3rd Virginia	110
	Died 15 January 1777	
MARMADUKE, Jesse	Soldier, 3rd Virginia	110
	Died 4 March 1777	
MARR, Thomas	Soldier, 3rd Virginia	110
	Died 1 February 1777	

Name	Remarks	Page
MARSHALL, Thomas	Major/ Lieutenant Colonel/ Colonel, 3rd Virginia	1, 2, 19, 27, 41–42, 51, 53, 59–60, 125–126, 132, 134–135, 140, 159
	Culpeper Minute Battalion	
	At Great Bridge, Virginia	15, 16
	Ordered to Hampton, Virginia	9
	His Negro slave, Major "desertion	14
	Major, Culpeper Minute Battalion	5, 15
	Major, 3rd Virginia	9, 17, 52
	Lieutenant Colonel, 3rd Virginia	52, 123
	Colonel, 3rd Virginia	42, 114
	Resigned to take up post in Virginia State Artillery	128–129
	Regimental Returns	42
MARSHALL, John		2
Maryland Troops	Action at Harlem Heights described	77
Maryland Continental Line	as part of Lafayette's 2nd Division at Monmouth	183
Maryland Council of Safety	Letter from Maryland Delegates of Congress, September 1776	80
Maryland Delegates of Congress	Letter to Maryland Council of Safety, September 1776	80
MASON, Benjamin	Soldier, 3rd Virginia Died 1 February 1777	110
MASON, Thomas	Private, 3rd Virginia	169, 171
Massachusetts Troops	In Major General Charles Lee's right wing at Monmouth	182
MASSEY, Burdett	Corporal, 3rd Virginia Died 1 February 1777	111
MATLOW, John	Soldier, 3rd Virginia May have died 31 December 1776	111
MATTHEWS, Chichester	Sergeant, 3rd Virginia	140
MATTHEWS, Dudley	Private, 3rd Virginia Died 1 February 1777	110

Name	Remarks	Page
MATTHEWS, John	Private, 3rd Virginia Wounded at Brandywine, September 1777	138
MAUZY, Peggy	Intended bride of Nathaniel Ashby, former 3rd Virginia lieutenant	173
MAXFIELD, Willoughby	Private, 3rd Virginia Died 3 March 1777	110
MAXWELL's Brigade	Part of Lafayette's advanced corps at Monmouth	185
MAXWELL, William	Brigadier General, Continental Army At Germantown Court of Inquiry for conduct at Germantown on complaint of Lieutenant Colonel William Heth of 3rd Virginia Court Martial for conduct at Germantown, October 1777; Acquitted Letter from General Washington, December 1776	133 133–134 152 152 97
MAY, George	Private, 3rd Virginia	169
McCOMB, James	Private, 3rd Virginia Died 15 January 1777	111
McCULLOUGH, William	Private, 3rd Virginia	170
McDANIEL, Elijah	Private, 3rd Virginia May have died 6 February 1777	111
McDONALD, Angus	Private, 3rd Virginia	121
McDONALD, Colbert	Private, 3rd Virginia	170
McDOUGAL, Alexander	Brigadier General, Continental Army At White Plains, October 1776	83, 143
McKINNEY, William	Private, 3rd Virginia Died 7 January 1777	111
McLANE, Allan	Captain, Patton's Continental Regiment	177
McWILLIAMS, William	Captain, 3rd Virginia Promoted to Brigade Major, Stirling's Brigade	18, 29, 35, 52 121
MEADE, ——	Militia Captain at Great Bridge	11

NAME	REMARKS	PAGE
MERCER, Hugh	Colonel, 3rd Virginia	17, 52
	Captain, Fredericksburg Independent Company, April 1775	3
	Brigadier General	27, 52, 93–94
	Wounded at Princeton	109
	Death at Princeton	53, 103, 108
	Mourned by 3rd Virginia	114
	Body taken to Philadelphia, January 1778	108
	Interment with military honors	108
MERCER, John Francis	Lieutenant/ Captain, 3rd Virginia	29, 36, 38, 39, 45, 71, 139, 171
	Adjutant, Caroline Minute Battalion	4
	Wounded at Brandywine	135
Metuchin Lines, New Jersey		60
MIFFLIN, Thomas	Philadelphia merchant and Militia General	104, 175
MILBURN, Thomas	Soldier, 3rd Virginia May have died 1 March 1777	112
MILES's Battalion	1st and 2nd Battalion, a Pennsylvania Rifle Regiment, part of Lord Stirling's Brigade	84
MILHOUSAN, Abram	Private, 3rd Virginia, in Morgan's Rifle Corps	206
Military Stores in Philadelphia		90
MILLER, David	Lieutenant/ Captain, 5th Virginia, transferred into 3rd Virginia, September 1778	19, 45
MILSTEAD, Leonard	Private, 3rd Virginia Died 15 January 1777	111
MOFFETT, Henry	Sergeant, 3rd Virginia	17, 20
Monmouth Court House	Description of Battle, 28 June 1778	67, 68, 181–189
	Woodford's Brigade at Monmouth	186–189
	General Charles Lee's conduct at	184–186, 188
	Letter from General Washington to President of Congress, June 1778	184
MONROE, James	Lieutenant, 3rd Virginia	99–101, 102
	Part played at Trenton	114
MOORE, Peter	Private, 3rd Virginia Wounded at Brandywine, September 1777	138
MOORE, William	Sergeant, 3rd Virginia Promoted to Ensign, 3rd Virginia	140

NAME	REMARKS	PAGE
MORGAN, Daniel	Colonel, 11th Virginia	3, 60, 198, 203
	Colonel, Independent Rifle Corps	124–125, 197
	3rd Virginia men selected for his Rifle Corps	31, 121, 124
	At Piscataway	124
	At Saratoga	64, 198–200, 201–202
	Arrival at Washington's main army At White Marsh after Saratoga	65, 164–165, 203
	Skirmish at White Marsh	204
	At Monmouth	68, 188, 207
	Letter from General Washington, June 1777	197
	Relinquishes command of Rifle Corps	207
	Promoted to Colonel, 7th Virginia	207
MORRIS, Anthony	Major, 1st Continental Infantry In Lafayette's corps, wounded at White Marsh, December 1777	204
MORRIS, Robert	Pennsylvania Delegate to Congress	102, 104–105
	Letters to General Washington and Silas Deane	107
MORRISON, Andrew	Soldier, 3rd Virginia Died 15 February 1777	110
MORRISON, John	Soldier, 3rd Virginia Died 1 February 1777	110
Morristown, New Jersey		56–57
MORTON, John		52
MOUNTJOY, Allan/ Alvin	Lieutenant, 3rd Virginia	32, 57, 61, 112 127
	Resignation 10 December 1777	168
MOUNTJOY, William	Paymaster, 3rd Virginia	19
MUENCHAUSEN, —	Hessian Captain at Germantown	135
MUHLENBERG's Brigade		122, 183
MUHLENBERG, Peter	Brigadier General, Continental Army	122
	Brigade Returns	180
	Commander, 1st Virginia Brigade	122
	Composition of	122
	Intrigue with Woodford over Woodford's Promotion	174
	Part of Lafayette's 2nd Division at Monmouth	183

NAME	REMARKS	PAGE
MURPHY, Jesse	Soldier, 3rd Virginia Died by 1 April 1777	111
MURPHY, John	Private, 3rd Virginia Wounded at Brandywine, September 1777	168, 173
MURPHY, Tim	Rifleman in Morgan's Rifle Corps, who fatally wounded British Captain Simon Fraser of 24th Regiment at Saratoga	202
MURRAY, John	Private, 3rd Virginia Died 15 January 1777	111
MURRAY, John, Lord Dunmore See also DUNMORE, Lord		1, 3
MUSGRAVE, Thomas	British Lieutenant Colonel at Germantown	145

N

NAME	REMARKS	PAGE
NASH, Francis	Brigadier General, Continental Army Died at Germantown, October 1777	151
NELSON, Thomas		2
NELSON, William	Lieutenant, 3rd Virginia	17, 52
New Hampshire Continental Line	1st, 2nd and 3rd New Hampshire, part of Enoch Poor's Division at Saratoga	201
New Jersey Brigade	At Monmouth	188
New Jersey Campaign		86–88
New Rochelle, New York	Skirmish, October 1776 Role of 3rd Virginia in	81–82 81–82
New York Convention	Letter from General George Clinton September 1776	79
Newark, New Jersey		57
Newtown, Virginia		7
NICHOLAS, ——	Captain, Minute man company	7, 10
NICHOLSON, —	Captain	106

Name	Remarks	Page
NOBLE, Daniel	Private, 3rd Virginia May have died 15 February 1777	111
NORMAN, William	Private, 3rd Virginia Wounded at Brandywine, September 1777	138
North Carolina Brigades	In Major General Charles Lee's right wing at Monmouth	182
North Castle		55
Oath of Allegiance	Required by Congress, February 1778 Officers in Woodford and Weedon's Brigade refuse to sign Officers, Woodford's Brigade reassured and sign oath	174 175 175
OBANNON, Andrew	Private, 3rd Virginia	17, 20
OBRYAN, Charles	Private, 3rd Virginia May have died 1 March 1777	111
Officers, 3rd Virginia	Refuse to take Oath of Allegiance when Colonel Woodford was promoted Officers reassured by General Washington and sign oath	174 175
Oneida Indians	Part played at Barren Hills, May 1778	177
Order of March	Order of March in Pennsylvania, December 1776	88
OREAR, Daniel	Private, 3rd Virginia	20
OVERALL, Nathaniel	Soldier, 3rd Virginia Died 15 January 1777	111

P

Name	Remarks	Page
PAGE, John	Letters from George Weedon Letter from George Wythe	59, 77, 81, 204 81
PANNELL, Emmanuel	Soldier, 3rd Virginia Died 15 January 1777	111
Paoli Massacre	Description, 21 September 1777	64
Paramus, New Jersey	Woodford's Brigade left there, July 1778	68
PATTERSON"s Brigade		182

Name	Remarks	Page
PAYNE, William	Captain, Fauquier company of Culpeper Minute Battalion	5
PEART, George	Private, 3rd Virginia May have died 15 February 1777	112
PEEBLES, John	British Army Captain	113
PENDLETON, Edmund	Letter from Colonel Woodford re Great Bridge, Virginia, December 1775	13
	Letter from Colonel Woodford re British bombing of Norfolk, January 1776	16
PENNINGTON, Daniel	Private, 3rd Virginia	173
Pennsylvania Troops	In Major General Charles Lee's right wing at Monmouth	182
Pennypacker Mills		64
PEYTON, George	Ensign, 3rd Virginia Died by 1 January 1777	108, 109, 111
PEYTON, John	Lieutenant/ Captain, 3rd Virginia Company Returns Wounded at Brandywine	18, 34, 36, 42, 45, 52, 53 108, 171 33, 36 135, 138
PEYTON, Robert	Ensign/ Lieutenant, 3rd Virginia Killed at Brandywine	32, 61 135, 138
PEYTON, Valentine	Lieutenant/ Captain, 3rd Virginia	19, 30–31, 34–36, 64 140, 173
PHELPS, Edward	Private, 3rd Virginia	170–171
Philadelphia, Pennsylvania		56, 58, 62, 64, 67, 75, 90 181–183, 204
PHILBERT, Obadiah	Private, 3rd Virginia	169, 171
PICKETT, Martin	Major, Fauquier County, Virginia Militia Captain, Culpeper Minute Battalion At Great Bridge Letter from Captain John Chilton, July 1777	20 5, 9 17 127
Piscataway, New Jersey	Description of Skirmish	60, 124–126

Name	Remarks	Page
POOR"s Division	At Saratoga	201
PORTERFIELD, Charles	Captain, 11th Virginia	133
POWELL, Benjamin	Private, 3rd Virginia In Morgan's Rifle Corps	168 204, 206
POWELL, Leonard	Private, 3rd Virginia Died 15 January 1777	111
POWELL, Levin	Major, Virginia Militia	52
POWELL, Robert	Lieutenant/ Captain, 3rd Virginia	18, 36, 39–42, 45, 61, 171
POWERS, James	Private, 3rd Virginia May have died 15 February 1777	111
President, Continental Congress	Letters from General Washington	78, 84, 86, 89, 91, 93–94, 101–102, 123–126, 129–131, 141–42, 160–165, 182
PRICE, David	Private, 3rd Virginia	170
PRICE, Elisha		109
Prince William County Independent company	Formation, Flag and Officers	3
Princeton, New Jersey	Battle at, Description	55–56, 75, 89, 93, 106–109
Proclamation freeing Slaves	By Lord Dunmore	8
Protest of Virginia Line	By Subalterns re reduction from ten companies to eight in Virginia Line, November 1777	162
PUTMAN, William	Private, 3rd Virginia May have died 1 February 1777	111
PUTNAM, Israel	Major General, Continental Army	89, 90

R

RALL, Johann Gottlieb	Hessian Colonel at Trenton	100

Name	Remarks	Page
RANDOLPH, John	Private, 3rd Virginia	173
RANDOLPH, Robert	Cadet, 3rd Virginia	121
READ(E), Isaac	Colonel, 1st Virginia	28, 42–43, 54, 82, 88
Reading Furnace, Pennsylvania	3rd Virginia encamped there, September 1777	64
Reorganization of Virginia Line	September 1778	190
Retreat into Pennsylvania	December 1776	88–94
RICE, Thomas	Private, 3rd Virginia Deserted 21 March 1778	172
RIKER, John (MD)	Part played at Trenton, December 1776	100, 101
RILEY, Edward	Private, 3rd Virginia Wounded at Brandywine, September 1777	137
RILEY, John	Soldier, 3rd Virginia	20
RINDE, Batt	Soldier, 3rd Virginia Died 15 January 1777	111
ROBERTSON, William	Cadet, 3rd Virginia, resigned April 1777	121
RODNEY, Thomas	Captain, Delaware Militia	104–105
ROGERS, John (2)	Private, 3rd Virginia Died 17 January 1777	110
ROGERS, Robert	British Major, Queen's American Rangers Escaped capture by 3rd Virginia Captain John Thornton	27, 82 114
ROSS, James	Colonel, 1st Pennsylvania	133
RUSH, Benjamin (MD)		108
RUSSELL, John	Private, 3rd Virginia	173
RUSSELL, William	Private, 3rd Virginia Deserted 20 February 1778	172
RUST, Vincent	Private, 3rd Virginia May have died 15 February 1777	111

Name	Remarks	Page
S		
Sandy Brook, New Jersey		62
SANFORD, William	Private, 3rd Virginia Wounded at Brandywine and died of wounds	137
Saratoga, New York	Description of Battle	64, 198–202
SCHUYLER, Philip	Major General, Continental Army Letter from General Washington, September 1776	80
SCOTT, John	Captain, Smallwood's Maryland Regiment Killed at White Plains, October 1776	83
SCOTT"s Virginia Brigade		122, 182
SCOTT, Charles	Brigadier General, Continental Army	68, 122, 174, 185
	Letter to Robert Southall Re Skirmishes of tories with Culpeper Minute Battalion	10, 11
	Lieutenant Colonel, at Great Bridge	9–10
SCOTT, James	Captain, Fauquier company, in Culpeper Minute Battalion	5, 19
SHARP, Thomas	Corporal, 3rd Virginia Died 15 February 1777	111
SHEPHERD, Richard	Private, 3rd Virginia Died 15 January 1778	172
SHOEMAKE, Spencer [aka SHUMATE]	Soldier, 3rd Virginia May have died 15 February 1777	111
SILVEY, Butler	Private, 3rd Virginia Prisoner of War, May 1777	124
SIMCOE, ——	British Major, Tory Queen's Rangers, At Skirmish at White Marsh	204
SIMPSON, Michael	Captain, 1st Pennsylvania	113
SLAUGHTER, John	Private/ Corporal, 3rd Virginia, in Morgan's Rifle Corps	206
SLAUGHTER, Philip	Member, Culpeper Minute Battalion	5
SLAUGHTER, Robert	Lieutenant, 3rd Virginia Resignation 10 December 1777	168

NAME	REMARKS	PAGE
SMALLWOOD, William	Colonel/ General, Maryland Militia Regiment	143
	At White Plains	83
SMITH, ——	Lieutenant	7
SMITH, Robert	Private, 3rd Virginia Died 17 January 1777	110
SMITH, William	Soldier, 3rd Virginia May have died 1 March 1777	111
Somerset Court House, New Jersey		56
SOUTHALL, Robert	Militia Captain Letters from Lieutenant Colonel Charles Scott, in Virginia Gazette, December 1775 re skirmishes of Culpeper Minute Battalion with Tories	10
SPENCER, Joseph	Captain, Culpeper Minute Battalion	9
SPILLER, Alexander	Private, 3rd Virginia May have died before 1 April 1777	111
SPOTSWOOD, Alexander	Lieutenant, Fredericksburg Independent company, April 1775	3–4
SPOTSWOOD, John	Major Account of skirmish at Great Bridge in Virginia Gazeete, December 1775	14
SQUIRES, Matthew	Captain of British sloop	6
St.CLAIR, Arthur	American General	98
STAMPS, William	Soldier, 3rd Virginia May have died 17 February 1777	111
STEELE, Alexander	Soldier, 3rd Virginia Died 15 February 1777	111
STEELE, Thomas	Private, 3rd Virginia Died in January 1778	172
STEPHEN, Adam	Major General, Continental Army	63–64, 91, 94, 98 100, 128–129
	Conduct at Germantown	145, 147
	Court Martial	151–152
	Dismissal from service	159

Name	Remarks	Page
STEUBEN von, Frederick William Augustus, Baron	Major General and Inspector General, Continental Army	175, 177 189–190
STEVENS, Edward	Colonel, Culpeper Minute Battalion At Great Bridge Brigadier General, Virginia Militia	2–3, 13 15 63, 175
STIRLING, Lord	aka William Alexander, Lord Stirling Brigade mentioned 3rd Virginia in his Brigade, October 1776 to May 1777 Commanded left wing at Monmouth	35, 43 51, 55, 98, 105 28 183, 186
STRIPLING, Robert	Soldier, 3rd Virginia Died 15 February 1777	111
STRONG, George	Soldier, 3rd Virginia Died 31 December 1776	110
STRONG, John	Private, 3rd Virginia	168
SULLIVAN, John	Brigadier General, Continental Army At Brandywine	98 134

T

Name	Remarks	Page
TALIAFERRO, Lawrence	Colonel, Culpeper Minute Battalion	9
TALIAFERRO, William	Major, 3rd Virginia	27
TAYLOR, Charles	Soldier, 3rd Virginia Died 1 February 1777	110
TAYLOR, Elijah	Private, 3rd Virginia	170
TAYLOR, Peter	Private, 3rd Virginia May have died 1 February 1777	111
TEBBS, John	Lieutenant/ Captain-Lieutenant, 3rd Virginia Supernumerary, October 1778	40, 61 190
TERRY, Stephen	Private, 3rd Virginia Wounded at Brandywine, September 1777	139
THARP, David	Private, 3rd Virginia, in Morgan's Rifle Corps	206
The Clouds	Battle, 16 September 1777	64
THORNBURY, John	Soldier, 3rd Virginia Died 14 February 1777	110

Name	Remarks	Page
THORNTON, John	Captain, 3rd Virginia	18, 29, 31, 35–36, 41, 45, 51–53, 103, 114, 121
	At Harlem Heights	77–78
	At White Plains	82
	Company Returns	36–37
	Letter from General Washington	121
	Men from his company selected for Colonel Morgan's Rifle Corps	197
	Part played at near capture of British Major Robert Rogers at New Rochelle	37, 82 114
	Promoted to Major, Grayson's Additional Continental Regiment	59, 121
TIBBS, ——	Virginia Lieutenant at Great Bridge	10
TOMLIN, Stephen	Private, 3rd Virginia	140
TOMLIN, William	Sergeant, 3rd Virginia	140, 168
TOWERS, John (1)	Private, 3rd Virginia	170–171
TRAVIS, Edward	American Lieutenant at Great Bridge	11
Trenton, New Jersey	Description of Battle 25–26 December	96–103
	British capture, December 1776	93
	Account of battle in Virginia Gazette 10 January 1777	101
Trenton, New Jersey		56
Trenton Falls		94
TRUMBULL, John	Governor of Connecticut Letters from General Washington, December 1776	94, 97
TRUMBULL, Jonathan Jr	Letter from William Williams, September 1777	110
TRUMBULL, Joseph	Letter from Eliphalet Dyer, re Brandywine, September 1777	140
TURNER, Daniel	Private, 3rd Virginia Wounded at Brandywine, September 1777	139
TURNER, Francis	Private, 3rd Virginia	173
TURNER, Thomas	Private, 3rd Virginia May have died 1 February 1777	111
Turtle Bay, New York	British land here in September 1776	76

Name	Remarks	Page
V		
Valley Forge, Pennsylvania	American winter quarters 1777–1778	67–68, 167
VAUGHAN, Listra [aka BAUGHAN]	Private, 3rd Virginia, in Morgan's Rifle Corps	205
VAUGHN, James	Private, 3rd Virginia Died 16 February 1777	111
VIGOR, John	Private, 3rd Virginia	170
Virginia Battalions	1st Virginia Battalion, Woodford's Brigade	29
	2nd Virginia Battalion, Woodford's Brigade	29
Virginia Brigades	1st Virginia Brigade	122
	2nd Virginia Brigade	122
	3rd Virginia Brigade	122
	4th Virginia Brigade	122
Virginia Gazette	Account of British Attack on Hampton	7–8
	Account of skirmish at Great Bridge	10, 12–14
	Account of Skirmish at New Rochelle	82
	Account Battle at White Plains	83
	Description of Fort Washington	86
	Accounts of Virginia Regiments	89, 91
	Account of Battle at Trenton	102
	Letter relating to battle at Princeton	106
	Account of Capture of General Mercer	108
	Reports of recovery of Virginia troops from smallpox	113
	Account of Battle at Brandywine	136
	Account of Battle at Germantown	148
	September 1778 Reorganization of Virginia Line	190
Virginia Regiments	3rd Virginia	53–54, 78, 84, 89, 91, 103 122, 135, 147, 190
	9th Viriginia	147
VON BREYMAN, Heinrich	Hessian Lieutenant Colonel at Saratoga	202

NAME	REMARKS	PAGE

W

WALLACE, —	British Lieutenant at White Bridge	10
WALLACE, Gustavus Brown	Captain, 3rd Virginia	18, 29, 37, 39, 42, 45, 51–54, 61, 101, 108, 121
	Letters to brother Michael Wallace	53–54
WALLACE, Michael	Letters from brother Captain Gustavus Brown Wallace	53–54
WALLIS, George	Captain, 4th Virginia	100
WALTON, John	Private, 3rd Virginia Deserted 10 April 1778	172–173
WASHINGTON, George	Commander in Chief, American Forces	1, 3, 18, 27–28, 53, 55–56, 58–59, 89, 93, 100–104, 107–108, 124–125, 141, 143, 160–164
	Account of action at Fort Lee	84
	Account of action at Harlem Heights	77–78
	Account of 3rd Virginia action at Harlem Heights	83
	Battle Orders, 10 September 1777	132
	Councils of War	68, 94
	General Orders	93
	Letter from General Gates, re Saratoga	200
	Letter from Robert Morris, December 1776	102–103
	Letter to Landon Carter, May 1778	181
	Letter to Governor Cook of Connecticut	76
	Letters to Congress	
	January 1777	101
	October 1777	160–162
	November 1777	162, 164
	December 1777	163
	Letters to General Gates, December 1776	97
	Letters to John Hancock	
	December 1776	89
	December 1776	97
	September 1777	136
	Letters to Patrick Henry	
	Re proposed resignation of Thomas Marshall, Colonel, 3rd Virginia	128–129
	December 1777	164

NAME	REMARKS	PAGE
WASHINGTON, George	Commander in Chief, American Forces	
	Letter to Marquis de Lafayette	175
	Letter to Henry Laurens	149–150
	Re Germantown, October 177	
	Letters to Charles Lee	87, 92, 95, 97
	Letter to New Jersey Governor Livingston about evacuation of Fort Lee	87
	Letter to Daniel Morgan, June 1777	197
	Letter to Lord Stirling, December 1776	95
	Letter to General Maxwell	97
	Letter to Commanding Officer, Morristown, December 1776	104
	Letters to President of Congress	
	September 1776	78
	November 1776	84
	Re Fort Lee	86
	December 1776	89, 91–94
	January 1777	101
	May 1777	123–124, 126
	June 1777	125
	August 1777	129–130
	September 1777	103, 131, 141–142
	October 1777	160
	November 1777	165
	December 1777	93, 102
	June 1778	182
	Letter to General Schyuler September 1776	80
	Letter to Major John Thornton March 1777	121
	Letters to Governor Trumbull December 1776	94, 97
	Letters to Brother John Augustine Washington	
	September 1776	76
	On loss of Fort Washington	85
	December 1776	87, 95–97
	June 1777	126
	October 1777	151, 167
	June 1778	181
	Letter to Lund Washington	
	December 1776	90, 92
	Letter to William Woodford	
	May 1777	121
	On duties of his new Brigade	122
	On the State of the Army	9
	Orders to Colonel Biddle for clothing for the army	180

NAME	REMARKS	PAGE
WASHINGTON, George	Commander in Chief, American Forces	
	Orders	84, 96
	To Colonel John Cadwallader	89
	To General Heath	89
	Orders	
	To General Charles Lee	87
	To General Woodford for clothing for army	160
	To Virginia Officers	180
WASHINGTON, John Augustine	Brother of George Washington	
	Letters from his brother	
	September 1776	76
	On loss of Fort Washington	86
	December 1776	87, 95-96
	June 1777	124, 126
	October 1777	151, 161
	June 1778	181
WASHINGTON, Lund	Letters from General Washington	90, 92
WASHINGTON, William	Captain, 3rd Virginia	38–39, 45, 52–53, 98–99 100–101, 123
	Company Returns	39
	Promoted out of 3rd Virginia	59, 121
WATERS, Richard	Lieutenant, 1st Maryland	83
WAYNE, Anthony	Brigadier General, Continental Army	
	At Piscataway	124
	At Germantown, October 1777	147
	At Monmouth	185, 187
	Harassment of British,	197
WEEDON, George	Lieutenant, Fredericksburg Independent company, April 1775	3
	Lieutenant Colonel, 3rd Virginia	17, 27
	Colonel, 3rd Virginia	5, 27, 35, 41–43, 52, 88 90, 100–101, 102
	At Harlem Heights	77
	Escort for Hessians to Philadelphia	103
	Regimental Returns	40–41
	Returns	53–56, 58–59, 58, 113–114, 121
	Adjutant General, Continental Army	
	Brigadier General, Continental Army	59, 121
	Brigade Returns	43, 97, 180
	In Weedon's Brigade	81–82
	In Lord Stirling's Brigade, October 1776 to May 1777	28, 82
	In Lafayette's Division at Monmouth	183

NAME	REMARKS	PAGE
WEEDON, George	Brigadier General, Continental Army	
	Intrigue in Woodford's promotion	174
	Letters	52
	Letters to John Page	59
	September 1776	77
	October 1776	81–82
	December 1777	204
	Prior military experience	52
	Resignation, resulting from promotion Of Woodford	174
WELLS, John	Private/ Sergeant, 3rd Virginia Died 31 May 1778	172–173
WEMMYS, James	Captain, Tory Queen's Rangers	133
WEST, Charles	Captain, Prince William Minute Battalion	5
	Captain, 3rd Virginia	40–45, 53, 109
	Action at Harlem Heights	77–78
	Company Returns	39–40
	Major, 3rd Virginia	27
	Promotion to Major, January 1777	27
	Resignation, July 1778	27
	Lieutenant Colonel, Virginia Militia	40
WESTALL, Henry	Private, 3rd Virginia	169
WESTBAY, —	Sergeant, Maryland troops, Killed at White Plains, October 1776	83
WESTFALL, Cornelius	Ensign, 8th Virginia	68
WHITE, Adam	Private, 3rd Virginia May have died 1 February 1777	111
WHITE, Joseph	Sergeant, Massachusetts Artillery, At Trenton	100–101
WHITE, William	Lieutenant, 3rd Virginia	63, 130
	Died 16 September 1777 from wounds at Brandywine	135, 139
White Creek	Skirmish	129–130
White Marsh	Skirmish 5–8 December 1777	166, 203–204
White Plains	Description of Battle 26 October 1776	54–55, 83
	American Casualties	83
	Woodford's Brigade's Role	70
	Account of Battle in Virginia Gazette	83

Name	Remarks	Page
WHITING, Matthew	Lieutenant, 3rd Virginia Resignation, March 1777	121
WHITLOCK, John	Private, 3rd Virginia Wounded at Brandywine, September 1777	139
WICKLIFFE, David	Private, 3rd Virginia Wounded at Germantown, October 1777	147
WILBURN, John	Private, 3rd Virginia Deserted in December 1777	172
WILKERSON, Isaac [aka WILKINSON]	Private, 3rd Virginia May have died 1 February 1777	110
WILKERSON, William	Letter from Cornelius Hammett about Brandywine	140
WILKES, James	Private, 3rd Virginia Reported sick, absent November 1777 too March 1778; Died 15 April 1778	169, 171
WILKINSON, James	Deputy Adjutant General, Northern Department; at Saratoga	199
WILLIAMS, Isaac	Private, 3rd Virginia Died 26 February 1777	110
WILLIAMS, James	Private, 3rd Virginia, in Morgan's Rifle Corps; Died 22 December 1777	206 203
WILLAMS, Jonathan	Private, 3rd Virginia Wounded at Brandywine, September 1777	138
WILLIAMS, Otho Holland	Major, Stephenson's Maryland and Virginia Riflemen; captured by British at Fort Washington Colonel, 6th Maryland	88 22, 88
WILLIAMS, Pearson	Private, 3rd Virginia, in Morgan's Rifle Corps	206
WILLIAMS, William	Private, 3rd Virginia Deserted 8 March 1778	172
WILLIAMS, William	Letter to Jonathan Trumbull Jr about Brandywine, September 1777	140
Williamsburg, Virginia	Arrival of Minute Battalions	5–6, 9
WILLIS, Lewis		40

NAME	REMARKS	PAGE
WILSON, James	Soldier, 3rd Virginia Died 1 February 1777	110
WINGATE, Martin	Private, 3rd Virginia, in Morgan's Rifle Corsp Discharge 1 December 1777	206 168, 204
WINKFIELD, William	Private, 3rd Virginia	17, 20
WOODFORD's BRIGADE	Mentioned Part of Lafayette's division on march to Philadelphia	44–45, 51 182

WOODFORD, William	Captain, Caroline Independent company
	Colonel, 1st Virginia
	   At Great Bridge
	   Letters to Edmund Pendleton
	   Brigadier General, Continental Army
	   3rd Virginia transferred to his brigade
	
	   Brigade at Germantown
	   Brigade Returns
	
	   Condition of 3rd Virginia
	   Brigadier General, 3rd Virginia Brigade
	      Councils of War for Monmouth
	      Role at Monmouth
	   Intrigue with Muhlenberg, Weedon, and
	      Scott involved in his promotion
	   Letter from General Washington about duties
	      of his new Brigade, May 1777
	   Orders from General Washington about
	      clothing for the Army
		4
		2, 8–10, 15, 42, 44
		12, 14–15
		9, 13, 16
		
		28, 36, 114,
		121–122, 159
		134, 147
		46, 65–68, 70, 114, 159,
		163–164, 167, 174,
		179–180
		167
		59, 122
		68, 183
		68, 186
		
		174
		122
		
		160

WOOLCOT, ——	Colonel, killed at Germantown	151
WRIGHT, Daniel	Private, 3rd Virginia Deserted 15 March 1778	169, 172
WYTHE, George	Letter to John Page, about death of Major Andrew Leitch, October 1776	81

Y-Z

NAME	REMARKS	PAGE
Yellow Springs,	Retreat to, 16 September 1777	64
YOUNG, John	Private, 3rd Virginia Wounded at Brandywine, September 1777	138
ZABRISKIE, Peter	House as Washington's Headquarters	85

BIBLIOGRAPHY

Online Resources

"Black Loyalists." *www.blackloyalists.com*. http://www.blackloyalists.com.
"Delinquent Tax Lists, 1799–1813, Pendelton County, Kentucky." *Rootsweb.com*. http://ftp.rootsweb.com.
"George Washington Papers, 1741–1799. Series 3b Varick Transcripts." *Library of Congress*, http://www.memory.loc.gov.
"George Washington Papers, 1741–1799. Series 4 General Correspondence, 1697–1799." *Library of Congress*. http://www.memory.loc.gov.
"George Washington Papers, 1741–1799. Diaries of George Washington." *Library of Congress*. http://www.memory.gov.
"John Francis Mercer of Stafford County: A Neglected Patriot." *Central Rappahannock Regional Library*. http://www.historypoint.org.
"John Francis Mercer." *Laughter and Lawter Genealogy Reference and Research Center*. http://www.laughtergenealogy.com
"Journals of Continental Congress." *A Century of Lawmaking for a New Nation: U.S. Congressional Documents and Debates, 1774–1875, Library of Congress*. http://www.loc.gov.
"Journals of the House of Representatives." *A Century of Lawmaking for a New Nation: U.S. Congressional Documents and Debates, 1774–1875, Library of Congress*. http://www.loc.gov.
"Journal of the Senate of the United States." *A Century of Lawmaking for a New Nation: U.S. Congressional Documents and Debates 1774–1875, Library of Congress*. http://www.loc.gov.
Milhollen, Hirst D. and Donald H. Mugridge. "Civil War Photographs, 1861–1865." *Prints and Photographs Division, LC–B811–02923 and LC–B 811–02924*, 1865. Library of Congress. http://www.memory.loc.gov.
"Monroe in the American Revolution (1776–1781)." *Wikipedia, the Free Encyclopedia*. http://www.en.widipedia.org.
"Original Members of the Culpeper Minute Battalion, 1775." *Culpeper Minuteman Chapter, SAR*. http://www.csmsar.com.
"Report on Relief for Andrew Leitch's Heirs, Serial Set v. 1075, 36–1, C.C. Rept 228." *Newsbank*. http://infoweb.newsbank.com.
"Revolutionary War Rejected Claims." *Library of Virginia, Rev Rej Claims*. http://www.ajax.lva.lib.va.us.
"Virginia Gazette." *Colonial Williamsburg Foundation*. http://research.history.org
"Virginia Soldiers of 1776." *Ancestry.com*. http://searchancestry.com.
Wikipedia, the Free Encyclopedia. http;// www.en.wikipedia.org..
Writings of George Washington from Original Manuscript Sources, Volumes 6–8. Electronic Text Center, University of Virginia. www.etext.virginia.edu.

CD Sources

Hening, William Waller. *The Statutes at Large, Being a Collection of all the Laws of Virginia from the First Session of the Legislature in the Year 1619*. Volumes 1-13, CD Rom 0878, Bowie, Maryland: Heritage Archives, 2003.
Lossing, Bernard. *Pictorial Field Book of the Revolution* CD 3261, Bowie, Maryland: Heritage Books, 2004.

Periodicals

L.G. Tyler, ed. "Diary of John Chilton, 3rd Virginia Regiment," *Tyler's Quarterly Historical and Genealogical Magazine*. XII, Richmond: Richmond Press, 1931.

Primary Sources

Force, Peter. *American Archives: A Collection of Authentick Records, State Papers, Debates and Letters and Other Notices of Publick Affairs.* 5th Series, Washington, DC: 1851.
Fauquier County, Virginia Court Records include Will Book and Marriage Bonds for 3rd Virginia officers and soldiers.
Heitman, Francis B. *Historical Register of Officers of the Continental Army during the War of the Revolution, April 1775 to December 1783.* Reprint of 1914 edition, Baltimore, Maryland: Clearfield, 1982.)
Library of Virginia. *George Weedon Papers, 1776-1789,* Accession 22954a, Personal Papers Collections.
National Archives and Records Administration. *Compiled Service Records,* M 881 MR 951-956, *Compiled Service Records, 3rd Virginia 1776-1778.*
Compiled Service Records, M 881 MR 956–962, *Compiled Service Records, 3rd and 4th Virginia Revolutionary War Rolls,* M 246 MR 97-98, *3rd Virginia Rolls.*
Revolutionary War Rolls, M 246 MR 137 *Returns of the Army under General Washington 1775-1782.*
Revolutionary War, Bounty Land Warrant Applications and Pensions, M 804, various microfilm rolls for pensions files for 3rd Virginia veterans.
Prince William County Court Records include Will Book, Minute, and Order Book entries.
University of Virginia. *Papers of the Wallace Family 1750-1888,* Accession 38150, Albert H. Small Special Collections Library.
U. S. House of Representatives. *Resolutions, Laws and Ordinances relating to the Officers and Soldiers of the Revolution,* Reprint of 1838 edition, Baltimore: Genealogical Publishing Company, 1998.
Virginia Historical Society, *John Chilton Papers,* Mss2c4395a1.
Keith *Family Papers,* Mss2c4394a1-11.
Virginia Historical Society, *David Griffith Papers, 1776-1778,* Mss2G8755b.

Derivative Sources

Barnes, Ian. *The Historical Atlas of the American Revolution,* New York: Routledge, 2000.
Berg, Fred A. *Encyclopedia of Continental Army Units,* Harrisburg, Pennsylvania: Stackpole Books, 1972.
Boatner, Mark *Encyclopedia of the American Revolution,* Mechanicsburg, Pennsylvania: Stackpole Books, 1994.
Bockstruck, Lloyd DeWitt. *Revolutionary War Bounty Land Grants Awarded by State Governments,* Baltimore: Genealogical Publishing Company, 1996.
Brown, Margie G. *Genealogical Abstracts Revolutionary War Veterans Scrip Act 1852,* Lovettsville: Willow Bend Books, 1997.
Buchanan, John. *The Road to Valley Forge,* New York: John Wiley and Sons, Inc, 2004.
Brumbaugh, Gauis Marcus. *Revolutionary War Records: Virginia,* Baltimore: Genealogical Publishing Company, 1995.
Cecere, Michael. *They Behaved Like Soldiers: Captain John Chilton and The Third Virginia Regiment, 1775–1778,* Bowie, Maryland: Heritage Books, 2004.
Cox, Ethelyn. *Historic Alexandria Virginia Street by Street: A Survey of Existing Early Buildings,* Alexandria: Historic Alexandria Foundation, 1976.
Drake, Paul. *What Did They Mean By That? A Dictionary of Historical Terms for Genealogists,* Bowie, Maryland: Heritage Books, 1994.
Dwyer, William M. *The Day is Ours: An Inside View of the battles of Trenton and Princeton, November 1776 to January 1777,* New Brunswick: Rutgers University Press, 1998.
Edgar, Gregory T. *The Philadelphia Campaign, 1777–1778,* Bowie: Heritage Books, 1998.
Fischer, David Hackett. *Washington's Crossing,* New York: Oxford University Press, 2004.
Fleming, Thomas. *Liberty: The American Revolution,* New York: Viking Press, 1997.
Fowler, William A. *Empires at War: The French and Indian War and the Struggle for North America 1754–1763,* New York: Walker and Co, 2005.

Grafton, John. *The American Revolution, A Picture Sourcebook,* New York: Dover Publications, 1975.

Gott, John and Russell, Triplett. *Fauquier in the Revolution,* Warrenton, Virginia: Warrenton Printing and Publishing Company, 1977.

Haller, Stephen E. *William Washington: Cavalryman of the Revolution,* Bowie, Maryland: Heritage Books, 2001.

Higginbotham, Don. *Daniel Morgan, Revolutionary Rifleman,* Chapel Hill, North Carolina: University of North Carolina Press, 1961.

Higginbotham, Don. *The War of American Independence: Military Attitudes, Policies and Practice 1763–1789,* Boston, Massachusetts: Northeastern University Press, 1983.

Hopkins, William Lindsay. *Virginia Revolutionary War Land Grant Claims 178 –1850, (Rejected),* Privately Printed, 1988.

Hurst, Harold W. *Alexandria on the Potomac,* Lanham: University Press of America, 1991.

Jones, Mary Stevens, ed. *An 18th Century Perspective: Culpeper County, Va,* Culpeper, Virginia: Culpeper Historical Society, 1976.

Ketchum, Richard M. *Saratoga: Turning Point of America's Revolutionary War,* New York: Henry Holt and Company, 1997.

Kinsey, Margaret B. *Mountjoy Omnibus,* Baltimore: Gateway Press, 2001.

Lefkowitz, Arthur S. *George Washington's Indispensable Men,* Mechanicsburg, Pennsylvania: Stackpole Books, 2003.

Leiby, Adrian C. *The Revolutionary War in the Hackensack Valley,* New Brunswick: Rutgers University Press, 1992.

Lesser, Charles H. ed. *The Sinews of Independence: Monthly Strength Reports of the Continental Army,* Chicago, Illinois: University of Chicago Press, 1976.

McGuire, Thomas J. *The Battle of Paoli,* Mechanicsburg, Pennsylvania: Stackpole Books, 2000.

McGuire, Thomas J. *Brandywine Battlefield Park: Pennsylvania Trail of History Guide,* Mechanicsburg: Stackpole Books, 2001.

McGuire, Thomas J. *The Surprise at Germantown,* Germantown: Cliveden for the National Trust for Historic Preservation and Thomas Publications, 1994.

Minis, M. Lee. *The First Virginia Regiment of Foot 1775-1783,* Westminster, Maryland: Willow Bend Books, 1998.

Mitchell, Joseph H. *Decisive Battles of the American Revolution,* Yardley: Westholme, 1962.

Mowday, Bruce E. *September 11, 1777: Washington's Defeat at Brandywine Dooms Philadelphia,* Shippensburg: White Mane Books, 2002.

Peters, Joan W. *The Tax Man Cometh: Land & Property in Colonial Fauquier County Virginia... 1759 – 1782,* Westminster, Maryland: Willow Bend Books, 1999.

Peters, Joan W. *Military Records, Patriotic Service & Public Service Claims from the Fauquier County Virginia Court Minute Books 1759–1784,* Westminster: Willow Bend Books, 1999.

Peters, Joan W. *Military Records, Certificates of Service, Discharge, Heirs, & Pension Declarations and Schedules from the Fauquier County Virginia Court Minute Books 1784–1840,* Westminster: Willow Bend Books, 1999.

Peters, Joan W. *Military Records, Pension Applications, Heirs at Law and Civil War Military Records from the Fauquier County Virginia Court Minute Books 1840–1904,* Westminster: Willow Bend Books, 1999.

Peters, Joan W. *Lost & Forgotten: Fauquier County, Virginia, French & Indian War, Revolutionary War, & War of 1812 Veterans from the Military Record Series of the Fauquier County, Virginia Clerks Loose Papers, 1759 –1825,* Westminster: Willow Bend Books, 2004.

Peterson, Harold L. *The Book of the Continental Soldier,* Harrisburg, Pennsylvania: The Stackpole Company, 1968.

Rae, John W. *Morristown: A Military Headquarters of the American Revolution,* Charleston: Arcadia Publishing, 2002.

Random House. *Webster's College Dictionary,* New York: Random House, 1991.)

Reid, Stuart and Zladich, Marko. *Soldiers of the Revolutionary War,* Oxford, Great Britain: Osprey Publishing Company, 2002.

Rhodehamel, John. *The American Revolution: Writings from the War of Independence,* New York: Library of America, 2001.
Rhodehamel, John. *George Washington: Writings,* New York: Library of America, 1997.
Sanchez-Saavedra, E. M. *A Guide to Virginia Military Organizations in the American Revolution, 1774–1787,* Richmond, Virginia: Virginia State Library, 1978.
Smith, Paul et als, eds. *Letters of Delegates to Congress 1774-1789.* 25 volumes, Washington, D.C: Library of Congress, 1977.
Smith, Samuel Stelle. *The Battle of Trenton,* Monmouth Beach: Philip Freneau Press, 1965.
Smith, William F. and Miller, T. Michael. *A Seaport Saga: Portrait of Old Alexandria, Virginia,* Norfolk: The Donning Company, 1989.
Symonds, Craig L. *A Battlefield Atlas of the American Revolution,* Baltimore: The Nautical and Aviation Publishing Company of America, 1986.
Taafe, Stephen R. *The Philadelphia Campaign,* Lawrence, Kansas: University of Kansas Press, 2003.
White, Virgil D. *Genealogical Abstracts of Revolutionary War Pension Files.* 5 Volumes. Waynesboro: The National Historical Publishing Company, 1990.
Wright, Robert K. Jr. *The Continental Army,* Washington, DC: Center of Military History, U.S. Army, 1985.
Wood, W. J. *Battles of the Revolutionary War 1775-1781,* New York: DeCapo Press, 1995.

Other Heritage Books by Joan W. Peters:

Abstracts of Fauquier County, Virginia Birth Records, 1853-1896

Being of Sound Mind: An Index to the Probate Records in Fauquier County Virginia's Clerks Loose Papers and Superior and Circuit Court Papers, 1759-1919

Fauquier County, Virginia's Clerk's Loose Papers: A Guide to the Records, 1759-1919

Military Records, Certificates of Service, Discharge, Heirs, and Pensions Declarations and Schedules from the Fauquier County, Virginia Court Minute Books, 1784-1840

Military Records, Patriotic Service, and Public Service Claims from the Fauquier County, Virginia Court Minute Books, 1759-1784

Military Records, Pension Applications, Heirs at Law and Civil War Military Records from the Fauquier County, Virginia Court Minute Books, 1840-1904

Neglected and Forgotten: Fauquier County, Virginia French and Indian War, Revolutionary War and War of 1812 Veterans

Prince William County, Virginia General Index to Wills, 1734-1951

The Tax Man Cometh—Land and Property in Colonial Fauquier County, Virginia: Tax List from the Fauquier County Court Clerk's Loose Papers, 1759-1782

The Third Virginia Regiment of Foot, 1776-1778, with Flags Flying and Drums Beating Volume One: A History

The Third Virginia Regiment of Foot, 1776-1778, with Flags Flying and Drums Beating Volume Two: Biographies

www.ingramcontent.com/pod-product-compliance
Lightning Source LLC
Chambersburg PA
CBHW071424150426
43191CB00008B/1034